Unacknowledged Kinships

The Tauber Institute Series for the Study of European Jewry

JEHUDA REINHARZ, General Editor
CHAERAN Y. FREEZE, Associate Editor
SYLVIA FUKS FRIED, Associate Editor
EUGENE R. SHEPPARD, Associate Editor

The Tauber Institute Series is dedicated to publishing compelling and innovative approaches to the study of modern European Jewish history, thought, culture, and society. The series features scholarly works related to the Enlightenment, modern Judaism and the struggle for emancipation, the rise of nationalism and the spread of antisemitism, the Holocaust and its aftermath, as well as the contemporary Jewish experience. The series is published under the auspices of the Tauber Institute for the Study of European Jewry—established by a gift to Brandeis University from Dr. Laszlo N. Tauber—and is supported, in part, by the Tauber Foundation and the Valya and Robert Shapiro Endowment.

For the complete list of books that are available in this series,
please see https://brandeisuniversitypress.com/series/tauber

STEFAN VOGT, DEREK J. PENSLAR, and ARIEH SAPOSNIK, editors
Unacknowledged Kinships: Postcolonial Studies and the Historiography of Zionism

*MARAT GRINBERG
The Soviet Jewish Bookshelf: Jewish Culture and Identity Between the Lines

SUSAN MARTHA KAHN, editor
Canine Pioneer: The Extraordinary Life of Rudolphina Menzel

ARTHUR GREEN
Defender of the Faithful: The Life and Thought of Rabbi Levi Yitshak of Berdychiv

GILAD SHARVIT
Dynamic Repetition: History and Messianism in Modern Jewish Thought

YOSEF HAYIM YERUSHALMI in Conversation with SYLVIE ANNE GOLDBERG
Transmitting Jewish History

CHARLES DELLHEIM
Belonging and Betrayal: How Jews Made the Art World Modern

CEDRIC COHEN-SKALLI
Don Isaac Abravanel: An Intellectual Biography

CHAERAN Y. FREEZE
A Jewish Woman of Distinction: The Life and Diaries of Zinaida Poliakova

CHAVA TURNIANSKY
Glikl: Memoirs 1691–1719

*A Sarnat Library Book

Unacknowledged Kinships
Postcolonial Studies and the Historiography of Zionism

Edited by STEFAN VOGT, DEREK J. PENSLAR, and ARIEH SAPOSNIK

Brandeis University Press
WALTHAM, MASSACHUSETTS

Brandeis University Press
© 2023 by Brandeis University Press
All rights reserved
Manufactured in the United States of America
Typeset in Empirica by Tobias Frere-Jones and Nina Stössinger
and Garamond Premier Pro by Robert Slimbach

For permission to reproduce any of the material in this book,
contact Brandeis University Press, 415 South Street, Waltham MA 02453,
or visit brandeisuniversitypress.com

LIBRARY OF CONGRESS CATALOGING-IN-PUBLISHING DATA
Names: Vogt, Stefan, 1968– editor, author. | Penslar, Derek Jonathan, editor, writer of introduction. | Saposnik, Arieh Bruce, 1966– editor, writer of introduction.
Title: Unacknowledged kinships : postcolonial studies and the historiography of Zionism / edited by Stefan Vogt, Derek J. Penslar, and Arieh Saposnik.
Description: Waltham : Brandeis University Press, 2023. | Series: The Tauber Institute series for the study of European Jewry | Includes bibliographical references and index. | Summary: "A ground-breaking collection of essays regarding the history, implementation and challenges of using 'antisemitism' and related terms as tools for both historical analysis and public debate. A unique, sophisticated contribution to current debates in both the academic and the public realms regarding the nature and study of antisemitism today" — Provided by publisher.
Identifiers: LCCN 2023002749 | ISBN 9781684581542 (paperback) | ISBN 9781684581559 (cloth) | ISBN 9781684581566 (ebook)
Subjects: LCSH: Antisemitism — Historiography. | Zionism — Historiography. | Jews — Historiography. | Jews — History — Study and teaching.
Classification: LCC DS145.U525 2023 | DDC 305.892/400722 — dc23/eng/20230131
LC record available at https://lccn.loc.gov/2023002749

5 4 3 2 1

Contents

Acknowledgments   vii

1 Introduction: Unacknowledged Kinships
STEFAN VOGT, DEREK J. PENSLAR, and ARIEH SAPOSNIK   1

Part I · Conceptualizations

2 A Rebellious "Tied-Up Beast": German Zionist Concepts of Authenticity as Counternarratives
MANJA HERRMANN   29

3 Zionism as "Positioning": Reconceptualizing Zionist Identity Politics
STEFAN VOGT   51

4 Postcolonial Parallels in Albert Memmi's Portrait of Frantz Fanon: Negotiating Négritude, Nativism, and Jewish Nationalism
ABRAHAM RUBIN   73

Part II · Looking West, Looking East

5 Blyden and Pissarro on St. Thomas: Pan-Africanism, Zionism, Diasporism, and the Sephardic Caribbean
SARAH PHILLIPS CASTEEL   95

6 Mapping Zionism: The "*Ostjude*" in Zionist History and Historiography
MAŁGORZATA A. MAKSYMIAK   119

7 Central European Zionisms and the Habsburg
   Colonial Imaginary
   SCOTT SPECTOR						139

8 "The Spoken Hebrew Here Is Not a Language":
   On Gershom Scholem and Oriental Hebrew
   GHILAD H. SHENHAV					161

Part III · Palestine and Israel between Empire and Decolonization

9 The Return of Modernity: Postcolonialism and
   the New Historiography of Jews from the Levant and Egypt
   ORIT BASHKIN						187

10 Between Monumentalism and Miniaturization:
   Israel's Settlement Project and the Question of
   Third World Colonialism
   JOHANNES BECKE					215

11 A Part of Asia or Apart from Asia?
   Zionist Perceptions of Asia, 1947–1956
   REPHAEL G. STERN and ARIE M. DUBNOV		233

Part IV · Conversations

12 An Interview with Dipesh Chakrabarty		275

   Afterword: Intellectual Journeys
   ATO QUAYSON						291

   Bibliography						303
   Contributors						333
   Index							339

Acknowledgments

This book began its life in the summer of 2018 as an international conference titled "Unacknowledged Kinships" at Goethe-University Frankfurt am Main, hosted by the Martin Buber Chair for Jewish Thought and Philosophy. We wish to thank Christian Wiese, who holds the Martin Buber Chair, for making this conference possible. We also wish to thank the conference donors: the Fritz Thyssen Foundation, the Foundation for the Promotion of International Relations at Goethe-University, the Ignatz Bubis Foundation, the Association of the Friends and Benefactors of the Goethe-University, the FAZIT Foundation, and the Wissenschaftliche Arbeitsgemeinschaft of the Leo Baeck Institute in Germany. We wish to especially thank the Ignatz Bubis Foundation for allowing us to use parts of its grant to help finance the editing of this book. The production of this book was also made possible by grants from the History Department at Harvard University and the Ben-Gurion Institute for the Study of Israel and Zionism at Ben-Gurion University of the Negev. We express our deep gratitude for this support.

The book would not have been possible without the kind and constant support of the staff at Brandeis University Press. We are particularly grateful to Sue Ramin, Sylvia Fuks-Fried, and Anthony Lipscomb. The editors also wish to express their gratitude to Talia Penslar for her deft stylistic editing.

Last but not least, our thanks go to the contributors to this book as well as to the participants in the conference that kicked off the process culminating in this volume's publication. Working with these scholars was an exceptionally pleasant and inspiring experience. We are extremely grateful for the patience and persistence with which they committed themselves to the creation of this book.

STEFAN VOGT, DEREK J. PENSLAR, ARIEH SAPOSNIK

Unacknowledged Kinships

1

Introduction

Unacknowledged Kinships

STEFAN VOGT, DEREK J. PENSLAR,
and ARIEH SAPOSNIK

In July 2000, a few weeks after the Israeli Defense Forces withdrew from Lebanon and only days before the beginning of the eventually failed peace talks between Israel and the Palestinian Authority at Camp David, a photograph appeared in a number of media outlets showing a man with a baseball cap who was just about to throw a stone. The man was the cultural and literary studies scholar Edward Said, who, as the author of the book *Orientalism* and other path-breaking works, is considered one of the founders of the discipline of postcolonial studies. The picture was taken in Southern Lebanon, close to the Israeli border. Said threw the stone in what he later described as a "symbolic gesture" toward Israel.[1]

In fact, the gesture could not have been more symbolic. A great amount of politically motivated reservation or even suspicion is at work between the academic fields of postcolonial studies and the study of Zionism. Postcolonial studies is considered by many of its protagonists, but also by many scholars of Zionism, as clearly anti-Zionist in its political positions and intentions. This is not an unfounded assumption. Postcolonial scholars often characterize Israel and Zionism as prime examples of colonial and postcolonial oppression.[2] At the same time, from a Zionist perspective, postcolonial studies are often reduced to anti-Zionist bias and dismissed

I

as pure ideology, without discussing their more substantive claims and findings.[3] For many protagonists and observers, postcolonial studies and the historiography of Zionism are not on speaking terms. They don't find it worthwhile, or even legitimate, to engage in a dialogue. This book contests this notion. It claims that there is an "unacknowledged kinship" between Zionism and postcolonial studies, a kinship that deserves to be discovered and acknowledged.

The book strives to facilitate a conversation between the historiography of Zionism and postcolonial studies by identifying and exploring possible linkages and affiliations between their subjects as well as the limits of such connections. The authors of the essays in this volume discuss central theoretical concepts developed within the field of postcolonial studies, use these concepts to analyze crucial aspects of the history of Zionism, and contextualize Zionist thought, politics, and culture within colonial and postcolonial histories. While the main purpose of the book is to test the applicability of postcolonial concepts to the history of Zionism, it also traces vectors that move in the opposite direction. Postcolonial studies might have something to gain from looking at the history of Zionism as an example of not only colonial domination but also the seemingly contradictory processes of national liberation and self-empowerment. Postcolonial studies and the historiography of Zionism could profit from each other if they could bridge the political chasm that all too often underpins their disciplines. This does not mean that these fields should look upon each other without critical scrutiny. To the contrary, an open and critical exchange could help each discipline address its own limitations and weaknesses that, in both cases, often derive from tendencies to essentialization and self-affirmation.

This book is the first to systematically investigate the potential for a dialogue between postcolonial studies and the history of Zionism. It is also unique in suggesting that postcolonial concepts can be applied to the history of European Zionism just as comprehensively as to the history of Zionism in Palestine and Israel or in Arab countries. Most importantly, this book is an overture for a dialogue between postcolonial studies and the historiography of Zionism. Featuring an interview with the postcolonial historian Dipesh Chakrabarty and an afterword by the postcolonial literary scholar Ato Quayson, it is the first to directly engage in such a conversation.

We believe that this not only provides a significant addition to the existing scholarship but also serves an important political purpose. Perhaps, one hopes, it could help overcome the destructive competition that often exists between the struggles against racism and the struggles against antisemitism, in favor of a joint effort to confront past and present forms of exclusion, subordination, and persecution.

First Encounters

For a number of years now, there has been growing interest among scholars of Jewish history and culture in including concepts from postcolonial studies into their work. Already in the early 1990s, Daniel and Jonathan Boyarin suggested viewing Jewish history from a perspective inspired by a postcolonial understanding of Diaspora.[4] This concept linked Jewish history with postcolonialism, making use of the latter's robust theoretical toolbox. In a similar vein, Samuel Moyn and Susannah Heschel have proposed employing Paul Gilroy's appropriation of the concept of "Diaspora," which itself originated in Jewish history, as well as concepts such as "Third Space" (Homi Bhabha), "Orientalism" (Edward Said), and "Subalternity" (Gayatri Chakravorty Spivak), for the analysis and interpretation of Jewish history.[5] These suggestions have been taken up especially in scholarship on the history of Middle Eastern and Mediterranean Jewry, as well as the history of Jews in other non-European spaces.[6] In recent years postcolonial approaches have also gained currency in the historiography of pre-1948 Palestine and the State of Israel.[7] In addition to textual representations of identity politics or of social and cultural processes, aspects of material culture such as visual art, music, and food have been analyzed in this context, which constitutes another bridge to postcolonial studies where these issues are also central.[8] In Israel, there is an academic journal, *Theory and Criticism*, which is devoted to promoting postcolonial studies (along with other critical theories) across the humanities, including the fields of Jewish and Israeli history.[9]

While these developments constitute a historiographical trend, there remains much to be done to firmly establish colonialism as an essential context for the study of Israeli history, as well as postcolonial approaches as legitimate means to address that history. At the same time, these approaches are not always deployed in a sufficiently critical and nuanced way. In many cases, for instance, postcolonial concepts have been applied to the history of the Yishuv and the history of Israel in order to support the notion that the Zionist project was entirely and inseparably bound to the colonizing West.[10] The Yishuv and Israel are entangled with, and implicated in, colonial forms of domination, yet that entanglement is complex. Critiques of the colonial paradigm have argued that the social structures in Palestine were neither equivalent to those in European colonies, nor were the ideological motives of the Zionists for settling in Palestine or their economic goals comparable to those of the European powers.[11] More importantly, the colonial paradigm is problematic precisely because of its unambiguity. The preconceived decision, whether for political or methodological reasons (or both), to place Israel and the Yishuv squarely on the hegemonic side of the colonial divide contradicts an insight that has been established above all by scholars of postcolonial studies, namely that the border between the two sides of this divide is neither clear nor tight.[12] In addition, it prevents us from asking whether Zionism also included anticolonial or postcolonial elements. Recent research has revealed, for instance, important similarities and interrelations between Israel and postcolonial development regimes, at least in the first two decades after 1948.[13] The relationship of the Yishuv with the British colonial authorities in Palestine—as well as with the Ottoman state—cannot be adequately understood either if the Yishuv, and the Zionist movement in general, are seen exclusively as a colonial force.[14]

Equally problematic is the concentration of much of the work that emphasizes the colonialist character of Zionism on Palestine and the emerging national conflict there. In Europe, where the Zionist movement originated and where its organizational and ideological centers were located for many decades, its position was markedly different. Here, Zionism was a movement of a minority that had been otherized, discriminated against, and persecuted for centuries, sometimes in a colonizing fashion. This is why the Israeli historian Avi Bareli accused protagonists of the colonial paradigm of "forgetting Europe" when they label Zionism a colonialist movement.[15] Zionism was not least a movement that strove to reposition the Jews within European societies. Including Europe in the picture helps us see Zionism's quality as a subaltern strategy of self-empowerment. This observation, however, should not lead to replacing one false unambiguity with another. A perspective on the history of Zionism that centers around its European aspects should not "forget Palestine," that is, the fact that both the ideological focus of Zionism and the location where its ideas were turned into practice were outside of Europe, in a space that was the object of colonial interests and desires. Inside Europe, too, Zionism cannot be located entirely on the subaltern side of the colonial divide. The movement's entanglement with European colonialism and its integration into European bourgeois culture were too strong for this. If we look at Zionist history in Europe, it becomes obvious once more that it is impossible to make a neat separation between hegemonic and subaltern positions.

In the 1990s, scholars began to look at the interconnections between Jewish history and colonial history within Europe.[16] Much of this work has been inspired by impulses from postcolonial studies. In particular, these scholars recognized that if, as Ann Stoler and Frederick Cooper have famously argued, "Europe was made by its imperial projects, as much as colonial encounters were shaped by conflicts within Europe itself," then the situation of the Jews in Europe must also have been implicated by colonialism, and vice versa.[17] In the field of German-Jewish history, for instance, Jonathan Hess, Susannah Heschel, and Christian Wiese have shown that Jewish struggles for equality and recognition, as well as antisemitic attempts to deny these rights to Jews, were strongly entangled with colonial structures and ideologies and that postcolonial concepts can help to understand these entanglements.[18] With regard to France and Britain, too, a small but growing group of scholars uses empire rather than the nation-state as their point of reference for investigating the position of the Jews in these societies.[19] The same is true for Eastern European Jewish history, where the Russian and Habsburg Empires provide a political and cultural setting that encourages scholars to use postcolonial concepts.[20] Finally, scholars such as Michael Rothberg and Bryan Cheyette have applied these concepts to the study of memory culture and literary representations of Jewish history, showing that European Jewish history and postcolonial studies can be brought together in extremely productive ways.[21] Anthologies and special issues of journals dedicated to the relationship of Jewish history and colonial history have been published or are underway.[22]

In research on the history of Zionism in Europe, the application of concepts taken from postcolonial studies is still underdeveloped and very much at its beginnings. One exception here is Said's notion of Orientalism. Already in 1984, Paul Mendes-Flohr used it to analyze self-conceptions and strategies of self-affirmation in the thought of Martin Buber and other Central European Zionists.[23] A number of scholars have since followed this suggestion and published important studies on Zionist Orientalism in Europe and beyond.[24] Several important edited collections discuss the role of Orientalism in European Jewish history in general and Zionism in particular.[25] The study of Orientalist ideologies and structures in and around the Zionist movement not only revealed important insights into the self-image and positioning of Zionist Jews between the "East" and the "West." It also significantly advanced the concept of Orientalism since its introduction by Said. For instance, it has been shown that Orientalist tropes were as important in Central and Eastern European discourses as they were in France or Britain. Moreover, this research helps us understand that Orientalism, while a powerful tool for colonial domination, could also be used from a subaltern perspective to confront such domination.

The concept of "Orientalism" has also informed a number of studies that discuss the role of visual culture for Zionist identity politics in Europe.[26] Visual culture, as well as other forms of material culture such as music, food, fashion, or architecture, have always been fields in which cultural identities are developed and expressed, tested and contested, and, perhaps most importantly, mixed and rearranged. This hybridity is especially common among diaspora cultures, making these issues important for Zionism as well as in postcolonial contexts. For postcolonial scholars, material culture is a complex field in which processes of subordination, adaptation, subversion, and emancipation can take place.[27] Particular emphasis is given to popular culture as a means to construct anti-hegemonic concepts of identity.[28] In the history of Zionism, similar processes can be detected. Historians have looked, for instance, at cases of Orientalist self-fashioning or the reception of East European Jewish folklore in Zionist circles.[29] The study of visual and material culture thus involves substantial overlaps, and offers opportunities for a dialogue, between the study of Zionism and postcolonial studies.

However, only a handful of scholars of European Zionism have reached out more comprehensively toward postcolonial studies and attempted to systematically connect these two fields or engage in a discussion with postcolonial scholars and their ideas.[30] Their research clearly indicates that postcolonial studies can be used much more broadly in the historiography of European Zionisms and that they can contribute just as much here as they contribute to the historiography of non-European Zionisms. Zionism in Europe needs to be located in a tension-filled position between European colonialism, directed toward spaces and populations both within and beyond the continent, and the Jews' own experiences of being, after a fashion, colonized. Numerous parallels and structural connections between Zionism and anticolonial nationalisms have been detected, including the ambivalent relationship of these nationalisms to their European sources. European Zionism, it seems, was a subaltern nationalism and anticolonial liberation movement and at the same time an element of European bourgeois and colonialist cultures.

The notion that it was both, however, also points to the limits of a possible kinship between postcolonial studies and the historiography of Zionism. These limits originate mostly in the differences and sometimes even conflicts between their subject matter. Even if there are striking similarities between the experiences of the European Jews and of colonized peoples, these experiences have not been the same. Particularly in the nineteenth and twentieth centuries, the relationship between Jewish and non-Jewish populations in Europe were much more ambivalent than the relationship between Europeans and non-Europeans in the colonies. And although there are also striking similarities between Zionism and anticolonialism, these movements, too, were far from identical. In fact, significant parts of the Zionist movement have striven to distance themselves from colonized peoples and from anticolonialism. Moreover, just as Zionism adopted colonialist features from its European environment and also developed its own, antisemitism has not been alien to anticolonial movements, as well as postcolonial societies and states.[31] Political developments—most importantly the Israeli-Palestinian conflict, but also the Cold War, and more recently Islamist terror and the so-called "War on Terror"—have further distanced Zionism, or at least the State of Israel, from the struggle against colonialism and its consequences. These differences between the subjects of research limit the applicability of postcolonial concepts, which have been developed specifically for colonial and postcolonial contexts, to the history of Zionism. Any exploration of kinships between postcolonial studies and the historiography of Zionism will have to take these limits into account. However, they should not prevent such exploration in the first place. The claim of a kinship does not suggest the possibility of a seamless transfer of postcolonial concepts to the historiography of Zionism. Rather, it suggests a more or less intimate, sometimes uneasy, but often surprisingly productive connection between two different but related fields of scholarship.

Although most of the initiatives to reach out to the other discipline, whether related to the history of Zionism or Jewish history in general, have come from the field of Jewish studies, several postcolonial scholars have started to view Jewish history as part of their subject area. Notable authors such as Stuart Hall, Paul Gilroy, and Edward Said have made it clear that their findings were partially applicable to the situation of Jews. Hall, for instance, considered the Jews to be Europe's "own internal others," not identical, but certainly comparable to the colonized others.[32] One of the first systematic attempts to integrate Jewish history into the field of postcolonial studies was made by Aamir Mufti in his book *Enlightenment in the Colony*.[33] Mufti conceives of Jewish history as a paradigm of colonial and postcolonial minority histories that can serve as a prism for the contradictions of the universalism of European Enlightenment. Paul Gilroy has extended this linkage even to the history of Zionism. He suggests using the concept of diaspora as an instrument to explore the relationship of Black and Jewish experiences and the questions they pose about "the status of ethnic identity, the power of cultural nationalism, and the manner in which carefully preserved histories of ethnocidal suffering can function to supply ethical and political legitimacy."[34] Zionism, he argues, should be considered a worthwhile topic for postcolonial studies because it "share[s] many of its aspirations and some of its rhetoric" with Black nationalism.[35] Nevertheless, very few postcolonial scholars have followed up on these initiatives. Most have been reluctant to critically engage with the history of Zionism, and with Jewish history more generally, other than to identify colonialist elements in the origins and practices of the State of Israel. This often prevents scholars of postcolonial studies from seeing Zionism in all of its ambivalences, including those it shares with anticolonial nationalism and other subaltern movements. It is the hope of the editors of this book that it might trigger new interest among scholars of postcolonial studies and indicate a pathway to new critical and nuanced research in the history of Zionism.

Exchanges

What exactly do postcolonial studies have to offer for the scholarship of the historiography of Zionism? Even a preliminary answer to this question is complicated by the fact that postcolonial studies is a large and heterogeneous field. There is no consensus on the borders of this field or even on what the term "postcolonial" means. It is nevertheless possible to identify a number of important new perspectives that postcolonial scholars have introduced into social theory, cultural studies, and historiography. Perhaps one of the most crucial ones is that ambiguities should be seen not as problems, but rather as assets and resources for critical scholarship. More precisely, postcolonial studies have questioned the binaries that structured cultural relations in the colonial world and inspired their representations and that continue to do so after the end of formal colonial rule. As Stuart Hall puts it, "It is precisely this 'double inscription,' breaking down the clearly demarcated inside/outside of the colonial system on which the histories of imperialism have thrived for so long, which the concept of the 'post-colonial' has done so much to bring to the fore."[36] In this sense, the "post" in "postcolonial" does not refer to a situation after colonialism, even though the processes and consequences of decolonization are both an important subject of and a powerful impulse for postcolonial studies. Rather, it signals a decentered approach in which a multitude of histories, temporalities, and cultural connections challenge the predominance of Eurocentric narratives.

This has important consequences. First, postcolonial concepts can help us understand social relations and cultural representations before, during, after, and across the processes of decolonization. Second, they can be applied not only to colonized and formerly colonized societies but also to the societies in metropoles, and not only to social relations between the colonizing and the colonized societies but also to those within the colonizing and the colonized societies themselves. In this way, they identify colonialism as a constitutive element also of European and North American society and culture. Third, and most important, postcolonial concepts go beyond an analysis of the relationship between the colonizer and the colonized, or the colonizing and the colonized society, and look at the overlaps, intersections, and transformations between the two sides of the colonial divide. In their most sophisticated and interesting manifestations, postcolonial studies undermine the binary logic of colonialism without ignoring its binary-producing power. It is exactly this ambivalence that makes postcolonial studies attractive for historians of Zionism and that creates the room to include the history of Zionism into the subject area of postcolonial studies.

Let us, for instance, consider how Homi Bhabha has thought beyond colonial binaries. In his understanding, it is exactly the dualistic mechanisms of colonialism that unsettle the binaries they are meant to establish. Because colonialism constantly connects different spaces and cultures, it creates not only relationships of power and domination but also spaces of instability, ambiguity, and hybridity. These "in-between spaces" open up possibilities to redefine identities on a basis other than "origin" or "essence," and to reconfigure the relationship between societies and cultures. In so doing, they disturb and undermine the binary structure of colonialism.[37] Postcolonial theory, in this reading, strives to deconstruct colonialism by emphasizing these disturbances, the fissures that exist in the fabric of colonialism not despite but precisely because of its obsession to establish a strict distinction between the self and the other, between the colonizer and the colonized. Zionism can be understood as such a disturbance. It was a movement that, by means of colonization, strove to liberate the Jews from a condition of subalternity that at least partly followed colonialist patterns. It included hegemonial and colonialist, as well as anti-hegemonial and anticolonialist, elements and was therefore located on both sides of the colonial divide. Zionism clearly belonged in the colonial world but did not fit into the dualistic logic of colonialism.

In a different way, but also with great potentials for the study of the history of Zionism, Stuart Hall has tried to capture this ambiguity with his concept of identity politics in diaspora communities. Identities, he argues, are both the product of the disassembling and reassembling of communities through colonialism and a means of self-empowerment in the face of these often violently imposed processes. They are meant to withstand these fragmentations, but at the same time help reproduce them as long as they are based on the idea of fixed and stable cultures, histories, or races. Hall, in contrast, insists that identities have no such essence, but are a form of politics. They are ways to relate to, to position oneself, and to be positioned within a society or a social or cultural environment.[38] If identities are understood as positioning, they lose the unambiguity with which they have been furnished and become fluent and multivalent. It is now possible to conceive of a subaltern identity as comprising elements of distinction from, confrontation with, affirmation of, and even participation in the hegemonic society. This is exactly what we find in Zionist concepts of Jewish national identity.

Hall's understanding of postcolonial studies as a project aimed at decentering the hegemonic, Eurocentric perspective on culture and history has been implicitly shared by Dipesh Chakrabarty in his influential book *Provincializing Europe*.[39] Chakrabarty argues that European concepts of history, society, politics, and culture, while being indispensable to critically confront global structures of domination, are utterly insufficient to understand and eventually abolish them. They need to be complemented, scrutinized, and rethought from beyond Europe and "the West." It is easy to see that this "beyond" can be geographically located also inside Europe. Colonialism and globalization produced large and diverse migrant communities within European societies. What is more, there have always been marginalized groups among the population of the continent subject to exclusion, othering, and even colonization. Arguably, the most paradigmatic of these groups have been the Jews. Therefore, rethinking European history and thought from a Jewish perspective might very well be considered an important contribution to the provincializing of Europe. Zionism, as a form of Jewish identity politics, but also as a form of thinking about Jewishness and Jewish history, is certainly an important element of this perspective. Despite being implicated in the strengthening of the centrality of Europe, Zionism might thus also be one of the agents of its provincialization.

As a historian, Chakrabarty focuses particularly on the historicist understanding of the past that underlies most of European thought and that is unable to accommodate what he calls subaltern pasts. These are histories that resist integration into the historicist narrative and therefore remain ignored or subordinated.[40] This, too, can be expanded to include subaltern strands within European history, including Jewish history. Yet rather than just integrate these pasts into the hegemonial history, thereby subsuming them under the historicist perspective, it is necessary to acknowledge them in their difference. They are elements of "necessarily fragmentary histories of human belonging that never constitute a one or a whole."[41] Such an understanding not only rejects the holistic or unitary concepts of "belonging" and "nation" that have been developed in the European political tradition, but it also acknowledges diverse and fragmented ways of relating to this tradition. This raises the question of whether Zionism constitutes an example and a confirmation of this view. To be sure, Zionist intellectuals have also contributed to, and even co-constituted, the Eurocentric vision of history that Chakrabarty criticizes. However, if Jewish history was one of those subaltern pasts that have been excluded from or subordinated to the hegemonic concept of history, then Zionism could also be seen as an attempt to rewrite this history and therefore to confront this exclusion and subordination.

In this sense, Zionism may very well be understood as a project of self-empowerment, a subaltern nationalism, akin to the anticolonial nationalist ideologies and movements across the globe. At least, it makes sense to ask for similarities and differences, but also for interrelations with other forms of subaltern nationalism. Chakrabarty has pointed to the fact that "belonging" and "nation" can have different meanings in European and in colonial or postcolonial contexts. Indian nationalism, for instance, includes at least two ways to imagine a national community: one that places India in a historicist narrative and is heavily indebted to European nationalist traditions, and another that refers to non-European—in this case, Indian—spiritual practices and beliefs.[42] A similar plurality seems to be at work in some versions of Zionist nationalist thought. Zionists developed an ambivalent relationship to European nationalist thought, which combined a deep indebtedness to European nationalism, including its romanticist and neo-romanticist sources, with an awareness of its repressive consequences and an emphasis on the specifically Jewish roots of Zionist nationalism. Similarly, the inbuilt tension in Zionist nationalism between being on the one hand an emancipatory project that strives to empower a subaltern group and to provide it with agency, and on the other hand reproducing existing structures of domination by—deliberately or unwittingly—participating in the discourses and practices of hegemonial nationalism, including its inherent exclusionism and essentialism, can also be detected in many forms of anticolonial nationalism.[43]

To be sure, there are also many differences between Zionist and anticolonial nationalisms. Even though anticolonial movements, too, were able to make use of colonial structures to develop their own nationalist ideologies and politics, they could only in exceptional cases rely on the open support of European imperialist powers, which the Zionist movement at many points in its history could.[44] Moreover, Zionists could, and often did, imagine themselves as harbingers and pioneers of European culture within supposedly "uncultured" non-European spaces. Although Zionist thinking also included ideas of proximity and relatedness, or even belonging to the cultures of "the Orient"—thereby displaying a stark difference from European colonial thought—it could also contain notions of superiority. In this sense, the oft-noted Orientalism in Zionist thought had a distinctively ambivalent quality as well: It was a strategy of self-affirmation through identification with the "Oriental" other, but it also relied on the ideological structure of domination through othering so aptly described by Edward Said. This, again, underscores the necessity to think beyond the binaries that have characterized both colonialism and thinking about colonialism for so long. Instead of deciding whether Zionism is a colonial or an anticolonial movement, it is therefore necessary to situate it in the contested and ambiguous space "between colonial, anticolonial and postcolonial discourse and practice."[45]

Also geographically, Zionism cannot be located either exclusively inside or exclusively outside of Europe. It first emerged in Europe, albeit to a large degree at the eastern margins of the continent, where it continued to have its strongest base up until the devastations of World War II. Yet a new center also arose in Palestine, and in many other non-European spaces Zionist movements developed as well. Moreover, Zionists claimed a land outside of Europe not as a colony, but as their ancestral homeland. Zionism, thus, was in many ways at once a European and a non-European movement. Postcolonial theory seems to be particularly well equipped to accommodate this kind of ambiguity. It allows us to see the colonizing and the colonized parts of the world as an integrated space and emphasizes the multiple migrations of people, power structures, commodities, and ideas between them. And it pays specific attention to mutual influences and co-constitutions. Postcolonial theory, therefore, is as much a method to analyze European societies and cultures as it is a tool to understand the conditions of the colonies. Zionism, as a phenomenon of the European center and the European and extra-European peripheries, and of the spaces in between, thus seems to be a predestined subject for postcolonial studies.

After the foundation of the State of Israel, Zionism, it seems, gradually lost its in-betweenness and moved ever more closely toward "the West" as the hegemonic side of the colonial divide. Israel's collusion with the United Kingdom and France in the Suez crisis, alignment with the United States, support for the apartheid regime in South Africa, and, above all, its settlement policy in the territories conquered in the 1967 War make a strong case for this, as do remarks by leaders such as Ehud Barak about Israel being "a villa in the middle of the jungle."[46] Yet, here too, a closer look that is informed by postcolonial critique reveals a more complicated picture. In its profound economic challenges and veneration of technological development, Israel had much in common with other postcolonial states. During the 1960s, it provided technical assistance to African states, whose leaders hailed Israel as the successful product of an anticolonial liberation struggle.[47] The prehistory and the foundation of the state is also deeply embedded in the processes of decolonization and of the dissolution of the British Empire, as well as in the emergence of a new post-imperialist order after the war. The question whether postcolonial concepts can help us analyze and understand the history of Zionism is thus important not only for the early decades of this history, but also for its entirety, and it remains relevant in our own day.

New Explorations

The lack of conversation between postcolonial studies and the historiography of Zionism stems from a number of political factors. From the beginning, postcolonial studies had a decidedly political agenda: not only to analyze the deep and ongoing influence of colonialism on past and present societies and culture, but also to criticize and help abolish it. To a significant degree, their origins lay in anticolonial resistance movements or in the fight against racism in the metropoles, even if many of their protagonists taught at prestigious European or North American universities.[48] This has also meant that postcolonial scholars are usually supportive of the Palestinian struggle against Israel, which they often conceive of as perpetuating colonial rule.[49] Post-2000 developments such as the Second Intifadah and a sharp rightward turn in Israeli politics, but also a sometimes insufficiently complex view of the conflict, have intensified postcolonial studies scholars' pro-Palestinian sentiment and account for the popularity of the Boycott, Divestment, and Sanctions movement among them. In this heated atmosphere, it is difficult to argue in favor of recognizing ambivalence in both Zionist history and the history of colonialism. Ironically, to do so would necessitate a reaffirmation of the ambiguity that stood at the very foundation of postcolonial studies. In addition, it would mean a recognition of the diversity and contradictions that have characterized Zionist history from its inception. The essays collected in this book seek to enact this recognition. In this way, it might finally be possible to acknowledge, and to critically assess, the kinship between postcolonial studies and the historiography of Zionism.

Each of the three main sections of this book approaches this kinship from a different angle. The first section, "Conceptualizations," looks at specific postcolonial thinkers and/or concepts that are of particular interest for the study of the history of Zionism. Manja Herrmann investigates the notion of authenticity, an important trope in postcolonial contexts, in early German Zionist literature as a means of identity construction through counternarratives. Such counternarratives are commonly identified as anticolonial or antiracist strategies to confront the identity imposed on the subaltern group by the master narrative of the dominant or majority culture.[50] Herrmann sees a similar strategy at work in Zionist discourses, albeit appropriated for the specific purposes of Jewish identity politics in Europe. Stefan Vogt discusses the applicability and usefulness of Stuart Hall's work for the study of the history of Zionism. Focusing in particular on Hall's concept of identity politics as "positioning," he argues that looking at the history of Central European Zionism through the prism of Hall's work helps us understand the ambivalent character of Zionist nationalism, the position of Zionism within the European cultures in which it emerged, and the relationship of Zionism to anticolonial and postcolonial identity politics. Last, Abraham Rubin looks at an eminent

Jewish postcolonial thinker who later became a Zionist: Albert Memmi. This chapter explores the postcolonial and autobiographical threads of Memmi's Zionism by revisiting his renowned essay, "The Impossible Life of Frantz Fanon." Rubin analyzes Memmi's attempt to reconcile Zionism and postcolonialism, but also demonstrates the structural contradictions in his effort to situate Zionism within a Third World framework and dissociate the Jewish state from its Occidental origins.

Under the title "Looking West, Looking East," the chapters in the second section locate the Zionist imagination in between and at the same time on both ends of the East-West range. Postcolonial studies have long insisted on the significance of space and location as cultural categories.[51] Focusing on the "West" and the "East" as the most important spatial references in the context of the history of Zionism (and beyond), the essays in this section investigate both the imagery and the materiality of these locations in Zionist conceptions of Jewish identity. In so doing, they emphasize the ambiguities of these locations. Sarah Phillips Casteel opens this section by considering the Danish colony of St. Thomas in the Caribbean as a site of cross-cultural contact, influence, and interdiasporic exchange. She revisits two of its natives, the Afro-Caribbean intellectual Edward Wilmot Blyden (1832–1912) and the Jewish painter Camille Pissarro (1830–1903), who were both deeply affected by Zionist ideas, and explores how the figure of Zion travels between Jewish and Black intellectual and artistic traditions. In doing this, she also emphasizes the role of visual art for questions of identity. Małgorzata Maksymiak shows in her chapter how the term "*Ostjude*" was created and explores its impact on the Zionist social, cultural, and political program before World War I. In contrast to contemporary scholarship on European Zionism, however, which focuses on German-Jewish perceptions of the *Ostjude*, she gives voice to the Zionist *Ostjuden* themselves, presenting their own perception of the stereotype. This essay, too, follows the spatial turn in cultural history and postcolonial studies, but it offers the concept of mental mapping as an alternative to Orientalism.

In the third chapter of this section, Scott Spector presents the Habsburg Empire, or more accurately its Austrian, "Cisleithanian" half, which stretched from Tyrol to Galicia, as a space that itself spanned the range, both geographically and imaginatively, from the "West" to the "East." Using Memmi's twin portraits of the colonizer and the colonized, he analyzes the multiple ways in which Habsburg cultural Zionists conceptualized and fantasized "the East" with reference to Austria, Europe, Palestine, and even Asia.[52] Last, Ghilad H. Shenhav reads Gershom Scholem's early writings on the Hebrew language through a postcolonial lens, discussing in particular his reflections on the transfer of Hebrew from a liturgical and scholarly language in Europe to a secular daily one in Palestine. He shows how Scholem saw in the local, corporeal, and Oriental aspects of the Hebrew language something uncanny that threatened the Zionist movement from within. Scholem, Shenhav argues, attempted to suppress these threatening features of the language through the Occidental categories of German Romantic thought. Shenhav's essay demonstrates that exploring the relationship between textual and non-textual cultures is not only a core theme of postcolonial studies but also extremely fruitful for the study of Zionism.

The third section, "Palestine and Israel between Empire and Decolonization," focuses on a particular yet still expansive, heterogeneous, and highly ambivalent location: the Middle East. In the scholarship on Zionism in the Middle East, and especially in Palestine and Israel, a number of researchers have employed postcolonial methods. Their power to deconstruct nationalist historical narratives is considerable, yet they run the risk of establishing their own myths. In her review on recent work on Jewish history in the Middle East, Orit Bashkin describes how Zionist and Orientalist readings of Jewish histories were called into question by postcolonial theoreticians who discussed the ways in which Zionist historiography sought to undermine the significance of the Jewish past by subjecting it to a universalizing model of Jewish oppression under non-Jewish sovereignty. Yet just as Zionist historians identified the modernization of the Arab world with the rise of antisemitism, for the postcolonial school modernity was connected to the destruction of Middle Eastern Jewish communities and the Nakba of the Palestinian people. The recent scholarship that is discussed in her chapter emphasizes instead that Jews were attracted to new political frameworks that emerged in the late nineteenth and early twentieth centuries, namely Ottomanism, Arab nationalism, and local patriotism.

Johannes Becke, too, uses postcolonial concepts to challenge both Zionist and postcolonial certainties, this time regarding the State of Israel. His chapter compares the Judaization of the West Bank to other postcolonial expansionist state projects like the Moroccanization of Western Sahara and the Sinicization of Tibet. Becke argues that these state expansions after decolonization, though they differ in their degrees of success, share the contradictory features of a colonial projection of power and population, an anticolonial obsession with redeeming usurped ancestral homelands, and the postcolonial monumentalism inherited from high modernism. In the concluding chapter of this section, Rephael G. Stern and Arie M. Dubnov trace the history of Zionist Asianism from the end of the British Mandate through the early years of the State of Israel. Looking especially at Zionists' attempts to forge ties to the emerging postcolonial states in Asia, they compare and contrast the discourse and diplomatic activities of the Hebrew University's delegation to the Asian Relations Conference in 1947 with the way Zionism was imagined, and imagined itself, at the time of the Conference of Asian and African Nations in Bandung in 1955. Stern and Dubnov ask whether this history testifies to a relationship between Zionism and the postcolonial world that is even more complicated and ambivalent than the notion of an unacknowledged kinship is able to suggest.

The book's objective, however, is not only to discuss the existence and the extent of such kinship, whether between Zionist and colonial or postcolonial history, or between the historiography of Zionism and postcolonial studies. It also strives to encourage dialogue between those active in the two academic fields. The final section, "Conversations," intends to provide openings for such a dialogue. Two eminent postcolonial scholars, Dipesh Chakrabarty and Ato Quayson, have contributed to this section, offering their thoughts on the relationship between postcolonial studies and the historiography of Zionism. In an extended interview, Chakrabarty discusses intersections between the experiences of the Jews and of the colonized, and to what extent Jewish history, and the history of Zionism, can contribute to unsettle historicist perspectives on modernity und thus to "provincialize" Europe. Quayson adds his thoughts on the postcoloniality of Zionism in his insightful afterword. Chakrabarty and Quayson demonstrate that thinking together Jewish and postcolonial perspectives can have a great impact upon the understanding of and confrontation with structures of domination. Their contributions, along with the essays in this volume, clearly establish that acknowledging the kinship of postcolonial studies and the historiography of Zionism, including the limits and ambivalences of this kinship, is far more than merely an academic endeavor.

NOTES

1. The image can be accessed at www.gettyimages.de/detail/nachrichtenfoto/picture-obtained-by-afp-04-july-2000-shows-us-scholar-nachrichtenfoto/51396655?adppopup=true. Obviously, no one was in the area where the stone landed. On the incident and Said's reaction to the critique, see Sunnie Kim, "Edward Said Accused of Stoning in South Lebanon," *Columbia Spectator*, July 19, 2000, http://columbiaspectator.com/2000/07/19/edward-said-accused-stoning-south-lebanon.

2. See for example Aamir Mufti, *Enlightenment in the Colony: The Jewish Question and the Crisis of Postcolonial Critique* (Princeton, NJ: Princeton University Press, 2007), 9–10; Homi K. Bhabha, *The Location of Culture* (London: Routledge, 2004), 165; Robert J. C. Young, *Postcolonialism: A Very Short Introduction* (Oxford: Oxford University Press, 2003), 14–16; Achille Mbembe, "Necropolitics," *Political Culture* 15 (2003): 11–14. Also Stuart Hall, who is discussed in this book as an important reference for possible intersections between postcolonial studies and the historiography of Zionism, portrays Zionism as the imperialist antithesis to a postcolonial conception of diaspora. See Stuart Hall, "Cultural Identity and Diaspora," in *Identity: Community, Culture, Difference*, ed. Jonathan Rutherford (London: Lawrence & Wishart, 1990), 222–37, here 235. Partha Chatterjee and Ann Stoler, among others, are active supporters of the academic boycott movement against Israel, both citing their postcolonial perspectives as reasons for this. See Partha Chatterjee, "Why I Support the Boycott of Israeli Institutions," *Savage Minds: Notes and Queries in Anthropology*, September 9, 2015, http://savageminds.org/2015/09/09/partha-chatterjee-why-i-support-the-boycott-of-israeli-institutions; Ann Laura Stoler, "By Colonial Design," *Pulse*, September 10, 2010, https://pulsemedia.org/2010/09/17/eminent-scholar-ann-stoler-endorses-boycott-of-israel. Said was in fact much more ambivalent in his position toward Israel. He was very active in promoting Israeli-Palestinian reconciliation, yet he rejected the Oslo Peace Accords and advocated a binational state. See, for instance, Edward W. Said, *The End of the Peace Process: Oslo and After* (New York: Vintage Books, 2001).

3. See, for instance, Efraim Sicher, *Under Postcolonial Eyes: Figuring the "Jew" in Contemporary British Writing* (Lincoln: University of Nebraska Press, 2012); Philip Carl Salzman and Donna Robinson Divine, eds., *Postcolonial Theory and the Arab-Israeli Conflict* (London: Routledge, 2008).

4. Daniel Boyarin and Jonathan Boyarin, "Diaspora: Generation and the Ground of Jewish Identity," *Critical Inquiry* 19 (1993): 693–725.

5. Samuel Moyn, "German Jewry and the Question of Identity: Historiography and Theory," *Leo Baeck Institute Year Book* 41 (1996): 291–308; Susannah Heschel, "Jewish Studies as Counterhistory," in *Insider/Outsider: American Jews and Multiculturalism*, ed. David Biale, Michael Galchinsky, and Susannah Heschel (Berkeley: University of California Press, 1998), 101–15.

6. See, for example, Joel Beinin, *The Dispersion of Egyptian Jewry: Culture, Politics, and the Formation of a Modern Disapora* (Berkeley: University of California Press, 1998); Yehouda Shenhav, *The Arab Jews: A Postcolonial Reading of Nationalism, Religion, and Ethnicity* (Stanford, CA: Stanford University Press, 2006); Orit Bashkin, *New Babylonians: A History of Jews in Modern Iraq* (Stanford, CA: Stanford University Press, 2012); Sarah Abrevaya Stein, *Saharan Jews and the Fate of French Algeria* (Chicago: University of Chicago Press, 2014); Sarah Phillips Casteel, *Calypso Jews: Jewishness in the Caribbean Literary Imagination* (New York: Columbia University Press, 2016).

7. See, for example, Liora R. Halperin, *Babel in Zion: Jews, Nationalism, and Language Diversity in Palestine, 1920–1948* (New Haven, CT: Yale University Press, 2015); Dafna Hirsch, *"We Are Here to Bring the West": Hygiene Education and Culture Building in the Jewish Society of Mandate Palestine* (Sde Boker: Mahon Ben-Gurion, 2014) [Hebrew]; Ella Shohat, "Sephardim in Israel: Zionism from the Standpoint of its Jewish Victims," *Social Text*, no. 19/20 (Autumn 1988): 1–35. See also Arieh Bruce Saposnik, *Becoming Hebrew: The Creation of a Jewish National Culture in Ottoman Palestine* (New York: Oxford University Press, 2008). Most recently, Arie M. Dubnov has forcefully suggested analyzing the emergence of the State of Israel in the context of the decline of the British Empire. See Arie M. Dubnov, "Notes on the Zionist Passage to India: Or: The Analogical Imagination and its Boundaries," *Journal of Israeli History* 35 (2016): 177–214; Arie M. Dubnov, "On Vertical Alliances, 'Perfidious Albion' and the Security Paradigm: Reflections on the Balfour Declaration Centennial and the Winding Road to Israeli Independence," *European Judaism* 52 (2019): 67–110.

8. See, for example, Motti Regev and Edwin Seroussi, *Popular Music and National Culture in Israel* (Berkeley: California University Press, 2004); Dalia Manor, *Art in Zion: The Genesis of Modern National Art in Jewish Palestine* (London: Routledge, 2005); Yonathan Mendel and Ronald Ranta, *From the Arab Other to the Israeli Self: Palestinian Culture in the Making of Israeli National Identity* (Farnham: Ashgate, 2016).

9. See https://theory-and-criticism.vanleer.org.il. The journal was founded in 1991.

10. See, for instance, Ronen Shamir, *The Colonies of Law: Colonialism, Zionism and Law in Early Mandate Palestine* (Cambridge, UK: Cambridge University Press, 2000); Ilan Pappé, *A History of Modern Palestine: One Land, Two Peoples* (Cambridge, UK: Cambridge University Press, 2004); Shenhav, *The Arab Jews*; Nur Masalha, *The Palestine Nakba: Decolonising History, Narrating the Subaltern, Reclaiming Memory* (London: Zed Books, 2012). The colonial paradigm has also been applied to the history of Israel and the Yishuv without resorting to postcolonial concepts. See, for instance, Gershon Shafir, *Land, Labour and the Origins of the Israeli-Palestinian Conflict 1882–1914* (Cambridge, UK: Cambridge University Press, 1989).

11. See, for instance, Ran Aaronsohn, "Settlement in Palestine: A Colonial Endeavour?" in *Zionism: A Contemporary Controversy*, ed. Pinhas Ginossar and Avi Bareli (Sde Boker: Ben-Gurion Research Center, 1996), 340–54 [Hebrew]; Avi Bareli, "Forgetting Europe: Perspectives on the Debate about Zionism and Colonialism," *The Journal of Israeli History* 20 (2001): 99–120.

12. See, for instance, Stuart Hall, "When Was 'the Post-Colonial'? Thinking at the Limit," in *The Postcolonial Question: Common Skies, Divided Horizons*, ed. Iain Chambers and

Lidia Curti (London: Routledge, 1996), 242–60; Ann Laura Stoler and Frederick Copper, "Between Metropole and Colony: Rethinking a Research Agenda," in *Tensions of Empire: Colonial Cultures in a Bourgeois World*, ed. Frederick Copper and Ann Laura Stoler (Berkeley: University of California Press, 1997), 1–56; Bhabha, *The Location of Culture*, esp. 1–27.

13. See Feisal Devji, *Muslim Zion: Pakistan as a Political Idea* (London: Hurst & Company, 2013); Johannes Becke, "Towards a De-Occidentalist Perspective on Israel: The Case of the Occupation," *Journal of Israeli History* 33 (2014): 1–23.

14. For more nuanced views, see for instance Jonathan Marc Gribetz, *Defining Neighbors: Religion, Race, and the Early Zionist-Arab Encounter* (Princeton, NJ: Princeton University Press, 2014); Dubnov, "Notes on the Zionist Passage to India."

15. Bareli, "Forgetting Europe."

16. For early examples, see Derek J. Penslar, *Zionism and Technocracy: The Engineering of Jewish Settlement in Palestine, 1870–1918* (Bloomington: Indiana University Press, 1991); John M. Efron, *Defenders of the Race: Jewish Doctors and Race Science in Fin-de-Siècle Europe* (New Haven, CT: Yale University Press, 1994); David N. Myers, *Re-Inventing the Jewish Past: European Jewish Intellectuals and the Zionist Return to History* (New York: Oxford University Press, 1995).

17. Stoler and Copper, "Between Metropole and Colony," 1.

18. Jonathan M. Hess, *Germans, Jews and the Claims of Modernity* (New Haven, CT: Yale University Press, 2002); Jonathan M. Hess, "'Sugar Island Jews'? Jewish Colonialism and the Rhetoric of 'Civic Improvement' in Eighteenth-Century Germany," *Eighteenth-Century Studies* 32 (1998): 92–100; Susannah Heschel, *Abraham Geiger and the Jewish Jesus* (Chicago: University of Chicago Press, 1998); Christian Wiese, *Challenging Colonial Discourse: Jewish Studies and Protestant Theology in Wilhelmine Germany* (Leiden: Brill, 2005).

19. For France, see Ronald Schechter, *Obstinate Hebrews: Representations of Jews in France, 1715–1815* (Berkeley: University of California Press, 2003); Maud S. Mandel, *Muslims and Jews in France: History of a Conflict* (Princeton, NJ: Princeton University Press, 2014); Ethan B. Katz, *The Burdens of Brotherhood: Jews and Muslims from North Africa to France* (Cambridge, MA: Harvard University Press, 2015). Studies on Britain include David Feldman, "The British Empire and the Jews, c. 1900," *History Workshop Journal* 63 (2007): 70–89; Eitan Bar-Yosef and Nadia Valman, eds., *"The Jew" in Late-Victorian and Edwardian Culture: Between the East End and East Africa* (Basingstoke: Palgrave Macmillan, 2009); Abigail Green, "The British Empire and the Jews: An Imperialism of Human Rights?" *Past and Present* 199, no. 1 (2008): 175–205.

20. For Russia, see especially Israel Bartal, *The Jews of Eastern Europe, 1772–1881* (Tel Aviv: Ministry of Defense Publishing House, 2002 [Hebrew]; English ed.: Philadelphia: University of Pennsylvania Press, 2005). For Habsburg, see, for instance, Scott Spector, *Prague Territories: National Conflict and Cultural Innovation in Franz Kafka's Fin de Siècle* (Berkeley: University of California Press, 2000).

21. Michael Rothberg, *Multidirectional Memory: Remembering the Holocaust in the Age of Decolonization* (Stanford, CA: Stanford University Press, 2009); Bryan Cheyette, *Diasporas of the Mind: Jewish and Postcolonial Writing and the Nightmare of History* (New Haven, CT: Yale University Press, 2013).

22. See Stefan Vogt, ed., *Colonialism and the Jews in German History: From the Middle Ages to the 20th Century* (London: Bloomsbury Academic, 2022); Ethan B. Katz, Lisa Moses Leff, and Maud S. Mandel, eds., *Colonialism and the Jews* (Bloomington: Indiana University Press, 2017); "Jewish Studies and Postcolonialism," Special Issue, ed. Willy Goetschel and Ato Quayson, *Cambridge Journal of Postcolonial Literary Inquiry* 3 (2016).

23. Paul Mendes-Flohr, "Fin-de-Siècle Orientalism, the Ostjuden and the Aesthetics of Jewish Self-Affirmation," *Studies in Contemporary Jewry* 1 (1984): 96–139.

24. For uses of "Orientalism" in the study of European Zionism, see for example Nadia Malinovich, "Orientalism and the Construction of Jewish Identity in France, 1900–1932," *Jewish Culture and History* 2 (1999): 1–25; Markus Kirchhoff, "Erweiterter Orientalismus: Zu euro-christlichen Identifikationen und jüdischer Gegengeschichte im 19. Jahrhundert," in *Jüdische Geschichte als allgemeine Geschichte*, ed. Raphael Gross and Yfaat Weiss (Göttingen: Wallstein, 2006), 99–119; Małgorzata A. Maksymiak, *Mental Maps im Zionismus: Ost und West in Konzepten einer jüdischen Nation vor 1914* (Bremen: Edition Lumière, 2015); Stefan Vogt, "The Postcolonial Buber: Orientalism, Subalternity, and Identity Politics in Martin Buber's Political Thought," *Jewish Social Studies* 22 (2016): 161–86; Viktoria Pötzl, "From Pan-Asianism to Safari-Zionism: Gendered Orientalism in Jewish-Austrian Literature," *Journal of Modern Jewish Studies* 19 (2020): 205–23. For non-European Zionisms, see for instance Yaron Peleg, *Orientalism and the Hebrew Imagination* (Ithaca, NY: Cornell University Press, 2005); Saposnik, *Becoming Hebrew*.

25. Ivan Davidson Kalmar and Derek J. Penslar, eds., *Orientalism and the Jews* (Waltham, MA: Brandeis University Press, 2005); Ulrike Brunotte, Anna-Dorothea Ludewig, and Axel Stähler, eds., *Orientalism, Gender, and the Jews: Literary and Artistic Transformations of European National Discourses* (Berlin: De Gryter, 2015); Ulrike Brunotte, Jürgen Mohn, and Christina Späti, eds., *Internal Outsiders – Imagined Orientals? Antisemitism, Colonialism and Modern Constructions of Jewish Identity* (Würzburg: Ergon, 2017).

26. See, for example, Michael Berkowitz, *Zionist Culture and West European Jewry before the First World War* (Chapel Hill: University of North Carolina Press, 1993); Michael Berkowitz, *The Jewish Self-Image in the West* (New York: New York University Press, 2000); Brunotte, Ludewig, and Stähler, *Orientalism, Gender, and the Jews*; Lynne M. Swarts, *Gender, Orientalism and the Jewish Nation: Women in the Work of Ephraim Moses Lilien at the German Fin-de-Siècle* (New York: Bloomsbury Visual Arts, 2020).

27. For a recent collection in this field, see Midori Yamamura and Yu-Chieh Li, eds., *Visual Representations of the Postcolonial Struggles: Art in East and Southeast Asia* (London: Routledge, 2021). For an interesting collection that juxtaposes Black and Jewish practices of representation, see Nicholas Mirzoeff, ed., *Diaspora and Visual Culture: Representing Africans and Jews* (London: Routledge, 2000).

28. Classical accounts include Stuart Hall, "Notes on Deconstructing 'the Popular,'" in *People's History and Socialist Theory*, ed. Raphael Samuel (London: Routledge, 1982), 227–40; Paul Gilroy, *There Ain't No Black in the Union Jack: The Cultural Politics of Race and Nation* (London: Hutchinson, 1987). For a recent collection, see Nadia Atia and Kate Houlden, eds., *Popular Postcolonialisms: Discourses of Empire and Popular Culture* (London: Routledge, 2019).

29. See, for instance, Artur Kamczycki, "Orientalism: Herzl and His Beard," *Journal of Modern Jewish Studies* 12 (2013): 90–116; Noah Isenberg, *Between Redemption and Doom: The Strains of German-Jewish Modernism* (Lincoln: University of Nebraska Press, 1999); Jascha Nemtsov, *Der Zionismus in der Musik: Jüdische Musik und nationale Idee* (Wiesbaden: Hassarowitz, 2009).

30. An incomplete list includes Derek J. Penslar, "Is Zionism a Colonial Movement?" in Katz, Leff, and Mandel, *Colonialism and the Jews*, 275–300; Spector, *Prague Territories*; Stefan Vogt, *Subalterne Positionierungen: Der deutsche Zionismus im Feld des Nationalismus in Deutschland, 1890–1933* (Göttingen: Wallstein, 2016); Stefan Vogt, "Zionismusgeschichte und postcolonial studies: Überlegungen zu einem uneingestandenen Verwandtschaftsverhältnis," *Werkstatt Geschichte* 76 (2017): 43–58; Manja Herrmann, *Zionismus und Authentizität: Gegennarrative des Authentischen im frühen zionistischen Diskurs* (Berlin: De Gruyter, 2018).

31. In recent years, a great number of studies of varying quality has been published on "subaltern" antisemitisms, especially on antisemitism in Islamic cultures, societies, and states. Among the more nuanced and reliable are Doron Rabinovici, Ulrich Speck, and Natan Sznaijder, eds., *Neuer Antisemitismus? Eine globale Debatte* (Frankfurt am Main: Suhrkamp, 2004); Meir Litvak and Esther Webman, eds., *From Empathy to Denial: Arab Responses to the Holocaust* (New York: Columbia University Press, 2009); Francis R. Nicosia and Boğaç A. Ergene, eds., *Nazis, the Holocaust, and the Middle East: Arab and Turkish Responses* (New York: Berghahn, 2018).

32. Stuart Hall, "The West and the Rest: Discourse and Power," in *Formations of Modernity*, ed. Stuart Hall and Bram Gieben (Cambridge, UK: Polity Press, 1992), 275–320, here 280; Paul Gilroy, *The Black Atlantic: Modernity and Double Consciousness* (Cambridge, MA: Harvard University Press, 1993), 205–12; Paul Gilroy, *Between Camps: Nations, Cultures and the Allure of Race* (London: Routledge, 2000), 279–326; Edward W. Said, *Orientalism* (New York: Vintage Books, 1979), 27–28 and 234–35.

33. Mufti, *Enlightenment in the Colony*.

34. Gilroy, *The Black Atlantic*, 207.

35. Ibid., 205. One of the few scholars of postcolonial studies who has taken up Gilroy's suggestion is Ato Quayson; see Ato Quayson, "Comparative Postcolonialisms: Storytelling and Community in Sholem Alechem and Chinua Achebe," *Cambridge Journal of Postcolonial Literary Inquiry* 3 (2016): 55–77.

36. Hall, "When Was 'the Post-Colonial,'" 247.

37. Bhabha, *The Location of Culture*, 1–2. Concepts of ambiguity and hybridity as an alternative to colonial binaries have been introduced into Jewish history by scholars such as Sander Gilman and Tudor Parfitt. See, for example, Sander L. Gilman, *Multiculturalism and the Jews* (London: Routledge, 2006); Tudor Parfitt, *Black Jews in Africa and the Americas* (Cambridge, MA: Harvard University Press, 2013).

38. See, especially, Hall, "Cultural Identity and Diaspora"; Stuart Hall, "Introduction: Who Needs Identity," in *Questions of Cultural Identity*, ed. Stuart Hall and Paul Du Gay (London: Sage, 1996), 1–17.

39. Dipesh Chakrabarty, *Provincializing Europe: Postcolonial Thought and Historical Difference* (Princeton, NJ: Princeton University Press, 2000).

40. See ibid., 97–113. See also Hall, "When Was 'the Post-Colonial,'" 251–53.
41. Chakrabarty, *Provincializing Europe*, 255.
42. See ibid., 148–79. It is interesting to note that Chakrabarty here refers extensively to the Indian poet and philosopher Rabindranath Tagore, who repeatedly exchanged his views with the Austrian-German Zionist thinker Martin Buber. On this relationship, see Abik Rhoy, "Martin Buber and Rabindranath Tagore: A Meeting of Two Great Minds," *Comparative Literature East & West* 25 (2016): 30–42; Maurice Friedman, "Martin Buber and Asia," *Philosophy East and West* 26 (1976): 411–26.
43. This tension has been analyzed in detail for the case of German Zionism in Vogt, *Subalterne Positionierungen*. See also Christian Wiese, "The Janus Face of Nationalism: The Ambivalence of Zionist Identity in Robert Weltsch and Hans Kohn," *Leo Baeck Institute Year Book* 51 (2006): 103–30; Axel Stähler, *Zionism, the German Empire, and Africa: Jewish Metamorphoses and the Colors of Difference* (Berlin: De Gryter, 2019).
44. See Derek Jonathan Penslar, "Declarations of (In)Dependence: Tensions within Zionist Statecraft, 1896–1948," *Journal of Levantine Studies* 8 (2018): 13–34.
45. Penslar, "Is Zionism a Colonial Movement?"
46. Address by then Foreign Minister Ehud Barak to the National Jewish Community Relations Advisory Council, February 11, 1996, quoted in Eitan Bar-Yosef, "A Villa in the Jungle: Herzl, Zionist Culture, and the Great African Adventure," in *Theodor Herzl: From Europe to Zion*, ed. Mark H. Gelber and Vivian Liska (Tübingen: Niemeyer, 2007), 85–102, here 86.
47. Anat Mooreville, "Eyeing Africa: The Politics of Israeli Ocular Expertise and International Aid, 1959–1973," *Jewish Social Studies* 21 (2016): 31–71. See also Daniel Kupfert Heller, "Israeli Aid and the 'African Woman': The Gendered Politics of International Development, 1958–73," *Jewish Social Studies* 25 (2020): 49–78.
48. On the history of postcolonial studies, see Robert J. C. Young, *Postcolonialism: An Historical Introduction* (Oxford: Blackwell Publishing, 2001).
49. The fact that one of the "founding fathers" of postcolonial studies, Edward Said, was a Palestinian who left his native Jerusalem with his family after the war of 1948, has certainly added to this bias. For Said's biography, see H. Aram Veeser, *Edward Said: The Charisma of Criticism* (London: Routledge, 2010), as well as his autobiography: Edward W. Said, *Out of Place: A Memoir* (London: Granta Books, 2000).
50. Without using the term itself, the concept has been introduced most forcefully in Bill Ashcroft, Gareth Griffith, and Helen Tiffin, eds., *The Empire Writes Back: Theory and Practice in Post-Colonial Literatures* (London: Routledge, 1994). See also the applications of this concept to Jewish history in Susannah Heschel, "Jewish Studies as Counterhistory," in *Insider/Outsider: American Jews and Multiculturalism*, ed. David Biale, Michael Galchinsky, and Susannah Heschel (Berkeley: University of California Press, 1998), 101–15; David Biale, *Gershom Scholem: Kabbalah and Counter-History* (Cambridge, MA: Harvard University Press, 1979).
51. See, for instance, Andrew Taverson and Sara Upstone, eds., *Postcolonial Spaces: The Politics of Place in Contemporary Culture* (Basingstoke: Palgrave Macmillan, 2011); Bill Ashcroft, Gareth Griffith, and Helen Tiffin, eds., *The Post-Colonial Studies Reader* (Lon-

don: Routledge, 1995). See also Said, *Orientalism*, esp. 49–73; Bhabha, *The Location of Culture*, esp. 1–27, 199–244, and 303–37.

52. Albert Memmi, *The Colonizer and the Colonized*, trans. Howard Greengeld (London: Earthscan, 2003), first published in French as *Portrait du colonisé: Précédé du portrait du colonisateur* (Paris: Ed. Bichet/Chastel, 1957).

Part I
Conceptualizations

2

A Rebellious "Tied-Up Beast"

German Zionist Concepts of Authenticity as Counternarratives

MANJA HERRMANN

"The Zionist idea wants to provide the Jews with inner safety," I replied,
"it aims to remove the ambivalence in the Jew of our time;
unbiasedness and inner freedom are its companions."

KURT BLUMENFELD

The umbrella term "Zionism," though it refers to a specific political movement, carries additional, contested shades of subjective meaning. It was allegedly through Zionism, as Kurt Blumenfeld (1884–1963) demonstrated in the passage quoted above, that Jews could attain true freedom. Similar arguments were put forth by other intellectual advocates of Zionism. This belief refers not only to the vision of *a Jewish state*, where Jews could live freely, but also to *a state of mind*. The latter aspect of Zionism, which is often overlooked, can best be grasped by analyzing the concepts of authenticity and the search for the authentic self, both of which were of the utmost importance in the construction of Zionist thought.

Conventional research into German-Jewish notions of authenticity is dominated by the projection of "authentic Judaism" and "Jewishness" onto Eastern Europe. Accordingly, "the authentic Jew" is situated within the geo-cultural unit referred to as "the East."[1] Through an analysis of the German-Jewish nationalist and Zionist discourse of authenticity, I would like to call this assumption into question. Within German-speaking Jewish nationalism and Zionism, negotiations of authenticity are omnipresent, and German Zionist thinkers formulated their own understanding of "authentic Zionism" and of what traits define an "authentic Zionist."

The Jewish nationalist and Zionist discourse of authenticity did not arise in a vacuum but rather in close connection with the societal situation of the Jews.[2] Negotiations of emancipation, recognition, and self-assertion, as well as antisemitism and other societal restrictions, are part of this discourse. Following the Zionist sources, we begin to understand this relationship as one between "hegemonic" and "counternarrative" approaches, as has already been pointed out in several studies of both cultural history and German-Jewish history. Accordingly, within Zionist discourse, authenticities were constructed by means of counternarratives. In other words, the nationalist Jewish and Zionist discourses of authenticity are often directed against a majority culture, or against a "master narrative" or "dominant discourse."[3] In the strongest sense, this means a rebellion against master narratives; in the weakest sense, these discourses provide an alternative to a common narrative.

Among several other scholars of German-Jewish studies employing postcolonial perspectives in general and the hegemonic-versus-counternarratives model in particular, Susannah Heschel famously applied the framing of Jewish history as counter-history to her work.[4] In her 1998 monograph *Abraham Geiger and the Jewish Jesus*, which analyzes the *Wissenschaft des Judentums*, Heschel highlights that "postcolonial theory's recognition that minority literature is characterized by counterdiscursive practices helps to illumine Geiger's work, inasmuch as the logic of his historical arguments represented an inversion of accepted European self-understanding."[5]

This chapter will demonstrate how German Zionist counternarratives of authenticity evolved. In particular, it will show which people and practices were marked as inauthentic and opposed to Zionism, which was constructed as the only authentic form of Jewish existence and the only way to live a truly free life. As the cultural historian Regina Bendix puts it: "The notion of authenticity implies the existence of its opposite, the fake."[6] Zionist thinkers counternarrated everything that they considered to be "fake" or "inauthentic." Alongside counternarratives of Christianity and Christian culture, a variety of codes that denoted "inauthentic Jews" developed within Zionist thought. Among these are "assimilationists," "new Marranos," and "Philistines." Additionally, in Zionist counternarratives of authenticity, we can observe fundamentally different situations for women and men and clear gender boundaries that were drawn regarding the search for one's own Jewish self and for true freedom.

The Concept of Authenticity

In order to better understand the Zionist notion of "fake," it is necessary to delineate the concept of authenticity. The literary critic Lionel Trilling explains that the implicit ontological level of authenticity can be deduced from the ideal of sincerity.[7] Trilling observes that in the sixteenth century, due to societal changes, "the moral life of Europe added to itself a new element, the state or quality of the self, which we call sincerity."[8] The most important sources for this are to be found in the domain of theater, which, as Regina Bendix points out, is constructed of pretense and artifice, that is, "insincerity."[9] In this discourse, parallels were drawn between roles one plays in theater and roles one plays in society. This led, in Trilling's view, to the emergence of a new concept: authenticity. In Trilling's words:

> Society requires of us that we present ourselves as being sincere, and the most efficacious way of satisfying this demand is to see to it that we really are sincere, that we actually are what we want our community to know we are. In short, we play the role of being ourselves, we sincerely act the part of the sincere person, with the result that a judgment may be passed upon our sincerity that it is not authentic.[10]

In other words, questions arose as to whether, underneath the demands of civilization, layers of uncorrupted selfhood could be found. These layers, this state of being, can implicitly be called "authentic."

The philosopher Charles Taylor explains the process by which being in this authentic state and leading an authentic life became a moral obligation in modern times. Taylor refers to Johann Gottfried Herder and his essentialist idea that every human being has his or her own "measure." This idea burrowed deep into modern consciousness.[11] In Taylor's words:

There is a certain way of being human that is *my* way. I am called upon to live my life in this way, and not in imitation of anyone else's life. But this notion gives a new importance to being true to myself. If I am not, I miss the point of my life; I miss what being human is for *me*.[12]

In connection to this moral obligation, nationalist ideology, as Elie Kedourie states, produces the belief that the individual can only fulfill themselves as an authentic human being by being part of a nation.[13] The concept of authenticity therefore remained central in the nineteenth century, especially in the German territories. In German Zionism, this concept was of major importance.

Counternarrating Christianity and Christian Culture

The idea that a human being can only fulfill himself and achieve an authentic state of being in his own nation and culture appeared in German-Jewish discourse in the second half of the nineteenth century. Up until now, scholars working on this time period have mostly focused on Moses Hess (1812–1875) and his 1862 work *Rome and Jerusalem*, which is generally understood as the first published manifestation of modern Zionist thought and secular nationalist Judaism in the German territories.[14] In *Rome and Jerusalem*, Hess stressed the effects of national ideology on the self. Real freedom could, according to Hess, only be achieved when Jews lived in harmony with their "nature"—and this was impossible under the "external restraint" that characterized the so-called "German-Jewish experience."[15] As Hess writes: "We call every being free, in the natural sense, which can develop its own destiny, its inner calling, according to its natural inclinations, without any external restraint."[16] Few sources exist and little research has been conducted on the Jewish nationalist concept of authenticity during Hess's time. The rediscovery of Wilhelm Herzberg's (1827–1897) 1868 Jewish nationalist novel *Jüdische Familienpapiere: Briefe eines Missionairs* (translated in 1875 as *Jewish Family Papers; or Letters of a Missionary*)[17] was an important addition to the body of literature on this issue.[18]

Jewish Family Papers, an epistolary novel, was extremely successful in its time.[19] It revolves around the protagonist Samuel's search for authenticity and comprises twenty-nine letters that he addresses to his foster father in England. Samuel loses both parents at the age of five and is raised as a Christian in his foster home. At the age of twenty-five, he decides to visit his uncle, his father's brother, who is a rabbi in Germany. Initially, he intends to convert his uncle's entire family to Christianity. However, his visit turns out to be an emotional journey into his own authentic self. The novel brings ideas of authenticity and inauthenticity into close conflict. Thus, from the very beginning, the reader is faced with concepts that are antonymous to the idea of authenticity—namely, lies and deception—which, as the novel demonstrates, will necessarily lead to negative consequences. Samuel, whose Jewishness conflicts with his Christian upbringing, is dissatisfied, unhappy, and plagued by nightmares. In the first letter, he confesses to his Christian adoptive father that he has always considered "[Christian] Theology" to be "a book with seven seals."[20] The description of the crucifixion in particular is especially horrifying to Samuel and inspired the childhood nightmares he describes in one of his letters. While he is traveling to meet his uncle, these nightmares return and he once again hears "those fearful groans out of the corner of the room," illustrating his self-betrayal.[21]

Eventually, Samuel returns to his Jewish faith, but throughout the novel, we witness several discussions between Samuel and the rabbi that resonate with the discourse of authenticity. These discussions are closely related to the discourse of modernity and offer a critique of modern times. Samuel represents modernity, progress, the city, individualism, and detachment from traditions. His unhappy and unstable self embodies the so-called sickness of civilization. To the rabbi, Samuel's conflict is a symptom of the sickness of modernity that is often found in modern men. In his eyes, this sickness can only be healed through Samuel's rediscovery of his true self. Numerous Jewish nationalist sentiments and statements surround this gradual process of self-discovery, including "a wondrous vibration," which Samuel feels "was more than interest in a co-religionist, it was the spirit of common nationality, of common blood." Finally, his return to Judaism is described in the novel almost as a kind of enlightenment:

> At last the Lord opened my eyes, and lo! she lay before me, quite near to me. She was my inheritance from my fathers, I needed only to take her by the hand and she was mine. I was blind but now I can see: let me enjoy my untold fortune quietly. For the first time in my life, I AM HAPPY!

The "bliss" of experiencing the self in light of his Jewish national belonging cures Samuel of the sickness of modernity and the lie he had lived as a Christian. Nevertheless, this passage highlights the ambiguity of the concept of authenticity, particularly when placed in the context of the discourse of modernity. Samuel's apparent rejection of modern achievements is in fact connected to a uniquely modern concept—that of personal happiness. This ambiguity in counternarratives that attempt to construct conflicted characters who ultimately prove to have a hybrid nature is central throughout the Zionist discourse of authenticity.

Modernity is not the only idea that is counternarrated throughout the novel. The first edition was published under the pseudonym "Gustav Meinhardt," most likely because Herzberg did not want to expose himself to critics due to the harsh criticism of Christianity articulated in the book. In one of his letters, Samuel asks his foster father a provocative question: "Indeed, the unprejudiced inquirer into history must ask himself the question in all seriousness: did European civilization arise *through* Christianity, or *in spite* of it?"[22] He goes on to argue that Christianity has "fostered priestly tyranny and the ignorance and stupidity of the masses,"[23] and he summarizes: "Happy those who are repaid for the hypocrisy and wickedness of our lives by the glitter and show of our civilization! I am not!"[24] Additionally, here Christian civilization is presented as capitalistic, with "no other care than to make money" in "this noble race for wealth; without looking to the right or left, only to the golden goal, which the nearer we approach, recedes the farther," because where could "contentment" be "acquired with gain?"[25] In short, Christian civilization is harshly criticized in the novel and depicted as principally uncivilized and especially immoral.[26] Samuel, however, even after his return to Judaism, remains in close contact with his foster father, and in the last letter, we learn about an upcoming visit to England. Once again, this illustrates that however antagonistic certain entities in the novel were intended to be, ultimately it merely paints a picture of hybridity.

Counternarrating "Assimilation"

In Zionist discourse, it was not only Christianity and Christian culture that were counternarrated, but also the narrative of liberalism and its byword, "assimilation," which was perceived as hegemonic.[27] It was in Vienna during the early 1880s that the first German-speaking Jewish nationalist or Zionist newspapers—such as *Selbst-Emancipation*, edited by Nathan Birnbaum—began to appear, providing the discourse of authenticity with new channels of dissemination.[28] In the pages of these publications, Zionist thinkers began to put forth a distinctly Zionist understanding of the process of assimilation. In the ensuing years, Zionists established the process of assimilation and the assimilated Jew as the pinnacle of inauthenticity.

Approximately a decade later, in 1897, at the First Zionist Congress in Basel, Switzerland, the cultural critic and author Max Nordau delivered his famous speech right after Theodor Herzl's opening address. In this speech, Nordau gave the Zionist discourse of authenticity one of its core tenets, stating that "emancipation has totally changed the nature of the Jew, and made him another being."[29] Nordau's subsequent statement serves as an excellent example of the Zionist view of the loss of Jewish authenticity in modern times:

> The emancipated Jew is insecure in his relations with his fellow-beings, timid with strangers, suspicious even toward the secret feeling of his friends. His best powers are exhausted in the suppression, or at least in the difficult concealment of his own real character. For he fears that this character might be recognized as Jewish, and he has never the satisfaction of showing himself as he is in all his thoughts and sentiments. He becomes an inner cripple, and externally unreal, and thereby always ridiculous and hateful to all higher feeling men, as is everything that is unreal.[30]

Here, Nordau presented a dramatic and radical view of Jews' situation at the time, which he believed to be the cause of the condition he had described. By contrast, Zionism provided Jews with a necessary and welcome escape route from this desolate state. In Nordau's words:

> Others hope for the salvation from Zionism which is for them, not the fulfillment of a mystic promise of the Scripture, but the way to an existence wherein the Jew finds at last the simplest but most elementary conditions of life ... namely, an assured social existence in a

well-meaning community, the possibility of employing all his powers for the developments of his real being instead of abusing them for the suppression and falsification of self.[31]

The "New Marranos"

Max Nordau used the term "Marranos" to illustrate his characterization of the "inauthentic" human being—that is, the emancipated or baptized Jew. The "Marrano" had become a cipher in the discourse of modern Jewish cultural self-positioning through works such as Phöbus Philippson's *Die Marannen*.[32] Nordau invoked this figure—alongside the "emancipated Jew"—in order to draw yet another Jewish parallel to his definition of the "degenerate." In the first chapter of *Degeneration*, Nordau discussed the "gloom" of the fin-de-siècle.[33] As a physician, he diagnosed two diseased states of human existence: "degeneration" or "degeneracy" and "hysteria, of which the minor stages are designated as neurasthenia." Nordau quoted Benedict Augustin Morel (1809–1873), who coined the term "degeneration" to refer to "a morbid deviation from an original type."[34] "Degenerates" could supposedly be identified by both physical and mental symptoms.

In his speech at the First Zionist Congress, Nordau put forth his thesis that "all the better Jews in Western Europe" experienced "misery" due to their social situation and sought "alleviation," sometimes "by flight from Judaism"—that is, by being baptized—in order "to save" themselves. However, "racial antisemitism denies the power of change by baptism, and this mode of salvation does not seem to have much prospect." Nordau went on to explain that "in this way there arises a new Marrano, who is worse than the old." The "latter Marrano"—that is to say, that of the fourteenth and fifteenth centuries—had, according to Nordau, "an idealistic direction—a secret desire for truth or a heartbreaking distress of conscience, and they often sought for pardon and purification through Martyrdom."[35] However, the "new Marranos," the baptized Jews of nineteenth-century Europe, would lay down their Judaism "with rage," but "in their innermost heart, although not acknowledged by themselves," they would "carry with them their own humiliation" and "their own dishonesty." For Nordau, these Jews, through their forced baptism, represented the height of assimilation and consequently the height of "inauthenticity." According to Nordau, they were living a lie, which they experienced as feelings of humiliation and dishonesty.

Nordau also dreaded the "future development of this race of new Marranos,... whose soul is poisoned by hostility toward their own and strange blood" and "whose self-respect is destroyed through the ever-present consciousness of a fundamental lie."[36] In addition to clarifying his understanding of "inauthenticity," Nordau's radical remarks here allow us to draw conclusions about his idea of authenticity. Above all, Nordau's focus here seems to be his belief that baptized Jews were lying to themselves. From this, it can be deduced that for Nordau, a feeling of sincerity was an inherent and vital characteristic of an authentic person.

Nordau's elaborations on the "new Marranos" are well known in scholarship. However, a reference to the same code (or "cipher") made by Nahum Sokolov (1859–1936), a Hebrew-language writer from Russian Poland who later became president of the World Zionist Organization, illustrates the issue at hand in greater detail. In 1903, Sokolov published an article in *Die Welt* entitled "Automarrannen." Echoing Pinsker's *Autoemancipation*, this headline suggested that Jews were making themselves into "Marranos." In this article, Sokolov described his experience viewing a painting of a "secret Seder evening" by the Russian painter Moshe Maimon (1860–1924), stating: "The [concept of the] Spanish Marranos does not

FIGURE 2.1. Moshe Maimon, *The Marranos* (1893). Public domain.

work anymore. It went on long enough."[37] He described the motif of the artwork as follows:

> And yet it attracts me—not the studious reproduction of the overly theatrically artificial and screwed-together [*verschraubt*] picture, but the motif. I mean: how the Jewish soul trembles and struggles to get to its source... The Jewish Passover and the Seder—that is essentially nothing less than the essence of the Jewish people, the Jewish human being, exposed in its innermost core of life. Pure instinct.[38]

For Sokolov, the painting represents authentic Judaism in two respects. On the one hand, authentic Judaism, or the authentic Jewish self, manifests in Passover, which marks the Exodus of the Israelites from Egypt and occupied a special place in the Zionist calendar as the ultimate festival of liberation; Sokolov claimed that Passover derived from the basic Jewish instinct. On the other hand, he considered the Conversos' Pesach Seder to be a heightened expression of authentic Judaism because it was celebrated in secret: "A human being, like a growling, *tied-up beast* dragged along by strangers, how it then rebels against the compulsion that restricts a free spirit and shrivels it up. Here lies the grandiose and shocking inspiration, the tremendous force and fanatical enthusiasm of the Marrano Seder."[39] In other words, here the "Marrano Seder" epitomizes the liberating aspect of Passover. Despite their external acceptance of Christianity and the invisibility of their Jewishness, the Conversos nevertheless secretly celebrated Passover. In the face of social coercion, they celebrated the festival of liberation and showed it to be a festival of freedom in the prison of society.

As the article continues, Sokolov draws an analogy between the past and the present. He describes how he initially thought that a friend's family chose not to celebrate Passover in their own home but rather in the grandmother's home because the latter, which was far more modest, served as a kind of traditional idyll. Later, he discovered that they had moved their celebration because they did not want their servants and other outsiders to know that they were Jewish. When Sokolov and some Christian friends of the family unexpectedly visited the grandmother's home, the family tried to hide objects and food that were part of the Passover celebration. Sokolov comments: "I see a weak generation [*Geschlecht*] walking on crooked paths."[40] He continues: "A person may own a magnificent home, lead a carefree existence, feel an unclear longing for activities with his own kind, and transform his own home into a glittering cage for self-mutilation [*Selbstverstümmelung*]."[41] Both the painting and the story are about secret Seder evenings. The Conversos' Seder represents for Sokolov a rebellion against external compulsion and thus a symbolic force. Sokolov's friend's Seder, however, symbolized the exact opposite. The family was celebrating the Seder evening in secret not because of external coercion but rather because of an internal coercion, which he expressly calls "self-mutilation" and which leads to the emergence of the "Automarrannos."

Sokolov concluded his article with a wish that Jews would stop attempting to "assimilate" and instead proudly follow their own natures: "And I want to teach him how the artificial 'Israelite' breaks free from the gangs of ghostly delusions and awakens to a free, personal life. And I want to open his eyes to show him how he makes himself ridiculous and contemptible through his imitation. I want to teach him to be a free Jew."[42] Zionism, according to Sokolov's understanding, constitutes the only means of awakening Jews to live a "free [and] personal life."[43] Sokolov, like Nordau, succinctly formulated the attributes of Zionist authenticity: simple and traditional living conditions, social stability, a benevolent society, freedom, pride, a personal life, and the development of the authentic self. "Assimilation," or the negatively coded notion of imitation, makes Jews "ridiculous" and "contemptible," terms that describe "inauthenticity" in Zionist discourse.

The "Philistines"

Alongside Nordau's "new Marranos" and Sokolov's "Automarranos," Zionist authors employed another contemporary cipher, that of the "Philistine." This term, with its connotations of an "inauthentic person," had its origin in the academic milieu that produced many of the early Zionist thinkers in Germany. "Philistines," originally a biblical term referring to a particular people against whom the Israelites did battle, was adopted by theology students to denote "opponents of God's word." During the *Sturm und Drang* period, the term became associated with the "personified failure of art and love."[44] The 1856 *Herders Conversations-Lexikon* defined a Philistine as "every non-student, someone who is not a professor," "a synonym for bourgeois [*Spießbürger*]"—that is, a person "of narrow and limited views and aspirations" who is "the enemy of all the poetry of life."[45] "Philistine" was thus a pejorative term for people who could not gain much from art and aesthetics and who led petty bourgeois lives. The term fell out of favor at the turn of the century and was gradually replaced with the word "Spießer."[46]

Max Nordau was particularly keen to use this term—in addition to "new Marrano"—to describe a deeply "inauthentic" person. The second chapter of his work *Paradoxes*, entitled "Majority and Minority,"[47] served as a discussion of the phenomenon of the "Philistine." Antipodal to the genius, the Philistine represented the "majority," "the masses," the "perspective background in the painting of civilization,"[48] the "mediocre multitude,"[49] and the "soil that yields them [the geniuses] nourishment."[50] According to Nordau, this was due to a "biological cause,"[51] that of "the primal law of life" on the one hand and of "heredity" on the other.[52] An individual's congenital ability to perform higher or the highest tasks would ultimately be decided by the amount of "vital power" that he or she possessed.[53] In other words: "We pride ourselves far more upon being the founder of a race than one of the descendants, the original copy rather than an extract, and consider it far better to be the title page of a book, rather than one of the numbered pages bound in it."[54] Moses Calvary (1876–1944), a Zionist thinker of the so-called second generation, remarked in his essay "The New Judaism and the Creative Imagination" that only a genius could be "creative," "never the Philistine."[55]

In his famously smug manner, Nordau also gave the notion of the Philistine a gendered element: "Among those living beings divided into sexes, the female seems to have less life-force and its concomitant creative impulse than the male."[56] Accordingly, "Woman is as a rule, typical; man, individual. The former has average, the latter exceptional features."[57] Although he conceded that there were "some original women," Nordau recommended caution when dealing with them, since a "deviation from the type, in woman, is in eighty cases out of a hundred, an indication of disease... In the course of centuries," he continued, "one woman may be born who has ambition."[58] Thus, the woman is a Philistine above all and deeply "inauthentic" in her essence.

Gender-Specificity and the Female Assimilationist

As this chapter has demonstrated, the Zionist counternarratives of authenticity were directed against anything that was understood as "fake," namely, anything connected to assimilation. For Jewish women, a special standard was applied within this discourse.[59] First of all, Jewish women were accused of representing the worst of assimilationism.[60] Berthold Feiwel (1875–1937) described the Jewish woman as "vain and superficial, obsessive about cleaning, presumptuous, pressing, extravagant—but that is not enough: she is also a bad, despotic housewife, a bad wife and mother. She is the representative of the most morbid modernity, the bearer of the lax and sinful marriage, family, and social morality. She damages customs and good taste."[61] In this passage, Feiwel characterizes Jewish women as the ultimate in inauthenticity. He goes on to argue that these women pose the greatest threat to authentic Jewish existence:

> These women... consciously or unconsciously work in the inner Jewish family and in the smaller or larger circles of their society on the dissolution of Judaism.... It is de-Judaization on a small scale that each of these women accomplishes. And yet it seems to us that there is a far greater danger to nationalist Judaism emanating from these women than from the side of the male representatives of assimilation.... These women not only rid themselves of the ideals of Judaism, and therefore general human [ideals], not only are they becoming more and more external, more untenable, more superficial, de-Judaized, or, if you will, Jewish antisemitic—but they also destroy, apart from their own individuality, the personalities of their husbands, their sons, [and] especially their daughters.[62]

Expounding upon his essentialist idea of the "natural" role of women, Feiwel specified: "It is only natural that for women—women tend to think with the heart—the emotional is expressed before the rational. In the case of Jewish women, too, it is first and foremost emotions that develop and strengthen their realization of national belonging: religion and family are the grounds on which their consciousness of nationality is built."[63] The famous philosopher and historian of religions Martin Buber applied Max Nordau's notion of Jewish "degeneration" to women. Buber argued that the Bible painted a "royal" picture of Jewish women in antiquity, claiming that it was "characteristic" "that tradition attributes the liberation from Egypt to the merit of noble women." In the Talmudic period, "the esteem in which women are held becomes even stronger." However, "the woman attained the highest importance in the time of the ghetto. Here, life in its entirety is huddled together within the family [*Hier drängt sich alles Leben in der Familie zusammen*]."[64] Buber described the tasks of women in this idealized period as follows:

> Here, the woman appears as the creator of a closed family culture. She relieves the man of a large part of his responsibilities and enables him to live out his spiritual interests. In the midst of the hardest persecution, she gives him courage and confidence [*Zuversicht*]. She educates her children to be brave and steadfast Jews. She brings a wonderful natural freshness [*Naturfrische*] into the house, which replaces the lost young green of the homeland as much as possible. At the same time, she maintains the living connection with Mother Earth and shapes life to its fullest.[65]

According to Buber, however, contemporary women had become "degenerate."[66] The "fanaticism of assimilation [*Assimilations-Fanatismus*]" that had followed the Jews' attainment of legal equality was "most vividly shared by the women, who cling most easily to the environment and adopt its nature."[67]

Martin Buber believed he knew the solution to this "degeneration" of the Jewish woman. Through her specific qualities, "she could renew the living *Volksthum* out of love and the deep understanding of the mind."[68] However, this would only be possible "if she cultivate[d] and develop[ed] the Jewishness in herself."[69] According to Buber, therefore, the Jewish woman must begin by reflecting upon her Judaism. Accordingly, her tasks included "the raising of self-confidence, the lively study of Jewish history and literature and the Hebrew language, [and] the cultivation of a genuine Jewish conviviality."[70] In order to accomplish these goals, she would need "faithful living love for the great destinies of her people," "strong helpful love for its presence," and "hopeful work-loving love for her people's self-aggrandizing future."[71] Buber's conclusions went beyond even these far-fetched claims. Not only would the tasks he prescribed allow women to recover from their degeneracy, but the entirety of the "work over there" in Palestine—the "language," the "celebrations," and the whole of "life"—would be "under the sign of the Jewish woman."[72] Buber justifies this understanding with the following analysis:

> For the man may find and theoretically develop cultural ideas, but only the woman can realize them; only the woman can create a living, continuing culture.... But such a *culture of life* can only be created by that love which is stronger than death: the folk love of the new Jewish woman. *For Zion for Jewish women, is called love.*[73]

Here Buber glorified women's alleged "natural" characteristics. Thus, he acknowledged the importance of women's role in the nation and avoided excluding women in general, but their tasks remained as limited as those of women in the German bourgeoisie.

Women themselves similarly expressed their position within Zionism in the speeches delivered at association meetings. Frieda Rand stated in a speech at a meeting of the Moria Literary Society for Jewish Girls:

> We women and girls, we are also able to cooperate in the great project for the welfare of our people, and just as the profession of an advocate or doctor is not impaired by its involvement in the processes of time, so also the Jewish woman and the Jewish girl can be active in their framework for Judaism without neglecting their domestic duties—Yes! We must be concerned for our people, acquaint ourselves with its joys and sorrows, because in the future we will be called as mothers, thus as educators of the future Jewish generation, to exert an important influence on the feelings and character of our children through our clear and pronounced ideas, through our true views, in order to train them to be zealous representatives of the Jewish cause.[74]

Here, Rand's vision of women's role becomes clear: they were meant first and foremost to be the "educators of the future Jewish generation." The aspects that belonged to the Zionist discourse of authenticity were addressed as follows:

> Is it the role of a Jewess to be ashamed of the name "Jewess"? Is the role of a Jewess to have no idea of Jewish history, or to reject and laugh at everything Jewish, as both educated and uneducated girls do today? . . . If men unite to work together for the good of Judaism, if they have focused their attention on eliminating the useless ornaments of foreign nationality which prevent the Jews from rising above their fellow citizens by so much as a hair, why should we girls not do this in our circles, since we need it just as much as them? *Just as for them, the only motto is "be Jewish," so we too should only want to "be Jewish women" and nothing else.*[75]

Here we find the typical Zionist narrative, which tried to overcome the shame of being Jewish and to fight assimilation. The last sentence aptly summarizes this in the imperative to only "be Jewish" or "be Jewish women," a quasi-existentialist formulation of the discourse of authenticity; it is important to simply "be."

In other words, Jewish women wanted to participate in the pursuit of Zionist authenticity. Yet as these early sources make clear, women were commonly relegated to the realm of emotion. As I have pointed out, in the context of nationalist endeavors, the pursuit of authenticity was considered a male task, inaccessible to the nationalist woman, who was primarily passively moved by "emotions from the depths of the heart." The gendered ideology of nationalist theory does not leave much room for interpretation. It should be stressed, however, that this tendency within nationalist theory should not be read as a general exclusion of women—quite the opposite—but rather as a hierarchical distribution of roles based on essentialist ideas.[76]

Conclusion

For the German Zionist thinkers, the concept of authenticity was a driving force. In order to fulfill the ideal of authenticity on an individual and collective level, German Jews became Zionists. The Zionist narratives of authenticity evolved as counternarratives. The postcolonial model of counternarratives enables us to more clearly observe these dynamics in the development of Central European Zionist thinking and the inherent power relations that Zionist thinkers perceived between themselves and the Christian majority culture. On the one hand, they counternarrated antisemitic or exclusionary hegemonic narratives of authenticity—including those of Christianity, Christian culture, and modernity. On the other hand, they counternarrated dominant Jewish narratives, including those of liberal Jewish historiography and other forms of Zionism.

In the Zionist view, liberalism—often pejoratively referred to as "assimilation"—had forced Jews to become a "tied-up beast," which then had to rebel and break free of its oppression. However, as we have seen in Herzberg's novel, the concept of authenticity remained a rather hybrid entity. Herzberg stylized concepts of authentic and inauthentic Jewishness that were in reality more hybrid than opposed, thereby attenuating the contradiction. Furthermore, the German Zionist concept of authenticity was highly gendered. Jewish women were excluded from the search for an authentic self and assigned a fixed and limited place in the male search for authenticity. This aspect of the discourse in particular demonstrates the limits of the notion, propagated by many Zionist thinkers, of authenticity as personal self-fulfillment within one's own nation.

NOTES

Epigraph. Kurt Blumenfeld in a conversation with Albert Einstein; see Kurt Blumenfeld, *Erlebte Judenfrage: Ein Vierteljahrhundert deutscher Zionismus* (Stuttgart: Deutsche Verlags-Anstalt, 1962), 127.

This chapter is part of a larger project on the concept of authenticity in early German Zionism, the findings of which have been published in a monograph. See Manja Herrmann, *Zionismus und Authentizität: Gegennarrative des Authentischen im frühen zionistischen Diskurs* (Berlin: De Gruyter, 2018).

1. Accordingly, most studies on nationalist Jewish authenticity deal with the East-West discourse or Orientalism and stress the image of the "authentic Eastern Jew." In his 1982 classic *Brothers and Strangers*, Steven E. Aschheim wrote that in Western Zionism, the Eastern European Jew became "the embodiment of Jewish authenticity" and an "exemplar of the unfragmented self"; see Steven E. Aschheim, *Brothers and Strangers: The East European Jew in German and German Jewish Consciousness, 1800–1923* (Madison: University

of Wisconsin Press, 1982), 84. In his innovative 1998 study *Marketing Identities*, David A. Brenner explained how the stereotypical representation of a "western Jewish enlightened identity" was opposed to an "eastern Jewish traditional identity" as a means of creating an "ethnical pan-Judaism"; see David A. Brenner, *Marketing Identities: The Invention of Jewish Ethnicity in "Ost und West"* (Detroit: Wayne State University Press, 1998). Michael Brenner also refers to the "Jew as oriental" and the rhetoric of the "authentic eastern European Jew"; see Michael Brenner, *Jüdische Kultur in der Weimarer Republik* (Munich: Beck, 2000), especially 145–230.

2. The long nineteenth century witnessed numerous forms of Jewish modernization and redefinition. Among other things, Reform Judaism, the *Wissenschaft des Judentums*, and Neo-Orthodoxy emerged. Each of these redefinitions constructed its own conception of "true" or "authentic" Judaism. For an overview of the discussions within Jewish contexts that remain relevant to this day, see Stuart Z. Charmé, "Varieties of Authenticity in Contemporary Jewish Identity," *Jewish Social Studies* 6 (2000): 133–55. Charmé lists three main narratives, firstly one that makes *descriptive* claims about historical continuity with particular traditions of the past as a source of authority for the present (for example, "halakhic Judaism is more *authentically Jewish* than liberal [non-halakhic] Judaism"); secondly, one that makes *prescriptive* claims about the *normative* superiority of one form of Jewish life over another (for example, "religiously observant Jews have more *authenticity* than assimilated ethnic Jews," or "Jewish life in Israel is more Jewishly *authentic* than Jewish life in the Diaspora"); and thirdly, "existential claims about one's deepest values and sense of self" (p. 134). Regarding the first narrative, see also Daniel Mahla, *Orthodox Judaism and the Politics of Religion: From Prewar Europe to the State of Israel* (Cambridge, UK: Cambridge University Press, 2020), especially chapter 2.

3. In literary studies, master narratives can be called "plotlines" or "masterplots," but in a larger socio-psychological or cultural context, they are referred to as "dominant discourses." See Michael Bamberg, "Considering Counter-Narratives," in *Considering Counter-Narratives: Narrating, Resisting, Making Sense*, ed. Michael Bamberg and Molly Andrews (Amsterdam: John Benjamins Publishing Company, 2004), 351–71, here 359.

4. See Susannah Heschel, "Jewish Studies as Counterhistory," in *Insider/Outsider: American Jews and Multiculturalism*, ed. David Biale, Michael Galchinsky, and Susan Heschel (Berkeley: University of California Press, 1998), 101–15. David Biale also applied this model in his work; see David Biale, *Gershom Scholem: Kabbalah and Counter-History* (Cambridge, MA: Harvard University Press, 1979).

5. Susannah Heschel, *Abraham Geiger and the Jewish Jesus* (Chicago: University of Chicago Press, 1998), 3.

6. Regina Bendix, *In Search of Authenticity: The Formation of Folklore Studies* (Madison: University of Wisconsin Press, 1997), 9.

7. For this, see also Somogy Varga, *Authenticity as an Ethical Ideal* (London: Routledge, 2012), 15–17; Jacob Golomb, *In Search of Authenticity: From Kierkegaard to Camus* (London: Routledge, 1995), 2–17; Charles B. Guignon, *On Being Authentic* (London: Routledge, 2004), 7–13.

8. Lionel Trilling, *Sincerity and Authenticity* (Cambridge, MA: Harvard University Press, 1972), 2.

9. Bendix, *In Search of Authenticity*, 16.
10. Trilling, *Sincerity and Authenticity*, 10–11.
11. Charles Taylor, "The Politics of Recognition," in *Multiculturalism: Examining the Politics of Recognition*, ed. Amy Gutmann (Princeton, NJ: Princeton University Press, 1994), 25–73, here 30.
12. Ibid.
13. Elie Kedourie, *Nationalism*, 4th expanded ed. (Cambridge, MA: Blackwell, 1996).
14. Moses Hess, *Rome and Jerusalem: A Study in Jewish Nationalism*, trans. Meyer Waxman (New York: Bloch, 1918).
15. For the term "German-Jewish experience," see Steven E. Aschheim and Vivian Liska, eds., *The German-Jewish Experience Revisited* (Berlin: De Gruyter, 2015).
16. Hess, *Rome and Jerusalem*, 81.
17. For a biography, see Reuven Michael, "Dr. Wilhelm Herzberg (1827–1897). Eine lückenhafte Biographie," *Bulletin des Leo Baeck Instituts* 65 (1983): 53–85.
18. For the following discussion of Herzberg's novel and further details, see also Manja Herrmann, "Proto-Zionism Reconsidered: Wilhelm Herzberg's Early German-Jewish Nationalist Novel 'Jewish Family Papers' and the Discourse of Authenticity," *Leo Baeck Institute Year Book* 62 (2017): 179–95.
19. The numerous editions of the novel are evidence of its success. After its first anonymous publication in Hamburg by Otto Meissner in 1868, further editions of the novel appeared in 1873 (Hamburg: Otto Meissner), 1893 (Zurich: C. Schmidt), and 1879 (Frankfurt am Main: I. Kaufmann). Reuven Michael mentions English and Hebrew translations of the work: *Jewish Family Papers; or, Letters of a Missionary*, trans. Rev. Dr. Frederic de Sola Mendes (New York: American Jewish Publication Society, 1875); *Kitvei Mishpaha Ivri'im* (Jerusalem: Galilee Lodge, 1930). The work was also translated into Dutch: *Uit het leven van een Christelijk zendeling ter bekeering der Joden*, trans. B. Hildesheim (Rotterdam: Haagens, 1874).
20. Herzberg, *Jewish Family Papers*, 4.
21. Ibid., 6–7.
22. Ibid., 71.
23. Ibid., 70.
24. Ibid., 70.
25. Ibid., 71.
26. For more on the analysis and further aspects, see Manja Herrmann, "Emotions in Jewish Nationalist Garb. Wilhelm Herzberg's Novel Jewish Family Papers: Letters of a Missionary (1868)," in *Wegweiser und Grenzgänger: Studien zur deutsch-jüdischen Kultur- und Literaturgeschichte*, ed. Stefan Vogt, Hans Otto Horch, Vivian Liska, and Małgorzata A. Maksymiak (Vienna: Böhlau, 2018), 261–71.
27. For the following analysis and further aspects of the politicization of the concept of authenticity, see Manja Herrmann, "The Power of Authenticity: Individualism, Gender, and Politics in Early German Zionism," *Modern Judaism* 39 (2019): 93–113.
28. It is estimated that between 1897 and 1938, no fewer than thirty-nine Zionist periodicals appeared in Germany. See Jehuda Reinharz, "Ideology and Structure in German Zionism, 1882–1933," *Jewish Social Studies* 42 (1980): 119–46, here 125. See also Hagit

Lavsky, *Before Catastrophe: The Distinctive Path of German Zionism*, 2nd ed. (Jerusalem: Magnes, 1998), 22.

29. Nordau's speech at the First Zionist Congress, in *Zionisten-Congress in Basel* (29. 30. und 31. August 1897). *Officielles Protocoll* (Vienna: Verlag des Vereines Erez Israel, 1898), 9–20, here 14. My translation.

30. Ibid., 17.

31. Ibid., 18. My italics.

32. Florian Krobb, *Kollektivautobiographien, Wunschautobiographien: Marranenschicksal im deutsch-jüdischen historischen Roman* (Würzburg: Königshausen & Neumann, 2002), 49. In addition, Krobb puts forward the thesis that "in the course of the nineteenth century, an entire 'Iberian,' 'Marranian,' or 'Sephardic' field of association emerged in the collective consciousness of the Jewish community of Central Europe, starting from Philippson's *Marannen*, that could effortlessly and easily be recalled simply by mentioning a cipher" (ibid.). For a discussion of further German-Jewish novels, see Nitsa Ben-Ari, *Romanze mit der Vergangenheit. Der deutsch-jüdische historische Roman des 19. Jahrhunderts und seine Bedeutung für die Entstehung einer neuen jüdischen Nationalliteratur* (Tübingen: Niemeyer, 2006).

33. Max Nordau, *Degeneration*. Translated of the Second Edition of the German Work (New York: D. Appletin and Co., 1895), 6. On Nordau's concept of "degeneration," see for instance Christoph Schulte, *Psychopathologie des Fin de siècle: Der Kulturkritiker, Arzt und Zionist Max Nordau* (Frankfurt am Main: Fischer, 1997); P. M. Baldwin, "Liberalism, Nationalism, and Degeneration: The Case of Max Nordau," *Central European History* 13 (1980): 99–120; Petra Zudrell, *Der Kulturkritiker und Schriftsteller Max Nordau. Zwischen Zionismus, Deutschtum und Judentum* (Würzburg: Königshausen & Neumann, 2003).

34. Nordau, *Degeneration*, 16.

35. Nordau's speech at the First Zionist Congress, 17.

36. Ibid.

37. Nachum Sokolow, "Automarrannen," *Die Welt*, April 17, 1903, 2–3, here 2.

38. Ibid.

39. Ibid. My italics.

40. Ibid.

41. Ibid., 3.

42. Ibid.

43. Ibid.

44. Gerd Stein, ed., *Kulturfiguren und Sozialcharaktere des 19. und 20. Jahrhunderts*. Vol. 4, *Philister–Kleinbürger–Spießer. Normalität und Selbstbehauptung* (Frankfurt am Main: Fischer, 1985), 13–14.

45. *Herders Conversations-Lexikon*, vol. 4 (Freiburg im Breisgau: Herder, 1856), 527–28.

46. Stein, *Kulturfiguren und Sozialcharaktere*, 4:13–14.

47. Max Nordau, *Paradoxes: From the German of Max Nordau* (Chicago: L. Schick, 1886).

48. Nordau, *Paradoxes*, 33.

49. Ibid., 34.

50. Ibid., 35.

51. Ibid., 40.

52. Ibid., 42.
53. Ibid., 46.
54. Ibid., 47.
55. Moses Calvary, "Das neue Judentum und die schöpferische Phantasie," in *Vom Judentum. Ein Sammelbuch*, ed. Verein jüdischer Hochschüler Bar Kochba in Prag (Leipzig: Kurt Wolff, 1913), 103–16, here 103.
56. Nordau, *Paradoxes*, 48.
57. Ibid.
58. Ibid., 50, 52.
59. For the following analysis, see also Herrmann, "Power of Authenticity."
60. For a discussion of this assumption, see Marion Kaplan, *The Making of the Jewish Middle Class: Women, Family, and Identity in Imperial Germany* (Oxford: Oxford University Press, 1991), 64–84. See also Tamara Or, *Vorkämpferinnen und Mütter des Zionismus: Die deutsch-zionistischen Frauenorganisation 1897–1938* (Frankfurt am Main: Lang, 2009), 36–38; Małgorzata A. Maksymiak, *Mental Maps im Zionismus: Ost und West in Konzepten einer jüdischen Nation vor 1914* (Bremen: Edition Luimère, 2015), 166–83.
61. Bertold Feiwel, "Die jüdische Frau," *Die Welt*, April 26, 1901, 1–3, here 2. My translation.
62. Ibid., 2.
63. Ibid., 3.
64. Martin Buber, "Das Zion der jüdischen Frau," *Die Welt*, April 26, 1901, 3–5, here 3–4.
65. Ibid., 4.
66. Ibid.
67. Ibid. In fact, according to research in this field, women had to play a dual role. On the one hand, many Jewish women raised their children with the ideals of the bourgeoisie, but on the other, "many demonstrated their feeling of fellowship with other Jews and their Jewish self-consciousness," achieving this by, for example, "insisting on Jewish rituals and holidays in the home, sometimes long after their husband and children found these quaint at best." In short, they "forged a modern Jewish identity." See Kaplan, *The Making of the Jewish Middle Class*, 4. As Kaplan points out (for example, 11), it was not only the Zionist thinkers presented here who overestimated the extent of assimilation by focusing exclusively on men: historians are also often guilty of this. According to Paula E. Hyman, the fact that women were nevertheless held responsible for assimilation made it possible for men to "continue the process, and the project of Jewish assimilation" unhindered; see Paula E. Hyman, *Gender and Assimilation in Modern Jewish History: The Roles and Representation of Women* (Seattle: University of Washington Press, 1995), 49.
68. Buber, "Das Zion der jüdischen Frau," 4.
69. Ibid., 5.
70. Ibid.
71. Ibid.
72. Ibid.
73. Ibid. Emphasis in the original.
74. Anonymous, "Die nationale Lösung der Judenfrage. Vortrag, gehalten in der Versammlung des literarischen Gesellgkeitsvereines jüdischer Mädchen Moria," am 24.

April 1892, von Frieda Rand [The national solution to the Jewish question. Lecture given at the Meeting of the Moria Literary Society for Jewish Girls, April 24, 1892, by Frieda Rand]," *Selbst-Emancipation*, May 1, 1892, 3–5, here 4. My italics.
75. Ibid. Emphasis in the original.
76. On the individual activities of women in the Zionist context, see also Michael Berkowitz, "Transcending 'Tzimmes and Sweetness': Recovering the History of Zionist Women in Central and Western Europe, 1897–1933," in *Active Voices: Women in Jewish Culture*, ed. Maurie Sacks (Urbana: University of Illinois Press, 1995), 41–62.

3

Zionism as "Positioning"

Reconceptualizing Zionist Identity Politics

STEFAN VOGT

Until very recently, scholars of Jewish studies and scholars of postcolonial studies have not shown a lot of interest in each other's fields. In Jewish studies, including the historiography of Zionism, there is meanwhile a still limited, but steady development, especially among younger scholars, to open up to postcolonial approaches. In the field of postcolonial studies, such an openness is still quite rare. This, of course, has a lot to do with politics. If postcolonial scholars do address the history of Zionism, they usually place it squarely, and exclusively, into the category of European colonialism. This, however, is at odds with many of postcolonial studies' own insights, especially those rejecting a dichotomous distinction between colonized and colonizing societies.[1] Just as anticolonial and postcolonial nationalism, for instance, cannot be neatly separated from European colonialism and nationalism, Zionist nationalism, too, contains both colonialist and anticolonialist elements.[2]

A few prominent postcolonial scholars, however, have considered Jewish history as a possible part of their field. In his seminal book *The Black Atlantic*, Paul Gilroy has even called on his colleagues to analyze Zionism as a phenomenon that is related to Black nationalism.[3] Gilroy's teacher Stuart Hall, too, considered Jews to be the West's "own internal others," comparable to the colonized peoples of the "rest" of the world.[4] In this chapter, I will show that Hall's work, in particular, offers a number of concepts that are extremely helpful to analyze the history of Zionism. Much of Hall's work concentrates on the analysis of identity formation in postcolonial settings, especially in Great Britain. This focus, however, makes it highly relevant for the study of nationalism because it addresses important elements of both nationalist exclusions of minorities by hegemonial societies and collective resistance against these exclusions. I suggest that this makes Hall's work also very useful for the study of Zionist nationalism, especially its European variants.

In his well-known essay *Cultural Identity and Diaspora* from 1990, Hall gives a definition of cultural identities which provides an immensely useful starting point for the analysis of the history of European Zionism. "Cultural identities," Hall writes, "are the points of identification, the unstable points of identification or suture, which are made, within the discourses of history and culture. Not an essence but a positioning. Hence, there is always a politics of identity, a politics of position, which has no absolute guarantee in an unproblematic, transcendental 'law of origin.'"[5] This definition contains three concepts that are particularly important for the history of Zionism: identity, positioning, and identity politics. The first part of this essay takes a closer look at these concepts and their implications. In the second part, they will be applied to the Zionist case, specifically the history of German Zionism. This will be done by analyzing two exemplary aspects of this history, Zionist Orientalism and the Zionist strategy against antisemitism. In a final step, I will discuss, on a more systematic level, the possible advantages of an application of these concepts to the history of Zionism.

Stuart Hall

Stuart Hall arrives at his definition of cultural identities through a critical reexamination of the ways in which identities were understood in anticolonial and postcolonial struggles. Here, they usually meant a "collective one true self" that lay underneath the differences and misrepresentations imposed by the hegemonial culture and that had to be rediscovered.[6] It could become manifest, for instance, in the idea of an authentic "Blackness" that was based on a supposedly common history, culture, or "race" and that provided a stable and unchanging frame of reference. Hall concedes that this essentialist understanding of identities constituted an important resource for resistance against colonial and postcolonial oppression. However, even if identities are understood as an essence, they are in fact something entirely different. They are an always incomplete process, a "production," something that is being constantly "made." For Hall, therefore, "identity" is a strictly political concept. Identities, he writes, are "a way of imposing an imaginary coherence on the experience of dispersal and fragmentation, which is the history of all enforced diasporas."[7] They are a strategy to overcome this fragmentation and its disempowering consequences. By consolidating the different experiences of the Black diaspora into a unified "African" identity, for instance, it is possible to replace the shattered pasts of slavery and displacement with an imaginary coherent history and to turn this imagination into a resource of resistance. At the same time, identities are the direct product of this fragmentation, "of the marking of difference and exclusion" that took place in colonial power relations.[8] They can only be based on the exclusionary categories of nation, race, or culture that have been established and imposed by the colonial system itself. This makes identities a problematic concept. "Identities," writes Hall, "can function ... only because of their capacity to exclude."[9] They reproduce the hierarchies and the fragmentation they are meant to overcome.

Hall's understanding of identities, therefore, is a highly ambivalent one. Identities are both a consequence of colonial and postcolonial domination and a resource for the struggle against this domination. They are both elements of suppression and elements of liberation. It is clear for Hall, however, that only on the basis of a nonessentialist perception of identities is it possible to properly understand colonial and postcolonial experiences. This is because even if identities are sometimes considered as essence, they are nevertheless always constructed. "Though they seem to invoke an origin in the historical past with which they continue to correspond," he writes, "actually identities are about questions of using the resources of history, language and culture in the process of becoming rather than being."[10] They are therefore anchored in the present, not in the past. Most importantly, identities in no way provide a reference point outside the dominant structures of power and representation, but rather a concept that relates the colonial subjects, and through which these subjects relate themselves, to these structures. They are "not the so-called return to roots, but a coming-to-terms with our 'roots.'"[11] In a post-colonial context, identities are practices with which members of subaltern groups place themselves and are being placed in relation to the hegemonial societies. Identities, as Hall puts it in his definition, are therefore a "positioning."

The implications of Hall's concept of positioning are much less spelled out in his work than those of the concept of identity. Hall emphasizes that "positioning" has both an active and a passive meaning. "They try to position us," he writes from his own perspective as a member of the Black minority in Great Britain, "and we are trying to find some space within the positioning."[12] Positioning is always an interplay of an allocation to and an assumption of a specific position within a cultural or political field. The structures of this field do not completely determine this position, but they considerably limit the options for self-positioning. Conceiving of identity as positioning therefore emphasizes the significance of both social conditions and agency for being in a certain position. If identity is understood as positioning, this also implies a degree of participation in the fields in which the positioning is taking place. These fields, however, whether they are societies, institutions, or discourses, are never homogeneous or smooth. Rather, they are fundamentally uneven, rutted by conflicts and permeated by power relations. It makes a big difference, for instance, from which position within the discourse on "race" this category is being applied. Depending on this position, it can be used as a marker of exclusion or as an instrument for those who are excluded to gain access and space.[13] Identity as positioning takes into account the fact that there are hegemonial and subaltern poles in these fields and that the positions therein differ accordingly. It also acknowledges the possibility that a group or discourse belongs to a field and at the same time distinguishes itself from other positions within this field, up to the point of open conflicts. This means that also the subaltern pole in the discourse of "race" still contributes to constituting this discourse. Conceiving of identity as positioning thus allows for a complex understanding of the relationship between minorities and the hegemonial society that acknowledges the differences but refrains from assuming a dualistic opposition.

According to Hall, this also means that "there is always a politics of identity."[14] Or, to put it differently, identity must be understood as a political strategy. From a subaltern perspective, its aim is to replace the representation of the subaltern by the hegemonial culture with self-representation, and to change the negative and derogatory content of this representation into a positive one. Identity politics allow the subaltern to constitute themselves against the hegemonic culture as a self-conscious collective with its own agency, and thus to challenge the very rules of representation, as well as the structures of domination that are based upon them. A politics of identity, therefore, is always a way in which the subaltern relate to the hegemonic culture and position themselves within it.

Hall makes it clear that identity politics can work with both understandings of identity, with identity as essence and with identity as positioning. For instance, it can refer to "race" as a preexisting biological or cultural unity, or as a category that is constructed through common practice. Whereas for analytical purposes it is important to acknowledge that identity is always constructed, the situation is more complex in the realm of politics. Hall concedes that identity politics based on an essential understanding of identity—"Identity Politics One," in his terminology—can be legitimate or even necessary in order to create the possibility of self-representation. Nevertheless, even in this context Hall clearly favors a nonessentialist understanding of identity. Identity Politics One, he argues, not only tends to create new exclusions and hierarchies, especially among the subaltern themselves, but it also reproduces the dualistic and essentialist structure of the hegemonic forms of representation.[15] In his work, Hall searches for ways to contain these tendencies within postcolonial minority movements and ideologies by basing identity politics on notions of difference rather than unity and of positioning rather than essence. Most Zionists, however, just as many protagonists of anticolonial and postcolonial minority movements, readily embraced the essentialist version, and the essentializing effects, of identity politics.

Zionist Orientalism

A good example of Zionist identity politics is the appropriation of "the Orient" by the Austrian-German philosopher and Zionist activist Martin

Buber. Buber was one of many German-speaking Zionists who referred positively to the "Orient" as a constitutive element of Jewish identity. They claimed Oriental roots or Oriental characteristics for the Jews, used Oriental imagery for textual and visual representations of Jewish identity, and wrote about their fascination with the "Orient" and its culture. This was particularly the case among cultural Zionists who considered the revival of the Jewish people more urgent than the establishment of a Jewish commonwealth in Palestine. At the beginning of the twentieth century, this sort of Jewish Orientalism was fairly common in Zionist circles and beyond, especially in German-speaking Central Europe.[16] Martin Buber was among the Zionist intellectuals who developed this ideology most thoroughly and most clearly.[17]

In a speech published in 1916 as *Der Geist des Orients und das Judentum*, Buber presented the Orient as a distinct entity with a specific and intrinsic personality, and he juxtaposed the Oriental man, which included for him the Jews, and the Occidental man in dualistic opposition.[18] In doing so, he gave a textbook example for Said's definition of Orientalism as "a style of thought based upon an ontological and epistemological distinction between the Orient and the Occident."[19] The "basic psychic act" of the Oriental is, according to Buber, "centrifugal," emanating from his own soul and unfolding in the world as motion and deed. In contrast, the "basic psychic act" of the Occidental is "centripetal," as he takes in external notions that he grasps by means of abstract concepts.[20] To the Oriental, the world is a unity; to the Occidental, a plurality. As a consequence, the Oriental carries the "truth of the world" inside of himself, whereas the Occidental confronts this truth from the outside. Most importantly, the senses of the Oriental are "closely connected with each other and with the dark life of the organism," while the Occidental's senses are "separated from each other and from the undifferentiated base of organic life."[21]

In attributing to the Oriental a sensual and organic relationship with the world and to the Occidental an abstract and intellectual one, Buber replicated a very common cliché of the European discourses on the Orient.[22] Also Buber's identification of the Jews as Orientals was clearly in compliance with the Orientalist paradigm of the time. At the same time, however, Buber's Orientalism was in many ways specific. Buber's self-affirmation as an Oriental implied that the Jews themselves would take control of the construction of Jewish identity. The rediscovery of the Oriental essence of Judaism was, according to Buber, accomplished by the Jews themselves and therefore a result of their own agency. The Jews were also a major driving force behind the growing attraction of the European cultures to the "spirit of the Orient." In short, the reemergence of the historical and cultural relevance of the Orient, which was to the benefit of Jews and non-Jews alike, was basically the result of a Jewish endeavor. In this sense, Buber subverted the hierarchical structure of the relationship between the hegemonial and the subaltern sides of the colonial divide. His Orientalism was thus not meant as "a Western style for dominating, restructuring and having authority over the Orient," as in Edward Said's definition, but as a way for the Orient to reclaim this authority and to reject the West's attempts to dominate the Orient by defining it.[23] In a clear instance of subaltern identity politics, Buber here deployed a strategy of self-Orientalization that was meant to counter European Orientalism.

The reason for this was obvious. European Orientalist discourse in the nineteenth century usually depicted the Orient as an uncivilized and backward place from which the West could be favorably distinguished. Accordingly, identifying the Jews with the Orient was often meant to denigrate Jews and therefore motivated by antisemitism. Even as the neo-romantic discourse of the fin-de-siècle turned the Orient into a positive counterimage to the allegedly decadent West, the corresponding idealized perception of the Oriental as a noble other remained firmly inside the colonial imagery, reproducing also its hierarchies. Moreover, if Orientalist scholars referred positively to the Orient, they often did so by separating an idealized ancient version from an allegedly dilapidated contemporary one. In a similar way, they separated the "noble" ancient Hebrew from the "despicable" contemporary Jew.[24] Therefore, even in its positive version, European Orientalism was also a discursive strategy to exclude Jews. In addition, the openly antisemitic denigration of the Jews as Orientals persisted as well, especially in the guise of the denunciation of the so-called *Ostjuden*. In his *Unsere Aussichten*, Heinrich von Treitschke had notoriously invoked the "host of hustling, pants-peddling youth" that "year after year, streams out of the inexhaustible Polish cradle over our eastern border."[25]

For Buber, in contrast, the Orient was clearly the superior and more vital side of the colonial divide. This, of course, included the Jews. The

Jew, declared Buber, "represents the human type with the most distinctly pronounced motor facilities."[26] In his eyes, it was not the West that brought culture to the East, but the other way around. All major religious teachings, he claimed, originated in the Orient, and the creative core of Christianity was actually "Judaism's prime possession."[27] This was because the relationship of the Oriental man with the world was more fundamental and his connection to life more immediate. "It is this," he explained, "that is creatively enduring in the great Oriental teachings, and in them alone. They posit authentic life as the fundamental metaphysical principle, not derived from nor reducible to anything else."[28] Buber did not give up the dualistic structure of the Orientalist discourse or the essentialist conceptualization of its two poles, but he attempted to revalue them in a way that undermined the power relations of this structure. Most importantly, he aimed to replace the representation of the minority by the hegemonial culture with self-representation.[29] In this sense, Buber's strategy of identity politics closely resemble those of anticolonial and of postcolonial minority movements.

Although Buber's ideas, as well as similar ones of many other Central European Zionists, were clearly within the realm of the Orientalist discourse of their time, they also demonstrate the limits of Said's understanding of Orientalism. Buber's Orientalism was not just a method of imperialist subjugation, even if it operated in a field that was constituted by imperialism, and even if it followed the discursive rules established in this field. It was also part of an anti-hegemonial strategy. Stuart Hall's concept of positioning can help us understand this contradiction. It allows for a comprehension of politico-ideological fields such as Orientalism as dynamic and heterogeneous locations of conflict. This makes it possible to see that the Zionists spoke from a subaltern position within the hegemonial Orientalist field. They appropriated and even co-constituted elements of this field, but they also reinterpreted them in specific ways and with specific intentions. As members of the bourgeoisie, most of the Zionists in Central Europe were firmly integrated into the fields of colonialism, imperialism, and Orientalism. As Jews, they were positioned at the margins of these fields. Zionists such as Buber appreciated this marginal position, affirmed it as part of their self-understanding as members of an "Oriental" nation, turned it into a positive attribute, and made it the basis of an anti-hegemonial strategy.

Fighting Antisemitism as Jews

The second example of Zionist identity politics I wish to discuss here refers to German Zionists' attitudes toward antisemitism. German Zionists developed a specific strategy to confront antisemitism that was based on their understanding of Jewishness. One of the basic assumptions was that antisemitism was an inevitable consequence of the Diaspora. Everywhere where two nations border on each other, the difference between these nations would produce tensions, a *"Randspannungsgefühl,"* as Kurt Blumenfeld, who later became the chairman of the German Zionist Organization, wrote in 1915.[30] In the case of the Jews, Blumenfeld argued, this effect was particularly pronounced, because it was omnipresent. Because they were dispersed all over Europe and beyond, the Jews bordered on other nations everywhere, even inside states and societies. This, he claimed, made antisemitism inevitable. The mantra of the inevitability of antisemitism in the Diaspora was repeated numerous times in Zionist articles, pamphlets, and speeches.[31] It was based on the notion of essential difference between Jews and non-Jews. "The reality of our Jewish particularity," wrote Blumenfeld, "is the real reason for antisemitism. Antisemitism demonstrates that we are still an effective community. Our peculiarity is being felt by others."[32]

Of course, this was a highly problematic perspective. It implied that Germans and Jews were inescapably locked into their respective ethnic communities. Moreover, the Zionists claimed fundamental and insurmountable differences between nations, insinuated a quasi-natural tendency toward national conflicts, and thus shared significant ideological patterns with German *völkisch* nationalism and, indeed, antisemitism. This even led some Zionists to the assumption that it would make sense to discuss these issues with certain antisemites and to search for common ground with them.[33] Paradoxically, however, this perspective also led the Zionists to important insights into the ideological structure of antisemitism. For example, Zionist analyses of antisemitism focused on the role antisemitic ideology played for the construction and safeguarding of the inner coherence of the antisemitic collective, an issue that is central to the study of antisemitism today. Even more notably, the Zionists came to the conclusion that antisemitism was fundamentally independent from the actions and characteristics of the Jews. No matter how "well" or "unsuspicious" the Jews would behave, antisemites would still find their presence unacceptable.[34] This notion, too, has been confirmed by modern research on antisemitism. On this basis, the Zionists also rightly insisted that antisemitism was always directed at the Jews as such, not at some specific Jewish individual or group such as the *Ostjuden*.[35]

The Zionists' understanding of antisemitism was also the basis for their strategy against it. At the center of this strategy lay the notion of the "strengthening of Jewish self-confidence."[36] If the Jews would be more self-confident, it was argued, they would be less vulnerable to antisemitism. The duty of Zionism was thus to raise the feeling of dignity among the Jews. Because of the assumed inevitability of antisemitism and because neither rational argumentation nor "good" behavior of the Jews would convince antisemites that they were wrong, the Zionists directed their strategy quite logically almost entirely toward Jews. Instead of teaching non-Jews, their aim was to provide the Jews with an "inner security," as the Zionist Siegfried Kanowitz put it, as a protection against antisemitism.[37] A major way to achieve this was the promotion of solidarity among Jews. To contain the spiritual, political, and especially economic damages that antisemitism could inflict on Jews, the Zionists called on German Jewry to establish communal structures of Jewish self-help.[38]

Yet the Zionist strategy against antisemitism was not only directed inward. If Jews would be more self-confident, the Zionists argued, they would also be able to finally achieve *Ebenbürtigkeit*, an equal status and the appropriate respect.[39] Jews would then be able to confront other nations not as a powerless and discriminated minority, but on par. This, the Zionists believed, would in the end also lead the non-Jewish world to accept the Jews as Jews. The goal of the fight against antisemitism in this concept was not integration, but recognition. It was not equality, *Gleichheit*, but equivalency, *Gleichwertigkeit*. If integration and equality were illusions, and undesirable ones at that, then the insistence on difference remained the only viable way to confront discrimination and denigration and therefore to fight antisemitism. As Georg Landauer concluded in the guidelines he presented in 1931 to the Commission on Antisemitism that had been established by the German Zionist Association (*Zionistische Vereinigung für Deutschland*): "Our job is to show that the identification of *Deutschtum* and *Judentum* does not represent the reality and that any attempt to make people believe in this identification is a misguided speculation. Instead, we have to show that modern thought is based on the legitimacy and the freedom of particularistic groups, including national groups, and that it is therefore more promising to fight for equal rights and the acknowledgement of our national difference."[40]

The basic principle of the Zionist strategy against antisemitism was thus to confront antisemitism not as Germans, but as Jews. This is exactly what Stuart Hall describes as identity politics: The Zionist strategy was to avow identification as Jews, redefine it as a positive attribute, and insist on the separation from, and difference to, the non-Jews. On this basis, they aimed at confronting the non-Jews on eye level, challenging the very structure of the hierarchical relationship between the hegemonial society and the subaltern group. The goal of this strategy was not to overcome antisemitism, but to enable the Jews to brace themselves against its assaults and to eventually make them immune. This also means that the Zionist strategy against antisemitism suffered from the same problems that also haunted anticolonial and postcolonial identity politics. It necessarily reproduced the distinctions between "us" and "them" that were established by the hegemonial culture and their politics of identity. To be sure, there is a great difference between hegemonial and subaltern identity politics, and Zionist identity politics certainly was of the latter type. Both the Jews and the colonized had been the object of practices of othering already for centuries and were therefore not free to choose whether to reproduce these distinctions or not. And just as postcolonial identity politics was directed against racism, the Zionist version was meant to confront antisemitism and to defend the Jews against it. If Jews would avow their identity as Jews, it was assumed, it would provide them with agency and with a degree of self-determination vis-à-vis an increasingly hostile environment. The Zionists believed that this was a much more powerful and effective approach than trying to blend into the non-Jewish society.

Zionism as Positioning

Both of these examples, Buber's peculiar Orientalism and the German Zionists' strategy against antisemitism—and other examples could be added—show the fundamentally ambivalent character of Zionist identity politics. While it produced potentials for Jewish self-empowerment, it also created new forms of entanglement with the hegemonial culture. While it strengthened the agency of Jews, it also reinforced their dependency on conditions set by the social and political environment in which they had to act. This ambivalence of Zionist identity politics is exactly the reason why it should be understood as a "positioning," following Stuart Hall's definition. Zionism was a way Jews positioned themselves within, and were positioned by, the cultural and political fields that constituted the society they lived in, in this case German society. It was both an actively constructed identity and a product of the situation of the Jews in Germany. On both its active and its passive sides, it contained elements of separation and of integration. Zionism meant participation in the German debates on nation and nationalism, but from a specific position within these debates that made the Zionists both insiders and outsiders to it. Most importantly, Zionism addressed the question of who and what Jews would be in the present and future societies they lived in, or, in Hall's words, "not 'who we are' or 'where we came from,' so much as what we might become."[41] Even if the Zionists considered Jewish identity to be something essential and inalienable, it was in fact the—never complete, always reworked—result of a complex process of relating to, and confronting, this society, that is, of a process of positioning.

For the ideology and politics of German Zionism, this meant that it was possible to positively refer to, adopt, and sometimes even co-constitute elements of German nationalism, colonialism, race discourse, and antisemitism, while at same time, and through this very process of adopting and co-constituting, to confront these hegemonial discourses. German Zionists actively participated in the German debates on nation and nationalism, and their own nationalist thinking featured many similarities to German *völkisch* nationalism.[42] In the first of his famous Prague speeches from 1909, for instance, Martin Buber claimed that the awareness of one's being part of the Jewish nation requires the "discovery of the blood as the root-like, nourishing force inside of each person, the discovery that the most fundamental elements of our being is determined by the blood, that our thinking and our will is fundamentally influenced by it."[43] He thus embedded the quest for the essence of Judaism in the established *völkisch* discourse. Because this participation and appropriation were being done from a specific, subaltern position within this discourse, Zionist nationalism could nevertheless take on quite different meanings and intentions. It not only made it possible to combine it, as Buber did, with a messianic striving for the redemption of humanity as a whole.[44] Zionist nationalism also contained elements of self-assurance and self-empowerment against the oppressive forces of hegemonial culture that were so typical for anticolonial liberation movements. As a strategy to overcome Jewish subalternity and heteronomy, it could acquire an emancipative dimension that was totally alien to German *völkisch* nationalism.[45] In both cases, in the discourses of Zionism and of anticolonialism, nationalism was paradoxically considered both the problem and the solution. It was understood as a major marginalizing force and at the same time a means to overcome this marginalization. Both Zionist and anticolonial nationalism thus simultaneously subverted and affirmed hegemonial nationalism.[46]

In a similar fashion, German Zionists participated in the discourses and practices of German colonialism, and there is no doubt that German Zionists contributed to introducing colonialist elements into the relationship between Jews and Arabs in Palestine.[47] Some German Zionists, such as Otto Warburg, were also active members in the German colonial movement.[48] At the same time, however, the German Zionists never fully identified with the goals and the politics of German colonialism. Rather, they developed a degree of identification with colonized peoples outside of Europe, even in Palestine. This could range from an idealized vision of peaceful coexistence with the Arabs to the idea that the Arabs could even be a model for the Jews in their striving to become indigenous to Palestine again.[49] As illusionary and self-deceiving as it might have been, this was a completely different way to address non-Western cultures than the "*Herrenstandpunkt*" so common among German colonialists. Moreover, a number of German and German-speaking Zionists, among them Martin Buber, argued that Zionism should be part of the anticolonial movement that strove to liberate the "Orient" from Western hegemony.[50] This did not prevent the Zionists from adopting the typically colonialist idea of a European civilizing mission and from considering themselves as "teachers and educators" of the suppressed masses of Asia.[51] The Zionists were at the same time members of a colonialist society and of a minority in this society that was subjected to colonial power relations. They strove to overcome these relations by engaging in their own project of colonization. For many

German Zionists, Jewish identity thus implied a self-conscious positioning between the West and the "Rest," to use Stuart Hall's famous phrase.[52]

Finally, the affinities the Zionists felt toward some aspects of antisemitic ideology, including the various attempts made by Zionists to enter into a conversation with certain antisemites, must be seen in the same light. It is true that these affinities, especially the assumption of an essential difference between Germans and Jews, led some Zionists to the illusionary hope that it might be possible to reach a "modus vivendi" with the antisemites, and even with the Nazis, which would be based on the recognition of this difference.[53] At the same time, however, these very affinities were also the basis for a much more radical challenge to antisemitism than the mere insistence on equality. In a way that, again, resembles the claims of postcolonial minority movements, the Zionists insisted that equal rights and equivalency must not be conditioned on national, ethnic, or *völkisch* equality. Or, as the Zionist Felix Rosenblüth (later to be known as Israel's first minister of justice, Pinchas Rosen) had put it already in 1913: "Either one disavows Jewish nationality and thus admits implicitly that its existence would justify antisemitism,... or one concedes the existence of Jewish nationality but refutes that this gives any legitimacy whatsoever to antisemitism—this is the method of Zionism."[54] This connects the Zionist confrontation with antisemitism once again to anticolonial and postcolonial struggles. In refuting the principle of "acceptance only through assimilation," the Zionist contested not only a central element of "benign" antisemitism, but also of one of the major pillars of Western hegemony in general.

Conclusion

On a systematic level, the advantages of understanding Zionist identity politics as positioning pertain primarily to three fields: the character of Zionist nationalism, the relationship of Zionism to the European contexts in which it emerged, and the relationship of Zionism to anticolonial and postcolonial identity politics. With regard to the character of Zionist nationalism, the concept of positioning permits us to understand that Zionism was a part of the surrounding nationalist discourses, while at the same time it differed from these discourses in substantial ways and pursued its own agenda. In the German case, for instance, it allows one to fully acknowledge the significant extent of Zionist participation in the discourses of German *völkisch* nationalism without making Zionism into a Jewish version of this *völkisch* nationalism, as it also appreciates the specifically subaltern dimension of Zionist nationalism. Moreover, understanding Zionist identity politics as positioning helps avoid a false unambiguity, which characterizes Zionism as either a liberal or a *völkisch* nationalism, either a movement of colonization or of liberation, either an emancipatory or an anti-emancipatory ideology. Zionism, in fact, was both. If we consider Zionist identity politics as positioning, it is possible to appreciate this fundamental ambivalence and to arrive at a much more complex understanding of Zionist ideology and politics. At least in the German case, it becomes clear that while the Zionists operated within the field of hegemonial German nationalism and actively participated in it, they also developed a subaltern nationalism that made them, at the same time, protagonists of an anti-hegemonial project.

Understanding Zionist identity politics as positioning also emphasizes an aspect that has often been underestimated in the historiography of Zionism, namely that Zionism offered a means by which Jews could redefine their position within the European societies they lived in, as well as toward the non-Jewish majorities in these societies. Zionism was therefore much more than a movement to create a homeland, or a state, in Palestine. It was also not only an inner-Jewish phenomenon. If Zionist identity politics is understood as positioning, it can be identified as a mode of relationship between Jewish and non-Jewish members, segments, and dimensions of a specific society. In this light, Zionism becomes visible as a constitutive element of the societies in which it emerged, for instance the German society. This notion builds on the concept of "co-constitution," developed especially by Steven Aschheim, which in recent scholarship in this field has replaced notions of "contribution" to or "integration" into a preexisting society.[55] In this concept, Jews play an active and co-determining role in the negotiated construction of crucial elements of the emerging and developing societies. This can also be applied to Zionism. Understanding Zionism as positioning, however, develops this concept further in that it stresses that this co-constitution did not happen under equal premises. It recognizes the uneven structures of the societies, the asymmetries of power, and the dynamics of inclusion and exclusion that are at work in them and especially affected the Jews. Even if the situation of European Jews was significantly different from those of colonized peoples outside of Europe, they co-constituted their societies from a subaltern position.

Regarding the relationship of Zionism with anticolonial and postcolonial identity politics, finally, the concept of positioning not only exposes a surprising amount of similarities, in terms of both the strategies used and the aims aspired. It also reveals structural commonalities that have to do with the common subaltern position from which these politics are being developed.[56] These commonalities include the ambivalent relationship to the hegemonial culture, which in both cases comprises elements of participation, adaptation, and confrontation. Like colonized and postcolonial identities, Zionist identity has been both imposed by the surrounding society and actively constructed by its protagonists. Zionism was certainly entangled in different ways, and also much more strongly, with European colonialism than anticolonialism. Yet subaltern positions can be occupied by different groups with different histories and different degrees of marginalization. There can be quite different subaltern positions within one particular field.

In a more general sense, Stuart Hall's concept of positioning allows for a decidedly nonessentialist understanding of Zionist identity politics. It makes it possible to deconstruct essentialist notions and to identify their political and strategic objectives, even if the protagonists are not aware of them or insist on the meta-political origins of the Jewish nation. On this basis, Zionist discourses about Jewishness, about the "Orient," or about the relationship between Jews and non-Jews can be understood as elements of a project of self-essentialization that is partly a deliberate practice by its protagonists and partly a reaction forced on them by the surrounding society. Understanding Zionist identity politics as positioning thus enables acknowledgment of the reasons and the achievements of these politics of self-essentialization, without endorsing its essentialism. Conversely, it can also help contain tendencies within postcolonial studies that aim at a re-essentialization of the understanding of identity.[57] If identity is understood as a political practice that can be employed in similar ways by groups as different as European Jews, colonized peoples outside of Europe, and postcolonial minorities within Europe, it cannot be grounded in any historical, cultural, or otherwise meta-political essence. In this way, understanding

Zionist identity politics as positioning can also be helpful in breaking down the political barriers between postcolonial studies on the one hand and the historiography of Zionism on the other.

NOTES

1. See especially Homi K. Bhabha, *The Location of Culture* (London: Routledge, 1994). See also the classic account by Albert Memmi, *Portrait du colonisé: Précédé du portrait du colonisateur* (Paris: Buchet/Chastel, 1957).
2. The entanglement of anticolonial nationalism with colonial nationalism has been shown most convincingly in the case of India by the members of the Subaltern Studies Group. For an overview, see Ranajit Guha and Gayatri Chakravorty Spivak, eds., *Selected Subaltern Studies* (New York: Oxford University Press, 1988).
3. Paul Gilroy, *The Black Atlantic: Modernity and Double Consciousness* (Cambridge, MA: Harvard University Press, 1993), 205–12.
4. Stuart Hall, "The West and the Rest: Discourse and Power," in *Formations of Modernity*, ed. Stuart Hall and Bram Gieben (Cambridge, UK: Polity Press, 1992), 275–320, here 280.
5. Stuart Hall, "Cultural Identity and Diaspora," in *Identity: Community, Culture, Difference*, ed. Jonathan Rutherford (London: Lawrence & Wishart, 1990), 222–37, here 226.
6. Ibid., 223.
7. Ibid., 224.
8. Stuart Hall, "Introduction: Who Needs Identity?" in *Questions of Cultural Identity*, ed. Stuart Hall and Paul Du Gay (London: Sage, 1996), 1–17, here 4.
9. Ibid.
10. Ibid.
11. Ibid.
12. Stuart Hall, "Politics of Identity," in *Culture, Identity, and Politics: Ethnic Minorities in Britain*, ed. Terence Ranger, Yunas Samad, and Ossie Stuart (Aldershot: Avebury, 1996), 129–35, here 132.
13. See ibid., 131.
14. Hall, "Cultural Identity and Diaspora," 226.
15. See Stuart Hall, "New Ethnicities," in *Black Film, British Cinema*, ed. Kobena Mercer (London: Institute of Contemporary Arts, 1988), 27–31.
16. See Ivan Davidson Kalmar and Derek J. Penslar, eds., *Orientalism and the Jews* (Waltham, MA: Brandeis University Press, 2005); Yaron Peleg, *Orientalism and the Hebrew Imagination* (Ithaca, NY: Cornell University Press, 2005); Arieh Bruce Saposnik, "Europe and Its Orients in Zionist Culture Before the First World War," *The Historical Journal* 49 (2006): 1105–23; Ulrike Brunotte, Anna-Dorothea Ludewig, and Axel Stähler, eds., *Orientalism, Gender, and the Jews: Literary and Artistic Transformations of European National Discourses* (Berlin: De Gruyter, 2015); Lynne M. Swarts, *Gender, Orientalism and the Jewish Nation: Women in the Work of Ephraim Moses Lilien at the German Fin de Siècle* (New York: Bloomsbury Visual Arts, 2020).

17. Buber even labeled this kind of self-understanding "*Orientalismus*." Martin Buber, "Der Geist des Orients und das Judentum," in *Vom Geist des Judentums: Reden und Geleitworte* (Leipzig: Wolff, 1916), 9–48, here 43. On Buber's Orientalism, see Paul Mendes-Flohr, "Fin-de-Siècle Orientalism, the Ostjuden and the Aesthetics of Jewish Self-Affirmation," *Studies in Contemporary Jewry* 1 (1984): 96–139.

18. Buber, "Der Geist des Orients." The origin of this text is not completely clear. Buber himself claims that it was originally a talk given between 1912 and 1914; see ibid., 7. In his comment in Martin Buber's *Werkausgabe*, David Groiser assumes that it was based on a talk held in Berlin in 1915. See Martin Buber, *Werkausgabe*, vol. 2.1, *Mythos und mystik: Frühe religionswissenschaftliche schriften*, ed. David Groiser (Gütersloh: Gütersloher Verlags-Haus, 2013), 401.

19. Edward W. Said, *Orientalism* (New York: Vintage Books, 1979), 2.

20. Buber, "Der Geist des Orients," 12.

21. Ibid., 13.

22. See Said, *Orientalism*, 40, 49.

23. Ibid., 3.

24. See, for example, Wilhelm Martin Leberecht de Wette, *Biblische Dogmatik Alten und Neuen Testaments. Oder kritische Darstellung der Religionslehre des Hebraismus, des Judenthums und des Urchristentums: Zum Gebrauch akademischer Vorlesungen* (Berlin: Realschulbuchhandlung, 1813); Heinrich Ewald, *Geschichte des Volkes Israel bis Christus.* 3 vols. (Göttingen: Dieterich, 1843–1852); Julius Wellhausen, *Prolegomena zur Geschichte Israels*, 2nd ed. (Berlin: Reimer, 1883).

25. Heinrich von Treitschke, "Unsere Aussichten," *Preußische Jahrbücher* 44 (1879): 559–76, here 572.

26. Buber, "Der Geist des Orients," 22.

27. Ibid., 33.

28. Ibid., 31.

29. As many postcolonial scholars have shown, this structures of Western representation of the non-European other were at the heart of the colonial power system. See, among others, Said, *Orientalism*; Gayatri Chakravorty Spivak, "Can the Subaltern Speak?" in *Marxism and the Interpretation of Culture*, ed. Cary Nelson and Lawrence Grossberg (Basingstoke: Macmillan, 1988), 271–313; Stuart Hall, *Representation: Cultural Representation and Signifying Practices* (London: Sage, 1997).

30. Maarabi (Kurt Blumenfeld), "Antisemitismus," *Jüdische Rundschau*, July 23, 1915, 240.

31. See, for example, "Die antisemitische Welle," *Jüdische Rundschau*, July 11, 1919, 377; F. L., "Zur Situation in Deutschland," *Jüdische Rundschau*, February 6, 1920, 63; Arnold Zweig, "Die Summe," *Jüdische Rundschau*, November 20, 1923, 502.

32. Maarabi, "Antisemitismus," 240.

33. See, for instance, the correspondence between Martin Buber and Max Hildebert Boehm, or between Robert Weltsch, the editor of the *Jüdische Rundschau*, and Wilhelm Stapel. Letter from Martin Buber to Max Hildebert Boehm, May 16, 1916, Jewish National and University Library Jerusalem (henceforth JNUL), Buber Archives, Ms Var. 350 a3; letter from Max Hildebert Boehm to Martin Buber, May 16, 1916, JNUL, Buber Archives, Ms Var. 350 a2; letter from Martin Buber to Max Hildebert Boehm, May 25,

1916, JNUL, Buber Archives, Ms Var. 350 a3; Wilhelm Stapel and Robert Weltsch, "Liberalismus und Judentum. Ein Briefwechsel," *Deutsches Volkstum* 14 (1932): 944–46. This was also seen and harshly criticized by many liberal and non-Zionist German Jews. For two examples from different periods, see "Hauptversammlung des Centralvereins, Vortrag des Professors Dr. Falkenheim, Königsberg," *Im deutschen Reich*, no. 5/6, May 1913, 201–13; Victor Klemperer, *Ich will Zeugnis ablegen bis zum letzten: Tagebücher. Vol. 2, 1942–1945*, ed. Walter Nowojski, 6th ed. (Berlin: Aufbau-Verlag, 1996), 144–45 (entry of June 25, 1942).

34. See Felix Rosenblüth, "Nationaljudentum und Antisemitismus," *Jüdische Rundschau*, March 28, 1913, 127; "Rundschreiben an die Mitglieder des Landesvorstandes und des Zentralkomitees, an die zionistischen Ortsgruppen und Vertrauensleute," January 15, 1923, Schocken Archive Jerusalem (henceforth SAJ), 531/241; Fritz Bernstein, *Der Antisemitismus als Gruppenerscheinung. Versuch einer Soziologie des Judenhasses* (Berlin: Jüdischer Verlag, 1926), 220–21; "Innere Sicherheit," *Jüdische Rundschau*, February 3, 1933, 46.

35. See, for instance, Arnold Zweig, "Ostjuden—und Abwehr?" *Jüdische Rundschau*, November 11, 1923, 580; Zweig, "Die Summe," 501; Alfred Landsberg, "Zionismus und Umwelt. Referat von Dr. Alfred Landsberg auf der Zentralkomitee-Sitzung vom 1. Januar 1924," *Jüdische Rundschau*, January 4, 1924, 5.

36. See, for example, "Protokoll der Sitzung des Landesvorstandes," February 2, 1930, SAJ, 531/32; "Protokoll der Sitzung der Antisemitismus-Kommission," May 7, 1931, SAJ, 531/66; "Protokoll der Sitzung des Landesvorstandes," May 18, 1931, SAJ, 531/32; "Thesen 'Die Wirtschaftslage der Juden in Deutschland,'" no date (May 1930), SAJ, 531/31.

37. "Protokoll der 6. Sitzung des Geschäftsführenden Ausschusses," February 19, 1930, SAJ, 531/61. See also "Innere Sicherheit," 45–46.

38. See "Protokoll der 6. Sitzung"; s. n., "Im Kampf um die Selbstbehauptung," *Jüdische Rundschau*, March 3, 1930, 107; "Thesen 'Die Wirtschaftslage'"; "Der neue Reichstag und das deutsche Judentum," September 1930, Central Zionist Archives Jerusalem, Kurt Blumenfeld Archive, A 222/3-1; "Protokoll der Sitzung des Landesvorstandes," October 12, 1930, SAJ, 531/32; "Grundlinien des Referats der Antisemitismus-Kommission," May 4, 1931, SAJ, 531/66.

39. The term *"Ebenbürtigkeit"* featured very prominently in German Zionist texts. See, for instance, "Rundschreiben an die Mitglieder des Landesvorstandes und des Zentralkomitees, an die zionistischen Ortsgruppen und Vertrauensleute," January 15, 1923, SAJ, 531/241; Landauer, "Zionismus und Umwelt."

40. "Grundlinien des Referats der Antisemitismus-Kommission." See also Zweig, "Die Summe"; "Die innerdeutsche politische Tätigkeit der Zionistischen Vereinigung für Deutschland. Entwurf von Richtlinien für ein Tätigkeitsprogramm der vor uns liegenden Arbeitsperiode," October 10, 1932, SAJ, 531/231.

41. Hall, "Introduction," 4.

42. See, among others, Paul Mendes-Flohr, *From Mysticism to Dialogue: Martin Buber's Transformation of German Social Thought* (Detroit: Wayne State University Press, 1989); Mark H. Gelber, *Melancholy Pride: Nation, Race, and Gender in the German Literature of Cultural Zionism* (Tübingen: Niemeyer, 2000); Christian Wiese, "'Doppelgesichtigkeit des Nationalismus': Die Ambivalenz zionistischer Identität bei Robert Weltsch und Hans

Kohn," in *Janusfiguren. 'Jüdische Heimstätte,' Exil und Nation im deutschen Zionismus*, ed. Andrea Schatz and Christian Wiese (Berlin: Metropol, 2006), 213–52.

43. Martin Buber, "Das Judentum und die Juden," in *Der Jude und sein Judentum: Gesammelte Aufsätze und Reden* (Köln: Melzer, 1963), 9–18, here 13.

44. See, for instance, Martin Buber, "Das Judentum und die Menschheit," in *Der Jude und sein Judentum*, 18–27; Martin Buber, "Die Erneuerung des Judentums," in *Der Jude und sein Judentum*, 28–46.

45. Some Zionists, such as Robert Weltsch, even developed this into a—contradictory—concept of Zionism as an anti-nationalist nationalism. See Stefan Vogt, "Robert Weltsch and the Paradoxes of Anti-Nationalist Nationalism," *Jewish Social Studies* 16 (2010): 85–115.

46. In the context of anticolonialism, this paradox is discussed, for instance, by Partha Chatterjee, *Nationalist Thought and the Colonial World: A Derivative Discourse?* (London: Zed Books, 1986).

47. See especially Shalom Reichmann and Shlomo Hasson, "A Cross-cultural Diffusion of Colonization: From Posen to Palestine," *Annales of the Association of American Geographers* 74 (1984): 57–70; Derek J. Penslar, *Zionism and Technocracy: The Engineering of Jewish Settlement in Palestine, 1870–1918* (Bloomington: Indiana University Press, 1991); Yfaat Weiss, "Central European Ethnonationalism and Zionist Binationalism," *Jewish Social Studies* 11 (2004): 93–117; Stefan Vogt, *Subalterne Positionierungen: Der deutsche Zionismus im Feld des Nationalismus in Deutschland, 1890–1933* (Göttingen: Wallstein, 2016), 113–195.

48. Derek J. Penslar, "Zionism, Colonialism, and Technocracy: Otto Warburg and the Commission for the Exploration of Palestine, 1903–1907," *Journal of Contemporary History* 25 (1990): 142–60.

49. For the first case, see, for instance, Davis Trietsch, "Jüdische Kulturmission im Orient," in *Jüdische Emigration und Kolonisation* (Berlin: Orient-Verlag, 1917), 42–45; Willy Bambus, *Die jüdischen Kolonien in Palästina, ihre Entstehung und Entwicklung* (Wien: Kommandit-Gesellschaft Karmel, 1904), 9–10; Aaron Aaronson and Selig Soskin, "Die Rosinenstadt Es-Salt," *Altneuland* 1 (1904): 13–22; Elias Auerbach, *Palästina als Judenland* (Berlin: Jüdischer Verlag, 1912), 46–47; Arthur Ruppin, *Zionistische Kolonisationspolitik. Bericht an den XI. Zionistenkongreß* (Berlin: Jüdischer Verlag, 1914), 29–30. For the second case, see Martin Buber, "Jüdisches Nationalheim und nationale Politik in Palästina," in *Der Jude und sein Judentum*, 330–42.

50. See, for instance, Martin Buber, "In später Stunde," *Der Jude* 5 (1920/21): 1–5; Martin Buber, "Jüdisches Nationalheim"; Eugen Hoeflich, "Juden und Araber (Offener Brief an Professor Musil)," *Freie Zionistische Blätter* 1 (1921): 56–57; Robert Weltsch, "Anträge zur Araberfrage," 1921, Leo Baeck Institute New York, Robert Weltsch Collection, AR 7185/1/20.

51. Buber, "In später Stunde," 5.

52. Hall, "The West and the Rest."

53. Robert Weltsch, "Politik und Terrorakte," *Jüdische Rundschau*, August 5, 1932, 295. On the relationship of German Zionism and National Socialism, see Francis R. Nicosia,

Zionism and Anti-Semitism in Nazi Germany (Cambridge, UK: Cambridge University Press, 2008).

54. Rosenblüth, "Nationaljudentum und Antisemitismus," 127.

55. Steven E. Aschheim, "German History and German Jewry: Boundaries, Junctions and Interdependence," *Leo Baeck Institute Year Book* 43 (1998): 315–22, here 316–17. See also Till van Rahden, "Jews and the Ambivalences of Civil Society in Germany, 1800 to 1933: Assessment and Reassessment," *Journal of Modern History* 77 (2005): 1024–47; Steven M. Lowenstein, "Jewish Participation in German Culture," in *German-Jewish History in Modern Times*. Vol. 3, *Integration in Dispute, 1871–1918*, ed. Michael A. Meyer (New York: Columbia University Press, 1997), 305–35.

56. See, for instance, Derek J. Penslar, "Zionism, Colonialism and Postcolonialism," *Journal of Israeli History* 20 (2001): 84–98; Feisal Devji, *Muslim Zion: Pakistan as a Political Idea* (Cambridge, MA: Harvard University Press, 2013); Arie M. Dubnov, "Notes on the Zionist Passage to India, or: The Analogical Imagination and Its Boundaries," *Journal of Israeli History* 35 (2016): 177–214; Johannes Becke, "Beyond Allozionism: Exceptionalizing and De-Exceptionalizing the Zionist Project," *Israel Studies* 23, no. 2 (2018): 168–93. See also the chapters by Johannes Becke, Arie M. Dubnuv, and Rephael G. Stern in this volume.

57. Partha Chatterjee, for instance, insists on the existence of a "spiritual domain" of the colonized that contains "essential marks of cultural identity." See Partha Chatterjee, *The Nation and Its Fragments: Colonial and Postcolonial Histories* (Princeton, NJ: Princeton University Press, 1993), 6.

4
Postcolonial Parallels in Albert Memmi's Portrait of Frantz Fanon
Negotiating Négritude, Nativism, and Jewish Nationalism

ABRAHAM RUBIN

In September of 1971, Albert Memmi, the renowned French scholar and novelist of Tunisian-Jewish descent, published "The Impossible Life of Frantz Fanon."[1] This penetrating and empathetic portrait of Fanon became one of Memmi's most-cited essays. Memmi's essay has come to assume a central place in critical evaluations of Fanon's intellectual legacy and the scholarly efforts to explore the intersections between his life and thought.[2] The power of Memmi's penetrating and perceptive portrait of Fanon—a fellow anticolonial thinker and activist—can be attributed to the biographical and intellectual parallels he saw in his own life. In fact, a comparative reading of Memmi's autobiographical writings and his account of Fanon reveals the extent to which Memmi self-consciously structured his intellectual biography of Fanon around these very affinities. Bryan Cheyette has gone so far as to claim that "Memmi transforms Fanon into a 'family likeness,' the only transformation permissible by Memmi, as an imagined double."[3] The essay does not merely trace the course of Fanon's intellectual and political transformations, but seems to implicitly juxtapose their respective ideological and identitarian trajectories. Underlying Memmi's depiction of Fanon is a sense of intimate proximity and personal identification, but also the need to differentiate and distinguish his politics from a fellow Francophone postcolonial thinker, whose key works, *Black Skin, White Masks* and *The Wretched of the Earth* had been read alongside Memmi's *The Colonizer and the Colonized*.[4]

Reading Memmi's image of Fanon as the work of biographical and political misprision sheds light on his own attempt to justify the evolving arch of his intellectual career and affirm its ideological coherence against the foil of Fanon's life and legacy.[5] The question of continuity is one that has preoccupied both Memmi and critics, who have grappled with the relationship between his anticolonial and Jewish writings. While Memmi's *The Colonizer and the Colonized* and *The Pillar of Salt* have been read and celebrated as part of the anticolonial canon since their publication in the 1950s, his subsequent writings on Zionism and Jewishness have been largely ignored in the field of postcolonial studies. The indifference—if not outright disdain—toward Memmi's later work reflects a tendency to distinguish his literary production in the 1950s from his subsequent work from the mid-1960s onward. Underlying this attitude is the idea that Memmi's thought divides into two separate and irreconcilable ideological phases—the anticolonial and the Jewish.[6] This tale of two Memmis is encapsulated in Joan Cocks's account of his political self-transformation:

> In the 1950s and 1960s, Memmi ... allies himself culturally and economically with North Africa, supports the cause of national liberation for oppressed Muslims and other colonized peoples, and writes on behalf of all subjugated groups but against homogenizing universalist projects. Yet, over the course of the 1960s and 1970s, he increasingly identifies himself with the Jewish people as distinguished from the Arab people..., defends the Jewish national cause against its Arab opponents, and champions a Jewish state in Palestine...What accounts for this metamorphosis in self-conception, empathy and political commitment—if it is a metamorphosis?[7]

The notion of Memmi's "about-face" is symptomatic of the disciplinary divide between Jewish studies and postcolonial studies.[8] Scholars have mostly shied away from drawing analogies between these two archives of historical experience, or exploring the affinities between Jewish thought and postcolonial critique. Precluding the possibility of placing Jewish and postcolonial experience within a common analytic framework is the contemporary perception of Jews as Westerners, and the racial identification of Jewishness with whiteness. The alleged antithesis between Jewish and postcolonial history is enhanced by the regnant conception of Zionism as a European political formation, and of Israel as a foreign colonial transplant in the Middle East.[9]

The effort to bridge this gap and conceptualize the experience of Jewish marginality alongside the condition of colonial domination is a hallmark of Memmi's Jewish writings. Memmi seeks to rethink the meaning of Jewish national self-determination from a Third World perspective that identifies the establishment of the State of Israel as part of the postwar process of decolonization. Thus, contrary to the idea that Israel represented a foreign colonial presence in the Middle East that foiled the historical goals of decolonization, Memmi sought to affirm the conceptual interconnections between the two projects. In this regard, Memmi did not perceive his embrace of Zionism as a renunciation of the anticolonial position he espoused in the 1950s, but saw it as the logical consummation of that same stance.

Memmi's portrait of Fanon offers a critical vantage point from which to reevaluate Memmi's own thinking about Zionism and what he called "the Jewish condition."[10] In his Jewish writings, Memmi adopts a relational framework that explores the intersecting experiences of colonialism and racism among oppressed collectivities. The intersectional prism that informs Memmi's diagnosis of the "Jewish condition" also extends to his reading of Fanon, albeit implicitly. When reading Memmi's account of Fanon's "impossible life" in light of Memmi's earlier works—particularly those that acknowledge the presence of an autobiographical dimension—we see how Memmi fashions a figure of Fanon in relation to his own intellectual and ideological persona. Pointing out Fanon's "failures," Memmi turns Fanon's political trajectory into a negative image of the ideological metamorphoses that ultimately led him to Zionism. Despite the implied contrasts that structure Memmi's essay, I wish to argue that the blind spots and contradictions that Memmi identifies in Fanon's life and work were also very much his own.

Fanon's Failures, or Martinique as Metaphor

Memmi opens his essay attacking the cult of personality formed around Fanon, observing that his image as Third World revolutionary blatantly disregards the biographical, social, and historical contexts from which Fanon's politics emerged. Those who celebrate Fanon as "prophet of the Third World" and idolize him as "a romantic hero of decolonization" rarely pause to question his motives or the unique circumstances that led to his embrace of the distant and foreign cause of Algerian nationalism: "As if it went without saying that a Black West Indian intellectual could some day become an Algerian patriot, with so absolute a self-sacrifice that he would die from it."[11]

Memmi charts out the internal paradoxes of Fanon's politics, tracing these back to Fanon's lifelong effort to resolve the ambiguities of his own West Indian identity. Fanon's self-invention as Third World revolutionary is the story of his failed attempt to transcend his Black-Antillean origins. According to this interpretation, Fanon acts out his ambivalent and contradictory relationship to France and Martinique through his ever-evolving political commitments and his theories on anticolonial revolt. His transformations from French Republican to Algerian nationalist, pan-Africanist to advocate of a "new humanism," were all abortive attempts to resolve the drama of his own identity.

Fanon grew up in the French Department of Martinique thinking he was French and white only to discover that he was perceived as Black and West Indian in metropolitan France. In response, Fanon renounced his ties to France and Europe; yet, rather than embrace his West Indian and Black identity, like his teacher Aimé Césaire, Fanon took another path, aligning himself with the Algerians and their struggle for independence. Memmi blames Fanon for blindly ignoring the limits of such radical self-invention: "By what miracle, without changing his skin and losing all memory, was he going to transform himself into a white Arab, and Moslem to boot when he was Christian by birth?"[12]

Rebuffed by Algerian nationalists, Fanon then turns to devote himself to a "United Africa, where frontiers of skin and cultural prejudice would no longer count and where even a Black West Indian would belong."[13] Yet Fanon's utopian politics failed to resonate with the liberation movements spreading throughout the African continent, each seeking to establish its own independent and self-contained national identity. In his final work, *The Wretched of the Earth*, the imagined ideal of pan-African unity gave way to an even more radical vision—that of a "new humanity" forged in the flame of anticolonial violence. As Memmi explains: "In order to complete this forward movement, in order to resolve his personal predicament, what was left for him if not to propose a totally unprecedented man, in a totally reconstructed world?"[14]

In Memmi's narrative, Fanon's radical politics and his personal tragedy were inextricably intertwined. Both were the product of his stubborn refusal to accept himself as a Black West Indian and attest to the fact that he never succeeded in extricating himself from Europe. The France that Fanon so adamantly disavowed thus cast its long shadow on his subsequent revolutionary and political identifications, all of which manifest the dynamics of the colonized subject's self-rejection.[15] The turn to Algerian nationalism, the appeal to Pan-African unity, and the exhortation of a "new humanity" represent different efforts to transcend his own Blackness. The unresolved dualities and ambiguities that inflicted themselves on Fanon as a Black colonial subject could not be overcome because Fanon never "returned to Négritude and the West Indies."[16] Once removing the "white mask," he never recovered his "black skin."

Thus, the only authentic solution for Fanon would have been to return to the West Indies and identify with the revolt of his own people. Yet Fanon could not reconstruct that identity as a West Indian because Martinique was too integrated into the French community to view itself independently and too Creolized to recuperate an authentic native identity. It was "incapable of furnishing him with the psychological and historical remedy to his tragic situation."[17] Algeria was meant as a substitute for his "unattainable identification with Martinique," yet when Fanon joined the Algerian cause he did so on abstract principle alone.[18] There was nothing that tied him to Algeria, with the exception that the Algerians, like him, had been colonized and dominated by the French. He spoke no Arabic, and was foreign to North African Muslim and Berber culture. He did not belong, yet his editorials in *Al Moudjihad* refer to the Algerians in the first person plural, exclaiming "we Algerians," in an ironic echo of "our ancestors the Gauls."[19] With the publication of *The Wretched of the Earth*, Fanon's life had come full circle. As a youth, Fanon rejected his West Indian identity in the name of a universalist humanism. The revolutionary path he embarked upon after his disillusionment with France brought him back to the same Eurocentric universalism he revolted against.

Memmi's critique of Fanon's political and identitarian self-invention echoes his own pointed rejection of the figure of the Arab Jew. Paradoxically, Memmi described himself in the very terms whose reality he ostensibly denies: "Of course we were Arab Jews, or Jewish Arabs, in our customs, our culture, our music, our cooking."[20] What Memmi contested was the nostalgic idealization of Arab-Jewish history as one of harmony and symbiosis. Not only did this idyllic image of the Arab-Jewish past falsify the historical rifts and tensions between the communities, but it also served the distinct ideological purpose of delegitimizing Israel. Memmi repudiates the political viability of Arab-Jewish identity, arguing that the North African nation-states that arose in the wake of decolonization liquidated their Jewish communities.[21] Fanon in Algeria and Memmi in Tunisia—both confronted the reality of Arab-Muslim nationalist exclusivity and experienced themselves as outsiders within the anticolonial national movements they joined.[22]

The account of Fanon's abortive efforts to resolve his identitarian predicament by way of a nationalism (that was not his own) and a universalism (predicated on the erasure of difference) bears clear parallels to Memmi's ideological evolution, fictionalized in his semi-autobiographical *The Pillar of Salt*, and recounted in detail in *Portrait of a Jew* and *The Liberation of the Jew*.[23] As an adolescent, Memmi rejected his Jewishness because he identified it with a parochial backwardness. He believed that by cutting himself off from his Jewish background, cultural past, and family he would find liberation. Substituting his commitment to the Jewish people for that of humanity, the young Memmi believed in the promise of universal human emancipation. Yet after Vichy and World War II, Memmi realized that his "destiny did not necessarily coincide with the destiny of Europe," bringing him to return to his native Tunisia in 1949.[24]

The failed promise of European universalism and the prospect of assimilation into French society were followed by the cruel disappointment that awaited him upon his return to Tunisia. Between 1949 and 1956, Memmi lived, taught, and wrote in Tunis, aligning himself with the cause of Tunisian national liberation. Once Tunisia attained its independence, it defined itself as a Muslim-Arab nation-state. This new political formation ultimately led to the dissolution of the Jewish community, which dispersed to France and Israel. Neither the European-universalist nor the Tunisian-nationalist avenues offer a solution to Memmi's specifically "Jewish" problem. Both options require the effacement of Jewish difference. It is the recognition of this fact that leads Memmi to Zionism.

In *The Liberation of the Jew*, Memmi argues that Jewish life in the Diaspora constitutes an "impossible condition"—an assertion that both echoes and anticipates his diagnosis of Frantz Fanon's "impossible life."[25] The work offers a comprehensive analysis of the diasporic Jew's oppression, which encompasses his political, economic, cultural, and religious existence. It affects his relationship to Jews and non-Jews alike, distorting his personality and self-perception. It divides his existence and splits his private and public persona. Memmi explores different paths out of this "double oppression"—interior and exterior—only to judge them all insufficient. Intermarriage, conversion, self-rejection, assimilation, nationalism, Jewish communitarianism—all fail to resolve the tensions and contradictions of the Jew's individual and collective existence. The diasporic Jew, Memmi observes, is oppressed in all aspects of his existence, concluding that "the specific solution to the Jewish drama" is that of national liberation.[26]

When Memmi advocates the necessity of Jewish-national self-determination he does not do so as a disinterested observer. He proclaims it as the "way out" of his own identitarian impasse as a formerly colonized subject of French rule and a victim of Arab-Muslim hostility. Zionism is posited as the path to reclaiming his own agency and authenticity. Zionism is Memmi's "return to the self." Memmi's reclamation of his Jewish identity by way of Zionism stands in contrast to Fanon's evasion of his Creole West Indian heritage. Memmi's anticolonial politics—that is, his Zionism—succeed where Fanon's failed, because his own revolt against oppression was undertaken in the name of his Jewishness, conceived here as his primal identity. At first glance, this implied contrast allows Memmi to vindicate his personal and political trajectory. Yet a closer examination reveals that the paradoxes he identifies in Fanon are mirrored in his own position as well. The similarities emerge when we compare Memmi's critique of diasporic Jewishness with Fanon's attitude toward Négritude and nativism.

Négritude, Nativism, and Jewish Nationalism

In the backdrop of Memmi's critique of Fanon are their diverging views on Négritude, the cultural and political movement of Africana intellectuals, whose paths converged in 1930s Paris. The leading figures of the movement, such as Aimé Césaire and Léopold Sédar Senghor, responded to the denigration of Blackness and Black culture by searching for new modes of aesthetic expression and cultural creativity through which to revalorize African diasporic identity. It was a project that combined the aims of cultural recuperation and political emancipation. These thinkers sought to extricate Blackness from colonial-racial discourse and contest the exploitation and dehumanization of Black populations under French imperial rule. Négritude challenged colonialism's assertion of Black inferiority and humanism's erasure of Black difference under the guise of a colorless universalism.[27]

In "Négritude et Judéité," an essay dedicated to Léopold Senghor, Memmi acknowledges his debt to Négritude, noting that his thinking about Jewish identity and liberation was influenced by "the awakening of subjugated peoples" and "their discoveries about themselves."[28] Memmi sees a direct relationship between Zionism and Négritude as movements set upon liberating oppressed communities. He goes on to draw an analogy between the emerging African nation-states (which he misleadingly identifies with the Négritude movement) and the establishment of Israel. In associating Négritude with separatist and statist liberation, Memmi misrepresents the original aims of the movement, which were the attainment of civic equality under French rule and the affirmation of Black cultural identity within the political framework of imperial France.[29] When it arose in 1930s Paris, as a loose network of Black Francophone intellectuals, the Négritude movement sought to renegotiate the French metropole's relationship to its colonies and separate the demand for equality and citizenship from the expectation of assimilation. Its most enduring legacy, perhaps, was the effort to articulate Black diasporic cultural identity.

This recuperative dimension, which was so central to the Négritude movement, has no equivalent in Memmi's Zionism. There is no culturally affirmative aspect to Memmi's analysis of the "Jewish condition," which identifies the tradition, history, and ritual of diasporic Jewry with degradation, reification, and despair. Thus, whereas Memmi aligns himself with Négritude and against Fanon, his critique of Jewish diasporic culture is in fact far closer to Fanon's position. Fanon famously railed against Négritude in *Black Skin, White Masks* and *The Wretched of the Earth*, arguing that its romantic nostalgia of premodern Blackness peddled in the same racist myths propagated by the white colonizers.[30] He considered Négritude's revalorization of Blackness to be politically regressive and essentialist. He staunchly rejected the concept of Black peoplehood, arguing that no such entity ever existed, and those who claimed otherwise deprived the African diaspora of the possibility of individual self-expression. Fanon further rejected the possibility of returning to one's native culture as a means of self-affirmation. Under the colonial system, native culture had turned fixed, closed, and "mummified."[31] "The culture of the enslaved people is sclerosed, dying. No life any longer circulates in it."[32] The native identifies tradition with purity and salvation, and it serves as a defense mechanism in the struggle against the colonizer. Yet by falling back on the "archaic positions" of the valorized indigenous tradition, the native cuts himself off from the present.[33]

Memmi, for his part, saw Fanon's rejection of Négritude as hypocritical and shortsighted. How could Fanon criticize Négritude for its particularism at the same time that he embraced Algerian nationalism? These protestations notwithstanding, Memmi's categorical rejection of diasporic Jewishness in *The Liberation of the Jew* closely approximates Fanon's critique of nativism. Memmi dismisses the possibility of maintaining an authentically Jewish existence in the Diaspora, either by way of tradition or social affiliation. He characterizes communal Jewish life in the Diaspora in unambiguously derisive terms, calling it "a closed world, living painfully and disastrously within itself."[34] The communally affiliated Jew exists in a state of insularity and marginality, he is "a living fossil."[35] Traditional Jewish life "imposes one type of alienation in place of another."[36]

Jewish tradition and community offer no way out of the Jew's predicament, they only perpetuate it, leading to the Jew's withdrawal from the world around him. The tradition of the oppressed may provide him with psychological solace, but it is also the cause of cultural stasis. In the face of his marginalization, it is understandable that the Jew should revert inward and find refuge among his kin, community, and religious traditions. The countermyths of his tradition allow him to reclaim his dignity, but they perpetuate his political impotence. The modern Jew must thus choose "between liberation from that tradition and death, smothered in the bands of the tefillin."[37] The "encystment" lamented by Memmi finds its parallel in Fanon's critique of nativism, which he describes as a "culture put into capsules."[38] Memmi's attitude toward traditional Judaism mirrors Fanon's critique of Négritude and nativism. Both see the colonized subjects' religion and culture through the prism of modernization and secularization. Inherent in their postcolonial critiques of native and traditional culture is the logic of developmentalism. Fanon's vision of postcolonial liberation is decisively secular and modernist. He is averse to traditional culture and sees it as an obstacle to independence. This secular bias is equally apparent in Memmi's disdain for traditional Jewish culture.

Memmi accuses Fanon of reproducing the logic of Eurocentric universalism in his anticolonial writings. Noting the abstract character of Fanon's revolutionary vision, Memmi writes:

> His perception of African unity was in great part illusory or at least premature … he made little distinction between the social realities of the various peoples, states, and nations that make up this immense continent. Thus he grew impatient, he showed his scorn of regional particularism, of the tenacity of tradition and custom, of cultural and national aspirations, as well as of the play of frequently contradictory interests.[39]

Fanon's vision of a postcolonial humanity remains anchored to a universalist template. By disregarding the particularities of different subjugated populations, and the ways their self-determination is tempered by their cultural and geographical variations, Fanon falls into the same trap as humanism's image of an abstract humanity.

Memmi criticizes Fanon's anticolonial politics for its abstract conjectural character. His image of a supranational, post-ethnic, and determinately secular community, which was supposed to emerge from the revolution, was a messianic and ahistorical construct. In his dream of a postrevolutionary utopian society, Fanon failed to discern the true traits and aims of historically concrete collectivities that revolted in order to assert their particularistic religious and national identities. The irony underlying this well-argued critique is that Memmi's image of a liberated Jewish collective involves a similar historical abstraction.

In his analysis of the "Jewish fate," Memmi posits a singular Jewish experience, without much regard to the multiple diasporic, cultural, geographic histories of the Jewish people.[40] The universalism Memmi accuses Fanon of imposing on the postcolonial subject is reproduced in *The Liberation of the Jew*, which posits a universal Jewish condition that effaces intra-Jewish differences and reduces Jewishness to the experience of oppression. Thus, while Memmi argues against interpreting Zionism through a Eurocentric lens, he nevertheless reproduces the abstract universalist logic he associates it with when he homogenizes Jewishness into a national identity. Paradoxically, Memmi supports Zionism in the name of the Jews' cultural particularity, but effaces the very particularities that make up the Jewish world. He attributes an arbitrary universalism to Fanon's thinking, accusing his revolutionary theory of reproducing the very Eurocentric logic from which it seeks to break away. Yet Memmi's so-called particularist solution merely transposes this universalism to an intra-Jewish realm, homogenizing diasporic Judaism into one uniform entity defined by the fact of its oppression. Memmi interprets Jewish history in terms of lack, inauthenticity, and incompleteness. His critique of diasporic Jewish life reproduces the European tropes of Jewish primitivism and inadequacy. The idea that the Jewish people should be liberated by way of national autonomy reproduces the European master narrative of modernity.

Homelands Lost and Recovered

Memmi's work tends to blur the lines between sociology, autobiography, and literature. This mode of writing justifies interpreting his Zionism as a literary-autobiographical solution to his own identitarian dilemmas.[41]

Memmi writes that when he left Tunisia to study in France, "the dream of the West had turned into a nightmare," but that he could not turn back.[42] The impossibility of this return is indicated in the title of his semi-autobiographical novel, *The Pillar of Salt*, which recounts the story of a young man caught between two diametrically opposed worlds. Unable to sever his ties to his impoverished Jewish-Berber family and its superstitious traditionalism, nor willing to embrace Western modernity, with its false pretense of moral universalism, the novel's protagonist boards a ship to Argentina at the end of the novel.

Memmi identified himself with the protagonist of *The Pillar of Salt* in subsequent works and interviews. A quote from the novel that serves as the opening epigraph to *Portrait of a Jew* reads:

> Could I be descended from a Berber tribe when the Berbers themselves failed to recognize me as one of their own? I was Jewish, not Moslem; a townsman, not a highlander. And even if I had borne the painter's name, I would not have been acknowledged by the Italians. No, I'm African, not European. In the long run, I would always be forced to return to Alexandre Mordekhai Benillouche, a native in a colonial country, a Jew in an anti-Semitic universe, an African in a world dominated by Europe.[43]

In contrast to his fictional counterpart who seeks to overcome his existence as a "half-breed," caught between the conflicting currents of East and West, by moving to Argentina, Memmi the author settled in Paris, married a French Catholic, and became a French citizen. In the novel, Argentina holds the promise of new beginnings for Benillouche and the prospect of true liberation, beyond the dialectics of assimilatory self-negation and the nostalgic primitivism of nativist self-affirmation. Memmi considered *Portrait of a Jew* and *Liberation of the Jew* as part of the same autobiographical endeavor he began with *The Pillar of Salt*, describing all these texts as a search for a way out of his own condition of oppression. The novel portrays Argentina as a third space that allows Benillouche to overcome his entanglements with both France and Tunisia. In *Liberation of the Jew*, it is Israel that plays this role and assumes the emancipatory promise of a place that is neither North Africa nor Europe. In the words of Olivia Harrison,

"If Tunisian Jews could not be natives in Tunisia, they would become natives in Palestine, construed as the homeland of the Jewish people."[44]

Just as Benillouche's story ends with his departure to the unknown, Memmi's *Liberation* ends with the incontrovertible necessity of establishing a Jewish state to end the Jews' oppression. Memmi does not discuss its geopolitical realities or sociocultural complexities. Memmi's Israel has a heuristic, abstract quality to it. His pronouncements regarding its potential to liberate the Jews are declarative and hyperbolic. There is a prophetic tone to his analysis of the Jewish condition, which alternates between the idealistic, wistful, and tragic, but at no stage does *The Liberation of the Jew* grapple with Israel as a lived reality. Israel remains a blank space unto which Memmi projects the fantasy of Jewish existential authenticity.

What Algeria is for Fanon, Israel is for Memmi. Let us recall Memmi's account of the compensatory role Algeria had for Fanon:

> What an extraordinary encounter in a part of the world uniquely suited to Fanon's neurosis: a land where French was spoken but where one could hate France. Algeria was precisely the right substitute, in the negative and the positive sense, for Martinique, which had let him down; or rather Algeria was the embellished substitute of his lost homeland.[45]

Identification with Israel was a way for Memmi to symbolically resist assimilation, even after he resettled in France. Memmi's Israel becomes the imaginary location of a recovered authentic identity. It offers an alternative to France and Tunisia, the two sites that represent the self-negation of Memmi's Jewishness, allowing him to overcome the assimilatory imperative in France and the exclusionary Arab-Muslim nationalism of Tunisia. Like Fanon's Algeria, Memmi's Israel is invested with an overdetermined symbolism. There is no substantive meditation on its culture, politics, or intra-ethnic relations. Its lived reality is negligible in Memmi's analysis of Zionism as an existential solution to the Jewish condition. According to Memmi, Fanon's revolutionary politics were driven by his ambivalence toward Europe and Martinique. Memmi argues that Fanon sought to transcend his West Indian identity by constructing a messianic utopia that celebrated violence as a cathartic measure that would usher in a new postrevolutionary humanity. A biographical interpretation along similar lines can be applied to Memmi's case. The projective dimension Memmi attributes to Fanon is mirrored in his image of Israel, as a site "uniquely suited" to resolve the ambiguities of Memmi's own French, Jewish, Tunisian identity.[46]

Conclusion

"A colonized people is not alone. In spite of all that colonialism can do, its frontiers remain open to new ideas and echoes from the world outside," wrote Fanon in *The Wretched of the Earth*.[47] Guiding Fanon's theory of revolt is a recognition that the interconnections between anticolonial movements serve to advance and inspire their respective revolutionary causes. Underlying Memmi's reflections on Zionism is a similar impulse. In reformulating Zionism through the prism of postcolonial critique, Memmi seeks to challenge the identitarian and political boundaries of Jewish nationalism. This alternative vision of Zionism aspires to establish new lines of solidarity between Israel and the Third World. In construing Zionism as a postcolonial, national liberation movement, one that faces the same political and cultural dilemmas as the nascent nation-states of the Third World, Memmi's intellectual legacy forms part of a persistent yet oft-disregarded strain of thought within Zionism that sought to align the Jewish and Afro-Asian struggles for collective self-determination, and pursued the cultural and political integration of the Jews in the Middle East.[48]

Memmi's ideal of Israel was deeply intertwined with issues relating to his own autobiographical identity. His image of Zionism was inflected by a philosophical and sociological orientation that emphasized conceptual over historical analysis. The tension between Memmi's idealistic interpretation of Zionism and its fraught political reality remains unresolved.[49] Yet in spite of its contradictions, Memmi's thought offers an imaginative reformulation of Zionism that expands its conceptual possibilities by aligning it with the postcolonial. In addressing Zionism's political and cultural affinities to Third World nationalism, Memmi writes:

> The Zionists, and many Jews of the diaspora, assume that what is happening today to the Jewish people, and the Zionist solution that was chosen, are totally unprecedented events. I am sorry to disappoint them

and to remind them frequently that all this is not so very original. There are many oppressions throughout the world, and the nationalist solution is the most common. I am not saying this so as to disparage Zionism; on the contrary, I find it very reassuring and it legitimizes Zionism that much more, in case that were necessary. It is reassuring that the problems that one faces are being faced by other people too. And it is so convenient to compare one's own solution with other people's. Between Israel and the other young nations in the world today there are certainly some fruitful comparisons to be made.[50]

Guiding Memmi's analysis is the understanding that Israel is not historically unique and that the circumstances of its founding are in fact quite close to those of other national liberation movements and postcolonial states established in the wake of World War II. Memmi's comparative approach to Zionism seeks to demythologize the establishment of the State of Israel and place the historical and political circumstances of its establishment in a comparative and regional perspective. Alerting his audiences to the Mediterranean background of the majority of the country's population and drawing sociological parallels between Israel and its Arab neighbors, Memmi challenges the idea of Israel's "Westernness." Memmi's line of argument might be construed as an apologetic retort to accusations of Israel's colonial character and its foreignness to the region, but it is also more than that. It is an intellectual exercise that reframes and recontextualizes our geopolitical understanding of Israel. Memmi refuses to resign himself to *realpolitik*, or accept the Arab-Jewish conflict as an inevitable reality. In his conceptualization of Zionism as a form of Third World nationalism, Memmi envisions an alternative geopolitical reality for Israel's integration in the region.

NOTES

1. Albert Memmi, "La vie impossible de Frantz Fanon," *Esprit* 406 (1971): 248–73; Albert Memmi, "The Impossible Life of Frantz Fanon," *The Massachusetts Review* 14 (1973): 9–39.
2. See Henry Louis Gates, "Critical Fanonism," *Critical Inquiry* 17 (1991): 457–70; Françoise Vergès, "Creole Skin, Black Mask: Fanon and Disavowal," *Critical Inquiry* 23 (1997): 578–95; Bryan Cheyette, *Diasporas of the Mind: Jewish and Postcolonial Writing*

and the Nightmare of History (New Haven, CT: Yale University Press, 2013); Azzedine Haddour, "Sartre and Fanon: On Négritude and Political Participation," *Sartre Studies International* 11 (2005): 286–301; David Macey, *Frantz Fanon: A Biography* (London: Verso, 2012); Ann Pellegrini, "Between Men: Fanon, Memmi, and the Colonial Encounter," in *Performance Anxieties: Staging Psychoanalysis, Staging Race* (London: Routledge, 1997), 109–29.

3. Cheyette, *Diasporas of the Mind*, 48.

4. Albert Memmi, *Portrait du colonisé, précédé par portrait du colonisateur* (Paris: Buchet/Chastel, 1957); Albert Memmi, *The Colonizer and the Colonized*, trans. Howard Greenfeld (London: Earthscan, 2003).

5. My use of the term "misprision" is an allusions to Harold Bloom's theory of "poetic misprision," which argues that "poetic influence ... always proceeds by a misreading of the prior poet, an act of creative correction that is actually and necessarily a misinterpretation. The history of fruitful poetic influence ... is a history of anxiety and self-saving caricature, of distortion, of perverse, willful revisionism without which modern poetry as such could not exist." By analogy, Memmi's portrait of Fanon may be understood in terms of the dynamic of inter-poetic relationship theorized in Bloom's work. In his "strong misreading" of Fanon, Memmi rewrites his own political identity. See Harold Bloom, *The Anxiety of Influence: A Theory of Poetry* (Oxford: Oxford University Press, 1997), 30.

6. Olivia C. Harrison, *Transcolonial Maghreb: Imagining Palestine in the Era of Decolonization* (Stanford, CA: Stanford University Press, 2015), 82.

7. Joan Cocks, "Jewish Nationalism and the Question of Palestine," *Interventions* 8 (2006): 29–30; Lisa Lieberman, "Albert Memmi's About-Face," *Michigan Quarterly Review* 46 (2007), http://hdl.handle.net/2027/spo.act2080.0046.326. For a more generous assessment of Memmi's legacy, see Susie Linfield, "Albert Memmi: Zionism as National Liberation" in *The Lions' Den: Zionism and the Left from Hannah Arendt to Noam Chomsky* (New Haven, CT: Yale University Press, 2019), 165–96; Daniel Gordon, "Telling the Whole Truth: Albert Memmi," *Jewish Review of Books* 9 (Spring 2018): 27–30.

8. See Michael Rothberg, *Multidirectional Memory: Remembering the Holocaust in the Age of Decolonization* (Stanford, CA: Stanford University Press, 2009); Santiago Slabodsky, *Decolonial Judaism: Triumphal Failures of Barbaric Thinking* (New York: Palgrave Macmillan, 2014); Cheyette, *Diasporas of the Mind*.

9. There have been various attempts to complicate this Occidental image of Zionism and Israel on both conceptual and historical levels. See, for example, Derek Penslar, "Zionism, Colonialism, and Postcolonialism," *Israeli History* 20 (2001): 84–98; Stefan Vogt, "The Postcolonial Buber: Orientalism, Subalternity, and Identity Politics in Martin Buber's Political Thought," *Jewish Social Studies* 22 (2016): 161–86.

10. Albert Memmi, *The Liberation of the Jew*, trans. Judy Hyun (New York: Viking Press, 1973), 14.

11. Memmi, "The Impossible Life of Frantz Fanon," 13.

12. Ibid., 10.

13. Ibid.

14. Ibid., 11.

15. See Memmi, *The Colonizer and the Colonized*, 167–68.

16. Memmi, "The Impossible Life of Frantz Fanon," 16.
17. Ibid., 20.
18. Ibid., 17.
19. Ibid., 24.
20. Albert Memmi, *Jews and Arabs*, trans. Eleanor Levieux (Chicago: J. Philip O'Hara, 1975), 20.
21. Ibid., 23.
22. According to Gil Hochberg, Memmi's critique of the figure of the Arab Jew involves an historical omission of Europe's role in fomenting antisemitism in North Africa. She notes an ideological shift in Memmi's writings; whereas his early work associates the Jews and Muslims of North Africa as colonized subjects, his later essays turn the Arab Jew into an "impossible figure." She explains this transition as the result of a "forgetting" of Europe's role in importing antisemitism to North Africa. It is his blindness to the interdependency of antisemitism and colonialism, "this forgetting of Europe," she argues, "that eventually turns Memmi into an uncritical supporter of Zionism, blind to its evident Eurocentric disposition and explicit colonial implications." This critique fails to do justice to Memmi. His account of the Arab-Jewish rift is not grounded in the notion of some kind of ontological Jewishness; it is a diagnosis of a political reality that was forced upon the Jews of the Middle East and North Africa. In fact, Memmi's discussion of the Arab Jew challenges the assumption that Jews are foreign to the Middle East, and seeks to make the experience of Jews of Arab lands more visible. "We constantly hear of 'Arab lands' and 'Zionist enclave.' But by what mystical geography are we not at home there too, we who descend from the same indigenous populations since the first human settlements were made?" He contests the conceptual binary of a Muslim Orient versus a Judeo-Christian West that pits the Arab-Muslim world against a supposedly Western-Jewish one. See Gil Hochberg, *In Spite of Partition: Jews, Arabs, and the Limits of Separatist Imagination* (Princeton, NJ: Princeton University Press, 2007), 2l; Memmi, *Jews and Arabs*, 14.
23. Albert Memmi, *Portrait of a Jew*, trans. Elisabeth Abbott (New York: Orion Press, 1962); Memmi, *The Liberation of the Jew*; Albert Memmi, *The Pillar of Salt*, trans Edouard Roditi (Boston: Beacon Press, 1992).
24. Memmi, *Portrait of a Jew*, 5.
25. Memmi, *The Liberation of the Jew*, 263.
26. Ibid., 274. Even before his public embrace of Zionism in the 1960s, Memmi had already recognized the inevitability of the "national solution" to oppression. In *The Colonizer and the Colonized*, he writes: "For a number of historical, sociological and psychological reasons, the struggle for liberation by colonized peoples has taken on a marked national and nationalistic look." See Memmi, *The Colonizer and the Colonized*, 73.
27. See Gary Wilder, *The French Imperial Nation-State: Négritude and Colonial Humanism Between the Two World Wars* (Chicago: University of Chicago Press, 2005).
28. Albert Memmi, "Négritude et Judéité," *African Arts* 1, no. 4 (1968): 26–123, here 27.
29. Memmi equates Zionism with statehood. His unequivocally statist view of Jewish national self-sovereignty cannot be reconciled with the cosmopolitan and transnational orientation of the Négritude movement. Négritude's political and cultural aims seem

more consistent with various pre-state strains of Zionism that were critical of ethno-national sovereignty and sought to articulate alternative regional visions of a Jewish polity in Palestine. Some representative studies on counter-state Zionism include Noam Pianko, *Zionism and the Roads Not Taken: Rawidowicz, Kaplan, Kohn* (Bloomington: Indiana University Press, 2010); David N. Myers, *Between Jew and Arab: The Lost Voice of Simon Rawidowicz* (Hanover, NH: Brandeis University Press, 2008); Joshua Shanes, *Diaspora Nationalism and Jewish Identity in Habsburg Galicia* (Cambridge, UK: Cambridge University Press, 2012); Dmitry Shumsky, *Beyond the Nation-State: The Zionist Political Imagination from Pinsker to Ben-Gurion* (New Haven, CT: Yale University Press, 2018).

30. Frantz Fanon, *Black Skin, White Masks*, trans. Richard Philcox (New York: Grove Press, 2007), 199–202; Frantz Fanon, *The Wretched of the Earth*, trans. Richard Philcox (New York: Grove Press, 2004), 150–51.

31. Frantz Fanon, "Racism and Culture," in *Toward the African Revolution*, trans. Haakon Chevalier (New York: Grove Press, 1988), 29–44, here 34.

32. Ibid., 41.

33. Ibid., 42.

34. Memmi, *The Liberation of the Jew*, 129.

35. Ibid., 29.

36. Ibid., 134.

37. Ibid., 222.

38. Ibid., 297; Fanon, "Racism and Culture," 42.

39. Memmi, "The Impossible Life of Frantz Fanon," 36.

40. Scholars such as Amnon Raz-Krakotzkin and Ella Shohat have criticized Zionism's universal narrative of Jewish suffering that Memmi reproduces here. According to Shohat: "Within this view, the history of Sephardis/Middle Eastern Jews is largely subsumed into the story of a uniquely 'Jewish experience' modeled on the paradigmatic example of European anti-Semitism, now projected onto a very different Muslim world. The Israeli/Palestinian conflict is assimilated into the narrative of perennial Arab hostility to Jews and a trace-the-dot history of pogrom-like episodes." See Ella Shohat, *On the Arab-Jew, Palestine, and Other Displacements* (London: Pluto Press, 2017), 1; see also Amnon Raz-Krakotzkin, "The Zionist Return to the West and the Mizrahi Jewish Perspective," in *Orientalism and the Jews*, ed. Ivan Davidson Kalmar and Derek J. Penslar (Waltham, MA: Brandeis University Press, 2005), 162–81.

41. Memmi, *Portrait of a Jew*, 3; Memmi, *The Liberation of the Jew*, 11; Memmi, *The Colonizer and the Colonized*, 9.

42. Memmi, *Jews and Arabs*, 70.

43. Memmi, *Portrait of a Jew*, 2.

44. Harrison, *Transcolonial Maghreb*, 95.

45. Memmi, "The Impossible Life of Frantz Fanon," 25.

46. Memmi was a product of a culturally syncretic upbringing, but he was not a theorist of postcolonial hybridity. Thus, despite his transnational trajectory, Memmi portrays cultural ambiguity as a condition of confusion and conflict. Both Memmi and Fanon work with the rigid binary of particularity and universality. There is no acknowledgment of the fluidity of identity or the possibility of cultural hybridity.

47. Fanon, *The Wretched of the Earth*, 35.
48. See, for example, Hanan Harif, *For We Be Brethren: The Turn to the East in Zionist Thought* (Jerusalem: Zalman Shazar, 2019) [Hebrew].
49. For an elaboration of this problem, see Slabodsky, "Barbaric Paradoxes: Zionism from the Standpoint of the Borderlands," in *Decolonial Judaism*, 145–76.
50. Memmi, *Jews and Arabs*, 130.

Part II
Looking West, Looking East

5

Blyden and Pissarro on St. Thomas

Pan-Africanism, Zionism, Diasporism, and the Sephardic Caribbean

SARAH PHILLIPS CASTEEL

"This is my peace, my salt, exulting acre:
there is no more Exodus, this is my Zion"
DEREK WALCOTT, *Tiepolo's Hound*

"Why does it remain so difficult for so many people to accept
the knotted intersection of histories?"
PAUL GILROY, "Afterword" to *Modernity, Culture and "the Jew"*

Black nationalism and Zionism emerged at the same late-nineteenth-century moment. In the summer months of the year 1900, London played host in swift succession to both the first Pan-African Congress and the fourth annual Zionist Congress. These nascent nationalist movements not only coincided temporally but also informed one another, albeit in an asymmetrical fashion. Zionism offered some Black nationalist thinkers what Paul Gilroy describes as "an organisational and philosophical model for twentieth-century Pan-Africanism."[1] For their part, Zionists such as Theodor Herzl and Ahad Ha'am also invoked the African diaspora, although as Axel Stähler has shown, they did so in a manner that tended to reproduce Eurocentric and colonialist biases.[2] Disciplinary and political divides have obscured these interdiasporic crosscurrents and the extent to which Black thinkers in particular have articulated African diaspora predicaments and possibilities with reference to Jewish historical experience. Indeed, the centrality of analogical thought to the expression of antiracist and anticolonialist critique remains politically sensitive and therefore difficult to acknowledge, as the recent controversy surrounding the United States Holocaust Memorial Museum's disavowal of Holocaust analogies attests.[3]

In this essay, I want to suggest that a Caribbean lens proves advantageous in bringing submerged cross-cultural exchanges to light, including those between Black nationalism and Zionism. The Caribbean supports such a reframing in part because in that region, the relationship between African and Jewish diaspora experience is not one of abstract parallelism but rather of historical intersection and material proximity. This proximity is illustrated by the biographies of two seminal nineteenth-century Caribbean figures—one Black and one Jewish—from the Danish colony of St. Thomas. Although rarely discussed alongside one another, the pan-Africanist intellectual and statesman Edward Wilmot Blyden (1832–1912) and the Jewish Impressionist painter Camille Pissarro (1830–1903) were born just two years apart in the island's capital, Charlotte Amalie, where they were raised in the same early-nineteenth-century Sephardic Caribbean milieu. Living through both the St. Croix slave revolt and the Dreyfus Affair, Blyden and Pissarro became radical thinkers but followed opposite paths. While Blyden admired Zionism and advocated for the repatriation of African Americans to Africa, Pissarro sought to integrate himself into European cultural life.

A century later, Blyden, Pissarro, and the colonial Sephardic Caribbean setting that formed them were revisited by two key Caribbean diaspora thinkers in the name of a third path: diasporism. At the turn of the twenty-first century, a moment in which diaspora was being reconceptualized by cultural theorists as a positive rather than negative condition, the critic Paul Gilroy and the poet Derek Walcott recuperated Blyden and Pissarro respectively in order to articulate a cross-cultural discourse of diaspora. Rather than constructing a linear historical narrative, this essay will interweave these nineteenth- and twentieth-century figures to highlight how contemporary critical and artistic interventions can reshape our understanding of the past to uncover what Gilroy calls "the knotted intersection of histories."[4] Examining the nineteenth-century Zionist and assimilationist trajectories of Blyden and Pissarro in tandem with the late-twentieth-century diasporist projects of Gilroy and Walcott reveals how Black and Jewish thinkers have often, in Walcott's words, stood "doubled in each other's eyes"—how they have articulated their understanding of diaspora and return analogically and reciprocally.[5]

Edward Wilmot Blyden and "That Marvelous Movement Called Zionism"

Edward Wilmot Blyden was a founding figure of pan-Africanism whose cultural nationalism, advocacy for racial pride, and understanding of what he called "the African personality" shaped subsequent Black thought. Described by his biographer Hollis Lynch as "easily the most learned and articulate champion of Africa and the Negro race in his own time," Blyden influenced W. E. B. Du Bois's pan-Africanism, Marcus Garvey's Black Zionism, and Léopold Senghor and Aimé Césaire's Négritude (among other African diaspora thinkers and concepts).[6] Despite his centrality to Black intellectual history, however, Blyden is a somewhat neglected figure.[7] Those commentaries that are available tend to focus on his West African career as a Liberian educator and statesman while devoting relatively little attention to his early years in St. Thomas, where he was born free to a schoolteacher mother and a tailor father in 1832, sixteen years before Denmark abolished slavery. Relatedly, with a few exceptions, critical commentaries tend to downplay or ignore altogether Blyden's lifelong fascination with Jewishness and unequivocal support for Zionism, both of which were rooted in his early contact with Caribbean Sephardim.[8] Blyden's intensive study of Hebrew as well as Jewish literature and culture inspired his trip to the Holy Land in 1865–66, which he detailed in his travelogue *From West Africa to Palestine* (1873). Blyden also references Jewishness in his major work *Christianity, Islam and the Negro Race* (1887), where he cited George Eliot's Zionist writings to buttress his argument for African emigration.[9] Yet it was in his 1898 pamphlet *The Jewish Question* that he articulated his support for Zionism most fully.

Published in response to the Zionist Congresses of 1897 and 1898 as well as to an 1898 article by the Jamaican Jewish judge and politician Oswald John Simon entitled "The Return of the Jews to Palestine," Blyden's *The Jewish Question* opens with a dedication that is worth citing in full:

TO LOUIS SOLOMON, ESQ,
OF LIVERPOOL.

Dear Mr. Solomon,
An acquaintance of many years, beginning during your residence in West Africa, and the discussions we have had from time to time on the subject of religion, on the work and destiny of the Jews—a community to which you have always seemed to me proud to belong—and your deep interest in Africa and her people, have suggested to me the idea of presenting the following pages to you, that you and your friends may have the record of the views held by an African of the work and destiny of a people with whom his own race is closely allied, both by Divine declaration and by a history almost identical of sorrow and oppression; and that, if possible, members of the two suffering races—Africans and Jews—who read these pages, may have a somewhat clearer understanding and a deeper sympathy with each other.

This dedication to Louis Solomon, whom Blyden had met in the 1860s in West Africa when the Jewish Liverpool businessman was a trader there, introduces several key themes of the pamphlet that help to establish why for Blyden, the Jewish question is "the Question of Questions."[10] Blyden begins by noting the pride that Solomon takes in belonging to the Jewish people, a racial pride that Blyden evidently hopes his own people will acquire. He goes on to assert close parallels between "the two suffering races," who bear "a history almost identical of sorrow and oppression." The connections between the Jewish and African diasporas are not only historical but also ordained: as a result of their suffering, both are "spiritual races" rather than "imperial races," as he will argue later in the pamphlet.[11] Finally, the dedication signals the extent to which Blyden's personal relationships with Jews such as Solomon contributed to his understanding of the affinities between Blacks and Jews and to his support for Zionism.

This last point is underscored at the opening of the pamphlet, where Blyden explains that growing up in the Caribbean port city of Charlotte Amalie, which was home to a significant Jewish community, Jews were not just abstract figures from the Bible:

> I have for many years—indeed from my childhood—been an earnest student of the history of God's chosen people. I do not refer merely to the general teaching which every child brought up in the Christian religion receives in Old Testament History... but also to that special teaching, outside of books, which comes from contact with living illustrations.[12]

In *The Jewish Question*, Blyden vividly describes the physical proximity of Jews and Jewish religious ritual during his childhood in Charlotte Amalie and the "reverence" that the latter inspired in him:

> I was born in the midst of Jews in the Danish island of St. Thomas, West Indies. For years, the next door neighbours of my parents were Jews. I played with Jewish boys, and looked forward as eagerly as they did to the annual festivals and fasts of their Church. I always went to the Synagogue on the solemn Day of Atonement—not inside. I took up an outside position from which I could witness the proceedings of the worshippers, hear the prayers and the reading, the singing and the sermon. The Synagogue stood on the side of a hill; and, from a terrace immediately above it, we Christian boys who were interested could look down upon the mysterious assembly, which we did in breathless silence, with an awe and a reverence which have followed me all the days of my life.[13]

Thus unlike his fellow pan-Africanist and Zionist supporter W. E. B. Du Bois, who had little acquaintance with Jews before his graduate studies in Europe, Blyden's interest in Zionism is traceable to his early contact with Jewish people and the Jewish religion.[14]

After visiting St. Thomas in 1858, the English novelist Anthony Trollope described it as an "emporium, not only for many of the islands, but for many also of the places on the coast of South and Central America. It is a depôt for cigars, light dresses, brandy, boots, and Eau de Cologne. Many men therefore of many nations go thither to make money, and they do make it."[15] Indeed, as Judah Cohen explains in his history of the Jewish community of St. Thomas, nineteenth-century St. Thomas was an international hub whose status as a center of trade was reflected in its multilingual and cosmopolitan population. Contributing to this mix, Jews at times made up as much as 20 percent of the white population and were well integrated in the tolerant Danish colony so that it was a space of significant contact between Jews and non-Jews rather than ghettoization.[16] Accordingly, Blyden's account highlights the spatial adjacency of Sephardic Jews and New World Africans in St. Thomas. He recalls the warm relations that he enjoyed with his Sephardic neighbors, who bore prominent Sephardic Caribbean names such as Azevedo, Da Costa, and Wolf, and describes the genial greeting these neighbors gave him upon his return to the island after a twelve-year absence: "I remember how cordially I was received by my Jewish acquaintances.... I had not been in the house fifteen minutes before, through the thoughtful hospitality of a Jewish neighbour living opposite, tea and other refreshments were sent in to give me a practical, and what was of course to me, a most grateful welcome."[17] Blyden reports that not only was he favorably received by his Jewish compatriots but so was his book *From West Africa to Palestine*.[18]

Blyden's early contact with Jews in St. Thomas laid the foundation for his strong interest in Zionism, whose relevance to his own people he identifies in *The Jewish Question*:

> I have taken, and do take, the deepest possible interest in the current history of the Jews—especially in that marvelous movement called Zionism. The question, in some of its aspects, is similar to that which at this moment agitates thousands of the descendants of Africa in America, anxious to return to the land of their fathers. It has been for many years my privilege and my duty to study the question from the African standpoint. And as the history of the African race—their enslavement, persecution, proscription, and sufferings—closely resembles that of the Jews, I have been led also by a natural process of thought and by a

fellow feeling to study the great question now uppermost in the minds of thousands, if not millions, of Jews.[19]

Blyden proceeds to offer a detailed, positive, and predominantly spiritualist account of Zionism that simultaneously conveys his aspirations for the African diaspora. Discussing the writings of Britain's chief rabbi Herman Adler and other Jewish intellectuals, he asserts that "there is hardly a man in the civilized world—Christian, Mohammedan, or Jew—who does not recognize the claim and right of the Jew to the Holy Land."[20] Drawing inspiration from the Jewish example, Blyden opens it up to an analogic reading in order to shed light on the predicament of other minority populations. For as Benyamin Neuberger observes, "Theodor Herzl was for [Blyden] a shining example of a new Moses dedicated to the liberation of his oppressed people."[21] Particularly striking is Blyden's analysis of how Jews have internalized the dominant society's racist views and the implicit psychological parallel that he draws between Jews and Blacks in this regard: "It is probably true that the proscription and misappreciation of which for ages they have been the victims, have given to the Jews a timidity and a backwardness, and taught them to disparage themselves and their lofty mission. Because they nowhere hold a dominant political position, they seem to have lost self-assertion."[22] The Zionist movement, however, is working to "rais[e] them out of an indifferent materialism into spiritual contemplation, and to a more active sense of racial privileges and responsibilities."[23] Blyden sought to instill in New World Africans a similar sense of racial privilege and responsibility as well as cultural unity.

Growing up in St. Thomas, where (as elsewhere in the Caribbean) Jewish integration into colonial society included their participation in the slavery system, Blyden could not have been unaware of the position that Jews occupied as brokers of the colonial economy.[24] This awareness does not mitigate his unequivocally positive account of Zionism, however, nor does it dampen his enthusiasm for the Jews' spiritual mission—a mission "that will by no means exclude the colonisation of Palestine, but rather enlarge its scope."[25] At the end of *The Jewish Question*, Blyden strengthens the associations between Blacks and Jews by linking early Judaism to Africa and by positing a special role for Jews to play on that continent.

Earlier in the pamphlet he had quoted Dr. Felix Adler, founder of the Ethical Culture movement, regarding "the dream of world-wide international fraternization" that "was not to be restricted to the Jewish nation, but through them as agents, was to be extended to all the peoples of the earth."[26] In keeping with this dream as well as with Oswald John Simon's "sense of the ever-widening range of Judaism as a spiritual force in the world,"[27] Blyden concludes his pamphlet by calling on Jews to come to Africa and tend to its spiritual condition as an antidote to the debasing materialist influence of Christian European colonialism. Thus, anticipating the analogical strategy that would be adopted by mid-twentieth-century anticolonial thinkers such as Aimé Césaire, Blyden advances his critique of European colonialism with reference to Europe's internal Jewish other.[28]

Paul Gilroy and the "Intercultural History of the Diaspora Concept"

Almost a full century after Blyden had called for "a somewhat clearer understanding and a deeper sympathy" between Blacks and Jews,[29] the critic Paul Gilroy renewed Blyden's appeal in his groundbreaking study *The Black Atlantic* (1993). Moreover, Gilroy did so in large part by invoking Blyden himself and recuperating Blyden's early engagement with Caribbean Jewishness. In the course of unfolding a "genealogy of Black intellectuals' attempts at rewriting modernity,"[30] *The Black Atlantic* returns us in its concluding chapter to the late nineteenth century as the "period which saw the birth of modern Zionism and of the forms of Black nationalist thought which share many of its aspirations and some of its rhetoric."[31] Gilroy here recalls Blyden's interest in Zionism to illustrate the larger impact of Jewish thought on nineteenth-century Black nationalism. In so doing, he is careful not to posit a reductive or simplistic causality. Nonetheless, he suggests that "it seems important to consider how analogies derived from Jewish thought may have affected [Blyden's] thinking about the formation and transmission of what he calls racial personality."[32]

In *The Black Atlantic*, Gilroy draws attention not only to Blyden's engagement with Jewish thinkers but also to his own such engagement in order to illustrate "the gains involved in setting the histories of Blacks and Jews within modernity in some sort of mutual relation."[33] Like Blyden,

Gilroy catalogs points of connection between Black and Jewish experience, such as the Exodus narrative, the notion of return, and the "idea that the suffering of both Blacks and Jews has a special redemptive power, not for themselves alone but for humanity as a whole."[34] Unlike Blyden, however, Gilroy's late-twentieth-century response to Jewish thought is centered less on Zionism than on the condition of diaspora and the forms of memory and tradition that attend it. Gilroy opens his discussion of Blacks and Jews with the observation that "it is often forgotten that the term 'diaspora' comes into the vocabulary of Black studies and the practice of pan-Africanist politics from Jewish thought."[35] In keeping with other works of diaspora theory of the 1990s, notably that of Stuart Hall, Gilroy recasts diaspora as a positive condition as part of his larger critique of cultural nationalism. Unlike Hall, however, who defines a salutary Caribbean model of diaspora against a "backward-looking," imperialist Jewish form, Gilroy posits a fluid and reciprocal relationship between Black and Jewish conceptions of diaspora.[36]

Writing in the early 1990s at the height of Black-Jewish tensions in the United States, Gilroy is keenly aware that in drawing attention to "the intercultural history of the diaspora concept"[37] and the influence of Jewish thought on Black intellectuals, he is breaking a taboo:

> Some of these [Jewish] discussions, particularly the contributions from writers whose relationship to Jewish lore and law was remote or ambivalent, have been a rich resource for me in thinking about the problems of identity and difference in the Black Atlantic diaspora. In the preparation of this book, I have been repeatedly drawn to the work of Jewish thinkers in order to find both inspiration and resources with which to map the ambivalent experiences of Blacks inside and outside modernity. I want to acknowledge these debts openly in the hope that in some small way the link they reveal might contribute to a better political relationship between Jews and Blacks at some distant future point.[38]

As in the case of Blyden, despite the explicit and sustained nature of Gilroy's engagement with Jewish thought, his interest in Jewishness has tended to be viewed as extrinsic to his central concerns. Relatedly, in the quarter century since Gilroy issued his call to scholars to forego the divisive politics of competitive victimhood in favor of a comparative, relational approach to the study of racialization, few have responded.[39] Instead, we find perhaps the fullest reply to Gilroy's call not in theoretical writing but in imaginative literature—in particular in the poet Derek Walcott's verse biography of the nineteenth-century Sephardic Caribbean painter Camille Pissarro.[40]

Camille Pissarro's Vexed Project of Assimilation

In *The Black Atlantic*, Gilroy notes that Blyden grew up in the same Sephardic Caribbean community as the painter Camille Pissarro. Indeed, while commonly understood in the context of French modernism, Pissarro's aesthetic practice was rooted in St. Thomas, where he was born in 1830 as Jacob Abraham Camille Pissarro to a Sephardic Jewish family with Portuguese and French roots. Pissarro spent most of his youth in the Caribbean and Latin America, settling permanently in France only in 1855. Pissarro's great-grandfather, Pierre Rodrigues Alvares Pizarro, had fled Braganza, Portugal, for Bordeaux, France, in 1769. In 1824, Pissarro's father Frédéric in turn left Bordeaux for St. Thomas to assist his late uncle's widow Rachel Pomié Petit with the family business, which supplied hardware, linens, clothing, and other dry goods. Frédéric's controversial union with Rachel, a Creole Jew born in Dominica, caused a protracted dispute with the Kehilah Kedosha Beracha v'Shalom u'G'milut Chasadim (Holy Congregation of Blessing, Peace and Loving Deeds) synagogue in Charlotte Amalie. Nonetheless, the family prospered in the bustling port city. Growing up in St. Thomas, Blyden would have walked by the Pissarro family store, which stood on Charlotte Amalie's central commercial street at 14 Dronnigens Gade, and above which Frédéric Pissarro and Rachel lived with their children.[41]

If Blyden's interest in Caribbean Jewishness has been sidelined in mainstream commentaries, so too has Pissarro's early visual engagement with Caribbean Blackness and its role in shaping his artistic philosophy. Just as Blyden was in close contact with the Jewish community of Charlotte Amalie, so Pissarro, growing up in a slave society, was in close contact with Black St. Thomians. The young Camille received his early education at the Moravian Protestant school that was established in St. Thomas for the instruction of enslaved people and free Blacks. The art historian Richard

R. Bretell speculates that while attending a school whose population was predominantly of African descent, Pissarro "must have learned lifelong lessons of respect for and tolerance of others."[42] Yet as members of the colonial bourgeois class, the Pissarros also owned two enslaved people, and Rachel Pissarro later brought a freed slave with her to France.[43]

Pissarro's early artworks center on free Blacks and enslaved people, registering their significant presence in his youth. In a visual counterpart to Blyden's narrative representation of the proximity of Blacks and Jews on St. Thomas, Pissarro's drawings and oils such as *Woman Carrying a Pitcher on Her Head* (1854–55) feature sympathetic Black workers whom he observed on the island. These figures anticipate the unromanticized agricultural laborers who would later populate his French rural landscape paintings in keeping with his egalitarian political vision. Ralph Shikes and Paula Harper observe that in his early works, Pissarro presented Black figures "straightforwardly, without condescension: they seem to have been of much greater visual interest to him than whites were."[44] A recently discovered oil painting from this period, *Portrait of a Boy* (1852–55), provides further visual evidence of the extent to which Pissarro dignified and humanized his Black subjects.[45] During a two-year sojourn in Venezuela that coincided with the abolition of slavery there in 1854, Pissarro applied this sympathetic, antihierarchical gaze to Indigenous people and mestizos as well. Distanced from European cultural and artistic centers, Pissarro developed an innovative, closely observed mode of depicting ordinary working people that he subsequently brought with him to Europe.[46]

According to Shikes and Harper, "Young Pissarro's attitude toward slavery is unknown, but he pictured Blacks sympathetically, and later, in his political maturity, he was consistently opposed to colonialism and exploitation of natives."[47] In an essay that brings into focus Pissarro's Caribbean Jewish formation, Nicholas Mirzoeff goes further, asserting that Pissarro's political radicalism stemmed from his compassion for the enslaved, who were emancipated in St. Thomas in 1848 while Pissarro was resident on the island.[48] Mirzoeff offers a striking reading of Pissarro's *Two Women Chatting by the Sea, St. Thomas* (1856), which signals the social concerns that would run through his oeuvre. The painting presents a seaside scene in which two Black women conversing may be simply resting from their labors; alternatively, they may perhaps be plotting against the slavery system itself. Mirzoeff argues that Pissarro's ambiguous rendering of the scene requires the viewer to adopt an ethical position with respect to slavery.[49]

While Pissarro's early views on slavery remain murky because of an apparent lack of textual sources, what is clear is that his art, like Blyden's writing, recorded an environment of Black-Jewish contact amid asymmetrical relations of power. Pissarro's and Blyden's biographies were not only

FIGURE 5.1. Camille Pissarro, *Woman Carrying a Pitcher on Her Head* (1854–55). Courtesy of the Maidun Collection, Alamy Stock Photo.

FIGURE 5.2. Camille Pissarro, *Two Women Chatting by the Sea, St. Thomas* (1856). Courtesy of the National Gallery of Art, Washington, DC, collection of Mr. and Mrs. Paul Mellon.

shaped by this environment but also exhibit further parallels. Almost exact contemporaries, both men left the island in pursuit of education: Pissarro to boarding school in France in 1842 and Blyden to West Africa in 1850 after he was barred from enrolling at the Rutgers Theological Seminary in the United States because of his race. Both men also spent part of their early lives in Venezuela: Blyden accompanied his family there in 1842–44, while a decade later Pissarro escaped his bourgeois family's demands by running away to Venezuela in 1852 with the Danish artist Fritz Melbye. These Venezuelan experiences were critical in shaping each man's path. In Blyden's case, his discovery that Venezuela operated according to a racial hierarchy similar to that of St. Thomas contributed to his political awakening.[50] In Pissarro's case, the artistic method that he established in Venezuela would be one that he would sustain throughout his career.

Both Pissarro and Blyden originally were apprenticed to their fathers' commercial trades but ultimately chose a different course, becoming radical thinkers who challenged established political, social, and cultural norms. While Blyden contested European colonialist notions of African inferiority, Pissarro defied not only the art establishment but also what he described in a letter as the "bondage of bourgeois life."[51] Living through a period of social unrest and the assertion of popular sovereignty, both men were in St. Thomas during the 1848 slave revolt on the neighboring Danish colonial island of St. Croix that led to emancipation. Several decades later, both were in Europe during the Dreyfus Affair, which Du Bois also followed, and which induced a crisis for Pissarro.[52]

Thus, despite Pissarro's greater class and racial privilege, his and Blyden's biographies display certain commonalities that speak to their shared intellectual ambition and iconoclasm. Yet as their choices of adoptive homeland signal, their trajectories also significantly diverged from one another. While both men departed the Caribbean to permanently settle elsewhere, Blyden chose to make his home in the newly independent West African state of Liberia, in keeping with his belief in African diasporic return to the motherland. Although he spent considerable periods of time in Europe as Liberia's ambassador to England and France, Blyden remained committed to the pan-Africanist project. Pissarro, by contrast, chose the path of assimilation by immigrating to France and eventually entering the mainstream of French art—one of the first modern Jewish artists to do so.[53] This assimilationist trajectory is reflected in Pissarro's use of Camille over his biblical given names and eventual favoring of the French spelling of his surname over the Spanish orthography with which he had earlier flirted.[54] It is also reflected in Pissarro's profound engagement with the French landscape painting tradition and the countryside surrounding Pontoise and Louveciennes—an artistic practice that can be understood as a form of diasporic emplacement.[55] Yet as Mirzoeff notes, Pissarro "carefully constructed a French artistic identity, only to see it collapse due to a combination of family crisis and rising anti-Semitism."[56] In particular, the Dreyfus Affair, which deeply divided the Impressionists, exposed significant tensions surrounding the project of Jewish assimilation in France.

Derek Walcott's Diasporist Poetics

As we saw, in the early 1990s Gilroy somewhat paradoxically recuperated Blyden's Black nationalist interest in Zionism under the sign of anti-nationalist diasporism. A few years later, the St. Lucian poet Derek Walcott staged a similarly diasporist act of recuperation and Black-Jewish engagement in his book-length poem *Tiepolo's Hound* (2000). *Tiepolo's Hound*, a closely researched verse biography of Camille Pissarro, offers a deeply personal meditation on the nineteenth-century Jewish painter's legacy for the contemporary Caribbean writer. Like Gilroy, Walcott investigates African diaspora identity by returning us to a colonial Sephardic Caribbean milieu in which Black-Jewish interdiasporic contact was a shaping force. And like Gilroy, Walcott's meditation on Blackness, Jewishness, and European cultural inheritance ultimately supports a diasporist vision, in keeping with the late-twentieth-century moment of the poem.

Tiepolo's Hound is centrally preoccupied with memory: with its loss and recovery. In broken quatrains that follow an *abab* rhyme scheme, the poem's speaker at once reconstructs Pissarro's early life in St. Thomas and foregrounds the act of imagination that such a recuperation entails:

> I imagine him sketching the port, becoming a painter,
> as the trade wind polishes Charlotte Amalie,
>
> until the salt taste of the wind grows fainter
> than the voices of his Sephardic family.[57]

The difficulty of recapturing Pissarro's Sephardic Caribbean past and the danger of mythologizing or distorting it are emblematized by the poet's simultaneous, obsessive search for a hound that he recalls having once seen in an Old Master painting but now cannot locate. Dogs, especially mongrel dogs, are a figure in the poem not only for the slipperiness of memory but also for homelessness and diasporic movement, as the speaker, a stand-in for Walcott himself, traces both Pissarro's migrations and his own travels across the Caribbean, Europe, and North America.

Interweaving biography and autobiography, the poem presents pendant portraits of the Impressionist painter and the St. Lucian poet that generate both parallels and contrasts. Born a century apart, in 1830 and 1930, the painter and the poet are confronted with a common challenge as island artists: how to negotiate their relationship to European artistic tradition. The poet's connection with Pissarro is enhanced by the fact that Walcott also paints, as the watercolors that he includes for the first time in *Tiepolo's Hound* attest. More profoundly, the poet sympathizes with the crisis of confidence that Pissarro experiences like any island artist who longs for the center only to feel rejected by it. Arriving in Paris, Pissarro finds that "museums demean him. Island boy."[58] The marble statues in the museum "turn their heads away from him, / from ancient texts in his Sephardic eyes."[59] By portraying Pissarro as an "island artist," Walcott claims him for the Caribbean, insisting on his "tropical eyes"—on the Caribbean origins of his artistic vision.[60] In so doing, Walcott challenges Eurocentric art historical accounts of the emergence of French Impressionism that efface both Pissarro's Caribbeanness and his Jewishness.[61]

The Caribbean's claim on Pissarro also carries a sharp critical edge in the poem, however. Several stanzas present Pissarro as betraying his native island by resisting its entreaties to be its painter. While the poet sympathizes with Pissarro's feeling that "his very birthplace was an error," he contends that the New World has much to offer the aspiring painter.[62] As Pissarro contemplates flight to Venezuela with Fritz Melbye, the St. Thomian fishermen of Walcott's poem rebuke him in Creole: "'We know you going. / We is your roots. Without us you weak.'"[63] Pissarro and Melbye ignore the cries of the recently manumitted slaves, "float[ing] through their silent appeals."[64] In response, the ex-slaves beseech Pissarro to remain on the island and be the Giotto of the Caribbean:

Halt, one foot on the gangplank! Turn, become us,
master and patriarch, let bearded spray confirm it,

your birthright; be in obscure St. Thomas
our Giotto, our Jerome, our rock-hidden hermit![65]

In Walcott's rendering, then, the central dilemma that Pissarro confronts is whether or not to leave the Caribbean, as he decides to do at the end of Book One when he immigrates to France, following "the deep reversing road / of the diaspora, Exodus."[66]

The poem's commentary on Pissarro's decision to abandon the Caribbean is accompanied by a critique of his colonialist gaze. In Pissarro's early drawings of St. Thomas, created just after emancipation, we see "the torpor of ex-slaves / and benign planters, suffering made quaint / as a Danish harbour with its wooden waves."[67] Pissarro's drawings problematically make the newly freed slaves seem "painless."[68] In response, employing a characteristically postcolonial ekphrastic technique, Walcott reanimates the unnamed Black figures in Pissarro's artworks so that they can speak back to the Jewish painter. Particularly effective is a section in which the poet himself becomes one of the newly manumitted slaves in Pissarro's drawings, "anonymous as my own ancestor, / my Africa erased, if not his France."[69] Here Walcott emphasizes the power differential between Pissarro, Melbye, and their Black subjects: "I shrank into the posture they had chosen."[70] Black St. Thomians offer an opportunity for practice for the young artist, who remains deaf to their pleas not to leave them behind "for cities where our voices have no words."[71] Thus, while Walcott supports revisionist art historical accounts that attribute Pissarro's innovative artistic vision to his Caribbean origins, he casts doubt on the scholarly literature's perhaps overhasty celebration of Pissarro's enlightened visual portrayal of Black subjects.

In Book Three of *Tiepolo's Hound*, Walcott devotes significant space to the Dreyfus Affair, which exposes the limitations of the Jewish painter's project of assimilation. As his biographers have documented, Pissarro became a firm Dreyfusard, distressed by those of his fellow Impressionists, including Cézanne, Renoir, and Degas, who sided against Dreyfus.[72] The speaker of the poem imagines Pissarro responding to the trial, which painfully reveals the dream of "an equal France" to be a fiction:[73]

> The nation was in an uproar, in his quiet place
> the rumour besieged his windows, the starlings rose,
>
> adding clamorous opinions to the Dreyfus case
> over the chimney cannons and the trenches of Pontoise.
>
> Dreyfus was the subject of Emile Zola's *J'Accuse*,
> Zola claiming the army had falsified evidence;
>
> he shared the blood hatred, the family circumstance,
> the Sephardic separation, it cut to the bone.[74]

Suddenly, in the France of the Dreyfus Affair, Pissarro finds that his own status as well as that of his art is in jeopardy, as the ominous rhymed word pairs "condemned"/"end" and "Jew"/"true" portend:

> The minute the traitor Dreyfus was condemned
> he ceased being a Frenchman, a Jew.
>
> That is what it boiled down to in the end.
> That is what mattered, that's why it was true.
>
> Thus all his canvasses were forgeries
> the way that Dreyfus copied his own script[75]

Despite Pissarro's secularism, his Jewishness now reasserts itself, his "Sephardic eyes" detectable in his very brushstrokes. In this section of the poem, ancestral memories of European antisemitism surface, melding together in a multidirectional fashion with a scene of a slave auction in St. Thomas.

In keeping with the poem's larger strategy of seaming together European and colonial spaces, the speaker draws attention to the Caribbean location of Dreyfus's exile:

> Dreyfus was sentenced to his own paradise—
> the Caribbean, off the coast of Cayenne,
>
> On Devil's Island, where, if he dies, he dies
> in sea and sunshine, luckier than most men.[76]

As I have discussed elsewhere, the poem's crisscrossing of the Atlantic—its destabilization of the hierarchical opposition of metropole and colony—is expressed on the level of form through the cross-rhyme scheme, which draws the eye to the interstitial space between the couplets created by the broken quatrains.[77] This interstitial space is the uneasy, hybrid space of diaspora that both the painter and the poet must navigate—and that Pissarro and Blyden sought to resolve through their immigration to France and Liberia, respectively.

Against Disciplinary Thinking

Walcott's engagement with Jewish concepts and history, like that of Blyden and Gilroy, ultimately enables him to comment on Black experience and to recast the relationship between colonial culture and modernity. In *Tiepolo's Hound*, Walcott reads nineteenth-century Caribbean Jewishness analogically and contrastively, revisiting Pissarro's diasporic dilemma in order to chart an alternative path both to the Zionist model of return that Blyden advocated and to the European assimilation that Pissarro attempted. In an explicitly dialogic moment, the poet addresses the painter directly:

> I said, "You could have been our pioneer.
> Treacherous Gauguin judged you a second-rater.
>
> Yours could have been his archipelago, where
> hues are primal, red trees, green shade, blue water."[78]

While Pissarro exiles himself from St. Thomas and devotes his artistic career to the French landscape, Walcott embraces his native Caribbean locale with its "mongrel culture":[79]

> Ours was another landscape, a new people,
> not Oise, where a wind sweeps famous savannahs,
>
> with farms and poplars and a piercing steeple,
> but cobalt bays and roads through high bananas.[80]

After "wandering like a hound" across Europe, "homesick for my acre," Walcott returns to St. Lucia to portray the humble streets of Anse La Raye and Choiseul, "the thick flowers too poor to have a name."[81] *Tiepolo's Hound* concludes with the poet's declaration that he has found his Zion, not in Africa or Europe, but in the Caribbean:[82]

> I shall finish in a place whose only power
> is the exploding spray along its coast,
>
> its rotting asphalt and cantankerous poor
> numb beyond resignation and its cost,
> . . .
> This is my peace, my salt, exulting acre:
> there is no more Exodus, this is my Zion,

> whose couplets race the furrowing wind, their maker,
> with those homecoming sails on the horizon.[83]

In the poem's closing couplets, extending a tradition of Black-Jewish interdiasporic exchange that can be traced back to Blyden, Walcott articulates his Caribbean homecoming through the Jewish tropes of Exodus and Zion.

Walcott's invocation of these biblical tropes, like Blyden's embrace of Zionism, is a prime example of what the literary critic Bryan Cheyette calls "metaphorical thinking." According to Cheyette, in contrast to "the disciplinary thinking of the academy," which "confines different histories of diaspora to separate spheres," metaphorical thinking (which he associates with imaginative literature) sees "similarities in dissimilarities."[84] It bears emphasizing, however, that while exemplifying this relational mode of thought, the cross-cultural articulations of exile and return that I have discussed here are specifically rooted in a colonial Caribbean history of Black-Jewish encounter and entanglement. Academic disciplines have tended to separate Black and Jewish experience as well as the history of the metropole from that of the colony. Moreover, the Caribbean has traditionally been understood as a peripheral space, extrinsic to the main currents of culture and history. As a result, the impact of the Sephardic Caribbean milieu on both Pissarro's aesthetic vision and Blyden's intellectual formation largely has been overlooked. Twentieth- and twenty-first-century political contestations surrounding Israel-Palestine make it still more difficult to appreciate the appeal that Zionist thought held for a nineteenth-century Black thinker such as Blyden. In this context, Gilroy's and Walcott's late-twentieth-century recuperations of Blyden's and Pissarro's Sephardic Caribbean influences serve as an important corrective. In particular, Walcott's unorthodox presentation of Pissarro as a Sephardic Caribbean—rather than French—painter illustrates how artworks can make visible "the knotted intersections of history" and thereby trace alternative genealogies of modernity.

NOTES

My thanks to Heidi Kaufman and the volume editors for their comments on earlier drafts of this essay and to Judah Cohen for his advice regarding nineteenth-century St. Thomas.

1. Paul Gilroy, *The Black Atlantic: Modernity and Double Consciousness* (Cambridge, MA: Harvard University Press, 1993), 211. On African American engagements with Zionism, see Alex Lubin, *Geographies of Liberation: The Making of an Afro-Arab Political Imaginary* (Chapel Hill: University of North Carolina Press, 2014), ch. 1. See Seth Forman, *Blacks in the Jewish Mind: A Crisis of Liberalism* (New York: New York University Press, 1998), 180–81, on how civil rights–era Jewish leaders drew comparisons between Zionism and Black Power that sometimes conflated the two movements.
2. See Axel Stähler's analysis of Herzl's and Ahad Ha'am's invocations of "the Negro Question" in Herzl's 1902 novel *Altneuland* and in Ha'am's review of the novel. Axel Stähler, *Zionism, the German Empire, and Africa: Jewish Metamorphoses and the Colors of Difference* (Berlin: De Gruyter, 2019), 51–55.
3. In June 2019, the United States Holocaust Memorial Museum publicly rejected Holocaust analogies in response to the application of the term "concentration camp" to detention centers on the U.S.-Mexico border. The museum's position was challenged by numerous Holocaust scholars in an open letter published in *The New York Review of Books* on July 1, 2019.
4. Paul Gilroy, "Afterword," in *Modernity, Culture and "the Jew,"* ed. Bryan Cheyette and Laura Marcus (Cambridge, UK: Polity Press, 1998), 287.
5. Derek Walcott, *Tiepolo's Hound* (New York: Farrar, Straus and Giroux, 2000), 159.
6. Hollis R. Lynch, *Edward Wilmot Blyden: Pan-Negro Patriot 1832–1912* (London: Oxford University Press, 1967), vii.
7. See Teshale Tibebu, *Edward Wilmot Blyden and the Racial Nationalist Imagination* (Rochester, NY: University of Rochester Press, 2012), 7–8, on the paucity of Blyden scholarship.
8. Exceptions include Gilroy's *The Black Atlantic* (discussed below); Benyamin Neuberger, "Early African Nationalism, Judaism and Zionism: Edward Wilmot Blyden," *Jewish Social Studies* 47 (1985): 151–66; and Michael J. C. Echeruo, "Edward W. Blyden, 'The Jewish Question,' and the Diaspora: Theory and Practice," *Journal of Black Studies* 40 (2010): 544–65.
9. See Edward Wilmot Blyden, *Christianity, Islam and the Negro Race* (Edinburgh: Edinburgh University Press, 1967), 108.
10. Edward Wilmot Blyden, *The Jewish Question* (Liverpool: Lionel Hart & Co., 1898), 5. It was Solomon's firm, Lionel Hart & Company, that first published the pamphlet and distributed it. On Solomon, see Benjamin Sevitch, "W. E. B. Du Bois as America's Foremost Black Zionist," in *The Souls of W. E. B. Du Bois: New Essays and Reflections*, ed. Edward Blum and Jason Young (Fairfax, VA: George Mason University Press, 2009), 244–45.
11. Blyden, *The Jewish Question*, 12. On parallels between Black and Jewish suffering, see also Blyden, *Christianity, Islam and the Negro Race*, 120.
12. Blyden, *The Jewish Question*, 5.
13. Ibid.
14. Growing up in Great Barrington, Massachusetts, Du Bois had little interaction with Jewish people but came into contact with Jews in the early 1890s while studying at the Friedrich-Wilhelm-Universität in Berlin. See Sevitch, "Black Zionist," 237.

15. Anthony Trollope, *The West Indies and the Spanish Main* (London: Chapman & Hall, 1860), 152.
16. Judah M. Cohen, *Through the Sands of Time: A History of the Jewish Community of St. Thomas, U.S. Virgin Islands* (Waltham, MA: Brandeis University Press, 2004), xvi–xvii.
17. Blyden, *The Jewish Question*, 6.
18. Ibid.
19. Ibid., 7.
20. Ibid., 8.
21. Neuberger, "Early African Nationalism," 163.
22. Blyden, *The Jewish Question*, 11. On Blyden's analysis of Black people's internalization of racist images, see V. Y. Mudimbe, *The Invention of Africa: Gnosis, Philosophy, and the Order of Knowledge* (Bloomington: Indian University Press, 1988), 111.
23. Blyden, *The Jewish Question*, 8.
24. On the broader history of Jews in the colonial Caribbean, see Jonathan Schorsch, *Jews and Blacks in the Early Modern World* (Cambridge, UK: Cambridge University Press, 2004).
25. Blyden, *The Jewish Question*, 14.
26. Ibid., 10.
27. Ibid.
28. See Aimé Césaire, *Discourse on Colonialism*, trans. Joan Pinkham (New York: Monthly Review Press, 1972).
29. Blyden, *The Jewish Question*, dedication.
30. Gilroy, *Black Atlantic*, 197.
31. Ibid., 205.
32. Ibid., 209.
33. Ibid., 212.
34. Ibid., 208.
35. Ibid., 205.
36. Stuart Hall, "Cultural Identity and Diaspora," in *Identity: Community, Culture, Difference*, ed. Jonathan Rutherford (London: Lawrence and Wishart, 1990), 222–37, here 235.
37. Gilroy, *Black Atlantic*, 211.
38. Ibid., 205–6.
39. Exceptions include Bryan Cheyette, *Diasporas of the Mind: Jewish and Postcolonial Writing and the Nightmare of History* (New Haven, CT: Yale University Press, 2013), and Michael Rothberg, *Multidirectional Memory: Remembering the Holocaust in the Age of Decolonization* (Stanford, CA: Stanford University Press, 2009).
40. For a larger discussion of Caribbean writers' relational readings of African and Jewish diaspora experience as well as further analysis of Walcott's *Tiepolo's Hound*, see my *Calypso Jews: Jewishness in the Caribbean Literary Imagination* (New York: Columbia University Press, 2016).
41. In his biography of Blyden, Thomas Livingstone suggests that given his and Pissarro's similar ages and physical proximity, Pissarro "was in all probability familiar with the Blyden family." Thomas Livingstone, *Education and Race: A Biography of Edward Wilmot Blyden* (San Francisco: The Glendessary Press, 1975), 16.

42. Richard R. Bretell, "Camille Pissarro and St. Thomas: The Story of an Exhibition," in *Camille Pissarro in the Caribbean, 1850–1855: Drawings from the Collection at Olana*, ed. Richard R. Bretell and Karen Zukowski (New York: New York State Office of Parks, 1996), 8–17, here 11.

43. Ralph Shikes and Paula Harper, *Pissarro: His Life and Work* (New York: Horizon Press, 1980), 20, 51.

44. Ibid., 25.

45. See "Newly Discovered Work by Camille Pissarro," March 14, 2018, http://www.mynewsdesk.com/bruun-rasmussen-auctioneers/pressreleases/newly-discovered-work-by-camille-pissarro-2415881.

46. Shikes and Harper observe that "unlike academically trained artists who drew the figure by formula, Pissarro sketched his figures sometimes clumsily but always conscientiously, attempting to catch the natural movements and positions of his subjects without imposing any preconceptions on them." Shikes and Harper, *Pissarro*, 30.

47. Ibid., 25.

48. See Nicholas Mirzoeff, "Pissarro's Passage: The Sensation of Caribbean Jewishness in Diaspora," in *Diaspora and Visual Culture*, ed. Nicholas Mirzoeff (London: Routledge, 2000), 57–75, here 58. Similarly, Katherine Manthorne writes that his Caribbean youth "helped shape Pissarro's liberal political philosophy, which was predicated upon an abhorrence of social injustice and led eventually to his anarchist leanings." Katherine Manthorne, "Caribbean Beginnings: Camille Pissarro," *Latin American Art* 2, no. 3 (1990): 30–35, here 33. Kathleen Adler also cites Pissarro's opposition to slavery in her *Camille Pissarro: A Biography* (London: B. T. Batsford Ltd., 1978), 14. The sources on which these kinds of claims are based are not entirely clear, however.

49. Mirzoeff, "Pissarro's Passage," 62–63.

50. See Livingstone, *Education and Race*, 19; Blyden, *Christianity, Islam and the Negro Race*, 120.

51. Quoted in Adler, *Camille Pissarro*, 18.

52. In his autobiography, recalling the lynchings that took place while he was in college, Du Bois remarks that "some echoes of Jewish segregation and pogroms in Russia came through the magazines; I followed the Dreyfus case; and I began to see something of the struggle between East and West." *The Autobiography of W. E. B. Du Bois* (New York: International Publishers, 1968), 122.

53. Stephanie Rachum observes that in this regard Pissarro was a "path blazer for the many artists of Jewish origin who would come to Paris in the early twentieth century." Stephanie Rachum, "Camille Pissarro's Jewish Identity," *ASSAPH Studies in Art History* 5 (2000): 3–29, here 25.

54. On the variations in orthography, see Manthorne, "Caribbean Beginnings," 35. See also Mirzoeff, "Pissarro's Passage," 60.

55. Correspondingly, Mirzoeff reads Pissarro's later turn to urban settings as an expression of diaspora aesthetics, understanding these works as "scenes of circulation and movement, the statement of a diaspora artist exploring the meaning of his exile." Ibid., 73. Mirzoeff's diasporist recuperation of Pissarro and relational reading of the African and Jewish diasporas could be fruitfully compared to Gilroy's and Walcott's texts.

56. Ibid., 64.
57. Walcott, *Tiepolo's Hound*, 21.
58. Ibid., 34.
59. Ibid., 35.
60. Ibid., 56.
61. A 1997 exhibition organized by the Jewish congregation of St. Thomas drew attention to Pissarro's neglected Caribbean roots and to his early Caribbean works. See Richard R. Bretell and Karen Zukowski, *Camille Pissarro in the Caribbean, 1850–1855: Drawings from the Collection at Olana* (New York: New York State Office of Parks, 1996).
62. Walcott, *Tiepolo's Hound*, 30.
63. Ibid., 25.
64. Ibid., 28.
65. Ibid.
66. Ibid., 30.
67. Ibid., 16.
68. Ibid., 141.
69. Ibid., 138.
70. Ibid., 141.
71. Ibid.
72. On the Impressionists and the Dreyfus Affair, see Philip Nord, "The New Painting and the Dreyfus Affair," *Historical Reflections/Reflexions Historiques* 24 (1998): 115–36.
73. Walcott, *Tiepolo's Hound*, 104.
74. Ibid., 101.
75. Ibid., 102.
76. Ibid., 105.
77. See Casteel, *Calypso Jews*, ch. 1. See also Jim Hannan, "Crossing Couplets: Making Form the Matter of Walcott's *Tiepolo's Hound*," *New Literary History* 33 (2002): 559–79.
78. Walcott, *Tiepolo's Hound*, 142.
79. Ibid., 154.
80. Ibid., 70.
81. Ibid., 149, 152, 157.
82. Walcott famously made the decision to spend much of his career in the Caribbean, in contrast to many of his colleagues. Notably, while Africa does not figure as a place of homecoming in *Tiepolo's Hound*, Black Zionism, Rastafarianism, and the longing for Africa are explored in Walcott's plays *Dream on Monkey Mountain* (1967) and *O Babylon!* (1976). Derek Walcott, *Dream on Monkey Mountain and Other Plays* (New York: Farrar, Straus and Giroux, 1970); Derek Walcott, *The Joker of Seville & O Babylon!* (New York: Farrar, Straus and Giroux, 1978).
83. Walcott, *Tiepolo's Hound*, 162.
84. Cheyette, *Diasporas of the Mind*, xii, 6.

6

Mapping Zionism

The "*Ostjude*" in Zionist History and Historiography

MAŁGORZATA A. MAKSYMIAK

After the world of East European Jewry vanished in the wake of World War II, it was "revived" as a subject by academics in the 1980s and has since received scholarly attention at a rapidly growing pace. In monographs that are now considered classics, Steven Aschheim, Jack Wertheimer, Trude Maurer, Ludger Heid, and Ezra Mendelssohn laid the groundwork for subsequent research on Western Jews' difficult relationship with the East European Jewish masses.[1] Valuable though they were, the earlier works did not pay sufficient attention to East European Jews' conceptions of the West, which they frequently articulated. The spatial turn, which reached the field of Jewish studies at the beginning of this century, provided an opportunity to rectify that omission.[2] Nevertheless, the Eastern European perspective is still largely missing in research on Jewish conceptions of the East and the West.

This chapter attempts to help close that gap by presenting the East European conception of the West and its Jewry as conveyed in Zionist press narratives published in Galicia prior to World War I.[3] I begin by pointing to the origins of the dichotomization between the East and the West that emerged among European Jews in the context of Prussia's colonial expansion to the east, starting with the first division of Poland in

1772. I then highlight the close affinity between the German non-Jewish discourse on the East in the eighteenth and nineteenth centuries and the Jewish—and particularly the Zionist—discourse. In doing so, I introduce the concept of mental maps, with a focus on Eastern Europe as a colonial space. This application of the concept of mental mapping corresponds with the postcolonial analysis in Edward Said's *Orientalism*. However, here the perspective is flipped: The Eastern European Jewish mental maps of the West draw upon the position of the colonized, who could not escape the Western European discourse on the East and adopted the ideas of the colonizers to explain their own heterogeneity.

Prussian Discovery of the East and Its Jews

The origins of the Jewish East-West dichotomy can be found in non-Jewish society and culture at the end of the eighteenth century, where the notions of East and West emerged as part of the process by which the Western European world was reinventing itself. This process, which had started after the Middle Ages, encompassed the decline of feudalism in the West and the beginning of the European colonial endeavor.[4] In the eighteenth century, Prussia played a decisive role in the emergence of an East and a West in Europe. Bordering on lands populated by non-German speakers of Slavic languages to the east, Prussia sought to keep up with the major colonial states of Europe. Unlike the territories other European states were beginning to colonize, the East of Europe was not located overseas. Nevertheless, it was considered exotic enough to qualify as a subject of colonization, and the area was rich in resources, rendering it particularly attractive during the lean years of the 1770–72 famine.[5] Prussia's role in the First Partition of Poland in 1772 was therefore not only motivated by late-eighteenth-century European power politics but was also an act of colonization within Europe. The same can be observed in the case of Galicia. As Larry Wolff has pointed out, the idea of Galicia was born during the First Partition of Poland, when the Habsburgs renamed the newly acquired Polish province "Halych," the medieval name of the region.[6] The invention of Galicia brought with it the call to "civilize" the region: Galician barbarism and backwardness were to be corrected. Prussian and Habsburg rule of the contested regions was a form of inward colonization, and the accompanying attitudes toward those lands an inward Orientalism.[7]

The colonized and Orientalized others were primarily Poles, but Jews belonged to this group as well. In her monograph on the representation of Jews and Jewish emancipation in the reports written by Prussia's officers in the contested Polish lands, Marion Schulte concludes that the imagined figures of Poles and Polish Jews were used by these officers to create an opposition between the region and their Western home.[8] Understanding themselves as having come from the West, the colonizers reinvented themselves as modern, civilized, and progressive, drawing a contrast with Poles and Jews, who were supposedly lazy, stupid, and in need of civilization, as Frederick II had claimed.[9] But the king and his officers were not alone in stereotyping the Poles and Jews as animalistic and uncivilized. This Prussian conception of the newly discovered and contested East was supported by the writings of German academics, travelers to the East, commentators in the press, and a wide array of moral entrepreneurs.[10] Immediately after the First Partition in 1772, they recognized a threat posed by the neighboring "Orient" to the demographics[11] and moral well-being[12] of the German lands. A Cabinet Order of the King to one of his most high-ranking civil servants, Johann Friedrich von Domhardt (1712–1781), issued that same year states:

> The great number of Jews in West Prussia must be gotten rid of. This is to happen gradually. First this invasion of Jewish beggars from the far corners of Poland must be brought under control, and they must be prevented from coming and staying.... Next, we must turn attention to the settling of the frontiers by Germans, such that the Poles will be pushed out, for they are of no use in the borderlands.[13]

The stereotyping of the inhabitants of the newly acquired lands in the East was first and foremost a manifestation of Prussian superiority toward Poland, part of a mental mapping of the contested region. The concept of cognitive or mental mapping was first explored in 1971 by the geographer Roger M. Downs and the psychologist David Stea, who described it as "an abstraction covering those cognitive or mental abilities that enable us to collect, organize, store, recall and manipulate information about the spatial environment."[14] Mental mapping helps an individual maintain proper orientation in an unknown space and remain in communication with it. The geographer Yuval Portugali went on to define cognitive maps as internal representations of external environments.[15]

A map, whether iconographic or cognitive, is not an objective picture of the geographic reality, since maps "are never value-free images: except in the narrowest Euclidean sense they are not in themselves either true or false."[16] Yet the topographical signs on an iconographic map correspond with the codes of a mental map, providing a bundle of information about the space. The contested Polish lands on Prussia's mental map, for example, were coded as disorder—while the West was coded as order—in the pejorative expression "*polnische Wirtschaft*," which conveyed negative associations such as dirt, laziness, alcohol abuse, and bigotry.[17] The "Jew" was also marked on this mental map. In a letter written in 1772 to his brother Prince Heinrich, King Frederick II of Prussia reports of these newly won Polish lands: "It is an excellent and beneficial acquisition, both in political and financial regard. But to protect me from envy, I tell people that I have only seen sand, firs, heaths and Jews."[18] Frederick II was known for his anti-Polish attitude, especially as his view of Poland became increasingly marked by negative stereotypes after 1763.[19] It can be assumed that the king's stereotypes, like the notion that Poland was empty save for the Jews, were accepted by those in his retinue and soon spread more widely among Prussia's populace.[20]

Jews were in fact much more numerous in Poland than in the German lands.[21] They appeared to Western observers to be completely different from their German counterparts, as the following quotation from the 1775 memoirs of a convert to Christianity shows. Describing the daily life of his father in a small German town, Gottfried Selig notes:

> These rabbis, or rather *melamdim* and *shohets*, who entertain our German Jews in their homes, are generally poor Polish Jews...; but they tend to have very raw manners and sport greyish beards, always covered in their filthy Polish *kaftan*. Since the Jews let themselves be seen in places where few if any Jews resided, they were consistently subjected to the harshest insults. It is thus easy to imagine what awaits an unfortunate Polish Jew of that type there.[22]

Polish Jews did not escape German stereotyping of Eastern Europeans. They were perceived to be speakers of a "corrupted" German—Judeo-German, later called Yiddish—who wore dirty, long *kaftans* and pursued "suspicious" trade. But it was not only gentiles who were describing Polish Jews thus, especially as the nineteenth century approached.

German-Jewish Perceptions of the East

The increasing acculturation of German Jewry coincided with the adoption of non-Jewish discourses in debates among Jews. One of these was the German discourse on the East, whose widespread adoption led European Jewry to divide itself along an East-West axis. Historians such as Jacob Katz argue that by the end of the eighteenth century German Jews were well aware of the differences in language, customs, and rituals that distinguished them from Polish Jews but that this awareness did not manifest as hostility toward East European Jews, and Polish Jews in particular, until the beginning of the nineteenth century.[23] Archival documents from the eighteenth century, however—such as the holdings in the Central Archives of the former German Democratic Republic—show that within a decade following Prussia's acquisition of Polish territory in August 1772, German-Jewish perception of Polish Jews had become negative. For instance, in 1785 the Jewish community in Strelitz petitioned the duke of Mecklenburg-Strelitz to stop the migration of Polish Jews from Prussia, whom they called "infamous and desperate rabble," on the grounds that they would pose a danger to the Jewish community and the duchy alike.[24]

The negative perception of Polish Jews among the Western European Jewish communities was encouraged above all by policies toward Jews in the newly won Polish territories. The Prussian expulsion of Jews from these provinces[25] was followed not only by impoverishment, increasing crime, and the decay of Polish Jewish communities but also by a drastic intensification of illegal migration to the West.[26] This massive immigration of Polish Jews imposed so great a burden on German-Jewish communities as to economically threaten their very existence. The regions bordering on New Prussia, including Brandenburg and Mecklenburg-Strelitz, particularly struggled with such problems. The situation of the Jews in Galicia was similarly difficult, albeit in different ways. Here, they fled from increasing poverty and conscription into the Habsburg army. The historian Emanuel Ringelblum points out that Jewish immigration from Galicia to Poland was a frequently discussed topic of both the *Gazety Pisane* and the Polish *Sejm Wielki* (1784–88).[27]

In other words, the dualization of European Jews began as early as at the end of the eighteenth century and can be seen as a direct consequence of the First Partition of Poland. And the adoption of non-Jewish East-West discourse was not only nourished by the increasing acculturation of Jews in German lands but also by Jewish migration and direct contacts between Polish and German Jews.

During the subsequent decades of the nineteenth century, the image of Eastern Europe and its Jews became increasingly negative and rigid. The German-language Jewish newspaper *Allgemeine Zeitung des Judentums* (*AZJ*), founded in 1837, included reports about Polish Jews from its inception. But in the second half of the nineteenth century the image the writers and editors provided of their Polish coreligionists became much more negative. In 1862 the newspaper criticized Hasidism in Poland as a degeneration of Jewish tradition, describing it with familiar epithets previously applied to Poles in general. Heinrich Heine had quipped in 1822 that the Poles were very accomplished when it came to drinking.[28] A journalist writing forty years later in *AZJ* claimed the same with respect to the Polish Hasidim, who instead of performing the blessing over wine after the synagogue service, engaged in "constant drinking, [an] everlasting drunken feast."[29]

The reasons for the increasingly negative perception of Polish Jews in the second half of the nineteenth century were manifold. For one, the Crimean War put Russia on the front pages of German and other European newspapers, resulting in increased attention to the region east of Germany and its renaming from "Northern Europe" to "Eastern Europe."[30] Furthermore, the French notion of the mentally ill Jew, which was enthusiastically adopted by German antisemites, influenced the perception of Polish Jews among their German coreligionists.[31] Defending themselves from guilt by association, as it were, German Jews emphasized that the French scholars had developed the theory in reference to Eastern European Jews.[32] Given this broader context, publications such as Karl Emil Franzos's (1848–1904) short novels about Galicia, including *Halb-Asien*, or Leopold von Sacher-

Masoch's (1836–1895) Galician stories, in which Polish Jews and the Polish environment as a whole appear as a negative counterimage of the German Jew, were well received. This image of the Polish Jew was rapidly distilled into coded terms like "*cheder*," "ghetto," and "pogrom," all of which stood for both the Jewish Orient and Jewish Eastern Europe, even among German Zionists.[33]

German Zionists, Galician Zionists, and the *Ostjuden*

Before the first half of the nineteenth century, Eastern European Jews were classified as Polish, Russian, or Galician Jews. By the middle of that century, however, the Jews of Eastern Europe had been conceptually homogenized. All were referred to as *Pojlische*—Polish Jews. At the same time, the term "Eastern Europe" gained general acceptance. Following the development of this term, Polish Jews were transformed into *Ostjuden*.

The Zionist Nathan Birnbaum (1864–1937), who later turned to Yiddishism and Orthodoxy, took on the concept of the Eastern Jews, or *Ostjuden*, in his journalistic work as early as the 1890s.[34] In 1897, the adjective "*ostjüdisch*" appeared for the first time in Birnbaum's writings, and in 1904, he used the term "*Ostjude*" in his works. The term appears to have already been in general use at this time.[35] However, it was Nathan Birnbaum in particular who popularized the word, at least in Jewish journalism. The term "*Ostjude*" is absent in the vocabulary of Birnbaum's contemporaries, who also focused on Eastern European Jewish affairs. Fabius Schach (1868–1930), for example, exclusively used the term "*Juden des Ostens*" in his articles.[36] Also, Leo Winz (1876–1952), the editor of the journal *Ost und West*, seems to have no other term for the Jewish Eastern Europeans besides "*östliche Juden*."[37] Birnbaum's popularization of the term "*Ostjuden*," however, was not simply a semiotic innovation. Hand in hand with it went his wish to renew the image of the *Pojlische*.

Gradually returning to his family origins in Galicia, Birnbaum recognized the modern transformative processes that had taken place in Eastern Europe in the previous decades, evinced primarily by the emergence of a modern Jewish literature in Yiddish and Hebrew and in the secularization of Jewish everyday life.[38] Therefore, Birnbaum wrote in an article published under the pseudonym Pantarhei in 1901 in *Die Welt*, "Nothing is more false than to lump the group that is now being discussed [Eastern European Jews] together with the original oriental." He continues: "The error is approximately—but only approximately—the same as if one were to deny the Europeanness of Russians and Poles themselves and count them among the Asians."[39]

Birnbaum was not alone in appreciating that Eastern Europe was not the Orient.[40] Moreover, the Western Zionist concept of the East, which drew on a polarized opposition between Western Europe on the one hand and the notions of backwardness, Jewish authenticity, the Orient, and Eastern Europe on the other, was by no means an exclusively Western European affair. Members of East European Zionist circles, too, constructed mental maps that distinguished between the East and the West. In doing so, they paid exceedingly close attention to how Western Europeans thought about the East and developed their own concept of the West and of a "de-Orientalized" Jewish Eastern Europe.

The Galician Zionists, for example, who, like all Galician Jews, were perceived to be *Pojlische* and would later be referred to as *Ostjuden*, responded with their own concept of where the Galician Jewish community was to be marked on the European map. According to *Przyszłość*—the Lviv-based newspaper that was the mouthpiece of the Galician Zionists—Galicia belonged neither to the East nor to the West of Europe.[41] Instead, it was situated exactly on the border between the two. In its very first issue, the newspaper argued that the region's simultaneously Eastern and Western European character could be seen in its legal status and demography. On the one hand, many Galician Jews closely resembled their Russian—that is, Eastern European—counterparts in their customs and language. At the same time, however, Galician Jews shared with their German coreligionists the experience of having equal rights under the law.[42]

Yet the strongest tactic consistently employed by Galician Zionists was to make reference to the region's sociocultural character, which rendered Galicia an in-between space: "On the eastern boundaries of Galicia the surging roar of Asiatic barbarism can be heard, whereas the gentle wind of Occidental culture is blowing in from the west toward the beautiful Carpathians." Appearing in the Viennese journal *Selbst-Emancipation* in 1892 under the byline of a reporter from Cracow, the article continues:

"The Orient meets the Occident everywhere and intense wrestling ensues. This describes the situation in Galicia."[43]

Galicia was already heterogeneous in terms of its territorial composition. Located at the border to the Russian Empire, it consisted of Ruthenian territories with Lviv as the capital in the east and the Little Poland region with Cracow as the center in the west. Western Galicia was predominantly inhabited by Poles, while the Ruthenians dominated in the east. The religious and linguistic landscape was similarly diverse. The Roman Catholic Church shared the region with the Uniate Church. Residents of Galicia spoke Polish, Ruthenian, and, increasingly, German. This mosaic of religions and languages also influenced the ethno-religious minority of the Jews, who spoke Yiddish as their vernacular.[44]

The heterogeneity of the Galician Jewish population was the strongest evidence against the Western image of Jewish East Europeans as an undifferentiated mass. It was also why the stereotype provoked such harsh reactions from Galician Zionists. One of them, Adolf Stand (1870–1919), wrote in 1904:

> K. E. Franzos presented to us the Jew as a cheat, one who would trade in anything, one who is physically filthy, morally degenerate, and a spiritual dwarf. And his trivial, shallow observations, his feeble and doubtful jokes arrived in Europe and provided a window into the soul of the Polish Jew... And thus, while we imported Voltaire, Spinoza, Kant, and Hegel, Masoch and Franzos were exports.[45]

Stand directed his appeal to Western Zionists, and German Zionists in particular, because he knew that most of them took Franzos's depiction of Galicia and the Eastern Jew at face value. But by no means did Stand deny the existence of the ghetto, the *Kaftanjuden*, the *Luftmenschen*, or the *Chochmey Israel* in Galicia. His mission was to oppose the Western European belief that modernity had not yet spread beyond the eastern border of the German-speaking lands and to prove that the image of the Eastern Jew established in the West did not reflect reality. He persistently expounded upon this injustice to the readers of the Polish-language Zionist periodicals in Galicia. In 1917, for example, he complained in the pages of the youth magazine *Moriah* that the Western European Jewish parvenu believed that the *Pojlischer* has "the appearance of an Asian, the culture of a Negro, the ethics of a catty writer, the rules of a criminal; he avoids soap and comb; his body is dirty, his conscience is demoralized, his brain is distorted, his soul perverted."[46]

Adolf Stand was not alone in appealing to his Western counterparts to exclude Galicians from the category of *Ostjuden*, in spite of the prevailing Western perception. He was joined by many other Galician Zionists whose lifestyles did not differ from those of their Western European coreligionists and who therefore identified with the image of the Western Jew rather than that of the Eastern Jew. For them, as for Stand himself, the aporia of the Galician positioning within the East-West Jewish dichotomy seemed to culminate in the following consensus: "The people belong to the *Ostjuden* type, while the intelligentsia represents a *Westjuden* type."[47]

This open confession that the differentiation between East and West among European Jews was essentially a social distinction dates to 1917, but even in the decade before there was already a clear tendency among Zionists to separate the mass of Jewish people in Galicia, who were seen as *Ostjuden*, from the Jewish intelligentsia, who were considered *Westjuden*.[48] The Zionists perceived Galicia as a space located "in between" the East and the West. At the same time, the Zionist elite, who were often alumni of the universities in Vienna and Berlin, claimed to belong to the *Westjuden* due to their Western education while considering uneducated Jewish people to be Eastern Jews. An article published in 1903 in *Wschód*, "The Battle Between Light and Darkness," summarizes in its very title the prevailing perception among Galician Zionists of the region's Jewish society.[49] The "light" here stands for the Zionists of Galicia, while "darkness" represents the alleged backwardness of the traditional, religious Jewish community. According to the author of the article, S. Taubes, the Zionists' "task is therefore to teach the people to think and look at the world undisturbed, to give them confidence in their own powers, so that they no longer have to seek solace from the *Schmarotzers* [miracle rabbis]."[50]

The desire to help the people, that is, the *Ostjuden*, was in fact one of the most commonly expressed goals among Galician Zionists, which corresponded to the aim of "physical, spiritual and economic uplift of the Jews" (in the East) propagated by Western Zionists.[51] In articulating this desire, the Galicians distinguished between the "wealthy, cynical, German-speaking and jargon-loathing plutocrats, . . . the professional intelligentsia, and the proletariat," and they concentrated their efforts, at least according to their press narratives, on the "enlightenment" of the third group of Galicians, the so-called Jewish proletariat, including the Hasidim.[52]

The Galician Zionists clearly identified with their Western European, German-speaking colleagues in terms of their own sociocultural position among European Jews. They considered themselves educators and saviors of the majority of the Galician Jewish population: "The focus of our movement," argued the Zionist Philipp Menczel (1872–1941), who lived in Czernowitz, in eastern Galicia, "is naturally in the East. It would be a mistake to assume that education of these masses can enable them to steer their own fate. For a long time yet, they will be the object instead of the subject in our movement."[53] This self-positioning of Galician Jews between East and West, along with the Zionist elite's self-identification as Western Jews, did not necessarily indicate that everything in the West was considered good. On the contrary, the Zionist leadership in Galicia created its own concept of the West and its Jews. In the opinion of Galician Zionists, Western European Jews were overwhelmingly false, lacking "authentic Jewishness." Western Zionists, too, were considered inauthentic, because they derived their Jewish identity from the confrontation with antisemitism rather than from their inner Jewishness. "No! I did not become a Jew under the influence of Aryan students," wrote the Galician Zionist J. A. Łubecki (1876–1921) in a letter addressed to the Galician Zionist intelligentsia and published in the pages of *Przyszłość* in 1899, "and I did not become a Jew because of Aryan antisemitic parents who denied me the hand of their beautiful little daughter. I became a Jew through my Jewish father [*sic*] and through my Jewish rabbi!"[54]

Łubecki's accusation was considered to be especially true of the Western Zionist leadership. According to Łubecki, there was almost nothing Jewish about the Western European Zionists, including leaders such as Herzl and Nordau;[55] they were "fabricated Jews," "Jews, too," antipodal to "Jewish Jews" and "natural Jews."[56] Zionist newspapers in Galicia had for years demonstrated a consistent skepticism toward the movement's leadership, and Western Zionists in general, despite their widespread declaration of loyalty to Herzl and Nordau. In a 1917 article published in *Moriah*, entitled "Greetings to Achad Ha'am," the Cracow rabbi and Zionist Osias (Jehoshua, Ozjasz) Thon (1870–1936) wrote: "Zionism emerged of course among Eastern European Jews, but its leadership was taken over by Western European Jews. The content was familiar, Jewish, only its form was foreign, European. How could the powerful form displace the content? In fact, it happened."[57] In just a few sentences, Thon summarized the issue at the heart of the Galician relationship to the Western Zionists: The problem was not that Zionism's "Jewish content" hailed from the East and its modern form from the West. Rather, the Galician problem was that the form dominated the content and that Eastern European Jews felt patronized by the Western Zionists. Galicians, who positioned themselves between East and West, expected Zionism and its leadership to preserve the balance between European form and Jewish content, and therefore between West and East. That a balance of this type was possible seemed obvious to Galicians, and not only because of the location of their homeland. Galician Zionists also pointed to a specific individual among the Zionists who seemed to embody their claim, uniting East and West in Zionism: Achad Ha'am.

What fascinated Galicians about Achad Ha'am as a person and about his cultural Zionist ideology was the fact that he exhibited no "apparent contradictions," but instead "true spiritual harmony" and "true, unspoiled Jewish originality" from the East, alongside an "apparent harmony of thoughts and emotions" stemming from the influence of modern Western European culture.[58] Achad Ha'am impressed them as a Hebraist, too. Love of the Hebrew language and commitment to its revival were considered the most admirable expression of Jewish authenticity, whereas folklore was criticized in the strongest terms as superstition, a denial of modernity, and a form of primitiveness.[59] Modern Hebrew and Modern Hebrew literature were seen as equivalent to European literatures and their cultural languages and were therefore considered by the Galicians to be an indispensable accompaniment to the processes of modernization driven by Zionism.

For all these reasons, the Hebraist Achad Ha'am, who knew how to mold Jewish authenticity into a Western European form, was a respected personality among Galicians. Even his ideological opponents like Gershom (Gustav) Bader (1868–1953) supported him when he was publicly denigrated by Max Nordau. In his article "Altneuland, Achad Ha'am and Nordau," published in *Wschód* in the wake of the controversy following the publication of Herzl's utopian novel *Altneuland* in 1902, Bader compared the relationship between Nordau and Achad Ha'am to the relationship between East and West in Zionism:

> We [Galicians] are Zionists because we are Jews, because we want to build on and continue the history of the Jewish people. Our goal is not to create an asylum for our oppressed and hungry brothers, but a home for ourselves. In Zionism we are creators and thinkers, while they [Western Zionists] contribute nothing but unnecessary phrases.... For us, Zionism encompasses the whole of Judaism; for them, it is no more than the solution to the question posed by those Jews who cannot or do not want to assimilate.[60]

According to Bader, who echoes Lubecki's criticism, the Western Zionist is not a "true" Jew, but a philanthropist who wishes to provide Eastern Jews with quick relief from their distress—he is a "Rachmones-Zionist."[61] Moreover, he is not the equal of his Eastern European coreligionists because he lacks a Jewish education. In short, he does not possess the Jewish authenticity that exists only in the East, expressed in the Galician Zionists' dedication to the creation of a modern Jewish nation on the basis of the Hebrew language.

The Galicians responded to these alleged differences among Zionists by seeking to put Eastern Jewish content—Hebrew—into a Western Jewish form that would resemble artifacts of Western European culture. This effort included sharp criticism of assimilation in Western Europe, where "alien elements displace all originality and vitality, weaken them and invalidate the vibrancy of colors and mentalities."[62] All the same, this understanding also had room for an appreciation of the advantages of Western European culture. The Galician J. Grünbaum, for example, argued in 1901 in *Wschód*:

> We—the Eastern Jews—form congresses in a social way. They teach us to organize and to work together for the good of the people. Through contact with our Western brothers, who tower above us in terms of political culture, we learn to unify the social initiatives of individuals into a whole, to then carry this out according to a prepared plan.[63]

This homogenizing conceptualization of the West and Galicia's putative claim to both Europeanness and Jewish authenticity ignored the fact that in many respects the Galician Zionists' criticism of their Western European counterparts was also a self-criticism. Moreover, although the Galicians confessed that their own community showed a tendency toward assimilation and issued warnings in their press organs about the reprehensible example set by "Poles of Mosaic religion," they refused to confront the gap between political commitment to Zionism and their day-to-day lives. Only a generational change in the community's activists induced older members to take stock of their Zionism and Jewishness. For example, Gerschon Zipper—one of the earliest Galician Zionists—wrote in 1914:

> Our national language is terra incognita for us. The number of Hebrew speakers among us is vanishingly small, and Hebrew thinkers are almost nonexistent among us.... So it is no wonder that one of my Christian colleagues once wanted to convince me how Galician Zionists are such good Poles, because... in terms of language, customs, culture and especially pronunciation, they are so similar to the Poles. That's the end result of the last 20 years![64]

Zipper reveals the constructed character of East and West in relation to European Jews. According to him, the Galician Zionists are no less fabricated than their Western European coreligionists, and hence not authentic either. Just as the German Zionists were "good Germans," the Galicians were "good Poles" who embraced the Zionist idea not for themselves but on behalf of the Eastern European Jewish population more broadly. Zipper's criticism and similar arguments received little to no attention. Efforts to differentiate between Eastern and Western Jews along sociocultural and geographical lines, in contrast, became increasingly controversial, dominating the debates about the Zionist cultural, political, and social program.

Conclusion

The Zionist debates around East and West outlined here had their origins in the discourse about the division between Eastern and Western Europe that began with the colonial act of the First Partition of Poland in 1772.

From this point onward, the Prussian colonial mind-set and its mental maps of the East were transferred into intra-Jewish affairs. The constructed, negative image of the Polish Jew would later reappear, corresponding with the way Western Jews would come to imagine their brothers in the East. The coining of the term "Eastern Europe" in the middle of the nineteenth century was soon followed by the invention of the designation *Ostjude*. The motivation behind the emergence of each concept, however, was quite different.

Nathan Birnbaum, who popularized the latter term, sought a means to overcome the lived discrepancy and outright hostility between Polish and German Jews. Using the term "*Ostjude*" and describing all the Jews in the eastern part of the continent as belonging to a single sociocultural group with its own language and customs, he hoped to close the gap between the Jewish East and West in Europe. Unfortunately, however, he used the model of mental maps to promote a new image of the Eastern European Jew. He preserved the dichotomization and homogenization of European Jews and simply attempted to replace the negative characteristics associated in the Western European mental map with his Eastern coreligionists with positive ones. He defined this term, which was intended to replace the already established image of the half-Asian East European Jew, as follows: "*Ostjudenheit* is the name given to 9–10 million Jews ... because their type has its origin in the Slavic lands of Europe (including Romania), i.e., in Russia, Poland, Galicia, Bukovina, North-East Hungary, and Romania."[65] For Birnbaum, this "type" was characterized by the use of Yiddish and adherence to Jewish tradition—they were not "acculturated" or "assimilated." In using this new name for an old image, Birnbaum ignored the fact that the image of the East European Jew was bound up with the image of Eastern Europe. In other words, to change the image of Jews from Eastern Europe, it would have been necessary to effect a change in the image of Eastern Europe, too. Furthermore, Birnbaum realized neither that the root of the animosity between East and West lay in the dichotomization of European Jewry and the accompanying homogenization of each subgroup, nor that it was these two processes that were responsible for the distorted perception of the European East.

Consequently, Birnbaum's efforts did not close the gap between the Jewish East and West in Europe. As members of a national liberation movement of the Jews, the Zionists strove to create a postcolonial space in which they could exist without being subjected to colonialist domination. However, in this very process they reproduced the mental maps that had already structured the colonial space. Their attempts to de-Orientalize the Jewish East was still tied up with the mechanisms that Edward Said has described as Orientalism. The persistence of colonial relations in postcolonial spaces that has been analyzed by critical postcolonial theory can therefore be detected in the case of Zionism. Arguments between Polish and German Jews occurred not only in the Zionist movement but also in Palestine in the 1930s and even in the Nazi concentration camps during World War II. Birnbaum's "success" is to be found in his passing on a new name for an old image to subsequent generations of historians who, like Galician Zionists one hundred years earlier, even today try to grasp the heterogeneity of the Jewish world with overly simplistic mental maps.

NOTES

1. Steven E. Aschheim, *Brothers and Strangers: The Eastern European Jew in German and German-Jewish Consciousness, 1800–1923* (Madison: University of Wisconsin Press, 1982); Jack Wertheimer, *Unwelcome Strangers: East European Jews in Imperial Germany* (New York: Oxford University Press, 1987); Trude Maurer, *Ostjuden in Deutschland, 1918–1933* (Hamburg: Christians, 1986); Ludger Heid, *Maloche–nicht Mildtätigkeit: Ostjüdische Arbeiter in Deutschland 1914–1923* (Hildesheim: Olms, 1995).
2. See, for example, Katrin Steffen, "Zur Europäizität der Geschichte der Juden im östlichen Europa," *H-Soz-Kult*, June 6, 2006, https://www.hsozkult.de/article/id/artikel-742.
3. The essay is based on my German-language monograph, Małgorzata A. Maksymiak, *Mental Maps im Zionismus: Ost und West in Konzepten einer jüdischen Nation vor 1914* (Bremen: Edition Lumiere, 2015).
4. See Stuart Hall, "The West and the Rest: Discourse and Power," in *Formation of Modernity*, ed. Stuart Hall and Bram Gieben (Cambridge, UK: Polity Press, 1992), 276–320, here 276–77.
5. For more on this economic aspect of the colonization of the East, see Dominic Collet, "Hunger ist der beste Unterhändler des Friedens: Die Hungerkrise 1770–1772 und die erste Teilung Polens," in *Die Teilungen Polen-Litauens: Inklusions- und Exclusionsmechanismen, Traditionsbildung, Vergleichsebenen*, ed. Hans-Jürgen Bömelburg, Andreas Gestric, and Helga Schnabel-Schüle (Oldenburg: Fibre Verlag, 2013), 155–70.
6. See Larry Wolff, *The Idea of Galicia: History and Fantasy in Habsburg Political Culture* (Stanford, CA: Stanford University Press, 2010), 13.
7. In the case of Germany and Austria, Orientalism does not conform to Edward Said's definition of the term because "othering and orientalization were played out at home."

See Sheldon Pollock, "Deep Orientalism? Notes on Sanskrit and Power Beyond the Raj," in *Orientalism and the Postcolonial Predicament: Perspectives on South Asia*, ed. Carol A. Breckenridge and Peter van der Veer (Philadelphia: University of Pennsylvania Press, 1993), 76–133, here 77.

8. Marion Schulte, *Preußische Offiziere über Judentum und Emanzipation, 1762–1815* (Berlin: De Gruyter Oldenbourg, 2018), 330.

9. On Frederick II and his perception of the contested "new lands" in Poland, see Hans-Jürgen Bömelburg, *Friedrich II. zwischen Deutschland und Polen: Ereignis- und Erinnerungsgeschichte* (Stuttgart: Alfred Kröner Verlag, 2011), 89–107.

10. For a discussion of the term "moral entrepreneur," see Howard Saul Becker, *Outsiders: Studies in the Sociology of Deviance* (New York: Free Press, 1963), 147.

11. Robert Liberles, "From Toleration to Verbesserung: German and English Debates on the Jews in the Eighteenth Century," *Central European History* 22 (1989): 3–32.

12. See, for example, the Orientalist Johann David Michaelis's criticism of the proposal to "emancipate" the Jews, "Hr. Ritter Michaelis Beurtheilung: Ueber die bürgerliche Verbesserung der Juden," in Christian Wilhelm Dohm, *Ueber die bürgerliche Verbesserung der Juden. Zweyter Theil* (Berlin: Friedrich Nicolai, 1783), 31–71.

13. K. O. an den Präsidenten Domhardt, September 9, 1780, reprinted in Max Bär, *Westpreußen unter Friedrich dem Großen*, vol. 2 (Osnabrück: Otto Zeller, 1965), 413.

14. Roger M. Downs and David Stea, *Maps in Minds: Reflections on Cognitive Mapping* (New York: Harper & Row, 1977), 6.

15. See Yuval Portugali, "Inter-Representations Networks and Cognitive Maps," in *The Construction of Cognitive Maps*, ed. Yuval Portugali (Dordrecht: Springer, 1996), 11–43. For a detailed discussion of the applicability of the concept of mental maps on the history of Zionism, see Maksymiak, *Mental Maps im Zionismus*, vi–x.

16. J. B. Harley and Paul Laxton, *The New Nature of Maps: Essays in the History of Cartography* (Baltimore: Johns Hopkins University Press, 2001), 53.

17. See Tomasz Szarota, "Pole, Polen und Polnisch in den deutschen Mundartenlexica und Sprichwörterbüchern," *Acta Poloniae Historica* 50 (1984): 81–114. At the same time as the expression "polnische Wirtschaft" was used to stereotype Poles at the end of the eighteenth century, some German travelers also used its equivalent with regard to the Jews: "Judenwirtschaft." See, for example, Ernst Moritz Arndt, *Erinnerungen aus dem äußeren Leben* (Leipzig: Widmann'sche Buchhandlung, 1840), 126.

18. Cited in German, with the French original in a footnote, in Bömelburg, *Friedrich II*, 90. The translation from the German version is my own.

19. Ibid., 78–88.

20. Ibid., 93–4. On the role of Frederick II in spreading the negative stereotypes about Poles, see also Szarota, "Pole, Polen und Polnisch"; Hubert Orlowski, "Polnische Wirtschaft," in *Zum Polendiskurs der Neuzeit* (Wiesbaden: Harrassowitz Verlag, 1996).

21. Although the period under discussion is a "pre-statistics age" and the numbers are only approximate, the demographic difference between the Jewish population in the Polish Kingdom and that in the German lands is quite striking. However unevenly distributed, the number of Jews in the second half of the eighteenth century in both Poland and Lithuania prior to the partition in 1772 was 750,000 out of the multiethnic Polish

population of between twelve and fourteen million, i.e., 5 to 6 percent of the population. See Gershon D. Hundert, "The Largest Jewish Community in the World," in *Jews in Poland-Lithuania in the Eighteenth Century: A Genealogy of Modernity* (Berkeley: University of California Press, 2004), 21–31. In contrast, Jews constituted about 1.2 percent of the population in the German lands at the beginning of the nineteenth century. See Stefi Jersch-Wenzel, "Bevölkerungsentwicklung und Berufsstruktur," in *Deutsch-jüdische Geschichte in der Neuzeit 1780–1871*, vol. 2, ed. Michael Brenner, Stefi Jersch-Wenzel, and Michael A. Meyer (Munich: Beck, 2000), 57–66.

22. Gottfried Selig, *Geschichte des Lebens und der Bekehrung Gottfried Seligs, Lect. Publ. seiner drey Schwestern und einiger nahen Anverwandten, welche sämmtlich das Judenthum verlassen, und treue Bekenner Jesu geworden sind. Erster Theil* (Leipzig: Hertel, 1775), 33.

23. Jacob Katz, *Zwischen Messianismus und Zionismus: Zur jüdischen Sozialgeschichte* (Frankfurt am Main: Jüdischer Verlag, 1993), 37–38.

24. Letter from the Jewish community in Strelitz to the duke of Mecklenburg-Strelitz, March 18, 1785, Landeshauptarchiv Schwerin, "Judenangelegenheiten Mecklenburg-Strelitz," 4.11-46, no. 46, unpaginated.

25. See Gustav von Schmoller, *Umrisse und Untersuchungen zur Verfassungs-, Verwaltungs- und Wirtschaftsgeschichte besonders des Preussischen Staates im 17. und 18. Jahrhundert* (Leipzig: Duncker und Humblot, 1898), 593.

26. Emanuel Ringelblum, "Żydzi w świetle prasy warszawskiej XVIII wieku," *Miesięcznik Żydowski*, June 6, 1932, 489–518; Moses A. Shulvass, *From East to West: The Westward Migration of Jews from Eastern Europe During the Seventeenth and Eighteenth Centuries* (Detroit: Wayne State University Press, 1971).

27. Ringelblum, "Żydzi w świetle prasy warszawskiej XVIII wieku," 503.

28. Heinrich Heine, *Sämtliche Werke*. Vol. 4, *Reisebilder*, ed. Hans Kaufmann (München: Kindler, 1964), 196.

29. Wider den Chassidismus II, *Allgemeine Zeitung des Judentums*, February 4, 1862, 65–66, here 66.

30. Hans Lemberg, "Zur Entstehung des Osteuropabegriffs im 19. Jahrhundert: Vom 'Norden' zum 'Osten' Europas," *Jahrbücher für Geschichte Osteuropas* 33 (1985): 48–91.

31. For more on the "mentally ill Jew" and French anthropology in the nineteenth century, see Sander L. Gilman, *Jüdischer Selbsthaß: Antisemitismus und verborgene Sprache der Juden* (Frankfurt am Main: Jüdischer Verlag, 1993), 210–17.

32. Sander L. Gilman argues that Max Nordau's publication of the article Muskeljude was based on his belief in the founding concepts of French anthropology, but only with regard to the East European "ghetto Jew." See ibid., 17.

33. See Maksymiak, *Mental Maps im Zionismus*, 57–75.

34. Birnbaum began his categorization of European Jews as early as the 1890s. See B., 'Eintracht,' *Selbst-Emancipation*, July 16, 1890, 1–3.

35. For example, the Austrian Zionist Dr. Fink used the term "*Ostjuden*" as early as July 1903 in his speech, delivered at the Third Party Congress of the Austrian Zionists; see "Dritter Parteitag der österreichischen Zionisten," in *Die Welt*, July 10, 1903, 2–5.

36. See, for example, the articles by Fabius Schach in *Ost und West*: Fabius Schach, "Der

deutsch-jüdische Jargon und seine Literatur," *Ost und West* 1 (1901): 179–90; Fabius Schach, "Das jüdische Theater, sein Wesen und seine Geschichte," *Ost und West* 1 (1901): 347–58; Fabius Schach, "Die Ausländerfrage in Deutschland," *Ost und West* 2 (1902): 305–16; Fabius Schach, "Ein notwendiges soziales Hilfswerk," *Ost und West* 3 (1903): 423–26; Fabius Schach, "Ost und West," *Ost und West* 3 (1903): 577–88; Fabius Schach, "Die russischen Juden in Deutschland," *Ost und West* 5 (1905): 719–30.

37. See, for example, the letter from Leo Winz to Adolf Friedemann, July 24, 1903, Central Zionist Archives Jerusalem, A 8/24, unpaginated.

38. On Birnbaum's returning to his family roots in Western Galicia, his slow "conversion" from Zionist to Yiddishist, and his self-stylization as an Ostjude, see Jess Olson, *Nathan Birnbaum and Jewish Modernity: Architect of Zionism, Yiddishism, and Orthodoxy* (Stanford, CA: Stanford University Press, 2013).

39. Pantarhei [Nathan Birnbaum], "Die jüdisch sprechenden Juden und ihre Bühne," *Die Welt*, October 11, 1901, 10–12.

40. See, for example, the voices of Adolf Stand or Gershon Zipper mentioned below. Also, the Galician Zionist perception of the Arab people in Palestine as "Orientals" indicates the self-perceptions of the Galicians as Europeans of a "higher culture" than the Arab natives. See Maksymiak, *Mental Maps im Zionismus*, 143–47.

41. Given the variations of the name for this city, including Lemberg, Lwów, and Lviv, I use the contemporary Ukrainian name Lviv throughout this essay in order to avoid confusion.

42. "Zasady i zamiary," *Przyszłość*, October 5, 1892. During the so-called Uganda debate (1903), for example, the Galicians saw themselves as mediators in the conflict between the Action Committee of the Zionist Congress, which was predominantly occupied by German Zionists, and their Russian comrades: "For us Galicians who live between East and West, the task is to help to end this fight and to facilitate an understanding," writes Pawel Almoni (1869–1922), alias Abraham Korkis, in *Wschód* in 1904, the successor paper to *Przyszłość*. See Pawel Almoni, "Vor der Sitzung des A. C.," *Wschód*, March 30, 1904.

43. Migdalus, "Die galizische Judenheit und die Zionsidee," *Selbst-Emancipation*, August 5, 1892, 156–57.

44. On heterogeneity in Galicia, see for example Israel Bartal and Anthony Polonsky, "Introduction: The Jews of Galicia under the Habsburg Empire," *Polin: Studies in Polish Jewry* 12 (1999): 4–23; Wolff, *The Idea of Galicia*, 17.

45. Adolf Stand, "Po śmierci Franzosa," *Wschód*, February 3, 1904.

46. Adolf Stand, "Przegląd. H. P. Chajes," *Moriah*, no. 10/11, July–August 1918.

47. Wilhelm Berkelhammer, "Przegląd. Kilka słów o konferencyi syonistów niemieckich," *Moriah*, no. 4, February 1917.

48. See also Małgorzata A. Maksymiak, "Beggars, Nymphomaniac Women, Miracle Rabbis and Other East European Jews: The East as a Category of Social Difference," *Journal of Modern Jewish Studies* 19 (2020): 434–49.

49. S. Taubes, "Walka światła z ciemnością," *Wschód*, April 29, 1903.

50. Ibid.

51. See "Stenographisches Protokoll der Verhandlungen des V. Zionisten-Congresses," Dezember 26–30, 1901, Basel (Wien: Verlag des Vereiner Erez Israel, 1901).

52. O. A., "Jeden kierunek pracy," *Wschód*, August 16, 1905. The word "jargon" was a very popular means among so-called "assimilated Jews" to refer to Yiddish.

53. "Dritter Parteitag der österreichischen Zionisten."

54. J. A. Lubecki, "List do galicyjskiej inteligencyi syonskiej," *Przyszłość*, July 5, 1899.

55. Lubecki also directly addressed his critique to Max Nordau in a letter published in Achad Ha'am's journal *Ha'Shiloach*; see J. A. Lubecki, "Zionism and its Opponents (Open Letter to Max Nordau)," *Ha'Shiloach* 4 (July–December, 1898): 377–81 [Hebrew]. Nordau immediately responded to this "disturber of the peace," calling him a "dog-Jew" ("*Hundsjude*") whose life would serve no purpose, no higher ideal. See Dr. Max Nordau, "Regardung Zionism (Letter to the Editor)," *Ha'Shiloach* 4 (July–December, 1898): 553–56 [Hebrew]. Lubecki's letter to Nordau was also reprinted in the Lviv-based, Polish-language *Przyszłość*. See "List otwarty Lubeckiego do Nordaua," *Przyszłość*, April 5, 1899. The Viennese *Die Welt* published Nordau's response to Lubecki's criticism; see "Ein Brief Nordaus," *Die Welt*, January 20, 1899, 2–4.

56. J. A. Lubecki, "List do galicyjskiej inteligencyi syonskiej," *Przyszłość*, July 5, 1899.

57. Osias Thon, "Pozdrowienie Achad Ha'amowi," *Moriah*, no. 4, February 1917.

58. See M. Bienenstock, "Achad Ha'am (Ucher Ginzburg): Szkic biograficzno-literacki," *Wschód*, June 22, 1904.

59. See Maksymiak, *Mental Maps im Zionismus*, 59–66.

60. Gustav Bader, "Altneuland, Achad-Ha'am i Nordau," *Wschód*, April 2, 1903.

61. This was the common name among Zionists for "philanthropic Zionism," which, according to the Eastern European Zionists, was what characterized their comrades in the West. "*Rachmones*" is the Yiddish word for mercy or compassion; it is derived from the Hebrew "*Rachamim*." For an example of its use, see the speech by Samy Gronemann on the occasion of the Delegation Day of the German Zionists in Hamburg printed in *Die Welt*, June 3, 1904, 6–8.

62. Bader, "Altneuland, Achad-Ha'am i Nordau."

63. J. Grünbaum, "Kongresy syjonistyczne i znaczenie," *Wschód*, November 1, 1901. For earlier examples of the conceptualization of East and West within Jewry that appeared in the pages of Galician Zionist periodicals, see Abraham Salz, "W sprawie organizacyi naszej," *Przyszłość*, December 5, 1892; Ruben Brainin, "List żyda rosyjskiego do brata na zachodzie, tłum. A. Stand," *Przyszłość*, January 5, 1893.

64. Gerschon Zipper, "Z chwili," *Moriah*, no. 7, April 1914.

65. M. A. [Matthias Acher, one of Nathan Birnbaum's pseudonyms, M. A. M.], "Die Ostjuden," *Mitteilungen des Verbandes der jüdischen Jugendvereine Deutschlands* 5 (1914): 197–206.

7

Central European Zionisms and the Habsburg Colonial Imaginary

SCOTT SPECTOR

Geographies of Desire

The Austro-Hungarian Dual Monarchy was the home of many Zionist thinkers, from the most famous to the forgotten. It is easy to overlook the diversity of Zionism in the late nineteenth and early twentieth centuries. Some of its most diverse and creative intellectual formations emerged from the region encompassed until 1918 by that empire. Yet can one speak of "Habsburg Zionism"? The conceit of this essay is that a common thread runs through some of the particularly innovative cultural products of Central European Zionism, and that out of this thread was woven a cultural imaginary of the East rooted in the Habsburg imperial experience. That thread was spun out of an unconscious or at least an unarticulated impulse. Zionism was conceived and pursued as an international movement with the ambition to address the condition of all Jews in the Diaspora. The idea of national "schools" of Zionism would have been anathema to early adherents, even if historians have recognized that West European Zionists in particular could retain national distinctions due to cultural affiliation with the nations of which they were citizens.[1] How were certain creative and idiosyncratic variants of European Zionism—better put, Zionisms—linked to their common context, the specific geo-cultural imaginary of Austria-Hungary?

Two of the leading figures of the Zionist movement, Theodor Herzl and Max Nordau, were born in Budapest and worked largely in Vienna, but their works stand outside of the arc of thought I am considering. They each rejected European-Jewish assimilationism, and both thought of the movement as a source of inner regeneration of the Jewish people as well as a movement for a political solution to the so-called Jewish question. But in another way, they were assimilationist, yearning for a national Judaism that would put the Jewish people of Eastern Europe and the West, Oriental and Occidental Jewry, "back" on the normative path of the nation-state.

The arc of Zionist thought discussed here is Habsburg, but more specifically Cisleithanian (i.e., pertinent to the Austrian half of the Dual Monarchy); it bends from the western Habsburg cities of Vienna and Prague (whose Jews were assumed to be assimilated to the surrounding gentile culture) to the eastern provinces of Galicia and Bukovina (where Jews were predominantly, though not universally, traditional and religious, and culturally separate from the peoples among whom they lived). The "geography of desire" mapped in these Zionist fantasies entailed a complex interaction with the idea of the "East," understood in the loosest possible manner, in relation to the eastern provinces of their own Habsburg state, to the Middle East, or even to East Asia.

Many of us in Habsburg studies have argued for some time that the colonial dynamics of overseas empires were played out, if with some significant differences, in the continental imperial territory of Austria-Hungary.[2] The Tunisian Jewish theorist Albert Memmi's insights in *The Colonizer and the Colonized* may have something to teach us about these Habsburg Zionists.[3] To wit: Memmi's classic text offers structural-psychological insight into colonial dynamics by painting twin portraits of the shared assumptions and understandings of the subjects and objects of colonization. Memmi describes the mythology of colonization acting on the shifting ontology of the colonized person, from alter ego of the colonizer to pure object, a "colonized." The ideology is inevitably absorbed by the colonized subject—recognition of the colonizer's image of oneself leads inexorably to some form of identification.[4] But the process is not unidirectional. It destroys the colonized object no more than it "rots" the colonizer; as in the Hegelian master-slave relationship, each sees in the other his own distorted reflection.[5] Jean-Paul Sartre, whose introduction to the text became canonical along with it, described this as a "relentless reciprocity" of the two figures that Memmi brings to life in the book.[6] In his incisive account, Sartre made the colonizer-colonized dialectic into an explicitly Marxist one, in a way that Memmi does not quite articulate. Memmi's structural and psychological analysis of these reciprocal profiles is grounded, he confesses for the first time in his 1965 preface, in his own experience, from which he knows the colonizer from the inside almost as well as he knows the colonized.[7] His insights derive from his "attachments" as Jew and Berber, as a Tunisian living in and intending to stay in Paris. Memmi knows whereof he writes, for he is both subject and object of the reciprocal ends of the colonizer-colonized relation.[8]

French colonialism was supposed to differ from other overseas European ambitions (notably those of the British, the Dutch, the Belgians) through a Napoleonic fervor, a civilizing mission to transform the colonial subject. In practice, France's imperial competitors also engaged in the paternalistic ideology that justified annexation as a civilizing mission, and all of these imperialisms operated more alike than differently.[9] Any observer might agree that the European overseas empires adopted the logic and objectives of the Enlightenment. It is the reciprocal relationship of the myths of national identity and of the mission to civilize that so strongly mark the case Memmi discusses. The myth of the *mission civilisatrice* in relation to self-identity is critical to the dynamic he analyzes.[10] The Habsburg relationship to its eastern marches, while less violent, unfolded under the star of a similar myth. It regarded the crownland of Galicia as an integral part of the realm that was nonetheless primitive and worthy of contempt, and that accorded to the empire the task to raise them up.[11] The dialectical tensions in the particular Zionisms under study in this essay emerge from a specifically Habsburg Jewish condition of identifying both as subject and object of the Orientalist gaze.

Origins

To really speak of the "origins" of Zionism in the Habsburg Empire is to turn away from the founders of the first Zionist organizations and congresses and toward Eastern Europe, including the eastern provinces of the empire. Galicia's Jews enjoyed the political emancipation of those in Prague, Budapest, and Vienna, and at the same time lived communally, culturally, and religiously more like those in unemancipated Eastern Europe, in the

Pale of Settlement of the Russian Empire. The first grassroots associations of "lovers of Zion" (*Hovevei Zion* or *Hibbat Zion*), promoting Jewish emigration from the Russian Empire and settlement in the historic Land of Israel, emerged in 1881 in response to the pogroms.[12] In the 1880s, a branch of the movement in Galician Boroslav, as Yosef Salmon has reported, included both Maskilim and Hasidim, hence melding *Haskalah* (Jewish Enlightenment) with its native East European competitor of a renewal of Jewish religious mysticism.[13] In Vienna in the same period, Russian-born Hebrew author Peretz Smolenskin (1840/42–1885) and Salomon Spitzer (1825–1893), leader of Austrian Orthodox Jewry who had been born in Ofen, now the Buda half of Budapest, formed a branch with the name *Ahavath Zion*.[14] Zionism from the first, in other words, was constituted out of an interplay of East and West, of Eastern and Western European political and social conditions and cultural possibilities. From the start, it entailed Orientalist fantasies on the part of virtually all participants, evoking, as it must, an image of self-transformation to what was seen in Central Europe and also elsewhere as the primitive Near East.

The term "Zionism" itself can be located in the Habsburg realm quite precisely: The first recorded usage is by the Viennese writer Nathan Birnbaum (1864–1937). Birnbaum was born in the Leopoldstadt (Second District) to moderately Orthodox parents. His father was from a Galician Hasidic family (but in Birnbaum's own biographical sketch he says he was "a bit of a Maskil, but still very much a Jew"), his mother from an Orthodox Hungarian family. He was educated in a secular manner and setting: He went to a German school, followed by a focus on Oriental studies and philosophy at the University of Vienna.[15] Already in this compact description one can detect the self-conscious presence of putatively opposing forces: orthodoxy and secularism, Jewish communal identification and assimilation.[16] He describes this background from the perspective of an East-West dualism in his autobiography *Fun an apikoyres gevorn a maymin* (From Apostate to Believer): "Born of East European Jewish parents in the West European metropolitan Jewish community in Vienna, I grew up with the concepts, and amidst the practice, of traditional Judaism—yet in an environment that no longer retained much of that strong and vital Judaism we still find among the Jews of Eastern Europe."[17]

One thing that is surprising about this glowing account of the "strong and vital Judaism still found" in Galicia is that it was written in 1927, after the integral Jewish life that Birnbaum was romanticizing had been all but annihilated by the violence of World War I and its murderous aftermath.[18] But even more than this, the quotation is an illustration of the double consciousness I am describing, where East and West, traditional and modern, communal authenticity and assimilation, are simultaneously present in both places, and in multiple ways. Can this double consciousness and the dialectic it entailed be properly understood as an interior relationship of colonizer and colonized?

Birnbaum the younger rejected religiosity and entered the Leopoldstadt Gymnasium on track to become a typical second-generation, assimilated Viennese Jew.[19] Instead, his immersion in an environment characterized by intellectually precocious and unproblematically German-identified Jewish youth produced a tension within him that brought him back to a consciousness of Jewish difference. He formulated this difference as an explicitly national one. In university he was driven to explore his Jewish heritage further through a self-construed curriculum he embarked upon with a small group of like-minded Vienna students from Galicia, along with one from Bucharest. This activity led to the creation in 1882 of the student organization *Kadimah*, which had the character of a national student association.[20] It was officially incorporated in 1883. While the association repeatedly asserted in its statutes submitted to authorities that "the association excludes all political tendencies, having as its objective the cultivation of Jewish consciousness, the national unity of Jewish students, and the care of national history and literature," in its activities it revealed an interest in the political autonomy of the Jewish nation within the borders of the Habsburg Empire.[21] The name *Kadimah* was suggested by Smolenskin, who took interest in the group—the word has the double meaning of eastward (*kedmah*) and forward (*kidmah*). From the association's first proclamation in May 1883, we read:

> In the eighteen centuries since the Jewish people have lost their independence, there has been an unceasing process of persecution whose aim has been the destruction of Jewry... Indifference at the core of

Jewry competes with external animosities to achieve this goal... We must actively confront this indifference... Kadimah's goal is to raise and cultivate the spiritual well-being of the people.[22]

A similarly declarative editorial from January 1892 put it succinctly in the call:

Comrades of kin!
The Jewish people must find its salvation within itself![23]

Kadimah was the first Jewish-national student corporation in Central Europe (hence anywhere, it would seem) and its first, handwritten newsletter, *Megillah*, a clever student production full of irreverent parody, has been called the first Jewish nationalist periodical in Central Europe.[24] In the early 1880s, Birnbaum took over the presidency of the organization and also published a pamphlet called *Die Assimilationssucht* (The Craving for Assimilation), with the subtitle "A Word to the So-called Germans, Slavs, Magyars, etc. of Mosaic Confession," signed "by a Jewish-national student."[25] The basis of the argument rests on the tension between two motivations within all peoples: *Eigentümlichkeit* and *Fremdartigkeit*, or authenticity and foreignness. The pamphlet has the distinction of having been called the first Central European Zionist publication. It came out only very shortly after Leon Pinsker (1821–1891) had published his influential booklet *Autoemancipation* (1882), which was a clear inspiration for Birnbaum and for *Kadimah* in this period: In fact, Pinsker provided 150 copies of his tract to the student association in 1893, and it was clearly the model for their periodical *Selbstemanzipation*, although it would later be renamed *Die Jüdische Volkszeitung*. The turn to inner, spiritual renewal entails an external turn to the East: Birnbaum and *Kadimah* embraced a Zionist and also a Hebraist agenda. A few other points distinguishing Birnbaum's program are important to mention here. He advocated the mass political organization of Zionism rather than the small-scale, non-political "practical Zionism" of associations in Eastern Europe. He also founded the short-lived Austrian Jewish-National Party, which had the unique distinction of uniting Galician and Viennese Jewish nationalists and Zionists together in one political organization.

Publishing under the pseudonym Matthias Acher, and eventually a host of other pen names, Birnbaum became a prolific writer. Besides coining the term "Zionism," his writings were widely read and distributed—by many more people and in more venues than others whose names are more familiar today (such as Ahad Ha'am, for example).[26] In spite of his sometime leadership roles, Birnbaum's visible and lasting influence was hampered by the idiosyncrasy and inconsistency of his thought, and he was an ineffectual leader who found it hard to set aside differences; furthermore, the seismic ideological shifts of his life made him difficult for current and later observers to place.[27] How were these shifts linked to a peculiarly Habsburg ideological topography, or the imperial imaginary linking East and West as simultaneously native and foreign? The mutual reflection, projection, and fantasy between East and West engaged a variety of Habsburg Jewish actors, Birnbaum in particular, in salient and productive ways.[28]

Inward and Eastward

Birnbaum's dramatic intellectual shifts are often schematized into three periods. The Zionist phase ranged from 1883 to 1900. But by the meeting of the First Zionist Congress at Basel in 1897, he had already moved toward a "cultural Zionist" position and away from the political and diplomatic focus of Herzl and his circle.[29] Cultural Zionism emerged from the creative thought of East European writer Ahad Ha'am (the pen name for Asher Zvi Hirsch Ginsberg, 1856–1927), who argued for Jewish settlement in the historic Land of Israel as a precondition of an internal regeneration of world Jewry—a spiritual transformation.[30] This was sometimes ancillary, but often at odds with Herzl's conception of a Jewish nation-state that would be a refuge and potential home for Jews all over the world.

The second phase emerged out of the engagement with the soul of the Jewish people and its regeneration that was the focus of cultural Zionism. Ironically, it led to his embrace of Yiddish language and culture from the turn of the century through to the outbreak of World War I. Birnbaum, recall, was not raised in a Yiddish-language environment and had to learn it as a foreign language, which he eagerly did. The Yiddishist orientation implied a different political solution to Zionism, yet still a nationalist alternative: Jewish autonomy within Europe. It went hand in hand with "practical Zionism," or the practice of improving material and spiritual conditions of the Jewish people in the places where they actually lived; it also entailed a national pride focused on Yiddish language and culture. He was the organizer of the 1908 Czernowitz Conference, now well known as the first international Yiddishist conference in history.

Beyond his leading roles in Jewish nationalism, Zionism, and Yiddishism, Birnbaum played a key role in the designation and popularization of the East European Jew as figure. The image of the *Ostjude*, or "Eastern Jew," had its origins before World War I, and is largely thought of as a paternalistic mix of disdain and romanticization by assimilated Central European Jews and to a lesser degree their Christian neighbors. It is significant that this image was promulgated by Jews either from Eastern Europe or with ties to it. It was also the creation of Galician and Bukovinan Jews who moved west and wrote in German—most famously Karl Emil Franzos (1848–1904), but also others such as Leo Herzberg-Fränkel (1827–1915), not to speak of the voluminous literature of the ghetto.[31] Yet it was Birnbaum who admiringly, and on their behalf, popularized if not coined the term "*Ostjude*" as a noun (as opposed to the very frequently earlier invoked adjective "*ostjüdisch*"). Even before the mass migrations from Galicia to Vienna and other Central European localities that launched the massive dissemination of the figure of the *Ostjude*, Birnbaum lauded them as a people. In a polemical pamphlet of 1915 he argued that as an integral people ("not a mere faith community!") they were particularly bound to the Habsburg Empire as its most committed patriots, even as quintessential Habsburg subjects, representing the imperial spirit itself.[32] This was a strategic claim in other than the obvious ways. Birnbaum's claim about the Habsburg *Ostjude* was more than a recirculation of the commonplace about Jewish loyalty to the emperor; it announced to all readers the "meaning" of the empire itself, as revealed by the war. If the Russian Empire called its many non-Russian nationalities "foreign peoples," states of the modern West did the same in a different manner; Austria alone represented a novel idea for the future, realizing "the idea of a state released from the connection to the National, as a pure idea of a political organization of people historically united within a geographic and economic area, and at the same time asserting nationality as a protected personal right of the person, one that accompanies him everywhere he sets foot."[33] He continues later in the booklet:

> If Austria... has demonstrated itself to be the State in which the personal right of the person to his nationality independent of territory along with the corresponding guarantee of the realization of national cultural spheres come to fruition, then there is surely no people of the world that is so suited for this [*vorgezüchtet*] than the Eastern Jewish people. As the only civilized people that has been interterritorial for such a long and uninterrupted period, it appears categorically predestined to affirm and to love Austria.[34]

Yiddish and the immersion in East European Jewish life that it entailed led Birnbaum further in a different direction, namely that of religious orthodoxy. By the end of the War he emerged as a leading player in the *Agudas Yisroel* party, which asserted a politically antizionist position.

If Birnbaum's significance has been somewhat underestimated, this may be due less to his innovation and influence than to the mobility his innovating spirit enabled. For those wishing to place him—those in his own time and later historians—he was something of a moving target. Yet, running through each of his apparently contradictory commitments, there is a red thread that holds this life together. In it we identify a dialectical rather than a diacritical tension between Eastern and Western identifications, and the ultimate object of transformation—the appeal to mass political organization notwithstanding—is the Jewish self. His aim was ultimately the spiritual transformation of the subject.

Culture in the Middle

An important bridge to all of the Habsburg Zionisms discussed here is the particular Central European inflection of the broader movement of "cultural Zionism" mentioned above. In Central Europe, a powerful source of the mediation and elaboration of cultural Zionism, which both preceded and then competed with Herzl's more diplomatic-political vision, was Martin Buber (1878–1965). In the West and in Germany Buber is looked upon so much as a German thinker at times that it seems his deep Habsburg roots are overlooked. This is odd because it is in spite of the well-known facts of his childhood, split between Vienna and Lemberg. His life before Berlin was hence defined by the force field of alternation between a religious, traditional, and spiritual Eastern and a secular and modern Western Austro-Hungarian map. These strands, of course, were very much present in both places, but the fantasy of the dualism of these ends of the realm fueled the dialectic that was so apparent in his work. The so-called Jewish renaissance that he and others in Central Europe promoted does have these Habsburg roots: access to both secular philosophical discourse and religious tradition, German and Yiddish, Western Jewish metropolitan life (not to say necessarily assimilated or secular) and Eastern Jewish communal life. It was Buber's Prague visits—as early as 1903, but notably the three incredibly influential lectures between 1909 and 1911—that left such an impression on Shmuel Hugo Bergman (then Hugo Bergmann, 1883–1975) and others of his circle.[35] In the latter figure, too, the connection to the Eastern Habsburg is essential: In a transformative trip to Jewish Galicia, he is simultaneously repulsed and awed by what he takes to be spiritual authenticity. Of a visit to a *mikveh* (Jewish ritual bath) in a Galician village, he describes the site as "a filthy pool, that is the place of purification"—but he is drawn to a Galician city like Cracow, which "makes me feel at home."[36] The homeland in the exotic, the paternalistic gaze of the Westerner on Eastern poverty, these sentiments merge in so many reflections of Prague Jews of the period, and not merely Zionists.[37] Buber's three Prague lectures between 1909 and 1911 inspired the young Jewish nationalists of the city (Franz Kafka was notably not among those so impressed). Through Buber they came to understand Zionism and Jewish identity as problems internal to the Jewish individual and the Jewish community, and the key to the mystical and "dialogic" (Buber's term) relationship between humanity and God.

The German-language contributions to and transformation of cultural Zionism were dominated by voices emanating from the Habsburg Empire and its successor states. The Habsburg geographical imaginary as well as the sense of a state, as Birnbaum articulated, as civic and political union of ethnicities led in these many cases to a radically alternative vision of Zion. In fact, shortly after Herzl's death in 1904, the predominant Zionism of Galicia also turned away from the political-diplomatic direction and toward a Diaspora politics that focused on practical or cultural Zionism.[38] It is not for nothing that those Habsburg Zionists who made *Aliyah* (i.e., who immigrated to the historic Land of Israel) were disproportionately represented in *Brith Shalom*, the minority faction that favored a binational state of Jews and Arabs in an independent nation.[39] It seems at first to be a very curious fact that those who in the greatest numbers flocked to the idea of a "multinational" state in Palestine did so out of their experience with a failed multinational imperial space. But that is because the perspective that assumes that such a space was necessarily doomed, and that the empire fell under the weight of its own pluralistic ambitions, is not one that these inhabitants shared. It is instead the product of a different imaginary, a nationalist one that has vanquished alternatives in the eyes of most retrospective observers, including most historians until recently.[40]

As we have seen, this movement of cultural Zionism as it was both filtered and transformed by the Western Habsburg lens strongly influenced Nathan Birnbaum, and with him many younger creative souls. Buber's Prague lectures coincided with the emergence of literary expressionism, and there is arguably a philosophical confluence of these two Central European streams. In our final Habsburg Zionist exemplar, they merge as well with a revolutionary fervor that was also native to the time.[41]

EX ORIENTE LUX

The third and final station of this limited survey is a latter-born Viennese writer and publicist, Eugen Hoeflich, aka Moshe Ya'akov Ben-Gavriêl (1891–1965). After immigrating to Palestine and then in Israel, he remained a close associate of members of the Prague group, especially Felix Weltsch (1884–1964) and Max Brod (1884–1968), and was also active in *Brith Shalom*. Hoeflich's ideological trajectory is a fascinating one, and because he is born latest of those discussed here, seems to suggest where the line begun by Birnbaum and advanced by Buber and the Prague cohort would lead. He was born to a well-situated, assimilated family (his father was a *Medizinalrat*/state medical councilor) and had Eastern-oriented interests from early on. He began his university studies in Arabic, and his attraction toward the East was to travel both closer to home as well as further afield. Politically, he demonstrated strong socialist commitments, and these would become explicitly revolutionary by the end of World War I. Aesthetically, he was attracted to Expressionism. His prolific production of essays, poems, prose, and memoir material is marked by all of these tendencies, assimilated into an extraordinary and idiosyncratic amalgam. Hoeflich came to Zionism through the cultural Zionism discussed above. Like many Jewish Central Europeans of his generation, the Expressionist revolt against bourgeois materialism and the cultural Zionist call for spiritual renewal were fully integrated with one another.[42]

Early on in World War I, Hoeflich was stationed in Galicia, and in July 1915 was wounded severely enough to be declared unfit for field duty; in 1917 he was assigned as commandant of an Austrian regiment in Palestine.[43] It was here that his Orientalist self-identifications and concomitant reorientations of Zionism as an anti-imperial struggle took form. Moving on from cultural Zionism, he came to develop what he called a pan-Semitic conception, identifying Jews and Arabs in a single anticolonial struggle against Europe, to a broader and yet strongly defined *pan-Asiatic* Zionism.[44] Zionism, in this view, is part of a global rejection of European domination by Asian subalterns—not only the Arab revolt but also the struggle in India against the British, events in China, the leadership role Japan was taking in Asian self-determination, and so on.[45] From his first attraction to the ideology, but most powerfully during and at the end of World War I, Hoeflich/Ben-Gavriêl believed first and foremost in a revolutionary Zionism.[46] He was eventually sent home on account of his subversive pan-Semitic activity and banned from Mandate Palestine until 1927, when the ban expired and he moved permanently to Palestine. There he took the Hebrew name he had used as a pen name, although he would continue to write in German until his death in 1965.

Over the course of the war, he remained a committed Zionist, but he was also critical and even disdainful of political Zionism as it had developed. He rejected the rationalist and state-centered model of Jewish nationalism that had been borrowed from a Western tradition that he believed should be rejected. Or else, he thought, it was contaminated by Western antisemitism itself: "Just as European antisemitism was the result of technical-European feeling and thought, the product of rationalist-European development, so did Zionism have to go through the categories of thought of the West."[47]

The Balfour Declaration itself represented for Hoeflich a source of the decay of Zionism, a British imperial gesture that created a commercial stampede of *Novemberzionisten* (the veritable clearance sale opening the gates to an onslaught of adherents in the wake of the declaration on November

2, 1917). He disparages the presumed Zionist victory of the Balfour Declaration as a betrayal of the people's movement of Zion: "Short-sighted politics, driven by all human weaknesses, explicable by impatience or out of psychotic exhilaration, turned the Zionist movement into a diplomatic affair, so that it naturally and in equal measure distanced itself from the real people's cause [*wirklichen Volksangelegenheiten*]."[48] Zionism, in other words—the revolutionary expression of the Asiatic nature of the Jews against their Western colonizers—had itself degenerated into the spiritually impoverished categories of the West. As the British restricted immigration of Central European Jews to Palestine, and those resisting the materialist spirit of the European colonization were powerless, Hoeflich was trapped in his Vienna exile to watch helplessly as Palestine developed into "a European industrial colony in the most horrible sense of the word."[49]

The reference to his "captivity" in Vienna relates to the lack of recognition of any kind that the city and empire from which he hailed had any influence on his outlook. As an Expressionist, Hoeflich is still, at the end of the war, committed to the authenticity of subjective knowledge over scientistic objectivity. But his account of his own subjectivity and the access it provides to his critical understanding of the East-West dynamic excludes any reference to Habsburg or to his multicultural experience in Vienna. In his memoir, *The Way into the Land: Notes from Palestine*, he describes subjectivity as method, for objectivity is "inhuman" and impossible for someone who has experienced something himself, as the author has the East: "I experience the Orient from the standpoint of a Jew who is fully and completely aware of his Oriental descent, his Asian blood."[50] Has Hoeflich then repressed the experience of the East-West dialectic that he had experienced in Vienna, in the relationship to Galicia, in the Central European Zionism influenced by an equally Central European "Jewish renaissance"?

Whether repressed into the unconscious or tactically occluded, it could not be otherwise. Memmi's lesson that the Jews of Tunisia and Algeria identified with the European colonizers and (particularly in the Algerian case) assimilated would seem to suggest a contrary movement from Hoeflich's and his fellow middle-European Zionists.[51] Yet, this opposition might better be seen as an illustration of the dialectics at work. The *dissimulation* apparent in this quote and in so much of Hoeflich's work in this period exposes the European colonial context of pan-Semitic and then pan-Asiatic

Zionism. The French colonizers, as Memmi reminds us, never promoted the conversion of the Algerian population, because assimilation would have been a step toward the "disappearance of colonial relationships" that the colonizer needs to maintain at all costs.[52] The subjectivity that Hoeflich confects in this text along with many others transforms him from a European colonizing subject into a victim of colonial processes. It creates a novel kind of Zionist subjectivity out of the negation of colonizer and colonized; in its empathic projection into the Semitic figure, it sublates the patriarchal gaze that drives it.[53]

The precarity of Palestine, poised between two powers struggling against one another, is another geographical image of opposing ideas, spiritual and material. But it also invokes the self-image of Central Europe itself as the battleground of the West against the "Turk." Hoeflich also muses on the different kind of imperialism engaged by the Germans (and therefore Austrians): Unlike the British and French colonial powers, they focused on economic incursions, but did not touch culture or spirit.[54] The alliance of the Habsburg and Ottoman Empires in war reflects, in a way, the position of middle Europe between East and West; in a late memoir, Hoeflich will reiterate commonplaces about the last years of the doomed Habsburg Empire, comparing it specifically to that other "world-political curiosity," the Ottoman.[55]

Hoeflich's Orientalism, his Judaism, and his anti-imperialist revolutionary fervor were all of a piece, and his writing was incisively polemical. The revolution does not emerge out of material need, but rather spiritual need. As he formulated it as late as 1923:

> Yet I see many signs that the true revolution of the future is being prepared in the East. A revolution that we welcome like the rising sun after a night without hope, the rise of the East against Western technical power, a resistance that we join unconditionally.... the greed of European-American capitalism is clawing at the fundamental elements of our humanity; it is violating the Asiatic homeland of the blood that binds us with a thousand and many thousands of threads. That is why we are partisan, that is why we stand in irreconcilable opposition to the imperialist West.[56]

Conclusion

The historiography of the Dual Monarchy has been moving steadily toward a global approach, and study of the realm itself has often turned to the connections of the imperial center with its periphery. These contributions reinforce the claim that it does not take an overseas empire to be "colonial." Some work has even moved to apply the insights of postcolonial theory to Habsburg.[57] Quite a bit more work has dealt more specifically with the Balkans—the closest thing to a Habsburg colonial possession, in certain ways—and the relation of the core crown lands with Galicia and Bukovina has also been treated in this way. As Said's pioneering ideas taught us decades ago, Orientalism emerged from colonialism, but was not a mere superstructure reflecting it. It constituted an imaginary that was productive—a knowledge that had less to do with understanding others than it did with projecting the Western self.[58] As in Said's cases of overseas imperialism, this projection entailed distanciation as well as identification, or fantasies of opposition as well as of reflection.

Perhaps because of assumptions about the outward objectives of Zionism and its international character, the particular and novel forms of Zionist ideology that emerged in Austria-Hungary have not really been attributed to these conditions. These innovations within Zionism pertained to the Habsburg colonial imaginary of East and West as native and foreign at once. They shared ground with the vision of an imperial geography that was reflected in texts as diverse as the encyclopedic *Kronprinzenwerk* and the fictions of Joseph Roth.

The authors of these creative Zionisms often lacked concrete knowledge of the Eastern Habsburg Empire, although they all felt connections to that Jewish life they regarded as more grounded and authentic. Buber of course did know Galicia intimately, and Birnbaum came to be deeply familiar with it, but only after his early Zionist period. At the moment in which he was so instrumental to the origins of Zionism, he had access to East-Central European Jewish knowledges and experiences through friends and scattered reading; Hugo Bergmann felt it necessary to travel there but had no deep and lived experience of it. Hoeflich/Ben-Gavriêl was there briefly in wartime. Yet, their arguably superficial experiences of the East were absolutely central to their self-identities and their visions.

This is why Memmi's twin portraits of colonizer and colonized suit the Habsburg Jewish case so well. Like Memmi himself, Zionist innovators from Vienna and Prague could see themselves as both subjects and objects of the internal colonial project of this continental empire. This sensibility turned out to be more salient than actual experience in the production of their idiosyncratic Zionist ideas. In a way, this can be compared to the "Orientalism" within Zionist ideology *tout court*. The fantasy of Palestine was essential to the self-image of Jewish-national theorists and Zionist migrants. The particular connection of that imaginary to "colonialism" (a figurative colonialism, because the actual relation of metropole to colony was lacking) was a precondition of Hoeflich/Ben-Gavriêl's powerfully anti-imperialist critique. The fact that all of the Central European cultural Zionists to make *Aliyah* were drawn to *Brith Shalom* and a vision of Zion inclusive of the indigenous Arab population (Hoeflich/Ben-Gavriêl's novel "pan-Semitic Zionism" was an early and extreme example of that inclusivity) is a further marker of the ambivalent and ultimately dialectical relationship to coloniality.[59] A founding figure in this regard was another innovative Prague-born Zionist, theorist of nationalism and imperialism Hans Kohn.[60] The interplay of a dialectic of East and West along with a similarly complex relationship to settlement in Palestine was present in cultural Zionism well before Hoeflich/Ben-Gavriêl.

The genealogical connections are clear among the innovative ideological products running from Nathan Birnbaum's through cultural Zionism to Hoeflich/Ben-Gavriêl's pan-Semitic and pan-Asiatic variants. The picture we get from looking at them all together, however, goes beyond intellectual influences and personal networks. More than a familial resemblance unites these examples of Zionisms that each and in their own very different ways trafficked in alternating identification and disidentification with East and with West, in the promise of renewal and spiritual fulfillment, and in the dynamics of colonizer and colonized. The "East" in these fantasies of remade selfhood and futurity shifted wildly from the Eastern Habsburg frontier to the Middle East to, in the case of Hoeflich/Ben-Gavriêl, China, India, and Japan. The remaking of the West was illuminated by the rising sun of the East—as the title of one of Hoeflich/Ben-Gavriêl's poems heralded: *EX ORIENTE LUX*. The turn to Zionism was in these as in all Western European cases a rejection of assimilationism, or a declaration of the failure of the liberal emancipation project in Europe, but it was also a recognition of a darkness in the eveningland that went beyond Judaism.

NOTES

1. See Michael Berkowitz, *Zionist Culture and West European Jewry Before the First World War* (Chapel Hill: University of North Carolina Press, 1993).
2. I myself belong to this group; see Scott Spector, *Prague Territories: National Conflict and Cultural Innovation in Franz Kafka's Fin de Siècle* (Berkeley: University of California Press, 2000), 172–74. A symptomatic work relating to these questions is Johannes Feichtinger, Ursula Prutsch, and Moritz Csáky, eds., *Habsburg postcolonial. Machtstrukturen und kollektives Gedächnis* (Innsbruck: StudienVerlag, 2003).
3. Albert Memmi, *The Colonizer and the Colonized*, trans. Howard Greenfeld (London: Earthscan, 2003). It came out originally as *Portrait du colonisé: Précédé du portrait du colonisateur* (Paris: Bichet/Chastel, 1957). Sartre's preface appeared in both French and English editions. On Memmi, see also the chapter by Abraham Rubin in this volume.
4. Memmi, *Colonizer and Colonized*, 86–88.
5. Memmi, "Preface," in *Colonizer and Colonized*, xvii.
6. Jean-Paul Sartre, "Introduction," in Memmi, *Colonizer and Colonized*, xxviii.
7. Memmi, "Preface," xiii.
8. In an oft-quoted (yet hard to locate) confession of this origin of his creativity, Memmi in 1995 wrote: "All of my work has been in sum an inventory of my attachments; all of my work has been, it should be understood, a constant revolt against my attachments; all of my work, for certain, has been an attempt at ... reconciliation between the different parts of myself." See Gary Wilder and Albert Memmi, "Irreconcilable Differences," *Transition* 71 (1996): 158–77, here 158.
9. Kenneth Pomeranz, "Empire & 'Civilizing' Missions, Past & Present," *Daedalus* 134, no. 2 (2005): 34–45, argues with astonishing breadth that civilizing missions have been and continue to be central to all imperialisms, itself a category that he construes as loosely as possible. His description travels millennia and over every continent up to the present United States, wandering from political economy to military force to human rights discourses.
10. See, for example, Alice L. Conklin, *A Mission to Civilize: The Republican Idea of Empire in France and West Africa 1895–1930* (Stanford, CA: Stanford University Press 1998); Dino Costantini, *Mission civilisatrice: Le rôle de l'histoire coloniale dans la construction de l'identité politique française* (Paris: La Découverte, 2008).
11. A key player in the promulgation of this image and task was another Jew with origins in one world and an identification with the other, Karl Emil Franzos, who is referred to again below and dealt with in greater detail in a companion article to this; see Scott Spector, "The Return of the Prodigal Galician Sons: An Austro-Jewish Dialectic," *Austrian Studies* 28 (2020): 47–63.
12. Derek Penslar, *Zionism and Technocracy: The Engineering of Jewish Settlement in Palestine, 1870–1918* (Bloomington: Indiana University Press, 1991), 20–22. See also Benzion

Dinaburg [aka Dinur], *Hibbat Zion* (1932), cited in Yoav Gelber, "The History of Zionist Historiography: From Apologetics to Denial," in *Making Israel*, ed. Benny Morris (Ann Arbor: University of Michigan Press, 2007), 47–80, here 50n6. The informal network of Jewish nationalist societies emerging after 1881 was officially established by Leon Pinsker at a conference for the purpose held in Katowice/Kattowitz, Upper Silesia, in 1884.

13. Yosef Salmon, "Zionism and Anti-Zionism in Eastern Europe," in *Zionism and Religion*, eds. Shmuel Almog, Jehuda Reinharz, and Anita Shapira (Hanover, NH: Brandeis University Press), 25–43, here 34.

14. Joshua Shanes, *Diaspora Nationalism and Jewish Identity in Habsburg Galicia* (Cambridge, UK: Cambridge University Press, 2012), 51.

15. Birnbaum's account of his family background and the quote about his father is cited in the definitive volume by Jess Olson, but the same author questions the accuracy of the characterization. See Jess Olson, *Nathan Birnbaum and Jewish Modernity: Architect of Zionism, Yiddishism, and Orthodoxy* (Stanford, CA: Stanford University Press, 2013), 20–21.

16. See Francisca Salomon, *Blicke auf das galizische Judentum: Haskala, Assimilation und Zionismus bei Nathan Samuely, Karl Emil Franzos und Saul Raphael Landau* (Vienna: Literatur-Verlag, 2012), 177.

17. *Fun an apikoyres gevorn a maymin* (Warsaw, 1927), cited in Salomon, *Blicke auf das galizische Judentum*, 18. The translation is from the excerpt published by Lucy S. Dawidowicz, *The Golden Tradition: Jewish Life and Thought in Eastern Europe* (New York: Holt, Rinehart and Winston, 1967), 215–16.

18. For the classic account of the catastrophic effects on Jewish Galicia in World War I, see S. An-sky [Shloyme Z. Rappoport], *The Enemy at His Pleasure: A Journey through the Jewish Pale of Settlement during World War I*, ed. and trans. Joachim Neugroschel (New York: Metropolitan Books, 2003). The original Yiddish version appeared under the title "The Destruction of Galicia." For the postwar massacres, see Jeffrey Veidlinger, *In the Midst of Civilized Europe: The Pogroms of 1918–1921 and the Onset of the Holocaust* (New York: Metropolitan Books, 2021); William W. Hagen, *Anti-Jewish Violence in Poland, 1914–1920* (Cambridge, UK: Cambridge University Press, 2018); Giuseppe Motta, *The Great War against Eastern European Jewry, 1914–1920* (Newcastle upon Tyne: Cambridge Scholars Publisher, 2018).

19. In addition to the previously cited biographical work on Birnbaum by Jess Olson, an earlier study by Joshua Fishman, *Ideology, Society & Language: The Strange Odyssey of Nathan Birnbaum* (Ann Arbor, MI: Karoma Publishers, 1987) confirms many of these details and judgments.

20. The student association records at the Austrian State Archive, Erdberg (henceforth OeStA) preserve the record of its establishment, charter, membership, and leadership: Akademische Verbindung "Kadimah," 1883–1938, OeStA/AdR BKA BKA-I BPDion Wien VB Signatur XIV 202. See also "Wien: 'Kadimah,' [1894]–1898," Nathan and Salomon Birnbaum Archives, Toronto (henceforth NSBA); letter from Dr. N. Birnbaum on behalf of "Kadimah" to Marcus Ernst, February 28, 1894, NSBA. See *Festschrift zur Feier des 100. Semesters der akademischen Verbindung Kadimah*, ed. Ludwig Rosenhek (Mödling: Glanz, 1933), a rich source for understanding the creation and significance of the student organization.

21. The statutes are renewed regularly and always contain this paragraph. See Akademische Verbindung "Kadimah," 1883–1938, OeStA/AdR BKA BKA-I BPDion Wien VB Signatur XIV 202. See "Verbindung 'Nationale Autonomie,'" NSBA. A most useful source in the ample historiography of the association is the chapter in Robert S. Wistrich, *The Jews of Vienna in the Age of Franz Joseph* (Oxford: The Littman Library of Jewish Civilization, 1989), 347–80.

22. Cited in Wistrich, *The Jews of Vienna*, 347 (trans. adapted from Wistrich on the basis of the original).

23. Ibid., from Birnbaum's journal *Selbstemanzipation*, reproduced on page 388.

24. See Olson, *Nathan Birnbaum and Jewish Modernity*, 28–29. Manuscript copies of every issue are preserved in the NSBA.

25. *Die Assimilationssucht: Ein Wort an die sogenannten Deutschen, Slaven, Magyaren etc., mosaischer Confession von einem Studenten jüdischer Nationalität* (Vienna: D. Löwy, 1884).

26. See, for example, Matthias Acher [Nathan Birnbaum], *Zwei Vorträge über Zionismus* (Berlin: Hugo Schildberger, 1898). From the first and throughout, Birnbaum stressed the objective of Zionism to be a cultural and spiritual movement to transform Judaism internally.

27. See Olson, *Nathan Birnbaum and Jewish Modernity*, 118–22; Scott Spector, *Modernism without Jews? German-Jewish Subjects and Histories* (Bloomington: Indiana University Press, 2001), 26–28.

28. A key essay stressing this reciprocal structure in relation to Nathan Birnbaum's thinking is Nick Block, "On Nathan Birnbaum's Messianism and Translating the Jewish Other," *Leo Baeck Institute Year Book* 60 (2015): 61–78.

29. Beyond the two chief biographies cited here, see also Leo Herrmann, *Nathan Birnbaum: Sein Werk und seine Wandlung* (Berlin: Jüdischer Verlag, 1914); Henryk M. Broder, "Nicht alle Wege führen nach Jerusalem: Nathan Birnbaum—von der Geschichte vergessen," in *Die jüdische Moderne: Frühe zionistische Schriften*, ed. Nathan Birnbaum (Augsburg: Ölbaum-Verlag, 1989), 7–15.

30. Habsburg cultural Zionism will be discussed at greater length below. For an early history, see Josef Fraenkel, *Dubnow, Herzl, and Ahad Ha-Am: Political and Cultural Zionism* (London: Ararat Publishing Society, 1963). The definitive biography of Ahad Ha'am in English is still Steven J. Zipperstein, *Elusive Prophet: Ahad Ha'am and the Origins of Zionism* (Berkeley: University of California Press, 1993).

31. For more on this, see Spector, "The Return of the Prodigal Galician Sons."

32. *Den Ostjuden ihr Recht!* (Vienna: R. Löwit, 1915), 15, 24.

33. Ibid., 10–11.

34. Ibid., 23–24. While this publication focused on Galician and Bukovinan Jewry as *Ostjuden* and Austrians, a second, important (if short) pamphlet focused on their integral unity with Yiddish-speaking Jewry in the Pale of Settlement. See Nathan Birnbaum, *Was sind Ostjuden? Zur ersten Information* (Vienna: R. Löwit, 1916).

35. See Scott Spector, "Another Zionism: Hugo Bergmann's Circumscription of Spiritual Territory," *Journal of Contemporary History* 34 (1999): 85–106.

36. From Hugo Bergmann's diary of his voyage to Galicia, Shmuel Hugo Bergmann Archives, National Library of Israel Archives, Jerusalem, Arc. 4 1502, printed in full in

Shmuel Hugo Bergmann, *Tagebücher und Briefe*, vol. 1, ed. Miriam Sambursky (Königstein, Ts: Jüdischer Verlag bei Athanäum, 1985), 9–15, here 9–10.

37. Spector, *Prague Territories*, 160–94.

38. See Shanes, *Diaspora Nationalism*, esp. 193–96.

39. One of the best sources for this is unfortunately only available in Hebrew: Adi Gordon, ed., *Brith Shalom and Bi-National Zionism: The "Arab Question" as a Jewish Question* (Jerusalem: Carmel, 2008). Gordon himself has developed a thesis about the relationship of the *Brith Shalom* position to a critique of imperialism/colonialism.

40. Namely the recent school (if it is one) of Habsburg historiography that is most paradigmatically condensed in Pieter Judson, *The Habsburg Empire: A New History* (Cambridge, MA: Belknap Press/Harvard University Press, 2016).

41. Mikhail Krutikov discusses this convergence of Expressionism, the rejection of commercial capitalism, and turn to mysticism and Orientalism as a "generational Habsburg" phenomenon. See Mikhail Krutikov, *From Kabbalah to Class Struggle: Expressionism, Marxism, and Yiddish Literature in the Life and Work of Meir Wiener* (Stanford, CA: Stanford University Press, 2011), 3–38, 60–65.

42. I did not conduct research for this chapter in Israel; however, the contents of the archive can be gleaned from the register (*Findbuch*) at the Austrian National Library (Quartos room), Archiv M. Y. Ben-Gavriêl, Ms. Var. 365 (Israel National Library). Five pages describe eleven cartons. Further materials are at the Central Zionist Archives, some of which is mentioned below. An excellent overview from a scholar who has gone through the Israeli archival material thoroughly is Hanan Harif, "Asiatic Brothers, European Strangers: Eugen Hoeflich and 'Pan-Asian Zionism' in Vienna," in *Against the Grain: Jewish Intellectuals in Hard Times*, ed. Ezra Mendelsohn, Stefani Hoffman, and Richard I. Cohen (New York: Berghahn Books, 2014), 171–85.

43. Unterabteilung Grundbuchblatt, OeStA, Kriegsarchiv KA GBBL (Grundbuchblätter) Karton 1320 (misfiled in Hof-Hor).

44. For more on this, see the chapter by Arie M. Dubnov and Rephael G. Stern in this collection.

45. This new position, it should be noted, was not shared by other Habsburg cultural Zionists and others who would join *Brith Shalom*. This included Buber and especially Hans Kohn, who argued against it explicitly: "Die Ansicht, daß alles asiatische gut, alles europäische schlecht ist, kann ich nicht teilen." See Armin A. Wallas, "Der Pförtner des Ostens: Eugen Hoeflich. Panasiat und Expressionist," in *Von Franzos zu Canetti. Jüdische Autoren aus Österreich. Neue Studien*, ed. Mark H. Gelber, Hans Otto Horch, and Sigurd Paul Scheichl (Tübingen: Niemeyer, 1996), 305–44, here 333n114 and 115. Buber was not willing to "leave" Europe behind entirely, and Kohn was as skeptical of Japanese imperialism as he was of the British and French.

46. Eugen Höflich [spelling alternates], "Die Mission des Zionismus," *Der Friede* 2 (1918): 156–57.

47. Eugen Hoeflich, *Die Pforte des Ostens: Das arabisch-jüdische Palästina vom panasiatischen Standpunkt aus* (Berlin: Benjamin Harz, 1923), 19.

48. Ibid., 21–22.

49. Eugen Hoeflich, *Tagebücher*, ed. Armin Wallas (Vienna: Böhlau, 1999), 63, entry of

December 21, 1918: "Die Situation ist augenblicklich diese: Die Aussicht nach Palästina zu kommen ist momentan gleich null, die Engländer verhindern angeblich die Übersiedlung mitteleuropäischer Juden, der Kapitalismus ist im Begriffe Hand auf das Land zulegen und die wenigen die ihn zu bekämpfen als ihr Lebensziel sich gesetzt haben sind vollkommen machtlos... Ich sitze nun in Wien eingesperrt, vor meinem geistigen Auge die entsetzlichste Entwicklung Palästinas zu einer europäischen Industrialkolonie in der schrecklichsten Bedeutung des Wortes."

50. Eugen Hoeflich, *Der Weg in das Land. Palaestinensische Aufzeichnungen* (Vienna: R. Löwit, 1918), 1–2. The full quotation is: "Von der Ansicht ausgehend, daß Objektivität etwas Unmenschliches ist, daß Niemand aufrichtig objektiv sein kann, sonderlich in Dingen, die er selbst gesehen, erlebt hat, will ich im Eingange dieser Zeilen es ausdrücklich feststellen, daß ich den Orient vom Standpunkte des Juden erlebe, der sich seiner orientalischen Abstammung, seines asiatischen Blutes voll und ganz bewußt ist."

51. See Memmi, *Colonizer and Colonized*, 72–74.

52. Ibid., 73.

53. This gesture could be identified more clearly through an even superficial reading of a long list of the prolific Hoeflich's texts, but the most illustrative must be the novel set in Palestine during World War I: Mosche Ya'akov Ben-Gavriêl, *Jerusalem wird verkauft oder Gold auf der Strasse. Ein Tatsachenroman* (1917), ed. Sebastian Schirrmeister (Wuppertal: Arco, 2015), where Arabs are picturesquely depicted, and central, but never active. On this aspect of the novel, see also Viktoria Pötzl, "From Pan-Asianism to Safari-Zionism: Gendered Orientalism in Jewish-Austrian Literature," *Journal of Modern Jewish Studies* 19 (2020): 205–23. This tendency is equally apparent in *Der Weg in das Land* (1918), which reads as a patriarchal travelogue over long stretches.

54. Hoeflich, *Der Weg in das Land*, 8–10.

55. Mosche Ya'akov Ben-Gavriêl, *Die Flucht nach Tarschisch. Ein autobiographischer Bericht* (Hamburg: Hoffmann und Campe, 1963), 7.

56. Hoeflich, *Die Pforte des Ostens*, 7–8. The German quote reads: "Sehe ich doch aus manchen Vorzeichen, dass die wahre Revolution der Zukunft sich im Osten vorbereitet. Eine Revolution, die wir begrüßen, wie den Aufgang der Sonne nach hoffnungsloser Nacht, den Aufstand des Ostens gegen die westliche technische Macht, dem wir bedingungslos anschließen.... Wir stehen dem imperiokapitalistischen Okzident unversöhnlich gegenüber, nicht weil wir hungrigen Magens vor Schaufenstern standen und uns das Stückchen Brot, mit dem wir unsern jämmerlichen Hunger hätten stillen können, nicht kaufen konnten, sondern weil der Raubwille des europäisch-amerikanischen Kapitalismus nach den Urelementen unseres Menschentums greift, da er die asiatische Heimat unseres Blutes, mit den uns tausend und abertausend Fäden verknüpfen, vergewaltigt. Darum sind wir Partei, darum stehen wir dem imperialistischen Westen unversöhnlich gegenüber."

57. An important anthology is Feichtinger, Prutsch, and Csáky, *Habsburg Postcolonial*, cited above. Particularly useful to the treatment in this essay is Clemens Ruthner's contribution, "K.u.k. Kolonialismus als Befund, Befindlichkeit und Metapher: Versuch einer weiteren Klärung," ibid., 111–28.

58. See Edward W. Said, *Orientalism* (New York: Vintage, 1978), especially 1–28.

59. See Yfaat Weiss, "Central European Ethnonationalism and Zionist Binationalism," *Jewish Social Studies* 11 (2004): 93–117.

60. The classic primary source was the influential essay by Hans Kohn, "Zur Araberfrage," *Der Jude* 4 (1919): 567–69, although Kohn was to abandon Zionism altogether after eight years in Mandatory Palestine. The most articulate biographer of Kohn today, Adi Gordon, has identified the origins of *Brith Shalom*'s binational position to the combination of Zionism and an anti-imperialist critique that was explicit in Kohn's work. See Adi Gordon, "Nothing but a Disillusioned Love: Hans Kohn's Break from the Zionist Movement," in *Against the Grain*, ed. Mendelsohn, Hoffmann, and Cohen, 117–42. See also the important contribution to Kohn's only apparently contradictory thought on imperialism by Zohar Maor, "Hans Kohn and the Dialectics of Colonialism: Insights on Nationalism and Colonialism from Within," *Leo Baeck Institute Year Book* 55 (2010): 255–71.

8

"The Spoken Hebrew Here Is Not a Language"

On Gersholm Scholem and Oriental Hebrew

GHILAD H. SHENHAV

Beginning in the second half of the nineteenth century and continuing through the first few decades of the twentieth century, the Hebrew language underwent an unprecedented transition. In a relatively short period, the Holy Tongue, which had previously been used primarily in religious and liturgical contexts, became a modern language used for self-expression and communication in all areas of human experience. The renewal and secularization of the Hebrew language are interwoven with the emergence of the Zionist movement and the emigration of Jews from East and West European countries to Mandatory Palestine. Therefore, the study of the transformation of the Hebrew language involves not only the relationship between the holy and the profane but also that of the Orient and the Occident; it is the transition from the Ashkenazi accent in which the Scriptures were read in Western and Eastern Europe for centuries to the Sephardic accent that serves, with some modification, the speakers of Modern Hebrew to this very day. The major question that this article wishes to address is: "How does one experience the evolution of Hebrew when one is, oneself, in transit from the Occident to the Orient?" I study this transitional period in the history of the Hebrew language by focusing on one character and two languages. The protagonist of this discussion is the young German-Jewish thinker Gershom Scholem, who came to be the great scholar of Kabbalah and one of the most important Jewish intellectuals of the twentieth century. Before devoting his scholarly career to Jewish mysticism, Scholem invested much of his intellectual power in exploring and writing on questions concerning the essence of the Hebrew tongue. In these essays, which were written in German between 1916 and 1928, Scholem discusses the methods of learning Hebrew and the opportunities and dangers entailed in its secularization.

This article offers a new perspective on Scholem's early writings by examining them through the lens and sensibilities of postcolonial studies. I make use of the postcolonial critique, not in the interest of "catching" the young Scholem or "convicting" him of taking an Orientalist approach toward the Hebrew language, but in order to point out a specific complexity manifested in his early writings. I argue that in the second and third decades of the twentieth century, Scholem adopted a critical approach, warning his audience of the implications of the appropriation of the Holy Tongue for Zionist political purposes. However, Scholem's critical framework, which treats the Hebrew language first and foremost as a religious and spiritual entity, also displays a profound form of "blindness" toward the Oriental aspects of the language.

My study builds upon prior attempts to read Scholem's mature scholarly writings from a postcolonial perspective. Gil Anidjar, who was the first to explore this line of commentary, based an argument on the following controversial statement from Scholem's magnum opus *Major Trends in Jewish Mysticism*: "If one turns to the writings of great Kabbalists one seldom fails to be torn between alternate admiration and disgust."[1] Anidjar's assertion is that although Scholem acknowledged the Oriental origin of the mystical sources, he kept a distance from their locality: "The role the East gets to play in such genealogy," writes Anidjar, "becomes overdetermined by what the East came to fully produce in the West. The East is thus rearticulated as 'primitive origin' that 'matured' in the West."[2] Terms such as "symbol" and "myth," which Scholem used throughout his historiographic research, are part of a modernist conception of metaphysics, language, and history. Supposedly, these terms create the illusion of an origin while obfuscating the local Oriental features of the kabbalistic texts. Boaz Huss made an important addition to Anidjar's argument by emphasizing Scholem's "negation of contemporary Jewish mysticism." According to Huss, Scholem expressed complete disinterest in the modern, local, and concrete manifestation of Kabbalah either as a school of thought that continues to produce texts or as a belief manifested by novel or renewed rituals. Scholem cast the "East" as an "Oriental" origin, but he perceived the "Oriental" present of Kabbalah as "fossilized, degenerate, and backward."[3]

Anidjar and Huss's critique is based on two elements that are essential to my current discussion of Scholem's early conceptions of the Hebrew language: first, the suppression of the Orient as a living, contingent source for the renewal of tradition, and second, the Western model, namely the scientific framework, that enabled Scholem to attribute new meaning to the Oriental source material. Scholem, who had been educated in German universities, repeatedly criticized his predecessors—the German school of Wissenschaft des Judentums[4]—but still shared with them similar methodologies and a similar aspiration to reveal objective historical truths about the Jewish sources.[5] In this chapter I will discuss how these two aspects—the Western perspective and the suppression of the Oriental—come into play in Scholem's early reflections on the Hebrew language during his own migration from the Occident to the Orient.

The first and main part of this article offers a comparative reading between Scholem's writings from his teens and early twenties in Germany and his essays and notes from the few years after his immigration to Jerusalem in 1923. In texts written while he was still in Europe, Scholem criticized any attempt to treat the Hebrew language as a political tool. Instead, he believed that Hebrew should be experienced, acquired, and renewed primarily as Scripture (*Schrift*) and as a spiritual-religious entity, rather than a spoken language for daily communication. Surprisingly enough, Scholem maintained his "purist" approach even after his immigration, despite himself using Hebrew for mundane tasks. In Mandatory Palestine, Scholem adhered to an approach that on the one hand rejects the appropriation and politicization of Hebrew but on the other suppresses the local, corporeal, and communicational aspects of the language that he heard and spoke in the Orient.

The second and shorter part of this article examines how Scholem's approach, which gives written Hebrew priority over spoken Hebrew, became a theological and philosophical stance on the secularization of the Holy Tongue. In my discussion I show how Scholem adopted an ambivalent position in which he both feared and desired the revival of the divine Hebrew he learned from Scripture.

The Arab Question and the Hebrew Language

Although this article approaches Scholem's early writings from a postcolonial perspective, it is important to note that Scholem never held a naïve colonialist or Orientalist worldview. Not long after his immigration, the young Scholem became an active member of the *Brith Shalom* movement, which called for the establishment of a binational Jewish-Arab state.[6] In political op-eds that Scholem published on behalf of the movement, he criticizes the tendency to present the Arab leadership as mentally inferior to Jewish leadership. Moreover, Scholem explicitly condemns the notion that the Zionist project is best understood as an extension of British colonialism in the Orient.[7] However, Scholem's progressive and pragmatic approach toward Arab-Jewish relations seems to be detached from his views on the Hebrew language. In 1926, the twenty-nine-year-old Scholem addressed an open letter to the German-Jewish thinker Franz Rosenzweig. Writing in German from Jerusalem, Scholem describes to Rosenzweig the danger inherent in secularizing the Hebrew language: the Holy Tongue that was completely devoted to the liturgical sphere is now being reinvented as a spoken language of daily life. Although the language may become secularized, the original meanings of words and the baggage attached to them cannot be erased, and they are liable to erupt like a volcano and endanger the Hebrew-speaking people:

> This country is a volcano, and language is lodged within it. People here talk of many things that may lead to our ruin, and more than ever of the Arabs. But there is another danger, much more uncanny than the Arab nation, and it is a necessary result of the Zionist enterprise: what of the "actualization" of the Hebrew language? That sacred language on which we nurture our children, is it not an abyss that must open up one day?[8]

Scholem claims that the speakers of Modern Hebrew are using it as they would any other language while being blind to the religious-theological implications of their actions. However, I argue that the metaphor and comparison presented by Scholem in the opening paragraph of his letter demonstrate Scholem's own blindness and deafness. First, the metaphor of the volcano is not based in the local geography—the Land of Israel has been free of volcanic activity for thousands of years. The only mountains that Scholem climbed in the first years after his immigration to Mandatory Palestine are those of Jerusalem, foremost among them Mount Scopus, where Hebrew University was officially established in 1925. From these mountains, one cannot feel any physical volcanic reactions, but one can very well see the most concrete metaphorical volcano in Hebrew-Arabic relations, namely the Dome of the Rock and the remnants of the Temple.[9] Moreover, Scholem frames the revival of Hebrew as an issue "much more uncanny than the Arab nation." The act of prioritization ("more uncanny"/"*Unheimlicher als*") is also one of exclusion: The Arab is positioned as the "other," who is not part of this linguistic "home" and not part of the immediate encounter between the German in which the letter is written and the Hebrew that is its direct subject matter.[10] Scholem explicitly states that he will not discuss Arabic and the Arabs in this letter because of an urgent internal matter that might endanger those who have only recently adopted Hebrew as a language for communication.[11]

If Scholem's political approach does not ignore Jewish-Arab relations and supports a binational state, then how should we understand his opening statement in the letter to Rosenzweig? I argue that even though Scholem perceives the "Arab question" as an external matter, his statement teaches us something more profound about his inability to hear the "Arab" or "Oriental" sound within the Hebrew tongue.

In order to develop my argument, some historical context is required. The second and third decades of the twentieth century were a formative period in which the sound of the Modern Hebrew tongue was gradually and deliberately structured. This formative stage brought the European background of most of the settlers into tension with the Eastern context of the land and the language. In 1913 the Hebrew Language Council (*Vaad Ha-lashon Ha-ivri*) announced that the Sephardic accent would become the standard pronunciation system for the Hebrew language.[12] The council decided that "living Arabic" would serve as a model for pronouncing the Hebrew gutturals *ayin* and *het*.[13] The council's resolution was supposedly self-evident and merely standardized the way Jews had spoken Hebrew in the Orient since the middle of the nineteenth century.[14] Nevertheless, as Miryam Segal convincingly demonstrates, the pronunciation promoted by the council was different from the traditional Sepharadic accent. Segal shows how Eliezer Ben-Yehuda, who was one of the most prominent proponents of the Sepharadic accent, in practice created a Hebrew that derives many of its phonetic features from the Ashkenazi pronounciation.[15] In other words, the council's chosen accent sounded "Sepharadic" only to settlers of European origins.

Scholem took no such Orientalist approach, not because he had a strong view on the ideal system of Hebrew pronunciation, but because he experienced Hebrew very differently from his fellow Zionist settlers. I argue that Scholem perceived Hebrew first and foremost as Scripture (*Schrift*), an entity that did not negate but nevertheless suppressed the concrete vocal and communicational manifestations of the language. I propose that young Scholem's blindness toward the Arab or the Oriental is best understood as a symptom of his principal tendency to disregard in his early writings the corporeal, tonal, and communicational aspects of the Hebrew tongue. In other words, when Scholem differentiates between the Arabic and the Hebraic, he ignores a prominent aspect of the language that he himself spoke in Jerusalem.

Scripture Instead of Speech

Scholem's idea of "Hebrew as script" is grounded in his upbringing in early-twentieth-century Berlin in an assimilating Jewish family. Lacking a structured Jewish education, Scholem started to develop his ideas around the language as an adolescent who learned to read Hebrew, mostly alone, through the liturgical texts that were absent from his early childhood. When Scholem left Berlin and settled in Jerusalem, he could freely read, write, and converse in Hebrew. Nevertheless, because of his unique and solitary learning experience and his specific German background, he perceived the language differently from other prominent Jewish thinkers who immigrated to Mandatory Palestine. The older generation of thinkers, of Eastern

European origins, who struggled with questions regarding the revival of the language, had come from a profoundly different linguistic background than Scholem. Eliezer Ben Yehuda, Haim Nachman Bialik, Achad Ha'am, and others were raised from early childhood with the Hebrew texts of the Bible and the Talmud. They read and prayed in liturgical Hebrew, as a second or third language that was not used as a means of communication. The struggle of these thinkers was not to learn a language from scratch but to "invent" daily spoken Hebrew and to adapt their European tongues to the local, Sephardic, Oriental accent. In his early twenties, Scholem was already aware of the profound difference between himself and these East European Jews. In a rare diary entry in Hebrew he wrote, "I remember that we too wanted to establish a strict society which would bind its members to speak to each other in public only in Hebrew. However, it was not carried out! A sign that we were German Jews."[16] Moreover, the East European Jewish thinkers had some preparation for spoken Hebrew, as they conversed and wrote in Yiddish. Scholem, on the other hand, began to learn Yiddish only after achieving fluency in Hebrew and never used it as a daily language.

When Scholem reached the age of twenty, his lonesome experience of learning Hebrew gave rise to a critique of Jewish-Zionist education. Scholem developed his worldview in a series of polemical essays in which he criticized the German-Zionist youth movement *Blau-Weiß* (Blue-White).[17] *Blau-Weiß* was established in the second decade of the twentieth century and offered a Jewish version of the popular *Wandervogel* (Wandering Bird) movement.[18] The movement focused on creating a young Jewish-Zionist community through the experience of hiking in the German outdoors. Scholem was invited to join the movement but left after only two "trial hikes."[19] In March 1917 Scholem published in the journal *Der Jude* an essay entitled "Jewish Youth Movement" (*Jüdische Jugendbewegung*), in which he attacks *Blau-Weiß* for lacking a true decisive purpose and for neglecting the Hebrew language:

> The commitment to Hebrew has not been connected to...the realization that a youth movement that has not been fundamentally Hebraized is today no longer thinkable. Hebrew is held to be a more or less valuable side-business. It would be a sad undertaking for the

statistician to keep a record of the time it takes for us from the commitment to the youth movement to the time we actually practice Hebrew even as a sideline. It is certain that within such youth the fullness of Judaism and the abundance of its content cannot be born.[20]

At first glance, Scholem's critique appears rather straightforward. He argues that a Zionist youth movement must prioritize in its activities the teaching of the Hebrew language. However, *Blau-Weiß* instead turns the matter of learning Hebrew into a marginal aspect of the process of creating a young German-Jewish community. Scholem is not motivated by practical political concerns; he does not wish to prepare the Jewish youth for a life in Mandatory Palestine where Hebrew is spoken. Instead, he believes that Hebrew is necessary for the "wholeness of Judaism" to unfold. Scholem does not reject the spoken manifestations of the Hebrew language, but he most definitely does not emphasize their importance.

Scholem does not fully define the "whole" Judaism for which young Jews should supposedly strive, but we can learn more about it through the rest of his debate with the members of *Blau-Weiß*. Hans Oppenheim, one of the leading figures in *Blau-Weiß*, published an article responding to Scholem in which he justified some of his arguments but explained that his movement was only taking its first steps and thus could not yet make the Hebrew language into its "common property." Moreover, Oppenheim clarified that he saw in the Hebrew language "an essential means for the nationalization of the Jewish youth."[21] Oppenheim's response infuriated Scholem, who rejected any attempt to turn the Hebrew language into a means to an end or to "appropriate" the Holy Tongue for contemporary political purposes.[22] In another op-ed, Scholem asserted that those who undertook the study of Hebrew for the sake of "nationalization" would fail and pointed to what he saw as a proper motivation for learning the language:

> If I wanted and had to establish a plan, I would say: we learn Hebrew in order to be able to keep silent in Hebrew. That is a reason I understand because it has its root in the soul of each of us. The imaginary practical argument—the conception of Hebrew as a means—are the legitimate children of confusion.[23]

Those who read Scholem's text shortly after its publication most likely understood the category of silence mainly in a polemical context: If Oppenheim and his fellow German Zionists wished to teach the members of *Blau-Weiß* to speak and sing in Hebrew in order to arouse national sentiment, then Scholem urged his contemporaries to learn the Holy Tongue for its own sake. His rejection of an instrumentalized spoken Hebrew and his emphasis on silence are a form of resistance to an attempt to appropriate the language for worldly means. Silence ostensibly has no positive content and thus cannot serve any concrete communicative purpose.

In a diary entry dated May 16, 1917, Scholem adds another layer to his critique of Oppenheim and explicitly ties the concept of silence to the primacy of Scripture in the process of learning Hebrew:

> From studying Hebrew for "reasons" (a la Oppenheim) nothing has ever been gained, at most—a Hebraist. If one learns Hebrew in order to keep silent in Hebrew, that's fine ... Only he who learns Hebrew for the sake of the Torah is a learner, a student of the teaching. For only he who has attained the sphere of silence can enter into the sphere of Teaching. The Teaching is the only permitted argument, the only true compelling reason for Zionism.[24]

While making his case against the appropriation of Hebrew, Scholem alludes to a resemblance between the motivations of the Zionist youth movements and those of the "Hebraist" project. As a body of scholarship has shown, in eighteenth- and nineteenth-century Germany, Scripture and the Hebrew language served as a prominent influence for thinkers like Herder and Hamann, who used them in their attempts to rethink and renew the essence of the German language and the German national project.[25] The Zionist youth movement ostensibly undertook a similar project in appropriating the Hebrew language to promote a national project. Scholem offers an inversion of this approach: It is not the Scriptures that promote the Zionist enterprise, but rather the political project is meant to support the study of Torah.

Scholem's reflections on silence go beyond the polemical critique of the Jewish youth movements. Within the scope of this article, I must only briefly mention that in early essays and notes on Hebrew-language laments, Scholem offers an elaborate philosophical and theological account of silence. Scholem defines Hebrew laments as a form of Scripture that allows the reader to experience a hint of what is beyond the communicative capacity of human language. Scholem believes that, when the liturgical laments are read out loud, their repetitive structure and acrostic form enable the reader to engage with a glimmer of both the absolute silence and the divine voice in the moment of messianic revelation.[26] According to Scholem, being able "to keep silent" through the Hebrew Scriptures is a practice with great religious and spiritual value.

In Scholem's early writings, the project of mastering Hebrew is inextricably tied to his aspiration to elucidate and define his own understanding of Judaism. Scholem positions this spiritual-intellectual process in contrast to the secular-Zionist approach, which treats the Hebrew tongue as means for concrete ends. In an essay entitled "How should one learn Hebrew" (*Wie soll man Hebräisch lernen*), Scholem presents this opposition somewhat differently than he did in his dispute with the members of *Blau-Weiß*:

> The goal of learning Hebrew is not to acquire an ability to express oneself in it (which is, to a great extent, only the mechanical consequence of profound mastery), or to generally understand other people. Rather, it is much more important to perceive Hebrew in such a way that Judaism in its spiritual sense becomes one with its linguistic nature. The insight into the essence of Hebrew, not speaking it, is the goal. Only where the silent domains of this language have opened themselves to the student can one speak of attaining a substantial degree of learning. Since modern Hebrew is not something absolute but goes through various stages of emptying, and the danger of falling victim to modern conceptualization is significant, it is strongly discouraged to strive for it in the first place.[27]

Scholem points to the "proper" way of learning Hebrew as a spiritual language and prioritizes the practice of studying the Jewish sources over skill in speaking Hebrew. His description expresses contradictory ideas: On the one hand, Hebrew is abundant and multilayered, requiring attention to its silences. On the other hand, the spoken language is mechanical, and the essence of Hebrew is "not its speech." According to Scholem, Modern Hebrew attempts to empty the language of its richness. Therefore, he cautions against learning Hebrew only as a modern tongue without its religious and traditional background. Scholem specifies that in order to study Hebrew properly, one must begin by reading the Pentateuch and the prophetic books of the Bible, preferably with an Orthodox teacher. At the second stage of study, one may move on to the Talmud in its aggadic and halachic parts. Only after these steps is the student ready to approach modern works by authors such as S. Y. Agnon and others. Scholem does not reject Modern Hebrew, but he prioritizes its written and not its spoken form. He does not perceive Hebrew as a fossilized language but as a living entity whose written form is gradually evolving. In other words, Hebrew may describe the outside world, but it is not well served by daily, verbal communication.

The Hebrew Language and the Silent Golem

We have thus far seen how in his early essays Scholem understood Hebrew primarily as a written language for spiritual use and thus objected to the Zionist youth movement's aspiration to appropriate the language for concrete political purposes. Scholem's worldview is rooted in his unique Jewish education and the fact that, while living in Europe, he learned the Hebrew language not through interpersonal conversations but by studying the Scriptures, mainly alone. However, in 1923, Scholem immigrated to Jerusalem, where Hebrew was already used for quotidian activities and conversations. At this point I wish to examine how Scholem's "purist" approach to Hebrew was affected by direct interaction with the local Hebrew he spoke and heard in the Orient.

In the mid-1920s, Scholem returned to the question of learning Hebrew in an essay entitled "Remarks on Hebrew and Learning Hebrew" (*Bemerkungen über Hebräisch und Hebräisch lernen*). Even though he was then hearing and practicing spoken Hebrew on a daily basis, his approach in this essay appears more polemical than of his writings prior to his immigration to Jerusalem. Scholem opens his essay by posing the question, "Can we learn Hebrew?" This is an odd question, because in the 1920s Hebrew was already commonly spoken by Jews in Mandatory Palestine. However, by "learn Hebrew," Scholem does not mean the task of acquiring a language for communication but rather the process of studying the written corpus by which the Holy Tongue had revealed itself for centuries. Scholem differentiates between the "language of the book" and Hebrew as spoken in Mandatory Palestine. The first, he claims, evolves without any direct relation to the second: "While in the living tongues, the life of the literary language crystalizes itself out of the spoken... this does not yet apply to Hebrew."[28] The language spoken in Mandatory Palestine is positioned as "the other" which is external to the evolution of what Scholem categorizes as proper Hebrew. Scholem radicalizes his claim by rejecting almost any spoken form of the language: "The spoken language here, not that of a few chosen ones, but that language in which you speak to your neighbor (when you speak in Hebrew) is not a language. It is, one can say, the perfect Volapük, but a language in which a world can live and move, it is not."[29]

Scholem doesn't just prioritize the Jewish Scriptures and criticize the appropriation of the Holy Tongue; as we see here, he actively suppresses or at least marginalizes the local, physical features of language that are evident in ordinary conversation. He seems to be ideologically or metaphorically "deaf" to the vocal manifestation of the language—he cannot truly hear the voice of his fellow neighbors as long as they speak in the modernized Hebrew of the Orient. While Scholem lived in Germany, his critique was fueled mainly by theological and philosophical motivations; however, in Mandatory Palestine, it takes on a distinct Orientalist bent. Scholem arrives with an Occidental perspective on the Hebrew language that prioritizes its written, spiritual, and religious aspects, and he struggles to adjust in response to his new surroundings.

Another prominent example of Scholem's stance toward spoken, secularized Hebrew is revealed in his harsh criticism of Eliezer Ben-Yehuda, who was unofficially titled the "reviver of Hebrew language."

> In the course of the migration of language from the book into life, its "soul" has been lost. The thing we brag about is most definitely not worthy of it, for we have not revived Hebrew, but only a Golem of it, an Esperanto... Such language cannot withstand the competition with Arabic and English. The miracle of speech is nothing but a successful conjuring of a ghost—that is, not of a speech-body [*Sprachleibe*], of a soul. But summoning ghosts has no merit. Here lies the core of

misleading the [D]iaspora through our aspirations, because since our ghost sidesteps, it claims to be alive. And one believes in it. But where ghosts speak, the living must fall silent. Ben Yehuda—the new witch of Endor.[30]

Almost all of Scholem's metaphors allude to the negation of body and voice: The ghost, like the Hebrew language, returns from the dead and haunts the living but lacks a bodily, physical presence. The Golem, which also represents the revived Hebrew language, is, according to the Babylonian Talmud, a creature created by man through a unique speech act. However, what differentiates the Golem from its human creator is its inability to speak. Because of its muteness, the Golem is condemned in the Talmudic parable to return to ashes.[31] Scholem dubs Ben-Yehuda "the witch of Ein-Dor" (*Ba-alat Ha-ov M-Ein-Dor*). This refers to the biblical figure who, at the request of King Saul, conjures the spirit and not the body of the dead prophet Samuel. The witch performs an act of heresy, giving voice to the deceased representative of God who was meant to remain silent.[32] Ben-Yehuda's project can be seen in the same light: He aspired to revive spoken Hebrew by any means possible, including bringing in influences from Arabic and English. Scholem percieved such a project as an act of heresy, and he explains that Hebrew would not be expanded by the encounter with the local languages but would simply lose to them.

I believe that we can draw a throughline between Scholem's inability to truly hear the voice of his neighbors who spoke Hebrew in the streets of Jerusalem and his insistence on perceiving the neighboring language—Arabic—as a competitor that might defeat the Hebrew language. Like any good student of ancient philology in early-twentieth-century Germany, Scholem was aware of the ties and mutual influences of the two Semitic languages.[33] In a diary entry dated July 27, 1919, Scholem reports that he practices Arabic grammar and hopes to thereby arrive at a better understanding of Hebrew grammar. Scholem writes: "It is only natural, that one can learn about the structure of one language, by better knowing another (language). And because I really need to learn Arabic, I am in a good position."[34] When Scholem was living in Europe and focusing on the grammatical features of written Hebrew, Arabic functioned for him as a source of knowledge that could enhance the study of Hebrew. However, after his immigration, Scholem failed to transfer his philological knowledge about the neighboring Semitic languages into the realm of the spoken languages of the Orient. According to Scholem, in Mandatory Palestine, Hebrew did not gain from spoken Arabic but was instead threatened by it.

Revisiting Scholem's Stance on the Secularization of Hebrew

We have now seen how Scholem's specfic background enabled him to think of Hebrew as a script first and foremost and as a religious-spiritual entity. His approach insists that Hebrew must not be appropriated for external ends, be they commonplace communication or grand political causes. However, after Scholem's immigration, his "purist" apporach developed into a supression of the local, vocal, and Oriental features of the Hebrew spoken in Jerusalem. In what follows, I wish to go beyond pointing out Scholem's "Orientalist blindness" and discuss how his framework gives rise to a theological stance with regard to the secularization of Hebrew. Therefore, I return with new insights to Scholem's famous confessional letter to Franz Rosenzweig, in order to reexamine his anxiety regarding the Holy Tongue coupled with his desire for it.

The categories of speech, voice, and silence come into play as the letter to Rosenzweig takes its most prophetic and apocaplyptic twist. Scholem warns that Zionists who secularize the language are hastening the most radical religious outburst—the moment in which God will speak directly to his people in his own voice:

> When the day finally comes and the force shored up in the Hebrew language is unleashed, when the "spoken," the content of language, takes form once again, our people will find itself confronted anew with that sacred tradition, signifying the choice before them: either to submit or to perish. Because at the heart of such a language, in which we ceaselessly evoke God in a thousand ways, thus calling Him back into the reality of our life, He cannot keep silent. This inevitable revolution of language, in which the Voice will again become audible, is the only subject never discussed in this country.[35]

If up to this point I have demonstrated how Scholem prioritizes his idea of Hebrew as script over the spoken language, then his "apocalyptic prophecy" clarifies the way in which the spoken and the scriptural are dialectically tied to each other. We learn that Scholem's suppression of the local and verbal manifestation of Hebrew is motivated by his fear of the materialization of some of the aspects of the Holy Tongue that he has encountered in studying the Scriptures. His prophetic statement assumes that there is something demonic in the secularization and vocalization of Hebrew in the Orient. He appears to believe that as long as the Hebrew language is limited to the written form and the religious sphere, its apocalyptic power is kept in a "proper container." However, once the language is both secularized and vocalized, the volcanic, violent aspects of scriptural Hebrew are awakened; once the Zionists begin to speak in the language of God in his holy land, divine authority might reappear in the language that only appeared to have been secularized.

The "return" of God's voice corresponds with a timely understanding of the term "uncanny" (*unheimlich*), which appears at the beginning of Scholem's letter to Rosenzweig. In his 1919 seminal essay "The Uncanny" (*Das Unheimliche*), Sigmund Freud describes the experience of the uncanny as an anxiety caused by the unplanned return of a repressed secret.[36] However, at its core, the uncanny also contains a desire to return to a homelike, maternal, or primordial state of things.[37] If we adopt Freud's terminology for our discussion, we can identify anxiety and desire. While warning of what is "much more uncanny than the Arab nation," (*unheimlicher als das Arabische Volk*), Scholem presents an anxiety about the return of repressed theological baggage, but he also alludes to a possible desire: Although he speaks Hebrew and lives in Jerusalem, Scholem desires and fears another language—the Hebrew of the Scriptures; a Hebrew that emerges from the ancient Orient.

Scholem's ambivalent position between fear and desire is also embodied in the language in which this letter to Rosenzweig is written—German. The German language serves a distancing function in this letter. It affords a vantage point that enables Scholem to write about Hebrew from a certain distance and prevents him from turning his arguments against his own text. It seems that Scholem is perfectly aware of his vantage point, as he defines the Jews who took part in the revival of Hebrew as "the generation of transition" (*das Geschlecht des Übergangs*). This transition takes place at the verge of an abyss (*Abgrund*):

> If we, a generation of transition, revive the language of the ancient books for them, that it may reveal itself anew through them, shall not the religious power of that language explode one day? And when that explosion occurs, what kind of a generation will experience it? As for us, we live within that language above an abyss, most of us with the steadiness of blind men.[38]

In accordance with his own personal transition from his childhood in Berlin to his adult life in Jerusalem, Scholem represents a conflicted perspective: He defines himself as part of the "generation of transition," which is engaged in renewing the Hebrew language but will never experience it as a first language, as a mother tongue. The danger awaits the generations to come, those who will have only the Oriental Hebrew at the tip of their tongues and will not be able to find comfort like Scholem in the German Mutter-Sprache. The Occidental German perspective leads Scholem to supress the Oriental features of Hebrew, but it also enables him to endure its religious magnitude.

I argue that the letter to Rosenzweig does not only present a meta-argument but also implicitly exemplifies its own claims. The letter has a strong apocalyptic tone when read in the original German or even in English translation. Nevertheless, if one thinks about this text together with its scriptural connotations and without the distance afforded by the use of German, its apocalyptic tone is amplified by several degrees of magnitude. In the final part of this paper, I show how his German vocabulary enables Scholem to partially avoid such amplification, and thereby defer some of the scriptural connotations of his own text.

As we have seen, the two most vivid apocalyptic-prophetic "visions" in Scholem's letter are the opening of the abyss and the violent return of God's voice. Interestingly enough, Scholem seems to be actively seeking to prevent these two visions from merging with one another. He does this despite, and perhaps because of, the fact that the scriptural tradition prominently depicts a connection between God opening his mouth and the ground opening up like an abyss to swallow human beings. I refer here to the biblical story of Korah and his people. In the sixteenth chapter of the book of Numbers, Korah rebels against Moses' leadership and against his authority as the representative of God. Moses first tries to convince Korah and his allies Dotan and Aviram to withdraw from this endeavor. However, after failing to change their minds, he decides to demonstrate the authority and validity of his words. Moses puts his authority to the test and declares that if he speaks the words of the Lord, then the earth will swallow the rebels:

> If the LORD make a new thing, and the earth open her mouth, and swallow them up, with all that appertain unto them, and they go down quick into the pit; then ye shall understand that these men have provoked the Lord. And it came to pass, as he had made an end of speaking all these words, that the ground clave asunder that was under them: And the earth opened her mouth, and swallowed them up, and their houses, and all the men that appertained unto Korah, and all their goods. They, and all that appertained to them, went down alive into the pit, and the earth closed upon them: and they perished from among the congregation.[39]

The biblical text engages with divine speech and its potential to become a concrete form of divine violence. Korah, Dotan, and Aviram wish to present their own interpretation of the words of God. However, their punishment is supposed to teach us that in a moment of absolute divine revelation there is no room for ambiguity and interpretation. Moses speaks the words of God, declaring that the earth will open its mouth, and the earth immediately complies. The words of Moses coincide with those of God, who speaks through nature. The biblical story demonstrates the power of divine language and the stakes involved in abusing it.

We have good reason to believe that Scholem was aware of the biblical context when he wrote his letter to Rosenzweig, because the story of Korah plays a prominent role in Walter Benjamin's 1921 essay "Critique of Violence" (*Zur Kritik der Gewalt*), which the two thinkers discussed in several letters from the early 1920s.[40] Benjamin's text includes a series of definitions and classifications of forms of violence, and the last one he addresses is "divine violence." He provides only one example of the "divine violence"—the moment in which God opens his mouth in order to swallow Korah and his people. According to Benjamin, God "strikes privileged Levites, strikes them without warning, without threat, and does not stop short of annihilation."[41] The act of "divine violence" in the biblical scene is described as a power that transcends the common categories of law and language; it has no measure and is not limited by any boundaries.

Scholem's letter predicts a moment in which the secularization of language would lead to dramatic consequences. However, unlike Benjamin, Scholem consistently refrains from depicting the moment of violent outburst and pairing it with a specific scriptural reference. The German language serves Scholem in his attempts to defer the immediate scriptural connotations of his own text, as we can see in the following example from the letter:

> That sacred language on which we nurture our children, is it not an abyss that must open up one day?[42]
> *Muss nicht dieser Abgrund einer heiligen Sprache, die in unsere Kinder gesenkt wird, wieder aufbrechen?*[43]

Scholem makes use of the grammatical structure of the German language in order to create a space between the subject of the sentence—the *Abgrund* ("abyss") of the "Holy Language" (*heiligen Sprache*)—and the verb *aufbrechen* ("open up"). Moreover, the German language also allows Scholem to avoid anthropomorphizing the ground and portraying it as a "mouthlike" entity that opens in a moment of rage. In other words, German vocabulary and syntax enable Scholem to minimize the parallels between the letter and the biblical passage about Korah. According to Scholem, the abyss might reveal itself and God's voice might be heard again, but in his telling the two are not necessarily tied with each other. The German affords a platform that maintains the apocalyptic prophecy in an indistinct form.

Scholem's description of the abyss is not a singular case. The German language allows him to also defer the scriptural context of the phrase "generation of transition" (*Geschlecht des Übergangs*).[44] When we consider the Hebrew word for "generation" (*dor*) in relation to radical transitions, questions of language, and acts of transgression, at least three biblical generations come immediately to mind: the "Generation of the Flood" (*Dor*

Ha-Mabul) was wicked and thus God decided to erase it from "the face of the earth." The "Generation of Division" (*Dor Ha-Palaga*) built the Tower of Babel and was punished by losing its universal language. The members of the "Generation of the Desert" (*Dor Ha-Midbar*) refused to believe that God would bring them to the land of Canaan and were condemned to wander in the desert for forty years. They were an intermediate generation, a generation of transition.

Conclusion

At the outset of my discussion, I pointed to two structural aspects within postcolonial criticism on Scholem's Kabbalah scholarship that might also deepen our understanding of his early writings on the Hebrew language: (1) the suppression of the Orient as a living contingent source for the renewal of tradition, and (2) the Occidental perspective, which allows one to attribute new values to Oriental material. I am aware that in adhering to these two aspects of postcolonial criticism my line of argumentation might appear as an attempt to "catch" the young Scholem or even "convict" him of taking a colonial approach toward the Hebrew language. This was certainly not my purpose.

I believe that we should approach Scholem's views on language with a certain "generosity," especially when applying the theoretical tools of postcolonial criticism. The sensitivities of the postcolonial approach enabled me to pinpoint the ways in which Scholem's external, Occidental perspective "suffered" from a "colonial blindness" toward the Hebrew as well as the Arabic languages. However, after acknowledging the ways in which Scholem failed to hear the local and vocal aspects of the Holy Tongue, we still have room to acknowledge how his stance expanded the conversation on the Hebrew language. Throughout this article the postcolonial framework allowed me to describe how Scholem's "Orientalist perspective" was coupled with a worldview that valued the study of the Hebrew language and Scripture but strongly rejected any attempt to master or acquire ownership of either. Scholem presents a counternarrative to some of his Zionist contemporaries who believed in their ability to make the Hebrew language their own and to adjust its vocabulary, accent, and history for the sake of their national project. In contrast to them, Scholem challenged the assumption that by secularizing a language one can domesticate it and circumscribe its uncanny historical past. According to Scholem, the Holy Tongue has a power in itself, which can be fully realized, not by secularization, but only through forms of divine revelation. Scholem's position, with all of its "blind" and "deaf spots," was a unique and foreign voice in the Mandatory Palestine of the 1920s. Some aspects of this voice might remain relevant to theological and political discussions that we still face today.

NOTES

1. Gershom Scholem, *Major Trends in Jewish Mysticism* (New York: Schocken Books, 1995), 36.
2. Gil Anidjar, "Jewish Mysticism Alterable and Unalterable: On Orienting Kabbalah Studies and the 'Zohar of Christian Spain,'" *Jewish Social Studies* 3 (1996): 89–157, here 117.
3. Boaz Huss, "Ask No Questions: Gershom Scholem and the Study of Contemporary Jewish Mysticism," *Modern Judaism* 25 (2005): 141–58, here 146.
4. Scholem claimed that the German-Jewish scholars stabilized the field of Jewish studies in order to adjust it to the framework of the local Christian establishment. See Gershom Scholem, "Reflections on Modern Jewish Studies," in *On the Possibility of Jewish Mysticism in Our Time & Other Essays*, ed. Avraham Shapira (Philadelphia: Jewish Publication Society, 1997), 51–71.
5. Anidjar claims that Scholem not only shared a methodology with *Wissenschaft des Judentums* but also a similar "colonial" approach toward the "archaic" kabbalistic material. Anidjar, "Jewish Mysticism," 117–18.
6. For more on Scholem's involvement in the *Brith Shalom* movement, see Amir Engel, *Gershom Scholem: An Intellectual Biography* (Chicago: University of Chicago Press, 2017), 100–23.
7. Gershom Scholem, *Other Writings*, ed. Avraham Shapira (Tel Aviv: Am Oved, 1989), 63–4, 67 [Hebrew].
8. Gershom Scholem, "On Our Language: A Confession," trans. Ora Wiskind, *History and Memory* 2, no. 2 (1990): 97–99, here 97.
9. Amnon Raz Karkotzkin convincingly demonstrates in his work how the temple and the mosques surrounding it are almost completely absent from Scholem's scholarship. See Amnon Raz-Krakotzkin, "Between 'Brith Shalom' and the Temple: Redemption and Messianism in the Zionist Discourse—A Reading of the Writings of Gershom Scholem," *Theory and Criticism* 20 (2002): 87–112, here 96 [Hebrew].
10. Scholem's text was eventually published as an open letter dedicated to Rosenzweig for his fortieth birthday. However, the text has several earlier drafts that were not written in the form of letters. In one of these versions, Scholem emphasizes the existence of two "volcanos," the Hebrew and the Arab. Both of them might be activated as a result of the

precarious approach of the Zionist Jews toward the Hebrew language. See Gershom Scholem, "Das Selbe wie stets," in *Poetica: Schriften zur Literatur, Übersetzungen, Gedichte*, ed. Herbert Kopp-Oberstebrink (Berlin: Jüdischer Verlag, 2019), 283–84, here 284.

11. Galili Shahar defines the Arab and the Arabic as the third person, who is denied from the encounter between the German and the Hebrew tongues, but nevertheless must be taken into account. Galili Shahar, "'A Third Reading': The German, the Hebrew and (the Arab)," *Prooftexts* 33 (2013): 133–39, here 135.

12. In the discussion that led to the council's decision, David Yellin, one of its founders, explained that it is only natural that an "Oriental language would have an Oriental accent." David Yellin, "The Accent and the Script," *The Chronicles of the Hebrew Language Council* 3 (1913): 24–49, here 28.

13. Ibid., 49.

14. John Efron demonstrates how among both Zionists and Hebraists the allure of the Sephardic pronunciation was based on a romantic perception. They believed that Sephardic pronunciation was more authentic and closer to the way Hebrew was vocalized in ancient times. John M. Efron, *German Jewry and the Allure of the Sephardic* (Princeton, NJ: Princeton University Press, 2016), 48.

15. Miryam Segal, *A New Sound in Hebrew Poetry: Poetics, Politics, Accent* (Bloomington: Indiana University Press, 2010), 62.

16. Gershom Scholem, *Tagebücher: Nebst Aufsätzen und Entwürfen bis 1923. 2. Halbbd.: 1917–1923*, ed. Karlfried Gründer, Herbert Kopp-Oberstebrink, and Friedrich Niewöhner (Frankfurt am Main: Jüdischer Verlag, 2000), 440.

17. For a chronological description of the dispute between Scholem and the leadership of the *Blau-Weiß* movement, see Hannah Weiner, "Gershom Scholem and the Jung Juda Youth Group in Berlin, 1913–1918," *Studies in Zionism* 5 (1984): 29–42.

18. Robbert-Jan Adriaansen, *The Rhythm of Eternity: The German Youth Movement and the Experience of the Past, 1900–1933* (New York: Berghahn Books, 2015), 68–69.

19. Ibid., 73.

20. Scholem, *Tagebücher*, 516. Unless otherwise noted, the translation is mine with the help of Dana Rubinstein, to whom I am deeply grateful.

21. Hans Oppenheim, "Eine Kritik des Blau-Weiß," *Blau-Weiß Blatter (Führernummer)* 1 (1917–1919): 10–12, here 12.

22. A recent study shows how in the German Zionist youth movements the Hebrew language was used to write Zionist folk songs that were structured similarly to common German folk songs. See Edwin Seroussi and Meir Stern, "Songs That Young Gershom Scholem May Have Heard: Jacob Beimel's *Jüdische Melodieen*, Jung Juda, and Jewish Musical Predicaments in Early Twentieth-Century Berlin," *Jewish Quarterly Review* 110 (2020): 64–101.

23. Scholem, *Tagebücher*, 105.

24. Ibid., 15.

25. See, for instance, Ofri Ilany, "'Is Judah Indeed the Teutonic Fatherland?' The Debate over the Hebrew Legacy at the Turn of the 18th Century," *Naharaim* 8 (2014): 31–47.

26. Gershom Scholem, "On Lament and Lamentation," trans. Lina Barouch and Paula Schwebel, *Jewish Studies Quarterly* 21 (2014): 4–12.

27. Gershom Scholem, "Wie Soll Man Hebräisch Lernen?" in *Tagebücher*, 612–14, here 612.

28. Gershom Scholem, "Bemerkungen über Hebräisch und Hebräisch Schreiben" (n.d.), National Library of Israel Jerusalem, Gershom Scholem Archive, Arc4 1599/ 277 I Nr.25.1.

29. Ibid. Volapük is an artificial tongue, like Esperanto, but based on Germanic rather than Romance roots.

30. Gershom Scholem, "Bei der Wanderung der Sprache vom Buch ins Leben ist die 'Seele' verloren gegangen," in *Poetica: Schriften zur Literatur, Übersetzungen, Gedichte*, ed. Herbert Kopp-Oberstebrink, Hannah Markus, Martin Treml, and Sigrid Weigl (Berlin: Jüdischer Verlag, 2019), 299–300, here 299.

31. *Babylonian Talmud*, Tractate Sanhedrin, folio 65.b.

32. 1 Samuel 28, 3–25.

33. Scholem started to learn Arabic as early as 1916. See Scholem, *Tagebücher*, 257.

34. Ibid., 497–98.

35. Scholem, "On Our Language: A Confession," 99.

36. An early attempt to address this letter through psychoanalytic theory was offered by Stéphane Mosès, who located the letter in Scholem's archive and wrote the first interpretation of the text. Stéphane Mosès, "Scholem and Rosenzweig: The Dialectics of History," trans. Ora Wiskind, *History and Memory* 2, no. 2 (1990): 100–16, here 111.

37. Sigmund Freud, "The Uncanny," in *The Standard Edition of the Complete Psychological Works of Sigmund Freud*, vol. 17, trans. James Strachey (London: Hogarth Press, 1981), 219–56, here 255.

38. Scholem, "On Our Language: A Confession," 97.

39. Translation from the King James Bible, Numbers 16:30–33. I am using here the English translation in order to offer an easier reading experience of my text, but it should be mentioned that also the canonical "Luther Bibel" puts emphasis on the opening of God's mouth in the moment when Korah and his people are swallowed: "*Wird aber der HERR etwas Neues schaffen, dass die Erde ihren Mund auftut und verschlingt sie mit allem*" (Mose 4, 16:30). Die Bibel oder die ganze Heilige Schrift des Alten und Neuen Testaments. Revidierte Fassung der deutschen Übersetzung Martin Luthers (Stuttgart: Privilegierte Württembergische Bibelanstalt, 1912), http://www.zeno.org/Literatur/M/Luther,+Martin/Luther-Bibel+1912/Das+Alte+Testament/Das+vierte+Buch+Mose+(Numeri)/Numeri+16.

40. Walter Benjamin, *The Correspondence of Walter Benjamin, 1910–1940*, ed. Gershom Scholem and Theodor W. Adorno, trans. Manfred R. Jacobson and Evelyn M. Jacobson (Chicago: University of Chicago Press, 1994), 172–75.

41. Walter Benjamin, "Critique of Violence," in *Selected Writings*. Vol. 1, *1913–1926*, ed. Marcus Bullock and Michael W. Jennings, trans. Harcourt Brace Jovanovich (Cambridge, MA: Belknap Press, 2002), 236–52, here 250.

42. Scholem, "On Our Language: A Confession," 97.

43. Gershom Scholem, "Bekenntnis über unsere Sprache," appendix to Michael Brocke, "Franz Rosenzweig und Gerhard Gershom Scholem," in *Juden in der Weimarer Republik*, ed. Walter Grab and Julius H. Schoeps (Stuttgart: Burg Verlag, 1986), 127–53, here 148.

44. The distancing effect of the German language comes at a certain cost. When German-

Jewish thinkers like Scholem use the metaphor of the "abyss" (*Abgrund*), they echo a completely other set of meanings from German philosophy and literature. I discuss the context of the word "*Abgrund*" in the German-Jewish thought of the early twentieth century in Ghilad H. Shenhav, "Between Abgrund and Urwirbel: The Story of One Word in the Buber-Rosenzweig Bible Translation," *Naharaim* 14 (2020): 83–102.

Part III
Palestine and Israel between Empire and Decolonization

9

The Return of Modernity

Postcolonialism and the New Historiography of Jews from the Levant and Egypt

ORIT BASHKIN

This historiographical essay reviews books and articles dealing with Jewish history in Palestine, Iraq, Egypt, Syria, and Lebanon, which were published mostly in the last two decades in the Anglophone academic world. I argue that methodological shifts concerning the study of modern imperialism and nationalism instigated changes in broader Middle Eastern and Jewish historiography in ways that critiqued both nationalist and postcolonial approaches. Moreover, new historical studies of Ottoman modernity and the different kinds of Arab nationalism(s) that emerged in the post–World War I era affected how historians look at the Jews who lived in Muslim societies prior to their migration to Israel.[1]

A dominant narrative in the scholarship about the Jewish communities of the region underlined the inability of Jews to become modern citizens in Muslim nation-states. This narrative played a major role in Orientalism, as scholars argued that premodern forms of Arab-Jewish coexistence collapsed in the modern age, due to the rise of Arab nationalism and Zionism. In his important book, *The Jews of Islam*, Bernard Lewis thus suggested that antisemitic literature, brought to the region by Christian missionaries, found a ready audience in the Arab print market beginning in the late nineteenth century.[2] Historian Raphael Israeli summarized this argument:

> Recent Arab-Muslim anti-Semitism has taken some new forms concurrent with the enhanced anti-Semitic mood in the West. The main strata of inspiration have not changed substantially, and include Muslim sources, such as calling Jews "descendants of apes and swine," and borrowings from the Christian themes of blood libel, *The Protocols of the Elders of Zion*, the world Jewish conspiracy, and the various ideas of "poisoning." Muslims also continue to utilize the Arab-Israeli conflict to cloak anti-Semitism as anti-Zionism or anti-Israelism.[3]

The emphasis on the persecution of the Jews in the modern Muslim world was important, not only as a means of discrediting Arab and Muslim nationalism, but also as a way for Middle Eastern Jews to claim a place for themselves in the State of Israel, a major destination for many of these communities following their displacement after 1948. Joel Beinin has shown how this approach allowed Middle Eastern Jews to represent themselves as Zionists resisting the oppression prevalent in the Islamic Middle East in order to fit into Israeli national narratives.[4]

These Zionist readings of Jewish histories were called into question by important scholars, who, instead of using the larger categories of "the Jews of Islam," preferred focusing on the unique histories of particular Jewish communities in the modern Muslim world. Norman Stillman, Esther Benbassa, and Aron Rodrigue played pioneering and crucial roles in establishing the field of modern Jewish history of various Middle Eastern communities.[5] Another important historiographical phenomenon emerged in the 1990s and the early 2000s with the rise of postcolonial Mizrahi studies. Postcolonial critics and theoreticians like Ella Shohat, Sami Shalom Chetrit, and Yehuda Shenhav challenged the works of Lewis, Refaeli, and other scholars of the field and their assumptions about modern Jewish life in Muslim states.

While former scholars saw the rise of Zionism in the Middle East as an answer to the importation of antisemitism into Arab societies, for Ella Shohat, Jews from Muslim lands were "Zionism's other victims," because of the socioeconomic and cultural discrimination that members of Jewish communities faced in Israel.[6] Shohat discussed the ways in which Zionist historiography sought to undermine the significance of the Jewish past by subjecting it to a universalizing model of Jewish oppression under non-Jewish sovereignty. The imposition of a European linearity of progression from medieval persecution to modern antisemitism and then to Zionism misrepresented the richness of Mediterranean and Middle Eastern Jewish cultural existence and assumed, wrongly, that the Jews of the modern Muslim world needed to be rescued by their Western European brethren. To Shohat, moreover, *Haskalah*, the movement that some scholars defined as a movement of Jewish enlightenment, was Eurocentric. This movement, in her readings, was imposed on the indigenous Jewish populations of the Middle East by Europeans, such as teachers and journalists, and as such represents a rupture, rather than a continuum, in Jewish-Arab thought and history. Employing the term "Arab Jew" (also to mark her own identity), Shohat has shown that Middle Eastern Jews did not cease to be Arabs once they became Israeli citizens, but rather framed their Arab-Jewish identity in a new fashion.[7]

Sociologist Yehouda Shenhav's discussions of the concept of "the Arab Jews" expanded this critique. Like Shohat, he criticized the manners in which European Jews represented themselves as the liberators of Middle Eastern Jewry from oppressive Muslim societies. Shenhav, however, challenged the binaries that emerged from Shohat's work. Studying such phenomena as the activities of Zionist emissaries and workers in Yemen and Iraq and the manners in which Israel handled the question of Jewish property seized by the Iraqi state, Shenhav underlined important processes of appropriation and hybridity within Mizrahi communities themselves, and illuminated how they, too, came to speak in a Zionist language that articulated their demands in a way understandable to the Israeli state, especially in his studies of the organizations of Sephardi Jews that aimed to reclaim Jewish property confiscated by Arab regimes. Inspired by Talal Assad (especially his critique of secularism) and Homi K. Bhabha (the ideas of hybridity), he contested the assumption that the cluster Zionist/European/secular represented the opposite of the Mizrahi/Eastern/religious and analyzed the historical setting that gave birth to these modes of signification.[8]

The works of Shenhav, Shohat, and their students shared something in common with the works they sought to reconstruct: the approach to modernity. Just as conservative historians like Lewis identified modernity with the rise of antisemitism in the Muslim world, for the postcolonial school modernity was connected to the destruction of the Jewish communities of the Muslim world, and, more broadly, to colonialism, racism, and ethnic cleansing. Both the conservative and the postcolonial schools were highly critical of nationalism, Jewish and Arab alike, with the conservative historians focusing on the faults of Arab nationalism, and the postcolonial ones focusing on both Zionism and Arab nationalism. The postcolonial school initially focused on the Israeli archives, and on Ashkenazi representations of Mizrahi Jews,[9] although both Shenhav and Shohat have shifted in recent years to Arabic sources: Shohat to the study of Judeo-Arabic and the Arabic works of the Jewish-Iraqi writer Samir Naqqash, and Shenhav to the study of Palestinian and Arab novels, multilingualism, and translation. In fact, in recent years, Shenhav produced brilliant translations of Arabic prose into Hebrew, performing his Arab Jewishness in ways that inspire new reading practices in Israel. Their original studies, however, challenged, and were deeply connected to, the realities and modes of identities created by the Zionist movement and the Arab-Israeli conflict.

A literary scholar, Lital Levy, has articulated an important critique of the postcolonial approach. Following Ammiel Alcalay, whose pioneering work, *After Jews and Arabs*, underscored the importance of Arab-Jewish writings in medieval and modern times,[10] Levy argued that these postcolonial scholars evoke Arab-Jewish identities as part of a political project that evolved from Mizrahi activism in Israel, which responded to the discriminatory economic, social, and cultural treatment of Jews from Muslim lands. She suggested that the focus on the Israeli context led to nonengagement with sources written in Arabic, crucial to the recovery of Middle Eastern Jewish pasts. The solution she proposed, and which she followed very carefully with her own studies, was endowing such studies "with historic depth."[11] Many historians of Middle Eastern Jewish communities, in whose studies the promises of the modern age were explored in depth, have subsequently answered Levy's demand for greater contextualization and nuance, and turned to see how the modern age affected the lives and identities of Jews while they were still living in Muslim and Arab states. These historians were trained not only in Hebrew but also in Arabic and Ottoman Turkish, and based their research on archives in these languages. They showed that the views of Jews toward empire, nation, and modernity had been formed long before Zionism and that some of these formations continued existing alongside Zionism and Hebrew nationalism.

Imperial Jewish Subjects and the Project of Arab Revival, 1839–1914

Historians of Jewish life in the Levant were very much interested in the empire that predated imperialism, namely, the Ottoman Empire. Historians of Levantine and Egyptian-Jewish communities have been inspired by historians of the Muslim world who have critiqued Arab national historiography for representing the late Ottoman period as an era of perpetual decline that led to Western colonization and in which a nascent Arab nationalism manifested itself in opposition to Ottoman-Turkish nationalism. While acknowledging the empire's genocidal policies against its Armenian and Assyrian communities, they have stressed the degree of the Levantine and Egyptian identification with an Ottoman world of letters, as multilingual Arab elites in the Muslim world read and wrote in Ottoman Turkish. These historians have also pointed to the support the Ottoman Empire received during World War I from its Arab subjects (a support that deteriorated during the horrific realities of hunger and starvation created during the war itself), and the ways in which service in the Ottoman military against Western colonial powers (Italy in North Africa, France and England during World War I) shaped the mind-set of Arab nationalists and resistance fighters active in the Levant.[12] These insights were then transformed to the Jewish context of the Levant and Egypt. Jews were therefore not living in the oppressive Muslim regime of the "sick man of Europe," to be rescued by the West, but were rather imperial subjects coping with the new realities of the modern world.

Historian Ussama Makdisi has been instrumental in this regard. He underlined the differences between the violence typical of the empire's conduct in the Balkans and the ecumenical framework that came into being in the Levant. In this region, the empire's different religious communities, while cognizant of religious differences, sought ways of living together as modern subjects committed to a battle against religious fanaticism.[13]

In an earlier study on Ottoman Lebanon, Makdisi highlighted the constructed nature of sectarianism in the Ottoman Empire and offered a view of sectarianism as a practice that belongs to the realm of the modern.[14] Jewish-Muslim relationships, according to the pattern outlined by Makdisi, were not a manifestation of primordial concepts created during the time of the Prophet Muḥammad and his successors, but rather responded to new realities created during the modern age, such as, for example, different colonial powers using the defense of local religious communities as a pretext for Western intervention. The new literature on Jews in the Ottoman Empire has accepted the imperial logic that the Ottoman state was a Muslim empire where the hegemony of the ruling Sunni elites was at the core of the political system. Yet it has looked into two interconnected spheres: that of the Jewish communities themselves, where the meanings associated with being a Jew in a modern Ottoman society were constantly debated, and that of the empire, where various non-Jewish agents suggested numerous significations to Ottoman-Jewish identity (such as "Ottoman subject," "*dhimmī*," and "citizen"). The state, moreover, had the power to change the nature of the social hierarchies within the religious community.

Central to formation of new Jewish identities in the Muslim world were the *Tanẓīmāt* (1839–1876), a series of Ottoman reforms aimed at preserving the power of the Ottoman state through modernization, centralization, and the creation of a new imperial civic identity regardless of the subjects' religion. Jewish elites took advantage of the Ottoman reforms; some were appointed to official posts in the newly established administrative institutions in the provinces and the imperial center, and many benefited from educational institutions established by the state and by the colonial powers, most notably from the construction of French Jewish schools belonging to the French network *Alliance Israélite Universelle* educational system (established in 1860). Freed from national historiographies, the recognition that the Mashriqi Jewish context was multilingual has led to studies of multiple sources in Ladino, Arabic, Hebrew, Judeo-Arabic, and Ottoman Turkish. Historians showed that many Jews made use of the Modern Hebrew press, recognizing the fact that Hebrew had ceased to be solely a liturgical and religious language, and had evolved into a transregional language used by Middle Eastern Jews to communicate with Jews elsewhere in the world regarding a variety of phenomena relating to modernity in general and the nature of the Ottoman state in particular.[15]

The most radical change occurred on July 23, 1908, when a constitutional revolution changed the meanings of imperial politics by limiting the sultan's power and introducing electoral politics and new notions of citizenship. The 1908 revolution also marked a change in the cultural practices of Mashriqi Jews, in the sense that it accelerated the integration processes initiated by the *Tanzīmāt*. Situated against the background of Ottoman reforms and the 1908 revolution, Jewish history is no longer seen in isolated terms, but rather in comparative ones: The same changes that affected other ethnic and religious communities in the empire (Armenian, Kurdish, Arab, Shiite, Christian Orthodox, and so on) affected the Jewish community as well. The interest in comparative and relational histories of the various minority communities of the empire has established that Jews and Christians were not simply to be viewed as categorized legally and religiously *together* as the people of the book, but rather that the competition between Jews and Christians in the domains of commerce and foreign education, and the ways in which these communities acted within the same system, marked a new stage in the history of both Christians and Jews. Thus, Bruce Masters, in a thoughtful work on Christians and Jews in the Ottoman Arab Middle East that stretches from the early modern period to the modern era, has illustrated how colonialism, global trading networks, and rising notions of sectarianism changed both Jewish and Christian life during the nineteenth century, and, at times, increased the socioeconomic competition between these two communities.[16]

Egypt, nominally part of the Ottoman Empire, was likewise a location in which Middle Eastern Jewish modernity was reinterpreted. Egypt went through major modernization processes during the nineteenth century, similar to the Ottoman *Tanzīmāt*, although led by a different, increasingly autonomous, dynasty, and subsequently its Jewish populations became part of regional and transregional networks, with important ties to other Jews in the region. Joel Beinin's work on modern Egyptian Jews has pointed to the rise of Jewish bourgeoisie and upper classes in the region. Benin has underlined the process through which kinship connections throughout the Mediterranean, a historical tradition of diasporic commercial activity, and participation in both Levantine and French cultures, created a group of Jewish commercial intermediaries between Europe and the Ottoman Empire, a process during which Jews often obtained foreign citizenship. In his work, he followed this trend under British colonial rule (1882–1922), which enabled Sephardi Egyptian families to thrive.[17]

Following the integration of Jews into global trading networks, and the urbanization of Jewish communities, the nineteenth century was an era of social mobility. Middle Eastern Jews, like their Christian and Muslim peers, moved to a variety of locations across the globe, and to cities and towns in the Middle East, forming, and becoming parts of, local and global Middle Eastern networks. Yaron Harel has illustrated how Jews of Aleppo joined the migration waves going from Bilād al-Shā'm (Syria and Lebanon) to Europe in his study of the members of Aleppo's Jewish community in Manchester, England.[18] Ilham Khuri-Makdisi's study of radical networks in Cairo, Beirut, and Alexandria, which followed the movement of people and ideas in the nineteenth century, included Mediterranean Jews, who moved throughout the region as migrant laborers, radicals, and exiles together with other Middle Easterners and Europeans. Khuri-Makdisi's findings, similar to those of early studies of the Egyptian-Jewish communist Joseph Rozenthal by Joel Beinin and Zachary Lockman,[19] locate Jews within a multiethnic class system and shift our attention from such nostalgic concepts as "cosmopolitanism" to questions relating to the quotidian experiences of Jewish laborers and exiles and the interplay between class and ethnicity.[20]

Thus, the era of Ottoman reforms, in both the empire and in Egypt, complicated the East-West binary typical of postcolonial assumptions. Jews, this new literature showed, identified with the Westernization efforts of the Ottoman Empire, which were led by Muslim elites, who themselves became more Westernized. Concurrently, however, their transregional networks allowed them to take part in emerging Western markets, tie themselves to foreign and global trade, and enjoy Western education in colonial schools.

The most serious effect of both the *Tanzīmāt* and the 1908 revolution was the birth of a sense of Jewish Ottomanism. Ottomanism signified a patriotic and civic belonging to the empire by all its subjects, regardless of their religion. Ottomanism, the new scholarship suggests, opened up new possibilities for religious minorities to think about citizenship and identity within a larger Muslim imperial setting. Michelle Campos's pioneering *Ottoman Brothers: Muslims, Christians, and Jews in Early Twentieth-Century Palestine* thus showed what Ottomanism meant, and how Ottomanism was practiced, among the Sephardi community in Palestine, and how this ideology overcame, but also produced, tensions related to the rise of Arab nationalism and Zionism. Unearthing a whole range of activities within various Palestinian public spheres, Campos's discussions of the Ottoman context in which the Sephardis operated replaced a much narrower set of questions raised by prior historians, who focused on whether, and to what degree, Sephardi Jews were Zionists or anti-Zionists. Campos explained that these Sephardim felt they lived in a shared homeland with Muslims because of the discourse of Ottomanism and because of close sociocultural relations of indigenous Jews and Arabs in Ottoman Palestine. However, Campos also pointed out that each such group, especially after electoral policies were enacted, strove to ensure its own communal power. The terminology chosen by Campos is key here: She used neither "Sephardim" nor "Jews of the Land of Israel" to depict her historical subjects, but rather, respectful of their definitions of themselves, "Palestinian Sephardim."[21]

Studying a similar context, Abigail Jacobson's insightful work, which looks at the history of Ottoman Jerusalem from 1912 to 1920, pays attention to the Sephardi community of Jerusalem and its various ideological tendencies. She locates the history of the city as one between empires, the Ottoman and the British. Although pointing to the continuities between the Ottoman and British imperial periods, Jacobson underlines the processes ignited by World War I, with its food shortages, conscriptions, the stationing of Ottoman soldiers and commanders in Jerusalem, and, importantly, the transnational networks that Jerusalemite Jews operated in order to overcome the harsh realities of the war (with Ashkenazi Jews benefiting from relations with American Jewry). She thus illustrates how global, Ottoman, and Palestinian realities determined, and changed, Sephardi-Ashkenazi and Sephardi-Muslim-Christian dynamics in Palestine.[22]

The shift to the study of Jewish life in a late Ottoman context has likewise produced histories from below that focus on everyday practices and the commercial, cultural, and social interactions between Jews and Arabs in Palestine, which continued under the British Mandate. These interactions, in other words, survived colonialism in its initial stages. Salim Tamari's work on the history of Ottoman and Mandatory Jerusalem inspects how Jews integrated into their Palestinian-Ottoman society, especially in his thoughtful article on Isḥāq Shāmī, "a Palestinian Arab Jew." According to Tamari, the term was used to "designate a forgotten milieu of those Mashriqi Jews who identified themselves with the rising Arab national movement and its emancipatory programme, and who shared language and culture with their Muslim and Christian compatriots in greater Syria, Iraq, and Egypt, as early as the Ottoman administrative reforms of 1839."[23] A significant component in Tamari's body of work is his focus on the ways in which Jews, Muslims, and Christians lived together and apart in Ottoman and Mandatory Palestine, especially Ottoman Jerusalem. He discusses the musicians who appeared before mixed religious crowds, the doctors who treated patients of all religions, the leftists who believed in a shared Marxist vision, and the ways in which membership in British archaeological and cultural associations, where both Zionists and Arab nationalists met, shaped similar ideas in each movement as to authenticity and nativism.[24] Tamari's works, however, also chronicle the ways relationships between Jews, Muslims, and Christians deteriorated as the deadly conflict in Mandatory Palestine escalated.

Outside of Palestine, most notably in Iraq, Ottomanism, the *Tanzīmāt*, and the 1908 revolution profoundly impacted Jewish lives. The first to notice this trend was historian Elie Kedourie. Kedourie was no great admirer of Arab nationalism, to say the least, yet his Ottoman nostalgia pushed him to research Ottoman-Iraqi Jews who professed their loyalty to the Ottoman state and championed the creation of a nonsectarian education system.[25] Jonathan Sciarcon, who has argued that the failure of the 1908 revolution to meet their expectations pushed Jews toward the British, still underscored the hopes (rather than the realities) that the revolution generated. Sciarcon illustrated how the revolution convinced Baghdadi Jews that they could and should play an integral role in the Ottoman state. These new beliefs fit with ideas of civic equality and Westernization that had been circulating among these educated Jews since the arrival of the *Alliance Israélite Universelle* to Iraq in the 1860s. Jewish intellectuals, like many of the empire's Christians, looked to Ottomanism as their ticket to the twentieth century, which would place them on equal footing with their coreligionists in Western Europe.[26] More recently, Annie Leah Greene showed how Jews shared their enthusiasm for the 1908 revolution with Sunnis, Shiites, and Christians in Iraq, and how the revolution marks the shift into writing in Arabic and Turkish and the publishing of bilingual Arabic-Ottoman newspapers by Jews.[27] Mashriqi Jews, like their Muslim and Christian colleagues, came to be divided on the question of whether to support or oppose the revolutionary powers after 1908; the revolution also provoked tensions and conflicts between different religious communities. And yet the new scholarship has shown that without understanding the magnitude of the 1908 revolution, especially in Palestine and Baghdad, Sephardi and Mizrahi politics make very little sense.

The effects of the scholarship on the Mashriq and Egypt, however, go beyond the nostalgic celebration of Ottoman inclusiveness and Ottoman modernity. Studying the Ottoman imperial framework has also meant analyzing the ways in which religious and ethnic groups were marginalized, racialized, and disciplined within what Ussama Makdisi has termed "Ottoman Orientalism."[28] The Arab response to Ottoman Orientalism was not necessarily a linear process through which a full-fledged Arabic movement challenging the Ottoman state came into being. Nonetheless, as Rashid Khalidi has pointed out, in cities like Beirut, Damascus, and Jerusalem, new Arab public spheres, with their Arabic newspapers, societies, public events, and coffeehouses, began to take root.[29] The Arabic word *nahḍa*, usually translated as "renaissance" or "revival," came to signify the cultural elements of this process, that is, the Arabic literary and cultural renewal that occurred during the second half of the nineteenth and early years of the twentieth centuries.[30] Recent scholarship has argued that the *nahḍa* was not simply a precursor of Arab nationalism, but rather a new way of thinking about temporalities and spaces. Arab thinkers, moreover, did not merely adopt Western cultural and literary models imposed on them, but rather experimented, modified, and adjusted the idea of the European enlightenment to meet a whole range of local needs.[31]

The new scholarship has likewise identified the role of Jews within this renewed interest in Arabness and in Arab culture. Shaul Sehayek, in an outstanding study that inspired all the Anglophone scholars on the topic who followed him, has detailed the attentiveness of the pioneers of the Arab *nahḍa* to Jewish affairs and their public defense of the rights of

European Jews and published essays on Jewish history, both ancient and modern, and the Jewish faith.[32] Jewish intellectuals who wrote in Arabic were highly interested in this movement. Citing a wide range of examples, from Esther Moyal, a Sephardi Jewish journalist who published in Arabic and was mentioned by leading Muslim female writers, to Jewish rabbis in Baghdad and Jerusalem, Lital Levy demonstrates how the *nahḍa* transformed the Mashriqi Jewish sense of identity and how it framed their location in the modern world. While her focus on the category of the Arab Jew excluded various forms of identity, Ottomanism most notably, as well as local identities, Levy turns our attention to the ambiguities, tensions, and anxieties, as well as to the hopes and expectations, reflected in these texts and to the transregional networks in which they circulated.[33]

Historian Jonathan Gribetz continued this line of thinking by examining key intellectuals and their responses to Judaism, and the Jewish intellectuals who collaborated with them during this period. Focusing on the Palestinian context, he showed how the conflict should be situated within discussions about both race and religiosity.[34] In a study of translation and cultural transformation, he analyzed the translation of the Talmud into Arabic by the Jaffa-born Jewish writer Shim'on Moyal (born 1866); the Christian intellectual Jurjī Zaydān (1861–1914) initiated the project in order to dispel the slanderous rumors about the Talmud circulating among readers.[35] Gribetz's work was also influenced by studies on race and color within modern Arab thought, showing how racial discourses brought Jews and Arabs together. Studies, especially Eve Toutt Powell's works, examined how racial categories formed in Britain and France affected local debates and practices.[36] As C. Ernest Dawn and Nimrod Hurvitz have demonstrated, beginning in the late nineteenth century, and even more so in the interwar period, educated Arab elites were interested in Semitic cultures and Semitic linguistics.[37] These new theories, in turn, highlighted that a common Semitic origin, history, and culture linked the Jews with their Arab neighbors.[38]

Considering the involvement of Jews in the Arab *nahḍa*, the most daunting challenge for historians attempting to conceptualize the Jewish contribution to modern Arab thought is the career of one of Egypt's leading playwrights, satirists, and journalists, and a man deeply connected to the revival of its modern Arab culture, Ya'qūb Ṣannū' (1839–1912). An

Egyptian patriot, he supported pan-Islamic unity as a remedy for European colonialism and the corruption of the local Westernized elites. The focus on a Jew as a pan-Islamic thinker responds to new studies, which consider pan-Islamic movements in the Ottoman Empire as modern and anticolonial.[39] Ṣannūʿ's passionate support of this political option led many of his contemporaries to believe he was Muslim. How, then, are we to conceptualize his works? Lital Levy, as well as Zvi Ben Dor and Moshe Behar, locate him within the Middle Eastern Jewish canon.[40] Scholars of Egyptian history, on the other hand, place him and his work unequivocally in an Egyptian social and political context, pointing to his seminal role in gender history[41] and his contribution to an Egyptian public sphere that articulated the demands of a new Egyptian public in the colloquial, as Ziad Fahmy has brilliantly shown.[42] Such scholarship, moreover, pushes us to link his anticolonial and pan-Islamist activities to other Muslim and Christian intellectuals who shared his sociopolitical vision, like social thinker Faraḥ Anṭūn (1874–1922), a Christian intellectual who supported pan-Islamic political cooperation as an appropriate response to colonialism.[43]

Middle Eastern Jewish thought was conceptualized in a context where ideas about the need to reform Islamic practices, laws, and discourses in light of modern realities took shape. As shown by Beth Baron and Heather Sharkey, Jews, Copts, and Orthodox Christians were particularly ambivalent about Catholic and Protestant missionary education. While many Jewish students were eager participants in the education system of the *Alliance*, at places where such education was not available or too expensive, Jewish parents debated whether to send their sons and daughters to Christian missionary schools.[44] Furthermore, Middle Eastern rabbis responded to these difficult conditions with great openness, tolerance, and creativity. The scholars who have worked on modern Middle Eastern rabbinical literature came from the field of Jewish studies, and their training enabled them to read this literature in all its depth, while contextualizing it within Middle Eastern realities. Thus, the excellent studies of Yaron Harel have shed light on the manners in which nineteenth-century Ottoman politics affected rabbinical appointments and notions of leadership within the varied Jewish communities of the Mashriq.[45] The innovative study of Zvi Zohar has brought to the fore the great halachic creativity of Sephardi rabbis. While taking into account religious conservatism, Zohar pays indispensable heed to geniuses such as Rabbi 'Abdallah Somekh and his Baghdadi circle, the Syrian Rabbi Yitzhak Dayyan, and to questions relating to Arabic language and modern print discussed in Egypt. Zohar's discussions are rooted in his mastery of the halachic tradition with which his historical subjects grappled and through which they understood issues concerning the modern transportation system, technology, and communications. He demonstrated that many of these rabbis promoted the notion that there was no inherit contradiction between reason and revelation and between the Jewish faith and scientific and technological progress. Zohar's book has challenged Orientalist assumptions regarding Western superiority by insisting that the inventiveness typical of the Mashriqi and Egyptian traditions transformed modern Jewish thought. Most importantly, the study has pushed readers conversant in Middle Eastern history to draw parallels between these rabbis and Muslim reformers, 'ulamā,' and intellectuals like Jamāl al-Dīn al-Afghānī and Muḥammad 'Abduh (1849–1905), who dealt with similar questions and found similar solutions.[46]

Alongside these narratives of inclusion, however, other, negative, images of the Jews appeared in Arabic and Muslim public spheres. The toxic mixture of colonialism, missionary activities, and antisemitism originating from Europe encouraged the first blood libel in Damascus and the translation of antisemitic texts into Arabic.[47] The point of the new scholarship, however, is not to ignore these tensions, but rather to understand them as part of the new sociopolitical dynamics that shaped the sectarian realities of the nineteenth century. The halachic literature, which combined reason and revelation, new cultural practices like translation, writing in Arabic for Muslim and Christian publics, and ideologies like Egyptian patriotism, Ottomanism, and pan-Islamism, as well as migration, were all responses to these new conditions and situations.

The ability of minority groups to take part in, appropriate, and reproduce the discourses of imperial civic identity and the *nahḍa* reveal the open-ended, pluralistic, and heterogeneous nature of the *nahḍa* and the possibilities opened up during the eras of Ottoman reforms. And as pointed out by Annie Greene, Lital Levy, and myself, for Middle Eastern Jews, the *Haskalah* was not simply a Eurocentric venue through which they learned about European modernity, but rather a movement whose ideas made much sense to them because of the *nahḍa*.[48] Unlike both the postcolonial and the conservative schools, then, studies of nineteenth-century modernities, in their imperial, cultural, Arabized forms, enable us to see the many venues in which modernity manifested itself in the Middle East, and how each of these venues had immense influence on Jewish perceptions of self, other, homeland, and belonging.

Arab Nation-States, Producing Arab-Jewish Local Patriotism, and the Challenge of Zionism

Moving beyond the Ottoman period to the investigation of the lives of Jews in colonized and independent Arab states required scholars to think differently about Arab nationalism. The 1990s saw the emergence of a new interest in Arab nationalism that challenged the idea that Arab nation-states were artificial constructs created by British and French colonial interests and uniting diverse ethnic and religious groups that had little in common with one another. These "artificiality narratives" were challenged by the recognition, based on the work of social scientists like Anthony Smith, Ernest Gellner, Eric Hobsbawm, Miroslav Hroch, and Benedict Anderson, that most national narratives are products of the modern age and the minds of urban elites, and that artificiality, invention, and imagination are at the core of any national movement, both in Europe and in the Middle East. Israel Gershoni, a prominent historian of modern Egypt, has pointed out that alongside pan-Arab nationalism (*qawmiyya*), regional-patriotic (*waṭaniyya*) identities, such as Egyptian, Lebanese, and Iraqi forms of nationalism(s), came into being.[49] Thus, Jews had a wide array of national narratives to choose from; they could identify as Egyptian, Lebanese, or Iraqi patriots; they could highlight the Arab markers of their cultural identities (a processes that started already in the late nineteenth century); or they could emphasize more their identities as religious minorities within new nation-states. The Jewish-Zionist settlement project in Palestine, however, raised, in Arab circles, questions about their loyalties and complicated the ways in which they conceptualized Arabness, Jewish solidarity, and ideas about the homeland.

Many a Jewish intellectual emphasized the Arab features of their identity. In fact, the intellectual production of Jews in the Mashriq and Egypt is clear evidence that Jewish intellectuals adopted Arabic as their writing and speaking language. Some called themselves Arab Jews, while others did not; yet all were very much a part of the Arab culture of the interwar period. These Jews operated in the urban centers where Arab and local forms of nationalism were practiced and interpreted, namely, Cairo, Beirut, Damascus, Aleppo, and Baghdad. Many Jews benefited from the economies that emerged in the interwar period, working as lawyers, administrators, bureaucrats, and global merchants. These Jews very much supported the state, although other Jewish groups had different outlooks regarding authorities of the French and British Mandates. Writing in colonized and postcolonized states also compelled Jews to think about Jewish identity within the framework of the East-West binary and to define themselves as "Eastern." This trend began under the Ottoman Empire, but became more prevalent in the interwar period.[50]

Joel Beinin's important book on the Jews of Egypt suggested that ethnonational identities are historically and socially constructed. Beinin looked at Egypt, rather than the Land of Israel, as a center of Jewish life from which a Diaspora was generated. The community, to him, was a heterogeneous community of cosmopolitan hybrids and he saw this duality as both a strength of the community and one of the factors in its ultimate demise. Beinin outlined the ideological options Jews adopted at the time, such as Egyptian patriotism, nationalism, communism, and Zionism, and contextualized them within the socioeconomic, colonial, and anticolonial realities of modern Egypt. He showed how many Egyptian Jews identified as patriots and saw Egypt as a homeland and community whose past, present, and future related to theirs.[51]

The feelings of Jewish patriotism Beinin uncovered appealed to Jews in other Arab nation-states. Within the Iraqi context, both Reuven Snir and Aline Schlaepfer have analyzed the manners in which Jewish intellectuals offered a variety of Arab-Jewish visions. Both underlined the contribution of Jews to Iraqi journalism and literature during the years 1908 to 1951, as part of a broader Jewish involvement within the Iraqi public sphere.[52] Historian Aline Schlaepfer has shown in particular how these new literary and journalistic genres were used to articulate Jewish desires for political independence and social reform, desires that were voiced by other Iraqi patriots of various religions.[53]

Studying Iraq, both Schlaepfer and I have pointed to the fact that in the interwar period Arab national elites secularized the Islamic past. Thus, the Prophet himself, as well as the generals who conquered the Middle East during the period of the four righteous Caliphs, functioned as national and patriotic models with whom modern Arab patriots, including Jews and Christians, could, and should, identify. Their Arab-Jewish identity, however, was not a primordial identity forged since the days of *al-Andalus*, but rather a product of Arab-Iraqi nationalism. Moreover, the formation of political parties in Iraq during the mid-1940s and the activities of the illegal Iraqi Communist Party offered new ways for Jewish political participation. These new politics explain why the ideological response to a horrendous series of urban riots in the aftermath of a pro-German coup during which more than 170 Jews were killed in Baghdad (the *Farhūd*, June 1–2, 1941) was not only Zionism, but also social democracy and communism.[54]

The attraction of Jews to secular ideologies, the Left, and especially the communist movement in the Arab world has been studied in other contexts, especially by Joel Beinin and more recently by Rami Ginat. Ginat's work relies on meticulous archival work in several languages (including Russian), and studies various communist groups. Jews, he argues, assumed various roles in communist groups and defined, and debated, their position as Egyptian, radical, and Jewish activists.[55] Communism, in both Egypt and the Levant, was likewise a form of patriotism; it connected Jews, Sunnis, Shiites, and Christians (Armenians, Assyrians, and so on), who all worked together in trade unions, illegal and legal parties, and in cells, and who were willing to share their struggles. Communism, moreover, had a most crucial influence in Mandatory Palestine and later in the State of Israel. Challenging both Arab and Jewish nationalisms, communism offered another vision of a state and society for both Jews and Arabs, as it did in Iraq, Egypt, and Syria. Nonetheless, scholars, especially Zachary Lockman in a groundbreaking work, has underscored the potential for a shared, class-based struggle by both Palestinian Arabs and Jews, set against a Zionist ideology that saw the growth of an autonomous Jewish economy and an independent Jewish labor market as one of its chief national aims.[56] Furthermore, being the only legal non-Zionist party after the establishment of the State of Israel, the Israeli communist party emerged as the most important political and cultural organization for the Palestinians who remained in Israel and for Middle Eastern Jewish writers and activists. While this article is not about the history of Mashriqi and Egyptian Jews in Israel, it is essential to note that the new scholarship on communist Jews before their arrival in Israel has indicated that the choice of these Jewish intellectuals to side with communism in Israel was not merely the outcome of discrimination against non-European Jews in Israel. Rather, it related to a long and important history of Jewish radicalism in Arab countries.

Communism, however, competed with Zionism in both Palestine and the Arab world. The contribution of the new scholarship to how we think about Zionism and the anti-Zionist struggle in Arab countries is threefold. First, the new scholarship has highlighted the Jewish opposition to Zionism from a variety of Jewish elites based on religious, Arab national, local patriotic, and humanistic considerations. The reasons for objecting to Zionism in the Levant and Egypt were no different than the reasons that pushed interwar Jewry in the United States and Europe to resist Zionism. Religious Jews believed that only God should end the Jewish exile. Secularizing Jews, in the Middle East, Europe, and the United States, feared identifying with another national movement would curtail their integration efforts, make the majority community question their patriotism, and cement antisemitic notions about the inability of Jews to become loyal subjects and citizens. For this reason, communist Mashriqi Jews often used the very same arguments articulated by Bundists and other communist Jews in Europe. Nevertheless, the conflict in Palestine made this anti-Zionist position much more important to Mashriqi Jews (outside of Palestine) and Egyptian Jews, as the Palestinian issue became a Middle Eastern issue that occupied Muslim societies. As the public spheres in Damascus, Beirut, Baghdad, and Cairo showed their solidarity with the Palestinian people by organizing demonstrations in support of the Palestinians, writing op-eds and articles about the topic, and at times sending volunteers to help the Palestinians (especially during the Palestinian national revolution of 1936–1939), Jews felt that they had to react against Zionism, lest they pay the price for the actions of the European Jewish movement in Palestine in their Arab home countries. They had to insist on being loyal citizens to the countries in which they lived, and whose citizenships they shared with Muslims and Christians.[57]

Second, scholars have stressed the damage caused to Jews in Arab lands because of Zionist activities, like Operation Suzanna.[58] Postcolonial and post-Zionist scholars revisited state archives in order to learn how Zionist emissaries, bureaucrats working for the Jewish Agency, and Israeli politicians looked at Middle Eastern Jews, and examined the outcomes of these internal Jewish Orientalist discourses and practices on the process of migration. In the new scholarship, as in the postcolonial school, the process of migration has not been represented as an exodus from oppressive Muslim states, but rather as a political game in which *both* Arab ultranationalists and Zionists/Israelis came to identify every Jew as a Zionist, and where Jews paid the price for the recklessness and chauvinism of these two national movements.[59]

Finally, the new scholarship has recognized the existence of Zionist movements in the Arab world and discussed the meanings of Sephardi and Mizrahi Zionism within Palestine. Suffering from the identification between Judaism and Zionism, and critical of the national Arab elites who promoted this equation, Arab-Jewish Zionists suggested that Zionism would solve the ills that Middle Eastern Jews saw in their societies, such as the gaps between rich and poor and between men and women. After 1948, these Zionist movements became more radical and were willing to make bold moves in order to realize their goals. In Palestine, as the studies of Moshe Na'or, Abigail Jacobson, Michelle Campos, and Jonathan Gribetz have suggested, Sephardi Zionists were very different from their European brethren, whom they occasionally criticized for being arrogantly ignorant with respect to the Palestinian natives of the land.[60] While this position was very typical of Palestine, Jews in Syria, Lebanon, and Iraq also articulated it. This recognition, and the need to move beyond the binaries "settler colonialist Ashkenazi Zionist/Arab Jew," into debates about the complexities and inner contradictions in the world of Mizrahi Zionists, uncovered a whole world of Mizrahi Zionist thinkers, mediators, and writes, as shown in the works of Almog Behar, Yuval Evri, and Mostafa Hussein.[61] However, Hillel Cohen had pointed out that the violence of the Palestine national revolt of 1929, in which many Sephardi Jews were murdered by Palestinians, and where lynching and murders also typified the Jewish actions against the Palestinians, severely curtailed this vision.[62]

Scholars, especially ones coming from neo-conservative circles, linked the failure of the interwar Arab-Jewish project and the rise of Zionism in Arab states to the turn of radical Muslim and Arab elites to Nazism and Fascism. Whereas some scholars saw the attraction of certain Arab elites to Germany and Italy as an anti-British and anti-French strategy, neo-conservative scholars, using the pro-Fascist activities of individuals like the Palestinian grand mufti Amīn al-Ḥusaynī, Antūn Saʿadā in Lebanon, and Sāmī Shakwat in Iraq, linked medieval anti-Jewish sentiments to modern antisemitism within modern Arab and Muslim contexts.[63] Here is the late prominent scholar of Arabic literature, Shmuel Moreh, writing on the *Farhūd* as a manifestation of a primordial sectarian conflict:

> Muslims found many similarities between Nazi doctrine and Islamic military power: the rise of Islam as a doctrine which united all the Arab tribes, by a charismatic leader, which must be spread by the sword, protects its followers against hellfire... The Nazi doctrine advocated force, racism and superiority of the Aryan race and favored Germany and hatred of Jews.... Sunni Palestinians took over the school system and replaced Iraqi Shiites. The predominance of Jews in commerce and in the new state as directors of financial departments of all Iraqi ministries, bookkeepers and financial policymakers' advisers to the British in the running of Iraq's economy, aroused the envy and hatred of the people.... The Palestinians, headed by the Mufti of Jerusalem, Haj Amin al-Husseini [sic], were given a free hand.[64]

However, as Israel Gershoni, James Jankowski, Peter Wien, Götz Nordbruch, and Gilbert Achcar have illustrated, many prominent Arab and Muslim intellectuals and politicians challenged their peers who espoused Fascist views. Pro-British and pro-French political elites, liberals, and communists, as well as religious writers, rejected these antidemocratic ideologies. The occupation of Ethiopia by Italy indicated to them a severe colonial danger to the region. Muslim writers argued that any ideology that privileges one race and deifies its leader was antithetical to Islam. Based on their readings of publications from the public spheres of Damascus, Beirut, and Baghdad, these scholars provide ample examples from both the print culture and the colonial archive about resistance to Fascism and Nazism.[65] Significantly, these scholars explain *why* certain historians argued that the persecution of Jews in Arab lands was motivated by Nazi ideologies. In a brave essay, historians Ulrike Freitag and Israel Gershoni have thus proposed:

> The recent emergence of Islamicist global jihadism, particularly after the tragedy of 11 September 2001, gave birth to pseudo-academic studies that were heavily charged politically. These studies sought to establish an uninterrupted continuity between the present phenomenon of global terrorist jihadism and the Nazism and Fascism of the 1930s. The intention, though not always explicit, is to further demonize contemporary Islamism by anchoring it in the annals of National Socialism and its atrocities.[66]

Freitag and Gershoni went on to note that certain historical narratives, like a Zionist historiography that sought to represent Palestinian resistance as antisemitic or secular national elites who sought to discredit Islamism, constructed a historiography that spoke about Islamic Fascism and antisemitism, although this historiography did not address many of the actions, and publications, of intellectuals and politicians at the time.

The Middle East in the interwar period, moreover, was not only torn between rival political visions and different sets of colonizers, real and potential. Its Arab cultures continued to flourish. Studying Jewish contributions to Arab culture and Arabic thought and literature in the Mashriq and Egypt during the interwar period and the 1940s brought to the fore discussions about the relationships of their works to the Arabic literary canon. Scholars who studied Jewish intellectual production explored Jewish works that were in dialogue with the Arab intellectual and literary canon and texts that challenged the meaning of the canon altogether (like the transregional rabbinic writings that, while meant for Jewish consumption and written in Hebrew and Judeo-Arabic, reflect ideas current in circles associated with Islamic reform). Acknowledging this diversity, Moshe Behar and Zvi Ben Dor have published an exciting anthology, which, for the first time, looks at Jews from the Mashriq and Egypt as intellectuals, social critics, and political theorists, and not simply as chroniclers of the sociopolitical changes occurring in their societies.[67] Sasson Somekh and Deborah Starr have likewise dedicated much space to translating and commenting on the writings of Jacqueline Kahanoff (1917–1979), whose works also appeared in Behar and Ben-Dor's anthology. In particular, they show how Kahanoff, a literary critic, novelist, and theoretician who was born in Cairo, turned the word "Levantine," which to Israeli thinking signified the debased culture of the Orient, into a marker of the hybrid and pluralistic spaces typical of the Middle Eastern cultures she knew in Cairo.[68]

The renewed interest in Kahanoff, a woman writing about the Levant for Israeli and American audiences, reflects, in a way, this new scholarship's desire to reconstruct the lives of Jews in Arab societies as detached from Israeli historiography, with all its assumptions about the Levant, Arabs, and Muslims. At the same time, historical processes in the Arab world, especially the Arab-Israeli conflict, meant that these rich relationships, although very meaningful in the present, belonged to a different era, whose partial reconstruction can never quite fully capture its richness and its long and varied trajectories. More broadly, the studies of Middle Eastern Jewish communities showed different Jewish engagements with the nation, as local patriots, Arab Jews, and communists; the latter, while being critical of nationalism, evoked communism to highlight their participation in patriotic struggles for social justice. Finally, Zionism was not simply a foreign movement imported from Europe and Palestine, as the postcolonial school would have it, or a natural response to Arab Fascism, as the conservatives have argued. Rather it was a local option, one among many, that appealed to Jews, especially as Arab national elites let them down and as the conflict in Palestine seemed to have determined the lot of Jews outside it.

To conclude, the new histories of modern Mashriqi and Egyptian Jewry emerged as a response to historiographies that challenged national narratives and their sectarian notions. Moving beyond a conservative and postcolonial position that has tended to depict a Middle East in which modern subjects—Jewish, Muslim, and Christian—lived in a sphere essentially different than Europe, new studies have unpacked the ways in which these Jewish subjects lived in a globalized world. Moving from British and French Empires to an Ottoman one, and from one nation-state (Israel) to many nation-states, this scholarship has stressed that the modern era changed the ways in which these Jews thought about themselves, their relationships with the state in imperial and national forms, and their connections with Christians and Muslims.

NOTES

1. For a much shorter version of this argument, see Orit Bashkin, "Introduction to a Roundtable: Jewish Identities in the Middle East, 1876–1956: The Middle Eastern Shift and Provincializing Zionism," *International Journal of Middle East Studies* 46 (2014): 577–80.

2. Bernard Lewis, *The Jews of Islam* (Princeton, NJ: Princeton University Press, 1984), 154–93. A popular representation of the myth of persecution is Bat Ye'or's *Juifs et chrétiens sous l'Islam: Les dhimmis face au défi intégriste* (Paris: Berg International, 1994); see also Robert S. Wistrich, *Anti-Zionism and Antisemitism in the Contemporary World* (New York: New York University Press, 1990). Sylvia Haim acknowledged that Arab Muslim intellectuals showed great sympathy to the plight of the Jews, but maintained that Arab Christians were involved in the translation and propagation of antisemitic literature; see Sylvia G. Haim, "Arabic Antisemitic Literature: Some Preliminary Notes," *Jewish Social Studies* 17 (1955): 307–12.

3. Raphael Israeli, "The New Muslim Anti-Semitism: Exploring Novel Avenues of Hatred," *Jewish Political Studies Review* 17 (2005), https://jcpa.org/article/the-new-muslim-anti-semitism-exploring-novel-avenues-of-hatred.

4. Joel Beinin, *The Dispersion of Egyptian Jewry: Culture, Politics, and the Formation of a Modern Diaspora* (Berkeley: University of California Press, 1998), 1–30.

5. Norman A. Stillman, *The Language and Culture of the Jews of Sefrou* (Manchester: University of Manchester Press, 1987); Aron Rodrigue and Sarah Abrevaya Stein, eds., *A Jewish Voice from Ottoman Salonica: The Ladino Memoir of Sa'adi Besalel a-Levi* (Stanford, CA: Stanford University Press, 2012); Aron Rodrigue, *Jews and Muslims: Images of Sephardi and Eastern Jewries in Modern Times* (Seattle: University of Washington Press, 2003); Aron Rodrigue and Esther Benbassa, *Sephardi Jewry: A History of the Judeo-Spanish Community, 14th–20th Centuries* (Berkeley: University of California Press, 2000); Aron Rodrigue and Esther Benbassa, eds., *A Sephardi Life in Southeastern Europe: The Autobiography and Journal of Gabriel Arié* (Seattle: University of Washington Press, 1998); Aron Rodrigue, ed., *Ottoman and Turkish Jewry: Community and Leadership* (Bloomington: Indiana University Press, 1992); Aron Rodrigue, *French Jews, Turkish Jews: The Alliance Israélite Universelle and the Politics of Jewish Schooling in Turkey, 1860–1925* (Bloomington: Indiana University Press, 1990).

6. Ella Shohat, "Sephardim in Israel: Zionism from the Standpoint of Its Jewish Victims," *Social Text* 19 (1988): 1–35.

7. Ella Shohat, *Taboo Memories, Diasporic Voices* (Durham, NC: Duke University Press, 2006); Ella Shohat, "The Invention of the Mizrahim," *Journal of Palestine Studies* 29

(1999): 5–20; Ella Habiba Shohat, *On the Arab Jew, Palestine, and Other Displacement: Selected Writings* (London: Pluto Press, 2017); see also Sami Shalom Chetrit, *Intra-Jewish Conflict in Israel: White Jews, Black Jews* (London: Routledge, 2010).

8. Yehouda Shenhav, *The Arab Jews: A Postcolonial Reading of Nationalism, Religion, and Ethnicity* (Stanford, CA: Stanford University Press, 2006).

9. Adriana Kemp, "Talking Borders: The Construction of a Poilitical Territory in Israel, 1949–1957" (PhD diss., Tel Aviv University, 1997) [Hebrew]; Hannan Hever, Yehouda Shenhav, and Pnina Motzafi-Haller, eds., *Mizrachim in Israel: A Critical Observation into Israel's Ethnicity* (Jerusalem: Van Leer/Tel Aviv: Ha-Kibbutz ha-me'uhad, 2002) [Hebrew]; Oren Yiftachel and Avinoam Meir, *Ethnic Frontiers and Peripheries: Landscapes of Development and Inequality in Israel* (Boulder, CO: Westview Press, 1998); As'ad Ghanem, *Ethnic Politics in Israel: The Margins and the Ashkenazi Center* (London: Routledge, 2010); Aziza Khazzoom, *Shifting Ethnic Boundaries and Inequality in Israel: Or, How the Polish Peddler Became a German Intellectual* (Stanford, CA: Stanford University Press, 2008).

10. Ammiel Alcalay, *After Jews and Arabs: Remaking Levantine Culture* (Minneapolis: University of Minnesota Press, 1993); see also Gil Anidjar, *Our Place in al-Andalus: Kabbalah, Philosophy, Literature in Arab Jewish Letters* (Stanford, CA: Stanford University Press, 2002).

11. Lital Levy, "Historicizing the Concept of Arab Jews in the Mashriq," *Jewish Quarterly Review* 98 (2008): 452–69.

12. Annie Leah Greene, "Provincial, Not Peripheral: Ottoman-Iraqi Intellectuals and Cultural Networks, 1863–1914" (PhD diss., University of Chicago, 2018); Hasan Kayali, *Arabs and Young Turks: Ottomanism, Arabism, and Islamism in the Ottoman Empire, 1908–1918* (Berkeley: University of California Press, 1997); Michael Provence, *The Last Ottoman Generation and the Making of the Modern Middle East* (Cambridge, UK: Cambridge University Press, 2017).

13. Ussama Samir Makdisi, *Age of Coexistence: The Ecumenical Frame and the Making of the Modern Arab World* (Oakland: University of California Press, 2019).

14. Ussama Makdisi, *The Culture of Sectarianism: Community, History, and Violence in Nineteenth-Century Ottoman Lebanon* (Berkeley: University of California Press, 2000).

15. Julia Phillips Cohen, *Becoming Ottomans: Sephardi Jews and Imperial Citizenship in the Modern Era* (Oxford: Oxford University Press, 2014); Julia Phillips Cohen and Sarah Abrevaya Stein, *Sephardi Lives: A Documentary History, 1700–1950* (Stanford, CA: Stanford University Press, 2014); Lital Levy, "Jewish Writers in the Arab East: Literature, History, and the Politics of Enlightenment, 1863–1914" (PhD diss., University of California, Berkeley, 2007); Rodrigue and Stein, *A Jewish Voice*; Rodrigue, *French Jews*. See also Annie Greene's discussion of the activation of the Jewish press in Ottoman Iraq in Annie Greene, "Burying a Rabbi in Baghdad: The Limits of Ottomanism for Ottoman-Iraqi Jews in the Late Nineteenth Century," *Journal of Jewish Identities* 12 (2019): 97–123.

16. Bruce Masters, *Christians and Jews in the Ottoman Arab World: The Roots of Sectarianism* (Cambridge, UK: Cambridge University Press, 2001).

17. Beinin, *The Dispersion of Egyptian Jewry*.

18. Yaron Harel, "The First Jews from Aleppo in Manchester: New Documentary Evidence," *AJS Review* 23 (1998): 191–202; see also his *Syrian Jewry in Transition, 1840–1880* (Oxford: Littman Library of Jewish Civilization, 2010).

19. Joel Beinin and Zachary Lockman, *Workers on the Nile: Nationalism, Communism, Islam, and the Egyptian Working Class, 1882–1954* (Princeton, NJ: Princeton University Press, 1987).

20. Ilham Khuri-Makdisi, *The Eastern Mediterranean and the Making of Global Radicalism, 1860–1914* (Berkeley: University of California Press, 2010).

21. Michelle U. Campos, *Ottoman Brothers: Muslims, Christians, and Jews in Early Twentieth-Century Palestine* (Stanford, CA: Stanford University Press, 2011).

22. Abigail Jacobson, *From Empire to Empire: Jerusalem between Ottoman and British Rule* (Syracuse, NY: Syracuse University Press, 2011).

23. Salim Tamari, "Ishaq al-Shami and the Predicament of the Arab Jew in Palestine," https://www.palestine-studies.org/en/node/77952; Hannan Hever, "Yitzhak Shami: Ethnicity as an Unresolved Conflict," *Shofar* 24, no. 2 (2006): 124–39.

24. Salim Tamari, *Mountain against the Sea: Essays on Palestinian Society and Culture* (Berkeley: University of California Press, 2009).

25. Elie Kedourie, "The Jews of Baghdad in 1910," *Middle Eastern Studies* 7 (1971): 355–61.

26. Jonathan Sciarcon, "Unfulfilled Promises: Ottomanism, the 1908 Revolution and Baghdadi Jews," *International Journal of Contemporary Iraqi Studies* 3 (2009): 155–68.

27. Green, "Provincial, Not Peripheral."

28. Ussama Makdisi, "Ottoman Orientalism," *The American Historical Review* 107 (2002): 768–96.

29. Rashid Khalidi, "Arab Nationalism: Historical Problems in the Literature," *The American Historical Review* 96 (1991): 1363–73.

30. Albert Hourani, *Arabic Thought in the Liberal Age* (London: Oxford University Press, 1962).

31. Khuri-Makdisi, *The Eastern Mediterranean*; Marilyn Booth, *May Her Likes Be Multiplied: Biography and Gender Politics in Egypt* (Berkeley: University of California Press, 2001); Tarek El-Ariss, *Trials of Arab Modernity* (New York: Fordham University Press, 2013); Jens Hanssen and Max Weiss, eds., *Arabic Thought beyond the Liberal Age: Towards an Intellectual History of the Nahda* (Cambridge, UK: Cambridge University Press, 2016); Peter Hill, *Utopia and Civilisation in the Arab Nahda* (Cambridge, UK: Cambridge University Press, 2020).

32. Sha'ul Sehayyek, "The Figure of the Jew in the Arab Press in the Years 1858–1908" (PhD diss., Hebrew University Jerusalem, 1991) [Hebrew].

33. Levy, "Jewish Writers in the Arab East." On Jews and the nahḍa, see also: Orit Bashkin, s.v., "Arab Jews: History, Memory, and Literary Identities in the Nahḍah," *Oxford Research Encyclopedia of Literature*.

34. Jonathan Marc Gribetz, *Defining Neighbors: Religion, Race, and the Early Zionist-Arab Encounter* (Princeton, NJ: Princeton University Press, 2014).

35. Jonathan Marc Gribetz, "An Arabic-Zionist Talmud: Shimon Moyal's At-Talmud," *Jewish Social Studies* 17 (2010): 1–30.

36. Eve M. Troutt Powell, *A Different Shade of Colonialism: Egypt, Great Britain, and the Mastery of the Sudan* (Berkeley: University of California Press, 2003).

37. Ernest C. Dawn, "The Formation of Pan-Arab Ideology in the Inter-War Years," *International Journal of Middle East Studies* 20 (1988): 67–91; Nimrod Hurvitz, "Muhibb al-Din al-Khatib's Semitic Wave Theory and Pan Arabism," *Middle Eastern Studies* 29 (1993): 118–34; Orit Bashkin, "The Arab Revival, Archaeology, and the Ancient Middle Eastern History," in *Pioneers to the Past: American Archaeologists in the Middle East, 1919–1920*, ed. Geoff Emberling (Chicago: The Oriental Institute Museum Publications, 2010), 91–101. See also Orit Bashkin, "On Noble and Inherited Virtues: Discussions of the Semitic Race in the Levant and Egypt, 1876–1918," *Humanities* 10 (2021), https://doi.org/10.3390/h10030088. On the Semitic discourse in the interwar period, see Yoni Furas, "We the Semites: Reading Ancient History in Mandate Palestine," *Contemporary Levant* 5 (2020): 33–43.

38. Jonathan Marc Gribetz, "'Their Blood Is Eastern': Shahin Makaryus and Fin de Siècle Arab Pride in the Jewish 'Race,'" *Middle Eastern Studies* 49 (2013): 143–61.

39. Cemil Aydın, *The Politics of Anti-Westernism in Asia: Visions of World Order in Pan-Islamic and Pan-Asian Thought* (New York: Columbia University Press, 2007).

40. Levy, "Jewish Writers in the Arab East"; Moshe Behar and Zvi Ben-Dor Benite, eds., *Modern Middle Eastern Jewish Thought: Writing on Identity, Politics and Culture, 1893–1958* (Waltham, MA: Brandies University Press, 2013).

41. Beth Baron, "Nationalist Iconography: Egypt as a Woman," in *Rethinking Nationalism in the Arab Middle East*, ed. James Jankowski and Israel Gershoni (New York: Columbia University Press, 1997), 105–24.

42. Ziad Fahmy, *Ordinary Egyptians: Creating the Modern Nation through Popular Culture* (Stanford, CA: Stanford University Press, 2011).

43. Orit Bashkin, "My Sister Esther: Reflections on Judaism, Ottomanism, and the Empire of Egypt in the Works of Farah Antun," in *The Long 1890s in Egypt: Colonial Quiescence, Subterranean Resistance*, ed. Marilyn Booth and Anthony Gorman (Edinburgh: Edinburgh University Press, 2014), 315–41.

44. Beth Baron, *The Orphan Scandal: Christian Missionaries and the Rise of the Muslim Brotherhood* (Stanford, CA: Stanford University Press, 2014); Heather J. Sharkey, *American Evangelicals in Egypt: Missionary Encounters in an Age of Empire* (Princeton, NJ: Princeton University Press, 2008); Mehmet Ali Doğan and Heather J. Sharkey, eds., *American Missionaries and the Middle East: Foundational Encounters* (Salt Lake City: University of Utah Press, 2011).

45. Harel, *Syrian Jewry in Transition*.

46. Ibid.; Zvi Zohar, *Rabbinic Creativity in the Modern Middle East* (New York: Bloomsbury Publishing, 2013). Menashe Anzi has made similar claims about Yemen in this context; see Menashe Anzi, "From Biblical Criticism to Criticism of the Kabbalah: Colonialism and Interreligious Interactions in the Indian Ocean and Yemen," *Journal of Levantine Studies* 10 (2020): 91–110

47. Jonathan Frankel, *The Damascus Affair: "Ritual Murder," Politics, and the Jews in 1840* (Cambridge, UK: Cambridge University Press, 1997); Ronald Florence, *Blood Libel: The Damascus Affair of 1840* (Madison: University of Wisconsin Press, 2004).

48. Levy, "Historicizing the Concept of Arab Jews"; Green, "Provincial, Not Peripheral"; Orit Bashkin, "Why Did Baghdadi Jews Stop Writing to Their Brethren in Mainz? Some Comments about the Reading Practices of Iraqi Jews in the 19th Century," *Journal of Semitic Studies* 15 (2004): 95–111.

49. Israel Gershoni, "Rethinking the Formation of Arab Nationalism in the Middle East, 1920–1945: Old and New Narratives," in Jankowski and Gershoni, *Rethinking Nationalism*, 3–25. On the historiography of Arab nationalism, see Khalidi, "Arab Nationalism: Historical Problems"; see also the discussion among Fred Halliday, Fred H. Lawson, James L. Gelvin, and Youssef M. Choueiri in a special roundtable on Arab nationalism, *International Journal of Middle East Studies* 41 (2009): 10–21.

50. Orit Bashkin, *New Babylonians: A History of Jews in Modern Iraq* (Stanford, CA: Stanford University Press, 2012), 1–21.

51. Beinin, *The Dispersion of Egyptian Jewry*.

52. Reuven Snir, *Arab-Jewish Literature: The Birth and Demise of the Arabic Short Story* (Leiden: Brill, 2019).

53. Aline Schlaepfer, "Between Cultural and National Nahda: Jewish Intellectuals in Baghdad and the Nation-Building Process in Iraq (1921–1932)," *Journal of Levantine Studies* 1 (2011): 59–74; Aline Schlaepfer, *Les intellectuels juifs de Bagdad. Discours et allégeances (1908–1951)* (Leiden: Brill 2016).

54. Schlaepfer, *Les intellectuals juifs*; Bashkin, *New Babylonians*.

55. Rami Ginat, *A History of Egyptian Communism: Jews and Their Compatriots in Quest of Revolution* (Boulder, CO: Lynne Rienner, 2011). See also Masha Kirasirova, "An Egyptian Communist Family Romance: Revolution and Gender in the Transnational Life of Charlotte Rosenthal," in *The Wider Arc of Revolution, Part 1*, ed. Choi Chatterjee, Steven G. Marks, Mary Neuburger, and Steven Sabol (Bloomington, IN: Slavica Publishers, 2019), 309–36. On Jewish-Iraqi communism, see Bashkin, *New Babylonians*, 141–82.

56. Zachary Lockman, *Comrades and Enemies: Arab and Jewish Workers in Palestine, 1906–1948* (Berkeley: University of California Press, 1996).

57. Esther Meir-Glitzenstein, *Zionism in an Arab Country: Jews in Iraq in the 1940s* (London: Routledge, 2004), 10–64; Bashkin, *New Babylonians*, 183–229; Beinin, *The Dispersion of Egyptian Jewry*, 60–90.

58. Beinin, *Dispersion of Egyptian Jewry*, 90–121.

59. Yehouda Shenhav, "The Jews of Iraq, Zionist Ideology, and the Property of the Palestinian Refugees of 1948: An Anomaly of National Accounting," *International Journal of Middle East Studies* 31 (1999): 605–30; Bashkin, *New Babylonians*, 182–228; Abbas Shiblak, *The Lure of Zion: The Case of Iraqi Jews* (London: al-Saqi Books, 1986), 67–71, 103–27.

60. Abigail Jacobson and Moshe Naor, *Oriental Neighbors: Middle Eastern Jews and Arabs in Mandatory Palestine* (Waltham, MA: Brandeis University Press, 2017); Campos, *Ottoman Brothers*; Jacobson, *From Empire to Empire*; Gribetz, *Defining Neighbors*; Menachem Klein, "Arab Jew in Palestine," *Israel Studies* 19 (2014): 134–53.

61. Mostafa Hussein, "Intertwined Landscape: The Integration of Arabo-Islamic Culture in Pre-State Palestine," *Israel Studies Review* 33 (2018): 51–65; Mostafa Hussein, "The Integration of Arabo-Islamic Culture into the Emergent Hebrew Culture in Late

Ottoman Palestine," *Jewish Quarterly Review* 109 (2019): 464–69; Almog Behar and Yuval Evri, "From Saadia to Yahuda: Reviving Arab Jewish Intellectual Models in a Time of Partitions," *Jewish Quarterly Review* 109 (2019): 458–63; Allyson Gonzalez, "Abraham S. Yahuda (1877–1951) and the Politics of Modern Jewish Scholarship," *Jewish Quarterly Review* 109 (2019): 406–33; Michal Rose Friedman, "Orientalism between Empires: Abraham Shalom Yahuda at the Intersection of Sepharad, Zionism, and Imperialism," *Jewish Quarterly Review* 109 (2019): 435–45.

62. Hillel Cohen, *Year Zero of the Arab-Israeli Conflict 1929* (Waltham, MA: Brandeis University Press, 2015).

63. Stefan Wild, "National Socialism in the Arab Near East between 1933 and 1939," *Die Welt Des Islams* 1 (1985): 126–73; Reeva Simon, *Iraq between Two World Wars: The Creation and Implementation of a Nationalist Ideology* (New York: Columbia University Press, 1986). For a critique of these narratives, see Peter Wien, "Coming to Terms with the Past: German Academia and Historical Relations between the Arab Lands and Nazi Germany," *International Journal of Middle East Studies* 42 (2010): 311–21; Götz Nordbruch, "'Cultural Fusion' of Thought and Ambitions? Memory, Politics and the History of Arab–Nazi German Encounters," *Middle Eastern Studies* 47 (2011): 183–94; Joel Beinin [book review], "*Nazi Propaganda for the Arab World* by Jeffrey Herf; *From Empathy to Denial: Arab Responses to the Holocaust* by Meir Litvak and Esther Webman," *International Journal of Middle East Studies* 42 (2010): 689–92.

64. Shmeul Moreh, "At Shavuot We Remember the Farhud," http://jewishrefugees.blogspot.co.il/2012/05/at-shavuot-we-remember-farhud.html.

65. Israel Gershoni and James Jankowski, *Confronting Fascism in Egypt: Dictatorship versus Democracy in the 1930s* (Stanford, CA: Stanford University Press, 2009); Götz Nordbruch, *Nazism in Syria and Lebanon: The Ambivalence of the German Option, 1933–1945* (London: Routledge, 2009); Gilbert Achcar, *The Arabs and the Holocaust: The Arab-Israeli War of Narratives* (New York: Metropolitan Books, 2010); Peter Wien, *Iraqi Arab Nationalism: Authoritarian, Totalitarian and Profascist Inclinations, 1932–1941* (London: Routledge, 2006); Peter Wien, "Arabs and Fascism: Empirical and Theoretical Perspectives," *Die Welt Des Islams* 52 (2012): 331–50; Israel Gershoni, ed., *Arab Responses to Fascism and Nazism* (Austin: Texas University Press, 2014).

66. Ulrike Freitag and Israel Gershoni, "The Politics of Memory: The Necessity for Historical Investigation into Arab Responses to Fascism and Nazism," *Geschichte und Gesellschaft* 37 (2011): 311–31, here 312.

67. Behar and Ben-Dor Benite, *Modern Middle Eastern Jewish Thought*.

68. Sasson Somekh and Deborah Starr, eds., *Mongrels or Marvels: The Levantine Writings of Jacqueline Shohet Kahanoff* (Stanford, CA: Stanford University Press, 2011).

10

Between Monumentalism and Miniaturization

Israel's Settlement Project and the Question of Third World Colonialism

JOHANNES BECKE

Israel's military occupation and colonization of vast territories captured in the Six-Day War (the Gaza Strip, the West Bank, the Sinai Peninsula, and the Golan Heights) continues to mark a watershed in the political and scholarly perception of the Zionist project: Pre-1967 Israel had almost been invited to the Bandung Conference, but post-1967 Israel would systematically be excluded from the thought, practice, and theory of postcolonialism.[1] Israeli expansionism in the occupied territories seemed to confirm that Zionism should indeed be read through the lens of settler colonialism, as Marxist anti-Zionists had always argued.[2] Ever since, comparative studies of Israel's occupation regime have privileged the comparison with classic forms of European settler colonialism, if not even South African apartheid.[3]

In contrast, as part of an emerging research agenda that reintegrates Israel into the context of postcolonial state formation, this chapter argues that Israel's settlement project followed a broader pattern of expansionism that was typical throughout the process of decolonization.[4] Similar to the Israeli case, core members of the Non-Aligned Movement actively pursued irredentist ideologies, captured contested territories, and engaged in large-scale projects of demographic engineering—whether in Tibet, East Timor, or Western Sahara. Awet Tewelde Weldemichael has described this paradox of expansionism in postcolonial times as "Third World colonialism," "no less colonial and ... no less imperially grandiose than Europe's [policies]."[5]

In order to integrate the exploration of Israel's settlement project into the study of "Third World colonialism," the chapter proceeds as follows: First, the chapter briefly sketches how the study of Israeli state-building was disconnected from the broader analysis of postcolonial state formation, whether through a process of culturalist othering (Occidentalization) or through a deliberate project of self-Westernization (and perhaps self-whitening).[6] Second, it describes the shared features of expansionist projects carried out by postcolonial states, including irredentist ideologies, patterns of coercive rule (frequently in defiance of international law), and demographic engineering.[7] Third, the chapter links the phenomenon of "Third World colonialism" to James Scott's influential diagnosis of "authoritarian high-modernist schemes" in Eastern Europe and the developing world: For expansionist states likes Morocco, Indonesia, and Israel, the deployment of massive state resources in captured territories fits into a broader pattern of monumentalist state projects, shaped by high modernism, authoritarian state power, and a cult of feasibility.[8] Fourth, it locates the distinctive feature of Israel's settlement project in its fusion of political monumentalism and architectural miniaturization: In sharp contrast to Indonesia, Morocco, or China, Israel was unable to engage in a process of full-scale territorial incorporation of the occupied territories. Consequently, the settlement project could be interpreted as a tacit admission of political failure, as "a retreat to the realm of appearances and miniatures—to model cities and Potemkin villages, as it were."[9] The conclusion argues that comparative scholars of Israeli expansionism could learn from the study of "Third World colonialism" by exploring the processes of Moroccanization, Sinicization, or Indonesianization as alternative pathways (or "the roads not taken") of the Israeli case. At the same time, scholars of "secondary colonialism" (whether in Morocco, Indonesia, or China) might fruitfully explore the very ambivalence at the heart of Zionism and apply it to their own cases: Derek Penslar defines the Zionist project as "historically and conceptually situated between colonial, anticolonial, and postcolonial discourse and practice."[10] If we apply this analytical matrix to Israeli, Moroccan, or Indonesian expansionism, we might learn that "Third World colonialism" in the West Bank, Western Sahara, and West Papua consists of a distinctive blend of a decidedly *colonial* projection of power and population, an *anticolonial* obsession with redeeming usurped ancestral homelands, and the *postcolonial* monumentalism inherited from high modernism.

Studying Israel as a Postcolonial State

When Indonesia, China, Morocco, and Israel adopted wide-ranging policies of territorial expansionism and demographic engineering amid the process of decolonization, nationalist movements in the newly conquered territories of East Timor, West Papua, Tibet, Xinjiang, Western Sahara, or the West Bank almost immediately described their insurgencies as a rebellion against neo-colonialism, secondary colonialism, or Third World colonialism: Maronite intellectuals described the Syrian occupation of Lebanon as merely the latest stage of a "constant struggle against foreign occupiers" since the days of the Phoenicians.[11] Facing the Moroccan-Mauritanian invasion after the departure of the Spanish army, Sahrawi nationalists assailed the "colonialism of the 'brotherly' neighbors" that had come to replace the "colonialism of the foreign enemy."[12] Not to be outdone, the Palestinian National Covenant from 1968 described the Zionist movement as "racist and fanatic in its nature, aggressive, expansionist and colonial in its aims and fascist in its methods."[13] Ever since, scholars of postcolonial state formation tend to wring their hands over the question of how to deal with the eerie parallels between European colonialism and the postindependence expansionism of newly decolonized countries, with Robert Young opting for the careful label of "comparable, but somewhat different."[14] Instead, Weldemichael has argued forcefully for the category of "Third World colonialism," based on his comparison of Indonesian and Ethiopian expansionism. Weldemichael defines Third World colonialism as a form of secondary or derivative colonialism, based on the imposition of administrative structures, languages, and rituals; the cooptation of loyalist subjects as a form of (secondary) colonial mimicry; and the libidinal economy of demographic engineering. Of course, the label of "Third World colonialism" might not be entirely unproblematic: The analytical framework adopts a historically, culturally, and legally specific framework of foreign domination to analyze a process in a different time period, with a different cultural disposition and a different legal framework, thereby sometimes blurring the distinction between colonization (in the sense of demographic engineering) and colonialism (as a world system of racialized dispossession and oppression).[15] Nonetheless, as Weldemichael's study shows, much can be learned from colonial attempts at "right-sizing and right-peopling the State"[16] for our understanding of postcolonial state expansions, especially in terms of countermobilization: The formation of a nationalist Sahrawi consciousness, for instance, would have been impossible without its framing as an *indigenous* claim to national self-determination, struggling against Spanish and Moroccan colonialism alike.

Weldemichael's argument might be especially crucial as an intervention against the ongoing framing of Moroccan, Indonesian, or Chinese expansionism as idiosyncratic aberrations from the norms and values of a postcolonial world: Since the "Green March" in 1975, Morocco has deployed its entire military, economic, and propagandistic machinery to claim, capture, and colonize Western Sahara—but no self-respecting scholar of the modern Maghreb would seriously question Morocco's categorization as a postcolonial state. The same cannot be said for the Israeli case, where attempts to explore Israel as a postcolonial state tend to be met with high levels of resistance, if not outright derision.[17] After decolonization, nationalist insurgencies from Western Sahara to South Tyrol have claimed the mantle of anticolonialism,[18] but only the Palestinian national movement has succeeded in mobilizing a broad response of "transcolonial identification," defined by Olivia C. Harrison as "processes of identification that are rooted in a common colonial genealogy and a shared perception of (neo)colonial subjection."[19]

This attempt to disconnect the study of postcolonial state formation and the study of Israeli society can be traced back to two interrelated processes: First, ever since the days of Ben Gurion who argued *against* an understanding of Israel as a Middle Eastern society, the state-founding elites of the Zionist project have engaged in a project of systematic self-modernization and self-Westernization.[20] Second, this project of self-Europeanization as an imaginary "villa in the jungle"[21] was matched by an increasing Occidentalization of the Zionist project: While Ashkenazi Jews had long been portrayed as the "internal Orient" of Europe, Israeli Jews rapidly morphed into the "internal Occident" of the Middle East.[22] This culturalist pattern of othering even took on racialized undertones: Race theorists of the nineteenth and early twentieth centuries had famously categorized European Jews as an "*Orientalisches Fremdlingsvolk*" (a foreign Asiatic people).[23] In contrast, racialized discourse about Ashkenazi Israelis (especially among postcolonial authors) increasingly shifted to portrayals of a "white settler community in Palestine,"[24] arguing that Ashkenazi Israelis "look like other Europeans, ... they speak European languages."[25] Based on this reading of Israeli history through the lens of colonial whiteness, Zionism would no longer be compared to anticolonial forms of nationalism (like the Irish example) or anticolonial return migration (like the case of Liberia)—and Israel's settlement project would not be compared to the demographic Moroccanization of Western Sahara, but rather to the brutal colonial regime in French Algeria.[26]

However, this settler colonial reading of Israeli state formation in 1948 and Israeli state expansion after 1967 fails to capture the driving forces of both the Zionist movement and Israeli statecraft: In the eyes of a postcolonial world, Israel's settlement project (if not the State of Israel itself) indeed came to be understood as a ghostly (and in a Freudian sense *unheimlich*) return to colonial practices.[27] However, to the messianic ethno-nationalists of Gush Emunim, the settlement project was no colonial conquest, but rather a revivalist rebellion against civilizational atrophy and "Hellenization," built around the nativist fantasy of a return to the geographical and textual sources of Jewish peoplehood.[28] This distinction might seem irrelevant to the Palestinian population in the occupied territories, but it helps to understand the powerful endurance of expansionism in postcolonial times, whether in the West Bank or in Western Sahara: From a perspective of countermobilization and political resistance, the appeal of describing Morocco's rule over Western Sahara as "colonialism, Moroccan style" is obvious, in the same way that Tibetan nationalists may prefer to speak of a Chinese-orchestrated "genocide" in Tibet, echoing the jargon of Zionist "settler-colonialism" among both Palestinian ethno-nationalists and Jewish antinationalists.[29] From an analytical perspective, however, these mobilizational frames fail to acknowledge the specific normative and institutional context of state expansions *after* decolonization, including the appeal of territorial maximalism for anticolonial thinkers and the practice of large-scale projects of demographic engineering among postcolonial state elites. Given the sheer ubiquity of "Third World colonialism," the phenomenon might be more than an anachronistic vestige or a ghostly return of a bygone colonial era. Instead, we might have to realize that expansionist state projects formed a constitutive feature of postcolonial state formation.

Israel's Settlement Project in Comparative Perspective

How could we theorize irredentist fantasy and expansionist practice as integral elements of the postcolonial state? The best way to approach the paradoxical nature of state expansions after decolonization might consist in a closer look at one of the crucial debates in the history of the United Nations, the debate over the Declaration on the Granting of Independence to Colonial Countries and Peoples (Resolution 1514 [XV], 1960). In popular culture, the debate might be best known for the shoe-banging incident involving the Soviet premier Nikita Khrushchev, who became angry when other representatives effectively called for a decolonization of countries under Soviet domination.[30] However, the Soviet Union was not the only country that stood out for a peculiar mismatch between anticolonial rhetoric and expansionist state practice. In fact, in the middle of a pivotal UN debate about decolonization, many state leaders had only one thing on their mind: the capture of contested territory.

Morocco's permanent representative, Mehdi Ben Aboud, cautioned that colonialism, "though leaving by the front door, comes back through the window."[31] This warning, however, did not prevent Morocco's foreign minister, M'hammed Boucetta, from arguing that "Mauritania has at all times formed an integral part of Morocco."[32] In addition to claiming "what is nowadays presented as the independent State of Mauritania," Boucetta also made the case for Moroccan ownership of all of Spanish Sahara and significant parts of Algeria. The Indonesian president Sukarno denied that Indonesian nationalism would "seek to impose ourselves on other nations," but laid a determined claim to Netherlands New Guinea, "the one-fifth of our national territory which still labours under imperialism," "a colonial sword poised over Indonesia."[33] In a not-so-hidden reference to Ethiopian domination over Eritrea (formally joined into a federal framework), the Ethiopian permanent representative, Haddis Alemayehu, suggested that the "peoples in the liberated countries, left alone without interference from foreign intriguers, will settle their differences in no time."[34] The Somalian permanent representative, Hajji Farah Ali Omar, laid claim to the Somali-populated parts of Ethiopia and emphasized the hope of this compatriots "for an early, happy and peaceful unification with our other Somali brothers who are not yet autonomous."[35] Iraq's permanent representative, Adnan Pachachi, declared his country to be "in the forefront of the fight for the rights of the colonial peoples."[36] Nonetheless, only a few months later, Pachachi would describe Kuwait as "an integral part of our country" because Kuwait was "not more than a small coastal town on the Gulf. There is not and has never been a country or a national entity called Kuwait, never in history."[37] Israel's foreign minister, Golda Meir, claimed that it was "of course, untrue that Israel pursues expansionist policies of any kind," but her defense of the Zionist return to the Land of Israel/Palestine already foreshadowed Israel's attempt to capture the occupied territories after the Six-Day War: "And did the desert in Israel bloom as long as we were in exile? Did trees cover the Judean hills, were marshes drained? No—rocks, desert, marshes, malaria, trachoma—this is what characterized the country before we came back."[38]

It took only a few years for the visions of Greater Syria, Greater Ethiopia, Greater Indonesia, and, of course, Greater Israel to become reality. In 1962, Ethiopia abolished the federal framework between the two countries and formally annexed Eritrea.[39] In 1963, Indonesia took over West New Guinea (the former Netherlands New Guinea) and incorporated the territory by force and demographic engineering—a practice that would later be repeated in East Timor after its conquest in 1975.[40] In 1967, Israel occupied the West Bank, the Gaza Strip, the Sinai, and the Golan Heights and launched a large-scale settlement project.[41] In 1975, Morocco and Mauritania invaded Western Sahara (the former Spanish Sahara) and divided the territory among themselves.[42] In 1976, Syria intervened in the Lebanese civil war and continued to establish a long-term military occupation.[43] Colonialism, so it seemed, might have been over—but expansionist statecraft was clearly not.[44]

Facing the normative pressures of the decolonization regime and the political violence of armed insurgencies, most expanding states followed a generic template of renaming and resettling. First, all memories of previous territorial organization were wiped from the map. West New Guinea was turned into "Irian Jaya"; the West Bank was transformed into "Judea and Samaria"; the partitioned Western Sahara was reorganized into three Moroccan provinces in the North (El-Ayoun, Smara, Boujdour) and a single Mauritanian province in the South (Tiris El-Gharbia).[45] Second, political incorporation was enforced by demographic engineering, that is: colonization. Whether in Indonesia's "new provinces," in the "Moroccan Sahara," in Israel's "liberated territories," or in Chinese-controlled Tibet, for that matter, expanding states rapidly moved in large numbers of settler immigrants to permanently claim the newly acquired territories.[46]

Faced with organized political and military opposition, many expansionist projects rapidly fell apart. The Somalian-Ethiopian war of 1977–78 put an end to the vision of "Greater Somalia," and the Iraqi attempt to reincorporate Kuwait as its nineteenth province collapsed after only a few weeks in the Gulf War of 1990. Other attempts at territorial incorporation unraveled much more slowly: Sometimes expanding states were pushed back by prolonged insurgencies (like the Eritrean war against Ethiopia), and sometimes occupying powers were undermined by transnational mobilization (like the East Timorese campaign against Indonesia). Some states withdrew their military forces after decades of quasi-permanent occupation (Syria), while other states decided to entrench their control over captured and colonized territories even at high diplomatic and financial costs—among them both Morocco and Israel.

Monumentalism and Miniaturization

The irredentist fantasies that guided these expansionist projects were culturally specific: While the post-1967 vision of "Greater Israel" privileged the Zionist motif of a nativist return to the sources (enriched with an unhealthy dose of messianism), the post-1975 ideology of "Greater Morocco" emphasized the sacred nature of the monarch as protector of Morocco's territorial indivisibility. However, instead of giving in to "ethnographic dazzle"[47] by taking the idiosyncrasies of Gush Emunim or Morocco's palace historians too seriously, we should focus on the overarching structural similarities that unite a wide array of expansionist projects throughout the process of decolonization—namely, means (a mobilized state apparatus), motive (irredentist ideologies), and opportunity (territorial conflicts).

More specifically, James Scott's insightful analysis of "authoritarian high-modernist schemes" might be fruitfully applied to the emergence of Third World colonialism: "In sum, the legibility of a society provides the capacity for large-scale social engineering, high-modernist ideology provides the desire, the authoritarian state provides the determination to act on that desire, and an incapacitated civil society provides the leveled social terrain on which to build."[48] From this perspective, the monumentalist aspirations of Third World colonialism should be read through the prism of "huge development fiascoes in poorer Third World nations and Eastern Europe," typically producing "the debris of huge agricultural schemes and new cities (think of Brasília or Chandigarh) that have failed their residents."[49]

Indeed, crucial cases of Third World colonialism were breathing the unfiltered air of high modernism: The Indonesianization of East Timor, the Moroccanization of Western Sahara, and the Sinicization of Tibet were made possible by the same raw state power and the same cult of feasibility as other large-scale projects of the 1960s and 1970s, whether hydroelectric dams, desalination projects, or massive networks of frontier villages. Tellingly, Morocco's monumentalist reconstruction of the city of La'ayoune in occupied Western Sahara was centered on a "square of allegiance," built in the unmistakable style of architectural brutalism.[50]

In terms of the political, economic, and symbolic resources that were invested in the settlement project throughout the last fifty years, Israel's massive state policy of demographic engineering matches the unbridled monumentalism of Morocco, China, and Indonesia. At the same time, its architectural policy of exclavization (the establishment of Jewish settlements as ethno-territorial exclaves) points to a fusion of monumentalism and miniaturization as the distinctive element of Israeli expansionism: Unable to carry out a full-fledged policy of territorial, political, and demographic incorporation of the occupied territories and its Palestinian-Arab majority, Israel was limited to establishing small-scale miniatures of Jewish-Israeli towns and neighborhoods, ranging from Labor Zionist *kibbutzim settlements* (in the Jordan Valley) to American-Israeli *suburb settlements* (like Tekoa).[51] Instead of transforming Nablus into an Israeli town, Israel surrounded it with the Jewish-Israeli settlements of Elon Moreh, Itamar, and Yitzhar. This pattern of exclavization (*Judaization*) instead of incorporation (*Israelization*) clearly stands out: While Morocco invested systematic efforts in in attracting Moroccan settlers to Western Sahara, they were not housed in isolated exclaves—the same is true for Chinese rule over Tibet, Indonesian rule over West Papua, and India's slow-moving shift toward demographic engineering in Kashmir.[52]

To an extent, Israel's policy of exclavization since 1967 follows the historical precedent of previous Zionist settlement efforts, not least the wall and tower settlement drive throughout the British Mandate.[53] Other historical role models range from the covenantal "miniature commonwealths" of Jewish diasporic history to the Cossack military outpost.[54] However, from a comparative perspective, Israel's strategy of miniaturization primarily expresses the limitations of Israeli statecraft. For those who have visited a Jewish-Israeli settlement in the West Bank, Scott's analysis of miniaturization as a sign of defeat might sound strangely familiar:

> The pretense of authoritarian high-modernist schemes to discipline virtually everything within their ambit is bound to encounter intractable resistance.... Those who have their hearts set on realizing such plans cannot fail to be frustrated by stubborn social realities and material facts. One response to this frustration is a retreat to the realm of appearances and miniatures—to model cities and Potemkin villages, as it were... The effect of this retreat is to create a small, relatively self-contained, utopian space where high-modernist aspirations might more nearly be realized. The limiting case, where control is maximized but impact on the external world is minimized, is in the museum or the theme park.[55]

Israeli Settlements: Museums, Theme Parks, Model Cities

Scott's theory of "utopian miniaturization"[56] helps us understand the distinct architecture of Israel's settlements in the occupied territories as an expression of political failure: As a consequence of great power intervention, domestic infighting, and demographic anxieties, Israel remains unable to carry out an all-encompassing policy of territorial incorporation in the occupied territories. Instead, the settlement project consists of a large number of isolated and well-guarded miniature exclaves of Jewish-Israeli life in the midst of a Palestinian-Arab demographic majority. In addition to the prominent outposts of national-religious messianism (Yitzhar), these neo-Zionist Potemkin villages reflect almost the entire spectrum of Jewish-Israeli society: Labor-Zionist exclaves (the kibbutzim in the Jordan valley), Haredi exclaves (Betar Ilit), Middle Eastern Jewish exclaves (large parts of Ma'aleh Adumim), Russian-Jewish exclaves (large parts of Ariel), and, of course, American-Israeli outposts (Tekoa).

While the establishment of territorial, legal, and ethnic exclaves is fairly widespread among expansionist states, Israel's strategy of establishing miniature exclaves is indeed exceptional. Typically, territorial exclaves are relatively large and self-sufficient, ranging from entire provinces (like the Oblast Kaliningrad) to semi-independent quasi-states. In the case of Armenia and Turkey, for instance, the control over contested territory was legitimated by establishing and maintaining the largely unrecognized statelets of the "Turkish Republic of Northern Cyprus" and the Armenian "Republic of Artsakh." In contrast to these large-scale territorial exclaves, Israel's miniature exclaves combine the elements of museums, theme parks, and model cities: *Museums* in the settlements typically emphasize the continuity of Jewish life in the region, thereby framing Jewish settlement in the occupied territories as a living reconnection to the past, ranging from pre-1948 Zionist settlement (Gush Etzion) via the Hebron Massacre (1929) all the way to the biblical patriarchs. Shooting ranges, wine tastings, and movie rides (for instance, at the Hebron Heritage Museum) transform the Jewish settlements into live-action *theme parks* for visiting tourists. Finally, the combination of frontier village, military outpost, and covenantal commonwealth confer the settlements the status of *model cities*—even if only in the eyes of their inhabitants.

This architecture of exclavization has also shaped the Judaization and increasing "Disneyfication" of Jerusalem: Despite the de jure annexation of East Jerusalem in 1967, Israel has invested limited efforts in the Israelization of Jerusalem's Palestinian-Arab population, whether in terms of citizenship, education, or inclusion into formal and informal decision-making.[57] Instead, the ring of new Jewish-Israeli neighborhoods around Jerusalem (like Gilo, Ramot, and Neve Ya'akov) was complemented by miniature Jewish settlements within Palestinian-Arab neighborhoods, ranging from individual houses inside Jerusalem's Old City to growing exclaves like the City of David, located south of the Old City and in immediate proximity to the Temple Mount/Haram al-Sharif, where the City of David National Park is slowly emerging within the Palestinian-Arab neighborhood of Silwan.[58]

In recent years, the City of David has begun to form an integral part of many guided tours in Jerusalem, thereby normalizing a settlement policy that threatens the status of East Jerusalem as the future capital of a Palestinian state while at the same time condoning a highly revisionist form of memory politics that tends to erase almost two thousand years of history in the Land of Israel/Palestine. In the words of Elad, the "City of David Foundation":

> The story of the City of David began over 3,000 years ago, when King David left the city of Hebron for a small hilltop city known as Jerusalem, establishing it as the unified capital of the tribes of Israel. Years later, David's son, King Solomon, built the First Temple next to the City of David on top of Mount Moriah, the site of the binding of Isaac, and with it, this hilltop became one of the most important sites in the world. *Today, the story of the City of David continues.*[59]

With its entanglement of archaeological excavations and slow-moving demographic engineering, the City of David National Park crystallizes how Jewish settlement in the occupied territories combines the elements of museum, theme park, and model city: The creation of a Jewish-Israeli exclave in the Palestianian-Arab neighborhood of Silwan goes hand in hand with the creation of a museum and an archaeologic theme park, which might one day become accessible by cable car from the Old Railway Station (in West Jerusalem) via Mount Zion. While land purchases, financing, and institution-building are driven by private associations (in this case, Elad) that act as ideological entrepreneurs, their efforts are closely entangled with the support of Israeli state institutions, such as the Jerusalem Municipality, the Israel Antiquities Authority, the Education Ministry, and the Custodian of Absentee Property—including, of course, security arrangements by the Israeli police and the Israeli military to protect the ongoing settlement efforts in the area.[60]

Conclusion

In 2020, the nexus (or perhaps the *unacknowledged kinship*) between Israeli and Moroccan expansionism reached a new level of public visibility: While the breakthrough agreement between the United Arab Emirates (UAE), Bahrain, and Israel (the "Abraham Accords" from August 2020) ultimately preempted Israel's annexation plans in the West Bank (as part of the failed "deal of the century"), only a few months later, the normalization of Moroccan-Israeli diplomatic relations was secured through the formal US recognition of Moroccan sovereignty in the occupied Western Sahara—clearly as a result of Israeli lobbying.[61] To put it in the words of Noa Landau: "Official recognition of Israeli annexation is out, but Moroccan annexation is endorsed...Netanyahu said the agreements with the UAE amounted to 'peace in exchange for peace.' In this case it's occupation in exchange for occupation."[62] But apart from the curious alignment of interest between two US allies in the Middle East and North Africa, what might be the analytical benefit of exploring Israel's settlement project as a form of Third World colonialism? And vice versa, what might scholars of Moroccan, Indonesian, or Chinese expansionism learn from the Israeli case?

For scholars of Israel's settlement project, such a comparative venture might be a safe shipping route between the Scylla of settler-colonial dogmatism and the Charybdis of apologetic whataboutism: After all, the categorization of Israeli expansionism as a form of Third World colonialism fully recognizes Israel's nature as a postcolonial state, yet without denying the colonial nature of its long-term project of demographic engineering, military rule, and land expropriation in the occupied territories. More specifically, the comparison between the Israeli case and alternative pathways might be particularly instructive to illuminate the truly *distinctive* elements of Israel's settlement project: As pointed out above, Israeli expansionism stands out for a highly idiosyncratic fusion of monumentalism (in terms of high-modernist statecraft) and miniaturization (in terms of architectural exclavization). In addition, such a structured comparison might point to differences in the type of irredentist claim to the land: In contrast to Moroccan or Indonesian unification nationalism, the Israeli claim to the occupied territories ultimately rests on a covenantal understanding of exclusive ownership of the land, in the words of Chaim Gans, a form of proprietary Zionism.[63]

For scholars of Third World colonialism, the analytical benefit of a close reading of the Israeli case might consist in a stronger focus on the internal ambivalence of postcolonial state expansions: By applying Penslar's analytical matrix of the Zionist project ("historically and conceptually situated between colonial, anticolonial, and postcolonial discourse and practice") to Third World colonialism, the phenomenon might be distinguished more clearly as a distinctive blend of a decidedly colonial projection of power and population, an anticolonial obsession with redeeming usurped ancestral homelands, and the postcolonial monumentalism inherited from high modernism.[64] From this perspective, in addition to (neo-) colonial statecraft and the postcolonial cult of feasibility, scholars might have to take a closer look at irredentist nationalism as a crucial element of anticolonial thought: From 'Allal al-Fassi to Ze'ev Jabotinsky, anticolonial nationalists have been obsessed with the territorial expression of restoring a lost sense of honor, of recovering a lost sense of precolonial authenticity. Perhaps the most fitting critique of Israel's settler movement might therefore be found in Edward Said's scathing comments about anticolonial nativism: "[Often] this abandonment of the secular world has led to a sort of millenarianism if the movement has had a mass base, or it has degenerated into small-scale private craziness, or into an unthinking acceptance of stereotypes, myths, animosities, and traditions encouraged by imperialism."[65]

NOTES

1. Benjamin Rivlin and Jacques Fomerand, "Changing Third World Perspectives and Policies Towards Israel," in *Israel in the Third World*, ed. Michael Curtis and Susan Aurelia Gitelson (New Brunswick, NJ: Transaction Books, 1976), 318–60. See also the chapter by Rephael G. Stern and Arie M. Dubnov in this volume.
2. Maxime Rodinson, *Israel: A Colonial Settler-State?* (New York: Monad Press, 1973).
3. Ian S. Lustick, *Unsettled States, Disputed Lands: Britain and Ireland, France and Algeria, Israel and the West Bank-Gaza* (Ithaca, NY: Cornell University Press, 1993); Ilan Pappé, ed., *Israel and South Africa: The Many Faces of Apartheid* (London: Zed Books, 2015).

4. Oded Haklai and Neophytos Loizides, eds., *Settlers in Contested Lands: Territorial Disputes and Ethnic Conflicts* (Stanford, CA: Stanford University Press, 2015); Oren Barak, *State Expansion and Conflict: In and Between Israel/Palestine and Lebanon* (Cambridge, UK: Cambridge University Press, 2017); Johannes Becke, *The Land Beyond the Border: State Formation and Territorial Expansion in Syria, Morocco, and Israel* (Albany: State University of New York Press, 2021). See also Johannes Becke, "Beyond Allozionism: Exceptionalizing and De-Exceptionalizing the Zionist Project," *Israel Studies* 23, no. 2 (2018): 168–93.

5. Awet Tewelde Weldemichael, *Third World Colonialism and Strategies of Liberation: Eritrea and East Timor Compared* (Cambridge, UK: Cambridge University Press, 2013), 2.

6. Johannes Becke, "Towards a De-Occidentalist Perspective on Israel: The Case of the Occupation," *Journal of Israeli History* 33 (2014): 1–23; Johannes Becke, "Dismantling the Villa in the Jungle: Matzpen, Zochrot, and the Whitening of Israel," *Interventions* 21 (2019): 874–91.

7. Johannes Becke, "Varieties of Expansionism: A Comparative-Historical Approach to the Study of State Expansion and State Contraction," *Political Geography* 72 (2019): 64–75.

8. James C. Scott, *Seeing Like a State: How Certain Schemes to Improve the Human Condition Have Failed* (New Haven, CT: Yale University Press, 1988), 257.

9. Ibid.

10. Derek J. Penslar, *Israel in History: The Jewish State in Comparative Perspective* (London: Routledge, 2007), 91.

11. Asher Kaufman, *Reviving Phoenicia: The Search for Identity in Lebanon* (London: I. B. Tauris, 2004), 239.

12. Conseil National Provisoire Sahraoui, "Proclamation du gouvernement de la République Arabe Sahraouie Démocratique," March 4, 1976, reprinted in *Annuaire de l'Afrique Du Nord* 15 (1976): 917–18, here 917.

13. See Article 22 of the Palestinian National Covenant (1968), printed in Yehoshafat Harkabi, *Palestinians and Israel* (Jerusalem: Keter, 1974), 65.

14. Robert J. C. Young, *Postcolonialism: An Historical Introduction* (Oxford: Blackwell, 2001), 3.

15. Ran Aaronsohn, "Settlement in Eretz Israel—A Colonialist Enterprise? 'Critical' Scholarship and Historical Geography," *Israel Studies* 1 (1996): 214–29.

16. Brendan O'Leary, "The Elements of Right-Sizing and Right-Peopling the State," in *Right-Sizing the State: The Politics of Moving Borders*, ed. Brendan O'Leary, Ian S. Lustick, and Thomas Callaghy (Oxford: Oxford University Press, 2001), 15–73.

17. Joseph A. Massad, "The 'Post-Colonial' Colony: Time, Space, and Bodies in Palestine/Israel," in *The Persistence of the Palestinian Question: Essays on Zionism and the Palestinians* (London: Routledge, 2006), 13–40.

18. Johannes Becke, "Land and Redemption: The Zionist Project in Comparative Perspective," *Trumah* 23 (2016): 1–13.

19. Olivia C. Harrison, *Transcolonial Maghreb: Imagining Palestine in the Era of Decolonization* (Stanford, CA: Stanford University Press, 2015), 2.

20. Amnon Raz-Krakotzkin, "The Zionist Return to the West and the Mizrahi Jewish Perspective," in *Orientalism and the Jews*, ed. Ivan Davidson Kalmar and Derek Jonathan

Penslar (Waltham, MA: Brandeis University Press, 2005), 162–81. See David Ben-Gurion, "An Eternal People or a Mediterranean People," May 6, 1954, Ben-Gurion Archives, Articles Division [Hebrew]. Many thanks to Avi Shilon for bringing this essay to my attention.

21. Eitan Bar-Yosef, *A Villa in the Jungle: Africa in Israeli Culture* (Jerusalem: Van Leer Institute/Kubbutz HaMeuchad, 2014) [Hebrew].

22. Achim Rohde, "Der Innere Orient. Orientalismus, Antisemitismus und Geschlecht im Deutschland des 18. bis 20. Jahrhunderts," *Die Welt Des Islams* 5 (2005): 370–411; Becke, "Towards a De-Occidentalist Perspective."

23. Jehuda Reinharz and Yaacov Shavit, *Glorious, Accursed Europe: An Essay on Jewish Ambivalence* (Waltham, MA: Brandeis University Press, 2010), 136.

24. Roger Owen, *State, Power and Politics in the Making of the Modern Middle East*. 2nd ed. (London: Routledge, 2000), 19.

25. Joseph Massad, "History on the Line: Joseph Massad and Benny Morris Discuss the Middle East," in *The Persistance of the Palestinian Question: Essays on Zionism and the Palestinians*, ed. Joseph A. Massad (London: Routledge, 2006), 154–65, here 163.

26. Aidan Beatty, "Zionism and Irish Nationalism: Ideology and Identity on the Borders of Europe," *The Journal of Imperial and Commonwealth History* 45 (2017): 315–38; George Bornstein, *The Colors of Zion: Blacks, Jews, and Irish from 1845 to 1945* (Cambridge, MA: Harvard University Press, 2011). See Becke, "Dismantling the Villa in the Jungle."

27. Yoav Gelber, "Zionism and Colonialism," *Nekuda*, no. 245 (September 2001): 44–47 [Hebrew].

28. Gideon Aran, *Kookism: The Roots of Gush Emunim: Settler Culture, Zionist Theology and Contemporary Messianism* (Jerusalem: Carmel, 2013).

29. Deon Geldenhuys, *Contested States in World Politics* (Houndmills: Palgrave Macmillan, 2009), 199; Barry Sautman, "Colonialism, Genocide, and Tibet," *Asian Ethnicity* 7 (2006): 243–65.

30. "Khrushchev Bangs His Shoe on Desk; Khrushchev Adds Shoe-Waving to His Heckling Antics at U.N.," *New York Times*, October 13, 1960; "UN Adjourned in Disorder: Mr K. Bangs Desk with His Shoe, President Breaks His Gavel," *The Guardian*, October 13, 1960.

31. United Nations General Assembly, fifteenth session, 902nd Plenary Meeting, 1960, 686.

32. United Nations General Assembly, fifteenth session, 1384.

33. United Nations General Assembly, fifteenth session, 285 and 283.

34. United Nations General Assembly, fifteenth session, 1021.

35. United Nations General Assembly, fifteenth session, 33.

36. United Nations General Assembly, fifteenth session, 682.

37. United Nations Security Council, fifteenth session, 11.

38. United Nations General Assembly, fifteenth session, 767; United Nations General Assembly, fifteenth session, 593. Throughout this chapter, the term "Land of Israel/Palestine" will be used to describe the territory of "Eretz Israel" (Land of Israel) or "historic Palestine," the homeland claimed by both Jewish and Palestinian-Arab nationalism, an ethnic landscape that to varying degrees corresponds to the modern-day geographic entity of "Mandatory Palestine" that was established under British colonial rule. For a

discussion of the contested nature of geographic terminology, see Gideon Biger, "The Names and Boundaries of Eretz-Israel (Palestine) as Reflections of Stages in Its History," in *The Land That Became Israel: Studies in Historical Geography*, ed. Ruth Kark (New Haven, CT: Yale University Press, 1990), 1–22.

39. Ruth Iyob, *The Eritrean Struggle for Independence: Domination, Resistance, Nationalism, 1941–1993* (Cambridge, UK: Cambridge University Press, 1995), chapter 5.

40. Dale Gietzelt, "The Indonesianization of West Papua," *Oceania* 59 (1989): 201–21; David Hicks, *Rhetoric and the Decolonization and Recolonization of East Timor* (London: Routledge, 2015).

41. Idith Zertal and Akiva Eldar, *Lords of the Land: The War for Israel's Settlements in the Occupied Territories, 1967–2007* (New York: Nation Books, 2007).

42. Tony Hodges, *Western Sahara: The Roots of a Desert War* (Chicago: Lawrence Hill Books, 1983).

43. Rola El-Husseini, *Pax Syriana: Elite Politics in Postwar Lebanon* (Syracuse, NY: Syracuse University Press, 2012).

44. Neta Crawford defines the normative juncture of decolonization as follows: "In the sense that it is no longer acceptable for states to take territory against the wishes of the inhabitants and to govern the people there without political representation, colonialism is over." Neta C. Crawford, *Argument and Change in World Politics: Ethics, Decolonization, and Humanitarian Intervention* (Cambridge, UK: Cambridge University Press, 2002), 340.

45. See Jason MacLeod, *Merdeka and the Morning Star: Civil Resistance in West Papua* (St. Lucia: University of Queensland Press, 2015), xv–xx; Gershom Gorenberg, *The Accidental Empire: Israel and the Birth of the Settlements, 1967–1977* (New York: Times Books, 2006), chapter 4; Hodges, *Western Sahara*, chapter 26; Virginia Thompson and Richard Adloff, *The Western Saharans* (London: Croom Helm, 1980), 293–96.

46. Oded Haklai, "The Decisive Path of State Indecisiveness: Israeli Settlers in the West Bank in Comparative Perspective," in *Settlers in Contested Lands*, ed. Haklai and Loizides, 17–39; Ehud Eiran, "The Indonesian Settlement Project in East Timor," ibid., 97–113; Jacob Mundy, "Moroccan Settlers in Western Sahara: Colonists or Fifth Column?" *The Arab World Geographer* 15 (2012): 95–126; Mette Halskov Hansen, "The Call of Mao or Money? Han Chinese Settlers on China's South-Western Borders," *The China Quarterly* 158 (1999): 394–413.

47. Robin Fox, *The Search for Society: Quest for a Biosocial Science and Morality* (New Brunswick, NJ: Rutgers University Press, 1989), 18.

48. Scott, *Seeing Like a State*, 5.

49. Ibid., 3.

50. On the reconstruction of La'ayoune under Moroccan occupation, see Akbarali Thobhani, *Western Sahara Since 1975 under Moroccan Administration: Social, Economic, and Political Transformation* (Lewiston, NY: Edwin Mellen Press, 2002), 108–26.

51. Sara Yael Hirschhorn, *City on a Hilltop: American Jews and the Israeli Settler Movement* (Cambridge, MA: Harvard University Press, 2017). For an architectural reading of Israel's occupation and the settlement project, see Eyal Weizman, *Hollow Land: Israel's Architecture of Occupation* (London: Verso, 2007).

52. Kunwar Khuldune Shahid, "'Kashmir Is Palestine': Why Both India and Pakistan Want to Push This Ominous Comparison," *Ha'aretz*, August 14, 2019, 2022, https://www.haaretz.com/world-news/.premium-kashmir-is-palestine-why-india-and-pakistan-are-both-pushing-this-ominous-analogy-1.7683411.

53. Sharon Rotbard, "Wall and Tower (Homa Umigdal): The Mold of Israeli Architecture," in *A Civilian Occupation: The Politics of Israeli Architecture*, ed. Rafi Segal and Eyal Weizman (London: Verso, 2003), 39–56.

54. S. Ilan Troen, *Imagining Zion: Dreams, Designs, and Realities in a Century of Jewish Settlement* (New Haven, CT: Yale University Press, 2003), 14; Israel Bartal, *Cossack and Bedouin: Land and People in Jewish Nationalism* (Tel Aviv: Am Oved, 2007) [Hebrew].

55. Scott, *Seeing Like a State*, 257.

56. Ibid., 130.

57. Michael Kimmelman, "Cable Cars Over Jerusalem? Some See 'Disneyfication' of Holy City," *New York Times*, September 13, 2019, https://www.nytimes.com/2019/09/13/world/middleeast/jerusalem-cable-cars.html.

58. Nir Hasson, "In Jerusalem's City of David Excavation, Politics Is Never Absent," *Ha'aretz*, May 29, 2012, https://www.haaretz.com/1.5209581.

59. "About Us," City of David Foundation, n.d., http://www.cityofdavid.org.il/en/about (emphasis added).

60. Nir Hasson, "How the State Helped Right-Wing Groups Settle East Jerusalem," *Ha'aretz*, November 7, 2010, https://www.haaretz.com/1.5136031.

61. "United States Recognizes Morocco's Sovereignty over Western Sahara," *American Journal of International Law* 115 (2021): 318–23; "Netanyahu Sought Deal with US, Morocco to Allow Normalization of Ties - Report," *Times of Israel*, February 4, 2020, https://www.timesofisrael.com/netanyahu-sought-deal-with-us-morocco-to-allow-normalization-of-ties-report.

62. Noa Landau, "Peace for Peace? Israel-Morocco Deal Is Occupation in Exchange for Occupation," *Ha'aretz*, December 11, 2020, https://www.haaretz.com/israel-news/.premium-peace-for-peace-israel-morocco-deal-is-occupation-in-exchange-for-occupation-1.9364413.

63. Haim Gans, *A Political Theory for the Jewish People* (Oxford: Oxford University Press, 2016), 60.

64. Penslar, *Israel in History*, 91.

65. Edward W. Said, *Culture and Imperialism* (New York: Alfred A. Knopf, 1993), 276.

11

A Part of Asia or Apart from Asia?
Zionist Perceptions of Asia, 1947–1956

REPHAEL G. STERN and ARIE M. DUBNOV

Introduction: The Politics of Sartorial Choices

On March 23, 1947, the soon-to-be Indian prime minister Jawaharlal Nehru, wearing his staple mandarin-collared coat and white Gandhi hat, opened the Asian Relations Conference in Delhi. A self-proclaimed "great gathering of the nations of Asia," the conference brought together almost two hundred delegates from twenty-eight countries, many of which were in the midst of struggles for independence against the slowly receding European empires. A highly choreographed event, the conference fused old and new. From a stage built in the sixteenth-century stone fort of Purana Qila, Nehru proclaimed an independent "Asian" future. "Standing on this watershed which divides two epochs of human history, we can look back on our long past and look forward to the future ... Asia after a long period of quiescence has suddenly become important again in world affairs."[1] The conference also combined the local and the regional. Alongside the goal of joining together to break with the colonial past and bring about "an indestructible pledge of the unity of Asia," each attendee was encouraged to wear their particular traditional attire in order to underscore the conference's diversity.

Amid this forest of delegates from across the Asian continent was a ten-member delegation representing the Yishuv, the Jewish community in pre-1948 Palestine. It was chaired by Shmuel Hugo Bergmann (1883–1975), a German-speaking Jewish philosopher and Zionist activist from Prague, and a classmate and friend of Franz Kafka, who had immigrated to Palestine in 1919 and served as the director of the Hebrew University's library (now known as Israel's National Library) and a professor of philosophy. Among the Indian saris, Burmese longyis, and fezzes, the Jewish delegation from Jerusalem stood out, as Bracha Habas (1900–1968), one of its members, recalled, in their "European dress and... European complexion." Photos taken during the conference opening confirm Habas's account: Bergmann and David Hacohen (1898–1984), a Russian-Jewish Zionist diplomat trained at the London School of Economics who later became one of the founders of the Israeli Foreign Office, stood side by side next to Nehru in thick, heavy European suits. Perhaps seeking to compensate for the Zionist delegation's sartorial "Westernness"—and "violation" of the conference's dress code—Habas emphasized the Jewish delegates' "Eastern" distinctiveness: "The unique Eastern ring of our flowing and eloquent language attracts attention and slowly forces a unique definition, which we deserve despite the light color of our faces and our European dress."[2] Whether the delegation's rolling *r*s and guttural *kh*s succeeded in bridging this ostensible geographic and cultural divide is unclear—there was at least one public altercation between the Zionists and Egyptian participants during the course of the conference. Still, the presence of a Zionist delegation at what one prominent Indian scholar termed a "landmark in Asian history" points to an under-examined history of the "unacknowledged kinship" between Zionism and extra-European nationalist movements that extended into the post–World War I and postcolonial periods.[3]

This chapter sketches the history of Zionist Asianism: an effort to forge political ties and reimagine the Jewish political renaissance that would parallel and collaborate with non-European and non-Western nationalisms. We pay special attention to Zionists' attempts to establish relations with nascent Asian states during the decade extending from the 1947 Asian Relations Conference to the aftermath of the 1956 Suez War. We offer a mix of cultural and diplomatic history, for Zionist Asianism, as we define it, was as much a sentiment as it was a political strategy. It was predicated on and grew out of an inherent cultural ambivalence concerning the otherness of the Jew that animated Zionist thought from its inception. This

FIGURE 11.1. Shmuel Hugo Bergmann (left), Jawaharlal Nehru (center), and David Hacohen (right) at the Asian Relations Conference, New Delhi, March 1947. Courtesy of the Nehru Memorial Museum and Library.

ambivalence was tied to, and further fostered, an intra-Zionist discord; Zionist thought (and practice) swung like a pendulum between perceptions of the Jewish national project as a "Western" one and conceptions that emphasized the Jews' Semitic "Easternness." The general shift of the gaze eastward, and the Zionist encounter with decolonizing Asia in particular, was thus not simply a story of diplomacy; it was equally a cultural and intellectual enterprise.

The Zionist Asianist imagination was continuously informed by its proponents' intellectual sources—and limits—and by the elisions and ambiguities that pervaded the imagined notion of "Asia." The great majority of Zionist Asianists were Ashkenazi male writers and political activists of Eastern and Central European descent. Jews from North African and Middle Eastern countries, who were placed in the new category of "Mizrahim" ("Eastern Jews"), rarely participated in this discourse, even after the mass immigrations to Israel in the 1950s. In this respect, the present chapter does not seek to directly challenge the arguments made by Ella Shohat, Aziza Khazzoom, and others who pioneered the application of postcolonial critiques to the historiography of early Israeli statehood and showed how binary East-West cultural constructions translated into intra-Jewish patterns of hierarchy, exclusion, and institutional discrimination.[4] Even within the pre-statehood European Zionist milieu, Zionist Asianism never became a mainstream orientation. Rather, it developed through constant negotiation with other Zionists who generally denied any affinity between Jews and the peoples of the East.[5] Among those who rejected Zionist Asianism stood Theodor Herzl and Vladimir Jabotinsky. Each insisted that Jews would provide Europe with a bridgehead into the Middle East and function as a fence against "Asian barbarism."[6] By contrast, Zionist Asianists sought to position the Jewish national project within an imagined East that stood in contrast to Europe: an imagined space of plurality and diversity, an alternative primordial home free from antisemitism, hyper-rationalism, and ethnonational divides. In constructing their imagined "Asia," most of the proponents of an Eastern recalibration did not distinguish clearly between "Asia," "the Orient," and "the East." Exactly how these various imagined geographies interacted was rarely made clear in their words or, it seems, in their minds. We argue that the confluence of these two factors played a crucial role in what was, ultimately, the indeterminate fate—and multiple afterlives—of Zionist Asianism.

This chapter proceeds as follows: After situating Zionist Asianism within the longer arc of Jewish, European, and colonial history, we focus on the evolution of Zionist Asianism from the late 1940s through the mid-1950s. We examine three moments during that decade: the Asian Relations Conference (1947), the first year of Israeli statehood (1949), and the Bandung Conference (1955). In the conclusion we revisit the complex entanglements between Zionism and the postcolonial world, which continue into the present.

"Easternness," "Semitism," and "Pan-Asianism": A Half-Century of Ambivalence

The discursive foundations of Zionist Asianism were laid long before 1945. Lacking a single point of origin, they developed out of a series of cultural dispositions and intra-Jewish divisions: schisms between Sephardic and Ashkenazi Jews, between "Westernized" Jews (*Westjuden*, predominantly German-speaking and emancipated) and "Eastern" Jews (*Ostju-*

den, Yiddish-speaking residents of the Pale of Settlement), and between European Jews and Mizrahi Jews (the latter term being a catchall applied to Jews from roughly a dozen communities in Northern Africa and the Middle East). Taken together, these internal sociocultural divisions marked the Jews' ambiguous status as a minority group that did not fit well within traditional East-West typologies.

The emergence of a racialized imagination—and what Homi K. Bhabha aptly described as the "conflictual economy of colonial discourse"—did not mean that Jews' perceived Easternness was understood as synonymous with backwardness. Nor did it mean that the allure of the East was incompatible with the imperialist imagination.[7] Benjamin Disraeli, an outspoken proponent of British imperialism, was obsessed with both the Near East and the Far East. Famously—or rather, infamously—he used his family's origin story to create a racialized myth of Sephardi superiority.[8] A host of evangelical advocates of Jewish restoration soon followed with their own imagined syntheses of Jews, the East, and imperial ambitions. Thomas Clarke was among the first to connect India and Palestine, envisioning a "revival of the ancient high-way of traffic between the East and the West" that would be achieved by replanting Jews on the eastern shores of the Mediterranean.[9] More famously, George Eliot's self-absorbed and constantly searching Daniel Deronda reconnected with his Eastern ancestral home and embraced a racial vision of a Jewish "republic." These mid-Victorian musings—written before the term "Zionism" was even coined—emerged out of a longstanding Protestant fascination with the Holy Land, a nineteenth-century romantic nostalgia for the Crusades, a rise in millenarian expectations, and increased European political and economic involvement in the region. Together, they laid the foundations for later visions of Jews and the East.

Jews themselves did not shy away from these associations. Several postassimilatory Jewish authors, such as Simon Bernfeld and Mordechai Ben-Hillel Hacohen, paid tribute to Disraeli and found his Eastern obsession attractive.[10] Though it took almost two decades for the first full Hebrew translation of *Daniel Deronda* to appear, British Jews knew the novel well and received it with enthusiasm.[11] For many it provided the literary prism through which Zionist ideas were later seen. When Herzl visited Britain in 1895, many of his interlocutors assumed that he was reviving the idea of an

Anglicized Jewish colony in Palestine, sympathetic to and dependent upon Britain. Needless to say, they were surprised that he had not read George Eliot's novel.[12] Russia's humiliating defeat by Japan in 1905, which seemed to negate Western paternalism and racial hierarchies, further inspired both Jews and colonial subjects. It was in this context that the eccentric poet Naphtali Herz Imber (remembered today as the author of "Hatikva," the Israeli national anthem) cast himself as "The Child of Half-Asia." Imber authored the quasi-mystical poem cycle *Barkai the Third*, which described the dawn of a new age and was dedicated to Japan's Emperor Meiji.[13] A certain tension characterized these meditations and fantasies. While they exuded a profound contempt toward Czarist Russia and displayed a sense of Jewish self-assertiveness, they did not categorically reject imperial and colonial rule.

Indeed, this tension persisted after the collapse of the Ottoman Empire and the British occupation of Palestine in 1917. Against this new political backdrop, the 1919 publication of Nahum Sokolow's pioneering history of Zionism showed which way the winds of change were blowing: Abandoning his earlier criticism of Disraeli as a neo-Crusader Orientalist, Sokolow described him as a forerunner of Zionism and "a living monument of the greatness of the Jewish Race." Sokolow also appropriated and canonized George Eliot's novel, declaring that it would "take its place as the proudest testimony to English recognition of the Zionist idea" in the "Valhalla of the Jewish people."[14] The Hebrew translation of *Daniel Deronda*, published in Warsaw in 1893 by the non-Zionist critic and translator David Frischmann (who expressed his skepticism toward Zionists who praised Disraeli), suddenly became relevant.

Soon thereafter, Frischmann began publishing a stream of translations of short stories and poems of the Bengali Rabindranath Tagore. By the time Frischmann discovered him, Tagore had become an international literary celebrity—he had been awarded the Nobel Prize in Literature in 1913—who was considered a spokesman of Eastern spirituality and an advocate of inter-Asian cooperation and intellectual decolonization.[15] Frischmann did not translate the original Bengali texts but relied on Tagore's translations into English, thereby participating (albeit belatedly) in a broader "European" rediscovery of Tagore.[16] Furthermore, Frischmann's admiration of Tagore did not lead him to repudiate his admiration of Britain. Rather, it marked a new appreciation of "Asia," which, in earlier writings, signified backwardness and dilapidation.[17] Similarly, when visiting Shanghai in January 1935, journalist Itamar Ben-Avi (son of Eliezer Ben-Yehuda, the famous Hebrew lexicographer) also had no problem reverting to this imperialist discourse, declaring, that "[t]wo Jews—Lord Beaconsfield [Disraeli] and Lord Rothschild—had given control of the Suez Canal to Britain, and Jews now wanted to give other things to the world, too—a new thought, a new book, a new world," while adding that "the revival of Asia would follow on the revival of Europe, and it might well be that from Palestine the start of the revival would come."[18] The reclamation of a silenced, sublimated Eastern Jewish identity and the adoration of empire-building were thus by no means incongruous.

Other Jewish "self-Orientalizing" gestures existed alongside these British-inspired "re-Orientalizations." Numerous early Zionists and self-proclaimed "experts" on the Orient looked to German philologists and so-called "Arabists"—native and predominantly non-Ashkenazi Jews who spoke Arabic and were familiar with the everyday life of the indigenous Arab population. These Zionists often invoked the Orient as a metaphor for return and rejuvenation, describing it as an enchanted space populated by hybrid Jewish-Arab figures.[19] Non-Zionist Jews also participated in the culture of Jewish self-Orientalism. Two such figures were Lev Nussimbaum, the colorful Russian-Jewish adventurer who fled the Bolshevik Revolution, converted to Islam, and reinvented himself as "Essad Bey," and the architect Friedrich Arndt-Kürnberg, who converted to Islam, took the name Omar al-Raschid Bey, and created an Alpine colony that offered its visitors a mystical fusion of Islamic, Buddhist, and Hindu "eastern wisdoms."[20] Moreover, it was around this time that Hermann Kallenbach, a German-born architect who moved to South Africa, met Mohandas Gandhi, with whom he later developed an intimate relationship and an intellectual bond.

Within the Zionist movement, German-speaking Zionists played a particularly important role in promoting Jewish nationalism as a cultural reclamation of a repressed Eastern identity. The avant-garde magazines *Ost und West* (1901–1923) and *Der Jude* (1916–1928) and the teachings of Martin Buber helped popularize the idea of reclaiming the Jews' "Oriental" roots, making it both a strategy of radical self-affirmation and a "post-*Bildung*" battle cry against the bourgeois norms of their parents' generation.[21] Positive references to the East were rarely accompanied by Anglophilia. As Stefan Vogt has argued, Buber's early works "integrated the Jews into the politics of German imperialism while reinterpreting these politics as anti-imperialist" and regarded with suspicion the power granted to Great Britain by the League of Nations.[22] Early Buberian calls for Zionists to collaborate with the people of the Orient were as much about the metaphysics of Jewish authentic reaffirmation as they were about echoing German attempts to ally with non-European forces to counter French and British colonial expansion. In 1920, Buber warned that Zionist success depended on "whether we shall appear before the awakening East as hateful agents and spies or, rather, beloved pioneers and teachers," adding that the West "is doomed to destruction."[23]

It is important to note the distinctive German context in which this discourse developed. German-speaking Jewish intellectuals' embrace of their "Eastern" otherness was a response to negative depictions of the Jew as a Semitic, Oriental, and irrational alien by Kant, Hegel, Richard Wagner, Werner Sombart, and others.[24] Rather than a manifestation of "Jewish self-hatred," this Jewish response was an intellectual reorientation, which called for a critical, self-reflective reevaluation of earlier axioms concerning acculturation, bourgeois norms, and a sense of Jewish belonging in Europe. One participant in this trend was Jewish anthropologist Franz Baermann Steiner (1909–1952), the author of the classic study *Taboo* (1956). Steiner identified as an alien Eastern Semite planted in the West and as a primitive whose thinking and relation to the Divine did not fit the hegemonic European taxonomy. During his short time in Jerusalem, Steiner joined the *Brith Shalom* association, the movement known for its advocacy of binationalism. Like *Brith Shalom*'s leader Martin Buber, Steiner was insulted by Gandhi's description of Jews as Europeans imposing themselves on Palestine as voluntary proxies of Britain and the United States.[25] This disappointment notwithstanding, Steiner and other members of *Brith Shalom* persisted in recasting Zionism as a movement rooted in Asia. Buber himself would later employ this discourse in his reflections on his early years as a Zionist. Recalling his response to Herzl's call for Jews to import Western technology into the Middle East, Buber remembered himself saying, "No, not for such a purpose did we perform our services;

We did not emblazon the name Zion on our flag just to participate in the Americanization of Asia."[26]

If Buber's warning centered on the importance of Zionist relations with the "awakening East," it was the Viennese novelist and journalist Eugen Hoeflich (later known by his Hebrew name, Moshe Ya'akov Ben-Gavriêl) who made himself the leading advocate of pan-Asian brotherhood and further developed this form of Jewish-Zionist Orientalism into a comprehensive Zionist Asianist vision.[27] Writing in the wake of World War I, Hoeflich was arguably the first to import the concept of "pan-Asianism" into Zionist discourse. Pan-Asianism, according to Hoeflich, was a sentiment that had emerged in China, India, and the Near East and sought to "overthrow the hegemony of technology and capital over the oriental spirit" in an attempt to break down the fictitious divides between East and West and bring about a new age of "coexistence" (*Nebeneinanderleben*). The Jews, as "a part of the East scattered throughout the West," were expected to stand at the forefront of the "ethical mission" (*ethischen Sendung*) of "liberating the Orient from the paternalism of the Occident."[28] Like many European artists and art lovers, Hoeflich was also affected by *Japonisme*, the craze for Japanese art and design that swept Europe in the late nineteenth century. As Hanan Harif has shown, he was particularly inspired by Okakura Kakuzō, who saw clear connections between the aesthetic aspects of Japanese life and Japan's future role as the leader of the Asian awakening. Hoeflich was exposed to these ideas only after 1918, via the translation of *The Ideals of the East* into German (published in 1922), and was particularly taken by Kakuzō's insistence that Asia is, in essence, one unit.[29] Jews and Arabs in Palestine, he argued in his 1923 book *Die Pforte des Ostens* (The Gate to the East), should join arms and follow Japan's lead in its uncompromising, assertive rejection of European political and aesthetic imperialism.[30]

Like Hoeflich's relatively late discovery of Japan, India entered discussions about the future of Zionism only toward the end of World War I. Unsurprisingly, it was the British occupation of Palestine and the (informal) integration of Palestine into "Greater Britain" that made the imagined connections between Palestine and British India conceivable. To be sure, the imagined linkage lent itself to various political conclusions. Edwin Montagu, the Jewish secretary of state for India (1917–1922) and a fierce critic of the Balfour Declaration, relied on this interconnectivity to express

242 | BETWEEN EMPIRE AND DECOLONIZATION

his fear that antagonizing the Muslim population in Palestine might fuel anti-British sentiment among "the Mohammadanes" in India. Yet among Zionists the passage to India centered on ostensible similarities between Jews and India. Take, for instance, the Kovno-born and Frankfurt-trained Zionist educator and journalist Schlomith Flaum, who joined Rabindranath Tagore's school in Santiniketan in 1922. Flaum became convinced that there were undeniable parallels between the Jewish national project and the quasi-mystical revivalist language she was exposed to in Bengal, including a shared deep suspicion of Western forms of nationalism and hyper-rationality.[31] It seems that similar ideas motivated the founders of the Hebrew University of Jerusalem, who invited one of Tagore's closest collaborators—the Scottish town planner and sociologist Patrick Geddes—to provide architectural blueprints for the university campus.[32] When Lord Peel's 1937 commission of inquiry proposed partitioning Palestine, the parallel trajectories became more obvious, with partition in Palestine serving as a template of sorts for the partition of the Indian subcontinent.[33]

The invitation to participate in the Asian Relations Conference in 1947, then, did not come out of the blue, nor did it find the Zionist intelligentsia unprepared. What caught Bergmann and his peers by surprise, instead, was the tense atmosphere that made the conference a site of interdiction as much as a site of interaction.

New Delhi, Spring 1947

Beyond the exalted speeches about Asia's awakening, the Asian Relations Conference brought together multiple conflicting visions of international society and Asia's place therein. For one, the Indian organizers' vision of an Indian-led pan-Asianism sat uneasily upon the debris of previous movements. While Nehru viewed the conference as a revival of the USSR–organized 1927 League Against Imperialism, the Asian Relations Conference's focus on Asia did not cleanly map onto the previous global anti-imperial vision. Given the violent record of wartime Japanese pan-Asianism, the Indian iteration cast itself as "progressive pan-Asianism."[34] Eschewing irredentist politics and wars of aggression, Nehru proclaimed in his opening speech that Asia "will have to function effectively in the maintenance of peace."[35] To underscore this point, he made sure Japan was excluded from the conference.

Still, other conflicting territorial, political, and ideological conceptions of "Asia" came to the fore at the conference. Multiple parties that the organizers hoped would attend declined their invitations, including the vast majority of Muslim and Arab countries and, most visibly, the leadership of the Muslim League. Political divisions were apparent even among participating countries. It was widely speculated that China was competing with India over the "leadership" of the "Asiatic grouping."[36] In discussions of immigration and the ethnic boundaries of citizenship, a number of Southeast Asian countries voiced their opposition to the continued unregulated immigration of Indian and Chinese subjects.[37] A Burmese delegate went as far as to say that "it was terrible to be ruled by a Western power, but it was even more so to be ruled by an Asian power."[38] Moreover, the content of pan-Asianism, like the definitions of "Asian" culture and identity, was not clear. Aside from a shared experience of colonial subjugation by European powers, the countries represented at the conference seemed to have little in common. The lack of a shared language other than English—the colonial language par excellence—was readily apparent. (Bergmann, familiar with the politics of multilingualism, allegedly supported the use of Esperanto.) Even when the Indian organizers tried to enumerate fundamental Asian values, they "sought to include so many qualities ('faith in the unity of mankind') that the definition became too vague, and the line of enquiry [*sic*] was not pursued."[39]

These unsettled definitions provided room for Zionist participation and, at the same time, made the presence of the Jewish delegation conspicuous. The invitation was far from preordained. It was extended only after the intervention of Emanuel Celler, a United States congressman who authored the Luce-Celler Act of 1946 (which allowed Indian and Filipino immigrants to become naturalized US citizens) and played an instrumental role in cultivating trade relations between India and the United States. Celler reached out to Vijaya Lakshmi Nehru, making the case that "the Yishuv was definitely a part of the Asiatic world and should not be excluded."[40] Even then, the invitation was sent to the Hebrew University—an ostensibly less politically divisive entity than the *Va'ad Leumi*, the Zionist National Council, which was the leading political organ of the

Yishuv.[41] Still, the name of the delegation, as Bergmann reported back to Jerusalem, was a source of contention:

> [I]n spite of our constant efforts to call ourselves "Jewish Palestine Delegation" and to maintain that we represent only the Jewish part of Palestine, we were considered, sometimes consciously and sometimes implicitly, as a delegation of Palestine as a whole. In my opinion, this slight falsification of the real position [we have] on the part of other members of the Conference has had a certain negative aspect, but it may have some positive results as well. (There can be no doubt the fact the Arabs of Palestine were not represented was a grave mistake on their part and a great disadvantage for the Arab cause, especially as other Arab countries also were not efficiently and adequately represented.)
>
> On the other hand, and in contradiction to our being called "Palestine Delegation," there has been a constant trend to refer to us as "Hebrew University Delegation," and to refrain from mentioning Palestine. The common ground for these two contradictory trends seems to me to be found in the endeavor not to mention and not to refer to *Jewish* Palestine, in order, thus, to avoid controversies.[42]

While Zionist Asianists viewed the invitation as an Indian acknowledgment of "the Jewish people as part of Asia, as indeed it is," the question of what Zionist Asianism exactly was remained murky.[43] To the contrary, the composition of the delegation, with its mix of professors, political activists, and diplomats, men and women, junior and senior, highlighted this uncertainty. Joining Bergmann was the Polish-born Immanuel Olsvanger (1888–1961), a fellow veteran of *Brith Shalom* and an acclaimed literary figure and Sanskrit scholar. Olsvanger had traveled to India in 1936 on behalf of the Jewish Agency in an early attempt to cultivate relations with the Indian National Congress, following Nehru's and Gandhi's statements in support of the Palestinians' demands.[44] Another academically inclined delegate was Alfred Bonné (1899–1959), a German-born economist who was the head of the Jewish Agency's Economic Research Institute and a member of the Agency's Planning Committee (1942–1946). A former binationalist, Bonné grew increasingly skeptical of proposals to establish a "Federation of Oriental Nations" during World War II and its immediate aftermath and had stressed the importance of population transfer and resettlement.[45] Economic ties were also central to the work of delegation advisor Fritz W. Pollack, a Berlin-born Zionist who was stationed in Bombay to strengthen trade relations with the Yishuv.[46] Meanwhile, members Ya'akov Shimoni, David Hacohen, and Bracha Habas identified with *Mapai*, the dominant political party in Jewish Palestine. Shimoni, who was born in Berlin in 1914 as Jaakow Simon, was a generation younger than the other members. Trained in Semitic languages, he became a leading Arabist and the general secretary of the intelligence branch of the paramilitary organization *Haganah*.[47] Hacohen, a Russian Jew who was educated at the London School of Economics, was also a man of action. During the war he served as the liaison between the *Haganah* and the Special Operations Executive, the British army organization in charge of conducting espionage and sabotage against the Axis powers in occupied Europe (and, later, also in occupied Southeast Asia). It was from Hacohen's private flat in Haifa that *Radio Levant France Libre* broadcasts were aired to Vichy-controlled Syria and Lebanon in preparation for the Allies' landing. When the relationship between the Yishuv and the British soured after 1945, Hacohen was one of the first to be arrested during Operation Agatha (known in Zionist sources as "the black Sabbath"), the infamous British attempt to crush Jewish anticolonial resistance.[48] Hacohen was married to Habas, who was born in Palestine and was a prominent journalist and writer.[49] Two other female delegates, the Canadian-born psychologist May Bere Merminsky (Merom, 1894–1986) and the Russian-born physician Anna (Hannah) Brachyahu (Borochov, 1887–?), were active members of Palestine's Jewish women's movement, and also tied, albeit indirectly, to the Labor Zionist movement.[50] Also fluent in English was the US-born veteran of the Jewish Brigades, Benjamin (Ben-Zion) Ilan (1913–1975), who was a member of kibbutz Afikim and the National Council of the Jewish labor party.[51] Unsurprisingly—given the growing tensions with Labor Zionism—there were no Revisionist Zionist representatives in the delegation.

If the delegation's diversity reflected the unsettled character of Zionist Asianism, then the presence of—and response to—the Zionist delegation at the conference further underscored the divides within Asianism writ large and the conflicting conceptions of postcolonial modernization. In their speeches, Bergmann and his colleagues focused on agricultural technology and economic reconstruction. Speaking the language of modernization seemed to be a prudent choice: no discourse could better fit an event planned by Nehru, who believed "the nationalist movement was designed to free this unity so that India could join the world-historical march towards modernity."[52] An ancient site like Purana Qila would permit them to speak about the way in which new technologies were crucial in connecting the past with the future. Though a British reporter who attended the meeting wrote that they "made a good impression," shortly after Bergmann spoke of a peaceful and tolerant Asia, Taqieddin al-Solh, the Arab League observer, criticized Zionism and the presence of the Hebrew University delegation at the conference. Echoing the broader discourse of Asian unity, al-Solh stated that the Arab states celebrated India's freedom "since your freedom is necessary for our freedom." Yet, al-Solh warned, Palestine was in a particularly precarious position. Due to the "Hebrew-Semitic" attempt "to take advantage as a special minority under the defence of British bayonets," Palestine "is more oppressed than any other country." Al-Solh appealed to the conference, saying, "We hope that you will stand by the side of right with us."[53] Karima al-Sa'id, an Egyptian delegate, voiced a similar reproof of Zionism: "We strongly object to any settlement in Palestine except for the Arabs ... We have had no trouble with the Jews at all ... but we do not want British rule to be replaced by that of European Zionists. We object to them as foreigners, as Europeans; not because they are Jews."[54]

The "New Delhi Incident"—as numerous Zionist newspapers termed al-Solh and al-Sa'id's speeches—brought to the fore Zionist Asianist thinking and its articulation in internal Zionist discourse. A considerable degree of anxiety was evident. *Davar* published a cartoon portraying the Indian organizers inviting the Yishuv delegation to sit on spiked chairs (figure 11.2). The fact that the Indian organizers did not prevent the incident but had allegedly facilitated the offensive Egyptian speech exacerbated this feeling of being ambushed.[55] So too did reports from delegation members Merminsky and Brachyahu of a similarly hostile anti-Zionist spirit at the Pan-Asiatic Women's Conference (convening in parallel to the main conference).[56] The widely read poet Nathan Alterman compared the Yishuv's presence at New Delhi with the ancient Israelites' "eternally publicized" appearance at Mount Sinai—both marked an "incident of a Jew on an

Asiatic stage." Moreover, according to Alterman, just as the Arabs had denounced the Yishuv delegation at the Asian Relations Conference, so too had the (ancient) "Egyptians" opposed the Israelites as they fled Egypt and made their way through the desert.[57] Ya'akov Shimoni expressed disappointment that Nehru and the other Indian leaders "stood on the side of the strong and not the side of the right and this is not a moral quality."[58] Nevertheless, Alterman's "Egyptian" criticism triggered an opposite response—a reassertion of the Yishuv's belonging within a heterogeneous Asia, albeit as an exceptional entity. Even if Asia was "a large and divided continent," the newspaper *Ha'aretz* asserted, it was nonetheless incumbent upon the Zionist leadership to operate with the "deep recognition ... that our tomorrow is somewhat tied to the world of tomorrow, which is rising around us through struggles and difficult battles." The Yishuv, according to the newspaper, belonged in Asia.[59]

For Bergmann, the head of the delegation, the apparent failure of the Zionists to forge a common anticolonial front with their Indian colleagues was especially frustrating. The delegation's exchange with Gandhi went particularly poorly. In response to David Hacohen's request that he "raise his voice in favor of our persecuted people," Gandhi mentioned "terrible" Jewish terrorist actions in Palestine and "hinted that as somebody would insist that he, Gandhi, should say something about the Palestine question, his words would necessarily be directed mainly against terrorism and therefore it would be better for our sake to leave him out of the picture." Beyond this, Gandhi asserted that Zionists' claims that they would halt their terrorist activity if the British increased Jewish immigration to Palestine were comparable to the flawed British rationale that by placating Hitler with the Munich Pact "everything would be alright [*sic*]."[60] Gandhi's choice of the Munich analogy—and the implicit comparison between Hitler's aggression and the Yishuv's resort to violence—as the basis for rejecting the Zionist delegation's claims was certainly striking on the rhetorical level. Moreover, his condemnation of the Jewish insurgency pointed to his continued belief that the Zionist enterprise lacked any underlying legitimacy. After all, India's leaders played a key role in forging anticolonial alliances and constructing a global interwar internationalism.[61] Notwithstanding Gandhi's commitment to nonviolence, he and the founding fathers of modern India were extremely sympathetic to the violent Irish rebellion against

British rule. The fact that Gandhi opposed Jewish anti-British violence both before World War II and the Holocaust and after ultimately spoke to the fundamental distinction that he saw between (legitimate) anticolonial violence and (illegitimate) Zionist violence. He famously wrote in November 1938 that "the cry for the national home for the Jews does not make much appeal to me" and that Jews should choose the path of nonviolent civil resistance in response to German persecution.[62] Although Bergmann would later convince himself that these frictions were minor and that the development of the Yishuv in Palestine was "the deepest expression of a true and complete return to the Asian homeland," this was certainly a blow.[63]

The desire to belong in Asia, and the anxiety surrounding exclusion from it, also came through in Bracha Habas and David Hacohen's serialized column about the conference. While the authors conveyed the sense that "we have encountered a world that is foreign and inaccessible to us," they simultaneously downplayed the degree of difference.[64] Some aspects of Indian culture, they asserted, were particularly admirable. "The cleanliness, the culture of relations, the lyrical Indian heads with their variety of coverings, the quiet and precise English in the mouths of Indian administrators—all of these inspire a respect for the inhabitants and their ways from one's first step on the ground of this country."[65] Moreover, they relativized the exotic nature of India by portraying the Yishuv as also being exotic, albeit in a different fashion. The Yishuv delegation was not simply European: "There is still something fundamental which separates us from the other groups of Europeans, the various observers and journalists. The unique Eastern ring of our flowing and eloquent language attracts attention and slowly forces a unique definition, which we deserve in spite of the light color of our faces and our European dress."[66] A central motif in this self-exoticization was the specifically Jewish roots of the Yishuv, which rendered it unique even in Asia. "Not only do these nations not have any contact with Jews, the teachings of Israel [*torat Yisrael*] and the heritage that it gave to the entire world had no influence on the Asian nations, their beliefs, traditions, and ways of life."[67] In fact, the Yishuv's difference within Asia, according to Habas, explained why Arab efforts to isolate it had been so successful.[68] Yet, Habas asserted, there were deep and substantive connections between the Yishuv and Asian countries—the Arabs notwithstanding. "Hindu intellectuals with influence in renewing India who are not ignorant of the essence of

משלחת הישוב בניו-דלהי
בְּבַקָשָׁה לָשֶׁבֶת. הַרְגִישׁוּ עַצְמְכֶם כְּמוֹ בְּבֵיתְו...

FIGURE 11.2. "Members of the Yishuv's delegation in New Delhi. Please be seated, feel at home!..." Caricature by Arie Navon, *Davar* weekend supplement, April 4, 1947, page 16. Courtesy of David Navon and the Archives of the Lavon Institute for Labor Research, Israel.

the Indian-Muslim conflict ... are open to relations and bold connections with our enterprise in Palestine. Our bold efforts in settlement, education, raising youth, developing the social structure of the village, and realizing socialism in many avenues of our lives in Palestine inspire curiosity, admiration and a desire for mutual relations."[69] Indeed, that the Zionist participants invoked the language of a return to ancient glories but did not consider themselves to be revivalists but rather modernists mirrored Nehru's suspicion of Hindu revivalist historiography that overemphasized India's spirituality and dwelled on its precolonial past. Ultimately, Habas and Hacohen acknowledged the challenges that the Yishuv faced if they wished to further integrate into Asia and warned the Yishuv not to place "exaggerated hopes" on the overall import of the conference.[70] Nonetheless, they concluded optimistically, "We did well to come here."[71]

Jerusalem, Fall 1949

This optimism soon gave way to increasing pessimism regarding Israel's place in Asia. In the crucial 1947 United Nations vote on the UNSCOP recommendation for partition, the vast majority of the Asian countries voted against partition (only the Philippines voted in favor while China abstained and Thailand was absent).[72] Thereafter, most Asian states opposed Israel's membership in the UN (it was eventually admitted in May 1949 under Resolution 273 with China and the Philippines being the only two countries in Asia voting in favor). Likewise, Israel was not invited to the second Asian Relations Conference in 1949.[73] Israel's pursuit of bilateral relations with Asian nation-states fared no better. Few countries in South and East Asia granted Israel recognition—by 1950 only the Republic of China, the Philippines, Burma, India, and Thailand had done so—and even once they did, diplomatic relations were not immediately established.[74]

Israeli attempts to establish diplomatic relations with India were even less successful. Encouraged by Taraknath Das, an Indian political activist and professor of political science at Columbia University, Zionist diplomats in Palestine and in the US reached out to a number of Indian politicians and diplomats in the months after the Asian Relations Conference.[75] At first these efforts led to minor achievements. Indian technocrats and politicians came to Palestine to study the Yishuv's agricultural and social institutions, including collective and cooperative settlements, and academic exchanges between the Hebrew University and a number of Indian universities were established.[76] Even as India passionately argued against the partition of Mandate Palestine at the UN, the Zionist-cum-Israeli leadership held out hope for warmer relations. The Israeli Orientalist journal, *ha-Mizrah he-Hadash* (The New East), routinely published news updates on South Asia. In India, the journal *India and Israel* (1948–1953) was partially funded by the Israeli government.[77] The journal included a smattering of original articles alongside selections and translations from the Israeli and Indian press. Yet, despite these successes, Israelis made little headway vis-à-vis Nehru and the Indian government. Until September 1950, Nehru refused to grant Israel recognition. When he finally acquiesced and recognized Israel—an event widely celebrated by the Israeli media and diplomatic community[78]—he made sure that Indian diplomats conveyed that they did not plan on sending a diplomat to Israel.[79] Thereafter, Nehru continued to give Israel the cold shoulder despite persistent Israeli diplomatic efforts and assertions that relations were just around the corner.[80] The 1952 official visit of Israeli foreign ministry director Walter Eytan to India and Moshe Sharett's multiple letters to Nehru during 1954 and 1955 failed to sway the Indian leader.[81] Perhaps unsurprisingly, Israeli officials gradually came to see this reality and crafted a narrative in which Nehru was the major stumbling block. To be sure, Ben-Gurion had already opined in 1949 that "the Indian intelligentsia is in our favor, not only due to political reasons but also due to social ones, but Nehru is cautious and is stalling."[82] Still, this discourse picked up in the early 1950s. For example, in 1952, Eliahu Eilat opined that establishing relations would be difficult given Nehru's belief that Israel was a Western-imperialistic element.[83]

Although Nehru's unwillingness to establish relations with Israel drew in part on his view of Israel as an imperial outpost, it was also part of his more fundamental turn away from Asianism. As T. A. Keenleyside has argued, Nehru's growing concern with securing aid and steering clear of the intensifying Cold War, in addition to the increasing number of conflicts between Asian states—including the Korean War, the Kashmir conflict, and the Israeli-Arab war—and those states' ensuing susceptibility to entanglement with the Cold War, made apparent "the impracticability of the vision of Asian unity."[84] Against this backdrop, Israeli frustration with Nehru and Indian diplomats grew; one Israeli diplomat blamed Indians' "small brains" for their reluctance to forge relations.[85]

Yet, despite these repeated rejections, Zionists did not fully give up on integrating into the budding inter-Asian society. If by the mid-1950s it was clear that Moshe Shertok's 1947 statement that the Yishuv sought to join Asia and assist in "bridging and connecting modern Asia to the rest of the world" was overly optimistic, then Zionists still sought to cast themselves as part of "Asia" and as a bridge between "Asia" and the "West."[86] This was most apparent in Zionist diplomatic efforts. In November 1949, the Foreign Ministry set up its Asian Division. Meanwhile, Israeli delegations participated in a variety of international and inter-Asian conferences and summits, including student conferences, jurists' conferences, conferences concerning housing and urban planning, and conferences hosted by the UN Economic Commission for Asia and the Far East.[87] Israel also sent a variety of experts to Asian countries and hosted large numbers of individuals and groups from Asian countries.[88] Trade between Israel and a number of Asian countries (Burma, Thailand, Indonesia, and Japan) also gradually increased during this period.[89] At the same time, Israel sought to join other nascent Asian states in international politics. Given that the Israeli government had adopted a policy of nonalignment in the years before 1952, various Israelis saw this development as a step toward conforming to the broader orientation of Asian countries, especially India.[90] In UN votes and resolutions, especially pertaining to colonialism and human rights, Israel voted with the vast majority of decolonizing countries (this voting alliance has been termed the "Afro-Asian bloc"). Israel, a leading intelligence agency officer later argued, was "eager to join the group, but was barred from doing so by the Arab members."[91] Still, there was a strain of optimism among Zionist-cum-Israeli Asianists. As one newspaper claimed, mixing historical fact with Asianist aspiration, Israel was "but one of the Asian states that received their independence in the four years after World War Two."[92]

Bandung, Spring 1955

When the Asian-African Conference convened in Bandung, Indonesia, in 1955 with much pomp and sartorial theater, there were no Israelis in suits on the stage. After all, the organizers of the conference did not invite Israel. Yet, exactly what this non-invitation signified was not entirely clear—to Israeli Asianists of the time or to historians writing since. Was it an Asian rejection of Israel? Bandung was certainly an important moment in the history of postcolonial internationalism. This much is clear from the sheer scale of the conference and the attention it received: Twenty-nine countries participated in Bandung, comprising a group nearly half the size of the UN and ostensibly representing an estimated 1.5 billion people. Still, that Bandung symbolized a unified "Asia" was far less clear. After all, as Christopher Lee and Naoko Shimazu have shown, Bandung's main success was on the symbolic level rather than on the practical political and strategic level.[93] Moreover, if Nehru began to distance himself from the idea of Asian unity after the Asian Relations Conference, by Bandung he had entirely divorced himself from this concept.[94] In fact, as scholarship from the 1960s and 1970s and more recent work have noted, far from embodying a spirit of unity, Bandung put the fractures and tensions of decolonizing Asia (and to a lesser extent Africa) on public display.[95] To be sure, there were areas of agreement—namely anticolonialism, vague discussions of racial solidarity, and the still popular concept of Asian unity—that would later enable the propagation of Bandung as a symbol of Third World unity.[96] Yet the conference was marked by rivalries between individual leaders as much as it was riven by territorial disputes and political divides. If Bandung offered Nehru an unparalleled opportunity to consolidate his image as a leader of this emerging international bloc, he was soon eclipsed by the new charismatic Egyptian leader Gamal Abdel Nasser and by the Chinese premier Zhou Enlai. Meanwhile, the Israeli-Arab conflict, the Formosa conflict, tensions along the Vietnamese-Chinese border, the Indian-Pakistani conflict, and the Korean War all cast a pall over the conference. Cold War tensions were also readily apparent. Against the backdrop of the recent formation of the Southeast Asia Treaty Organization (SEATO) and the Baghdad Pact, debate raged at the conference as to whether communism was a form of neocolonialism, and only after much political maneuvering was a compromise resolution drafted.[97] While India continued to serve as an example of postcolonial state-building, it was seen not only as an embodiment of anticolonialism but also as "a model for 'national self-sufficiency.'"[98] That this Indian self-sufficiency came at the expense of any willingness to join a large bloc—whether Soviet, Western, or nonaligned—illustrates the instability beneath the images of unity on display at Bandung.

It might, therefore, be less than productive to speak of Israel's non-invitation to Bandung as simply an Asian rejection of Israel. Indeed, if Bandung is to be cast as a moment of separation at all, then the story should really be one of mutual divorce. After all, the Israeli Foreign Office showed little interest in joining what one European observer called "a union of proletarian states."[99] Likewise, a year later, Israeli troops marched into Egypt, helping the British and the French restore Western control of the Suez Canal. As Zach Levey, Uri Bialer, and other historians of Israeli foreign policy have demonstrated, it was during this short but decisive period that Israel reoriented its position, unable to maintain neutrality vis-à-vis the new Cold War realities, which offered different iterations of the East-West binary.[100] Israelis, in other words, were happy to be left out of the new club retroactively tagged as the "Third World."[101]

Instead, it might be more beneficial to examine contemporary Israeli perceptions of the significance of the non-invitation to Bandung. Among Israeli Asianists, the non-invitation brought out both their lingering hopes and their growing cynicism regarding Asia. When the Colombo Powers announced in late December 1954 at the Bogor Conference that they would be convening an Asian and African conference in 1955, Israel was not on the list of invitees. Despite Israeli efforts to secure a spot, and despite the fact that Nehru and Burmese prime minister U Nu supported Israel's invitation, Pakistani prime minister Mohammad Ali Bogra had the final say in the matter.[102] Disappointing though it was, Israelis did not view this non-invitation as especially adverse. Journalist Azriel Carlebach, who was visiting India at that time in a semiofficial capacity, briefly conveyed his disappointment regarding Israel's non-invitation to Nehru before changing the topic.[103] Ya'akov Shimoni (who was then working in the Asian Division) doubted that the conference would have more than symbolic importance: "The conference's remaining value is as a protest and a symbol. However, its diplomatic, practical, and true importance, I believe, will necessarily remain extremely minor."[104] Even David Hacohen, who was serving as the Israeli delegate in Rangoon and who made a much more emphatic stand against the decision, ultimately saw the non-invitation as a pure political machination on the part of the Arabs: "We did not come out of this matter, in spite of the failure, beaten or weaker. On the contrary, our existence and pressure are increasingly demonstrated on the international level. And, the aggressiveness and crudeness of the Arabs are more apparent and more bothersome for all."[105]

Still, as the conference began, Israeli officials increasingly worried about the direction events were taking. In the lead-up to the conference, Israeli officials and newspapers speculated that Arab representatives would raise an anti-Israel resolution. These concerns were exacerbated by the recent Israeli Operation Black Arrow (February 28, 1955), which killed thirty-four Egyptian soldiers and officers in Gaza. In addition to being the deadliest attack since the end of the 1948 war, this clash would subsequently be seen as a turning point in Nasser's understanding of Israeli-Egyptian relations. Against this backdrop, Israeli diplomats frantically tried to preempt the anticipated blow.[106] These efforts, however, had little effect. In his speech at Bandung, Iraqi delegate Fadhil Jamali emphasized Zionism's perniciousness: "It is one of the blackest and darkest chapters in human history. It is the worst offspring of imperialism ... Zionism, however, with its state of Israel, has added to all these evils, the uprooting of a whole population and the expulsion by force of innocent peoples from their homes, thus making destitute and homeless nearly one million Palestinian Arabs."[107] Then, as part of his efforts to court Nasser, Chinese premier Zhou Enlai spearheaded an effort to adopt a more forceful resolution in support of Palestinian refugees.[108] While the Burmese and Indians moderated the resolution, the final communiqué (under chapter E, "Other Problems") declared support for the "Arab people of Palestine" and called for the "implementation of the United Nations Resolutions on Palestine and the achievement of the peaceful settlement of the Palestine question."[109] The Israeli government and press saw the resolution regarding the Arabs of Palestine as firmly anti-Israel, in spite of the fact that it was not placed under the heading of self-determination or "problems of dependent peoples," did not touch upon Israeli military rule, and explicitly asserted that the implementation of the UN resolutions should be through a peaceful settlement.

Yet, while Israeli officials and newspapers cast the Bandung resolution as a blow, they asserted that it was far from fatal. To be sure, Israeli officials portrayed the decision as unjust. As the Israeli ambassador to Japan told his Indian counterpart, by discussing Israel in its absence, the participants at Bandung had committed the very acts for which they criticized the Western powers: "That the future of Asian countries was decided in their absence and without their participation and that an aggressor was sometimes rewarded at the expense of the injured party."[110] On April 20, the lead editorial in *Davar* termed the resolution in support of the rights of the Arabs a "distortion of justice." At the same time, however, officials and newspapers downplayed the resolution by focusing attention on its ostensible instrumentality and merely declaratory nature. As *Davar* asserted, the conference comprised an "impure mixture [*sha'atnez*]" of nations, and the resolution was a "cold calculation" intended to paper over its deep fractures and find commonality among "nations and states the separation between which is so vast and pronounced that there is not even any meaning to their joint resolutions."[111] In addition to their doubts as to whether Israel was simply another Asian country, Israelis saw Bandung—and Asia—as a fractured entity in and of itself.

In turn, rather than view Bandung as a nail in the coffin of their overtures to Asian nation-states, Israelis recalibrated their efforts. In the wake of Bandung, Moshe Sharett implored Israeli diplomats to avoid "a historiosophic analysis of our nation and the nations of Asia and Africa" and instead pay heed to the fact that "experience has shown that the efforts invested in forging ties with Asian countries have been fruitful."[112] *Hatzofeh* held out the hope that the conference would induce Israel to embark on an extensive diplomatic campaign in the non-Muslim Asian countries. "The 'kick' that Israel received at Bandung can potentially become a blessing."[113]

Zeev (Walter) Laqueur put forth an even colder, realist view regarding the Israeli "orientation toward Asia":

> From a geographical point the state of Israel does not belong in the sphere of the Far East or Southeast Asia. The distance between us and Rome, Paris, and London is much shorter than that to Delhi, Jakarta, and Peking. Those who desire can obviously develop a mysticism of our belonging to the Asian lands, but in diplomatic terms there is no significance to this.

What is more, according to Laqueur, Israel did not suffer from the "retardation [*pigur*] in the diplomatic thinking of the ruling class in Asian countries." While acknowledging that there were strong anti-imperialist elements in Israel and that the Yishuv had exhibited anti-British zeal in the recent past, he implored Israeli leaders not to revert to this anticolonial thinking in order to be accepted within Asia. Rather, it was incumbent upon the Israeli leaders and public to exhibit "strong nerves" and patience.[114] Indeed, as we will show in the conclusion, the Israeli government did not understand Bandung as spelling an end to its activity in Asia.

Conclusion: Chronicles of the Non-Epic Encounter

Discourses of resemblance and mimicry, as critical theorist Homi Bhabha famously claimed, are constructed around an ambivalence. Mimicry, as opposed to fake, false, or fictitious identity, is the expression of a yearning to forge a new identity, "the desire for a reformed, recognizable Other, *as a subject of difference that is almost the same, but not quite.*" It often collapses into a paradox, namely "[t]he desire to emerge as 'authentic' through mimicry."[115] Following this insight, Daniel Boyarin has suggested reading Herzlian Zionism as a psychodrama of mimicry, an attempt to overcome Jewish ambivalence by imitating European colonial powers and ultimately being absorbed by them. Boyarin speculates:

> I ask of myself, [i]s the very desire to be in the "postcolonial club," to grab as a Jew some bit of moral high ground, ultimately any different from Herzl's desire to be in the "colonial club," to grab a bit of literal territory? Still seeking acceptance as a Jew, am I a specimen of "white skin, black masks," a postcolonial mimic, a talmudic Jazzjew?[116]

The Jewish past and present, no doubt, is an arena fraught with numerous unresolved puzzles and ambiguities of cultural difference. And yet, writing from privilege, the temptation of expropriating postcolonial critique as a form of virtue signaling is great, particularly among members of the middle-class, predominantly male, academic cosmopolitan elite. To be honest, we should also halt in our pursuit to identify an unacknowledged kinship between Jewish history and postcolonial literary critique and look in the mirror. Is this inquiry not a continuation of older strategies of appropriation, a recasting of the Jew as a subaltern, marginalized minority?

As we have attempted to show in this chapter, a certain degree of mimicry is an unavoidable feature not only of the colonial encounter with the other but also of the Zionist reimagination of the Jewish nationalizing subject itself. The eastward orientation of Zionism in general, and Zionist Asianism in particular, illustrate the pernicious nature if not the inevitability of the considerable degree of mimicry implied in the Jewish national project, whether it takes the colonial or the postcolonial mode. This eastward-looking gaze never developed into a full-fledged, systematic political theory. Most Zionist Asianists did not offer a clear distinction between "Asia" and the "East" but rather used these fluid categories interchangeably, for they were not denoting a clear geography as much as an abstract nexus of space and culture. It was, above all, an aesthetic sensibility and a cultural construct developed by Eastern and Central European Jews who were both participating in and taken aback by the metaphysics of "soil," "roots," and "autochthonousness" that characterized nineteenth-century romantic nationalism. It emerged in a European context, as response to a rising tide of *Völkisch* nationalism that rendered "the Jew," to use Étienne Balibar's wording, "a person in the 'wrong' soil," who had to be removed from it.[117] Paradoxically, it could also end up, as in the case of Buber, giving weight to theories concerning Jewish "racial power" (*jüdische Rassenkraft*), endorsing the idea that Jews constitute a "community of blood," and reaching a conclusion that there is an Eastern soul hiding within the body of every Jew, even those who bear the external appearance of Western bourgeois citizens.[118]

Jewish Orientalism, in short, was never an orientation devoid of internal contradictions. Yet unlike Edward Said's totalizing binary view of Orientalism and Occidentalism as two incompatible orientations, this was not an Orientalism that looked at the East only as an exotic space to be discovered, colonized, and ruled. Instead, the East was imagined by these figures as a place where Jews could find their roots and reclaim a forgotten, authentic Eastern identity—a "Semitic brotherhood." This quickly evolved into a belief in the possibility of a broader "revival of the East" of which Zionism would be part.

Post-1945 politics forced Zionist Asianists to recalibrate their positions and translate a racial aesthetic sensibility into the language of realpolitik and decolonization. The transition into the postcolonial age pushed them to abandon an enchanted view of common Eastern or Oriental origins and adapt themselves to the age of nation-states. Skeptical of nation-statism, Bergmann noted in his official report in 1947 that he was disturbed by the fact that stateless minorities such as the Kurds could not be represented at the conference, and that practically all the delegations and representatives "were of the unanimous opinion that in every country a homogenous unity should be created out of the existing groups, minorities and religions." His memo also highlighted the inapplicability of the idea of ethnically homogenous national units in Palestine:

> We pointed out in various private conversations that this could not apply to Palestine since in this country two different nations are living together, neither of which was prepared to assimilate or to amalgamate itself to the other. In the official deliberations of the conference, however, we saw no possibility of stressing this point. It would have given rise to a very controversial and difficult discussion, and since all of the discussions were centred around the problems of South East Asia [*sic*] only, we felt justified to avoid this controversy.[119]

The point arose in the final act of the conference and, Bergmann speculated, would no doubt come up in the future. He was not wrong.

On the one hand, contrasting the representation of Zionism in the inter-Asian conference in 1947 with its ultimate sidelining from Bandung seems to tell a story of mutual divorce. As we argued in this chapter, this is a story that goes beyond the chronicles of diplomatic history alone. Instead, it is one of a period of transformation. Zionists-cum-Israelis turned into "nervous outsiders," looking at the crystallization of a new language of "Third Worldism" and the creation of a new club of nations—more precisely, nation-states.[120] The discursive and theatrical dimensions of both conferences were an inherent and essential feature, and they serve as a reminder that these political spaces were created through both inclusions and exclusions. By the time of Bandung, Jews' place in the ethno-racial category of "European whiteness" had been cemented. Israel's ruling elite was not eager to join the new club and felt uncomfortable internalizing this ethno-racial assignment as part of the archetypical *sabra* (new Jew) identity. After the Suez War of 1956, and in light of its involvement in the establishment of the United Nations Emergency Force (UNEF), India was once again depicted in an Israeli newspaper as offering Israelis a seat on a bed of nails, while it sat comfortably on a cushion named Kashmir. In this cartoon, "Srulik," the famous character invented by the caricaturist Katriel Gordosh ("Dosh") to represent little Israel, was a prototypical Labor Zionist, coded as a young, light-skinned, somewhat naïve but always brave male pioneer (figure 11.3). Like the diplomatic summits, which offered theatrical stages to performances of difference, such images marked the move away from hybridity toward an intensification of the division between East and West. From the vantage point of Middle Eastern history, these heightened divisions were not divorced from the erosion and ultimate collapse of what historian Ussama Makdisi has described as a broader "ecumenical frame," in which religious differences did not collapse into sectarianism but provided room for cross-religious solidarity.[121] From the vantage point of Jewish history, the ossification of differences also marked, perhaps, the end of what the late Zygmunt Bauman considered to be the root cause of anti-Jewish prejudice throughout the age—"proteophobia," the fear of that which cannot be ordered or neatly categorized.[122] The fuzziness or oscillation of identity that shaped the ways in which numerous Jewish thinkers, including the early Zionist Asianists, thought about themselves and their political future was no longer viable.

On the other hand, this seemingly non-epic encounter sheds light on Zionist Asianism's indeterminate fate. Even if Israel's inability to secure an invitation to the Bandung conference exacerbated the doubts plaguing Zionist Asianism, it did not mark its ultimate demise. As far as diplomatic history is concerned, Bandung—and the subsequent crisis in Suez—did not clearly bring about Israel's "outsider status in the international community," nor did it constitute a mutual divorce between Israel and "Asia."[123] After all, as recent scholarship has shown, Bandung was as much a moment of unity among the nascent postcolonial states as it was one of divisions. By the mid-1950s, it became increasingly questionable whether "Asia" continued to be a clearly defined family of nations. The reorientation of Zionist Asianists, in other words, was intertwined with the question of whether there was ever a single "Asia" from which to separate. Moreover, Israeli connections with Asian and African nation-states were never entirely eradicated: Israeli diplomatic and military relations with Asia and, increasingly, Africa flourished during the late 1950s through the early 1970s, and Israel continued to be involved in South and Southeast Asia. Finally, the ostensible similarities and connections between Israel and Asia, as well as the composition of the Zionist Asianist faction, gradually changed. In the late 1950s, counter-establishment figures like Boaz Evron, Natan Yelin-

Figure 11.3. "The fakir: 'sit!'" Caricature by Kariel Gardosh ("Dosh"), *Ma'ariv*, February 17, 1957. Courtesy of Daniella Gardosh.

Mor, and Uri Avnery, all veterans of the anti-British underground groups Lehi (Stern gang) and Etzel (Irgun), took up the older eastward-looking discourse. In 1958, they published the "Hebrew Manifesto," which called for the political integration of the State of Israel with its Arab neighbors in a joint "Semitic Space" and for collaboration with Nehru's India and the Non-Aligned Movement.[124] The more recent past has witnessed what is, perhaps, a novel form of Zionist Asianism with the rise of populist and anti-liberal political alliances between Israeli and Indian leaders. Ultimately, then, rather than simply being a case of unacknowledged kinship, the story of post–World War II Zionist Asianism and its various afterlives points to a far more complex and ambivalent relationship between Zionism and the postcolonial world.

NOTES

The authors would like to thank David Armitage, Rotem Geva, Shimon Lev, Erez Manela, Sam Moyn, and Robert Vitalis for their valuable feedback on earlier drafts of this chapter.

1. Jawaharlal Nehru, "Asia Finds Herself Again [Speech Delivered at the Opening of the Asian Relations Conference at New Delhi, March 23, 1947]," in *The World's Great Speeches*, ed. Lewis Copeland et al. (Newburyport, MA: Dover Publications, 2012), 617–619, here 617. The full list of countries that sent delegates to the congress includes Afghanistan, Burma, Ceylon, China, Egypt, India, Indochina, Indonesia, Iran, Jewish Palestine, Korea, Malaya, Nepal, Outer Mongolia, Philippines, Siam, Soviet Asian republics (Armenia, Azerbaijan, Georgia, Kazakhstan, Tajikistan, Uzbekistan), and Tibet. In addition, the Arab League, Australia, Great Britain, Russia, Turkey, the United States, and the United Nations organization sent observers to the congress.

2. Bracha Habas and David Hacohen, *Twenty Days in India: March–April 1947* (Tel Aviv: Am Oved, 1947), 7–8 [Hebrew]. Unless stated otherwise, all translations from Hebrew and German in this chapter are ours.

3. Sisir Gupta, *India and Regional Integration in Asia* (Bombay: Asia Publishing House, 1964), 37. Cited in Vineet Thakur, "An Asian Drama: The Asian Relations Conference, 1947," *The International History Review* 41 (2019): 673–95, here 675.

4. Ella Shohat, *Israeli Cinema: East/West and the Politics of Representation* (Austin: University of Texas Press, 1989); Aziza Khazzoom, "The Great Chain of Orientalism: Jewish Identity, Stigma Management, and Ethnic Exclusion in Israel," *American Sociological Review* 68 (2003): 481–510.

5. For a slightly different take on the mainstream Zionist view of the "Orient," see Arieh Bruce Saposnik, "Europe and Its Orients in Zionist Culture Before the First World War," *The Historical Journal* 49 (2006): 1105–23.

6. Herzl described his Jewish state as an "outpost of civilization" (*Vorpostendienst der Kultur*), part of a "European barrier" against Asiatic barbarism (*ein Stück des Walles gegen Asien*). Theodor Herzl, *Der Judenstaat; Versuch einer modernen Lösung der Judenfrage* (Berlin: Jüdischer Verlag, 1920 [1896]), 24. Jabotinsky was no less decisive: "We Jews have nothing in common with the so-called East and thank God for that. If some of our uneducated masses are guided by spiritual ancient traditions and prejudices, reminiscent of the 'East,' we should help them recover from this addiction." Vladimir Jabotinsky, "The East," [1926], in *Guiding Principles to Current Problems*, ed. Joseph Nedava (Tel Aviv: Jabotinsky Institute, 1981), 91 [Hebrew].

7. Homi K. Bhabha, *The Location of Culture* (London: Routledge, 1994), 85.

8. Todd M. Endelman, "Benjamin Disraeli and the Myth of Sephardi Superiority," *Jewish History* 10 (1996): 21–35.

9. Thomas Clarke, *India and Palestine, or the Restoration of the Jews* (London: W. Bremner & Company, 1861); George Eliot, *Daniel Deronda*, 8 vols. (Edinburgh: William Blackwood and Sons, 1876).

10. Hanan Harif, *For We Be Brethren: The Turn to the East in Zionist Thought* (Jerusalem: The Zalman Shazar Center, 2019) [Hebrew]; Hanan Harif, "Asiatic Brothers, European Strangers: Eugen Hoeflich and Pan-Asian Zionism in Vienna," in *Against the Grain: Jewish Intellectuals in Hard Times*, ed. Ezra Mendelsohn, Stefani Hoffman, and Richard I. Cohen (New York: Berghahn, 2014), 171–85.

11. Shmuel Werses, "Daniel Deronda in the Hebrew Press and Literature," *Molad* 8 (1980): 39–40 [Hebrew]; Mikhal Dekel, "'Who Taught This Foreign Woman About the Ways and Lives of the Jews?': George Eliot and the Hebrew Renaissance," *English Literary History* 74 (2007): 783–98. We would like to thank Derek Penslar for turning our attention to these works. An earlier, incomplete attempt to translate Eliot's novel was made by Haim [sometimes cited as Henry or Hayyim] Guedalla (1815–1904), a prominent Anglo-Jewish philanthropist of Moroccan origins and one of the closest aides to Sir Moses Montefiore, with whom he was connected by marriage, accompanying him on several of his travels, including his 1855 visit to Jerusalem. For additional details, see Monika Mueller, *George Eliot U.S.: Transatlantic Literary and Cultural Perspectives* (Madison, NJ: Fairleigh Dickinson University Press, 2005), chapter 3; Abigail Green, *Moses Montefiore: Jewish Liberator, Imperial Hero* (Cambridge, MA: Belknap Press of Harvard University Press, 2010), 170, 400–402 and passim.

12. Arie M. Dubnov, "'True Art Makes for the Integration of the Race': Israel Zangwill and the Varieties of the Jewish Normalization Discourse in Fin-de-Siècle Britain," in *New Directions in Anglo-Jewish History*, ed. Geoffrey Alderman (Brighton, MA: Academic Studies Press, 2010), 101–34. Col. Albert W. Goldsmid, who converted to Judaism and became one of Herzl's few supporters in England, reportedly introduced himself to Herzl by saying, "I am Daniel Deronda." Theodor Herzl, *Tagebücher 1895–1904*, vol. 1 (Berlin: Jüdischer Verlag, 1922), 324 [entry of November 25, 1895]. Herzl had, however, previously taken the name Tancred when he joined the German-nationalist fraternity Albia in 1880. Derek Penslar speculates that he might have been familiar with Disraeli's 1847 book of that name. Derek Penslar, *Theodor Herzl: The Charismatic Leader* (New Haven, CT: Yale University Press, 2020).

13. "The Poet of Zion and 'Child of Half-Asia' Naphthali [*sic*] Herz Imber Drifts to New York," *New York Times*, June 26, 1904; Naphtali Herz Imber, *Barkai the Third, Or: The Blood Avenger, Poems* (New York: A. H. Rozenberg, 1904) [Hebrew]. Barkai is a Talmudic term for Venus, the morning star. In addition to the dedication, Imber included in the opening of his book a copy of his letter to the Japanese emperor, explaining that "[t]he horrors of Kishineff [*sic*, Kishinev pogrom], which took place a year before the outbreak of the present war, has inspired me to prophesize the punishment of the Russians in the victory of your Majesty's arms. There was another inspiration—the poem which your Majesty has published in three stanzas, which has inspired me to render them in the sacred language of the oldest nation of the world—the Hebrews." Ibid., preface.

14. Nahum Sokolow, *History of Zionism, 1600–1918*, vol. 1 (London: Longmans, Green and Co., 1919), 212, 140.

15. Pankaj Mishra, *From the Ruins of Empire: The Revolt against the West and the Remaking of Asia* (London: Penguin, 2013), chapter 5.
16. See Louise Blakeney Williams, *Modernism and the Ideology of History: Literature, Politics, and the Past* (Cambridge, UK: Cambridge University Press, 2009); Michael Collins, *Empire, Nationalism and the Postcolonial World: Rabindranath Tagore's Writings on History, Politics and Society* (London: Routledge, 2012); Priya Satia, "Byron, Gandhi and the Thompsons: The Making of British Social History and Unmaking of Indian History," *History Workshop Journal* 81 (2016): 135–70. A detailed account of the Hebrew reception of Tagore can be found in Shimon Lev, "'Clear Are the Paths of India': The Representation of Tagore in Jewish Literature," *The Journal of Indo-Judaic Studies* 15 (2015): 31–48.
17. A good example can be found in his 1912 travelogue, where he reported with alarm that "thus far, the country [Palestine] is desolate and forsaken, and everywhere one goes he will find an awful and worrying dilapidation, an Asian order and brutal life. (הסדרים סדרי אזיה והחיים מסביב חיי פראים)." Such backwardness would disappear, he added, only if "a miracle from heaven would occur overnight, and England [*sic*] will take all this negligence and turn it into its possession, and would make it an orderly and developed country (ארץ מתוקנה ושלמה), just as it did in Egypt." David Frischmann, *In the Land* (Warsaw: Ahisefer, 1912), chapter 3 [Hebrew].
18. Itamar Ben-Avi, "Palestine's Role in Coming Developments in Asia," *The Pagoda* [Shanghai Rotary Club magazine], January 17, 1935, 4, 5.
19. Gil Eyal, *The Disenchantment of the Orient: Expertise in Arab Affairs and the Israeli State* (Stanford, CA: Stanford University Press, 2006).
20. Tom Reiss, *The Orientalist: Solving the Mystery of a Strange and a Dangerous Life* (New York: Random House, 2005); Paul R. Mendes-Flohr, *Divided Passions: Jewish Intellectuals and the Experience of Modernity* (Detroit: Wayne State University Press, 1991), chapter 4.
21. We borrow the term "post-*Bildung*" from Steven E. Aschheim, "German Jews Beyond *Bildung* and Liberalism: The Radical Jewish Revival in the Weimar Republic," in *Culture and Catastrophe: German and Jewish Confrontations with National Socialism and Other Crises* (New York: New York University Press, 1996), 31–44.
22. Stefan Vogt, "The Postcolonial Buber: Orientalism, Subalternity, and Identity Politics in Martin Buber's Political Thought," *Jewish Social Studies* 22 (2016): 161–186, here 168.
23. Martin Buber, "In Später Stunde," *Der Jude* 5 (1920–21): 1–5, here 5 as translated by Vogt, "The Postcolonial Buber," 175.
24. Michael Mack, *German Idealism and the Jew: The Inner Anti-Semitism of Philosophy and German Jewish Responses* (Chicago: University of Chicago Press, 2013); Shulamit Volkov, "Antisemitism as a Cultural Code: Reflections on the History and Historiography of Antisemitism in Imperial Germany," *Leo Baeck Institute Year Book* 23 (1978): 25–46; Marc David Baer, *German, Jew, Muslim, Gay: The Life and Things of Hugo Marcus* (New York: Columbia University Press, 2020).
25. Franz Baermann Steiner, "Letter to Mr. Gandhi [1946]," in *Selected Writings*, vol. 2 (New York: Berghahn Books, 1999), 129–46; Martin Buber, *A Land of Two Peoples: Martin Buber on Jews and Arabs*, ed. Paul R Mendes-Flohr (New York: Oxford University Press, 1983), 106–26.

26. In the original: "לא, לא למען דבר כזה, מילאנו את שירותינו; לא כדי להשתתף באמריקניזציה של אסיה; חרתנו על דגלנו את שם ציון." Martin Buber, *Selected Writings on Judaism and Jewish Affairs*, vol. 2 (Jerusalem: Ha-Sifriyah ha-Tsiyonit, 1984), 247 [Hebrew].

27. On Hoeflich, see Scott Spector's contribution to this volume.

28. Eugen Hoeflich, "Panasien," *Der Jude* 6 (1921–1922): 764–67, here 764.

29. Harif, *For We Be Brethren*, chapter 7.

30. Moshe Ya'akov Ben-Gavriêl [aka Eugen Hoeflich], *Die Pforte Des Ostens: Das Arabisch-Jüdische Palästina Vom Panasiatischen Standpunkt Aus* (Berlin: Harz, 1923).

31. Schlomith F. [Frieda] Flaum, *Wandering Daughter of Israel* (Tel-Aviv: L. Meir, 1935) [Hebrew]. Rediscovered recently, Flaum's book was published in a new edition, edited by Ilan Bar-David and Noga Shevach (Beer-Sheva: Ra'av, 2019). The republication is a testimony to the renewed interest in the "Asian" dimension of Zionism. For discussion, see Nurith Govrin, *Forgotten Traveler: Schlomith F. Flaum: Her Life and Work* (Jerusalem: Karmel, 2005) [Hebrew]; Shimon Lev, *From Lithuania to Santiniketan: Schlomith Flaum & Rabindranath Tagore* (New Delhi: Lithuanian Embassy in New Delhi, 2018).

32. Volker M. Welter, "The 1925 Master Plan for Tel-Aviv by Patrick Geddes," in *Tel-Aviv, The First Century: Visions, Designs, Actualities*, ed. Maoz Azaryahu and S. Ilan Troen (Bloomington: Indiana University Press, 2012), 299–326.

33. Arie M. Dubnov and Laura Robson, eds., *Partitions: A Transnational History of Twentieth-Century Territorial Separatism* (Stanford, CA: Stanford University Press, 2019).

34. Vijay Prashad, *The Darker Nations: A People's History of the Third World* (New York: New Press, 2007), 27; T. A. Keenleyside, "Nationalist Indian Attitudes Towards Asia: A Troublesome Legacy for Post-Independence Indian Foreign Policy," *Pacific Affairs* 55 (1982): 210–30, here 212; G. H. Jansen, *Afro-Asia and Non-Alignment* (London: Faber and Faber, 1966), 51; Giri Deshingkar, "The Construction of Asia in India," *Asian Studies Review* 23 (1999): 173–80.

35. *Asian Relations, Being Report of the Proceedings and Documentation of the First Asian Relations Conference New Delhi, March–April, 1947* (New Delhi: Asian Relations Organization, 1948), 24.

36. See, for instance, "'A Third World' in Formation: The New Delhi Conference," *Palestine Post*, April 4, 1947; Mark A. Lawrence, "Pacific Dreams: The Institute of Pacific Relations and the Struggle for the Mind of Asia" (PhD diss., University of Texas at Austin, 2009), 124–25.

37. *Asian Relations*, 90–107.

38. Ibid., 96.

39. Jansen, *Afro-Asia and Non-Alignment*, 65.

40. Emanuel Celler to Eliahu Epstein, January 22, 1947, Central Zionist Archives Jerusalem (henceforth CZA), J1/30271; Eliahu Epstein to Moshe Shertok, January 24, 1947, CZA J1/30271.

41. Va'ad Leumi Directorate to Hebrew University Secretariat, January 8, 1947, CZA J1/30271; Naidu to Magnes, October 2, 1946, CZA J1/30226.

42. Shmuel Hugo Bergmann and Jaaqov [Jacob] Shimoni Housing, "Report on the Inter-Asian Conference (April 17, 1947)," CZA, S25/7485 (emphasis in the original). Bergmann

sent Chaim Weizmann a copy of his report, accompanied by a brief description of his meeting with Lord Mountbatten, the last Viceroy. Bergmann to Weizmann, April 24, 1945, Weizmann Archives, 5-2740.

43. Leo Kohn, "The Inter-Asian Relations Conference at New Delhi," *New Judea* 23 (April 1947): 134–35. See also Eliav to Ben Zvi, January 2, 1947, CZA J1/30271; "The Inter-Asian Conference," n.d., CZA J1/30271.

44. Olsvanger would later be involved in the migration of Jews from Kochin to Israel.

45. Alfred Bonné, *The Economic Development of the Middle East: An Outline of Planned Reconstruction after the War* (New York: Oxford University Press, 1945). Some of Bonné's suggestions, including his strong emphasis on Jewish immigration as an engine of industrialization and economic productivity, can be found already a decade earlier, in his study *Der Neue Orient: Eine Einführung in Das Wirtschaftliche und Staatliche Werden Der Orientlände* (Tel Aviv: Hitachduth Olej Germania, 1937). Preparing Palestine's transition from a wartime to a peacetime economy, however, was inherently tied to debates concerning Palestine's "absorptive capacity," which stood at the heart of the post-1939 Zionist-British debates concerning restrictive immigration quotas. From the evidence we gathered it seems that in the postwar years Bonné was still envisioning a loose regional federation or a single customs union that would include Palestine, Syria, Transjordan, Lebanon, and perhaps even Iraq, suggesting that the immigration of two million Jews into Palestine would not change the total "Oriental population" [*sic*] in that entire region. The study, however, did open with a quote from the American Declaration of Independence, which served as the book's motto. See also Nimrod Lin, "People Who Count: Zionism, Demography and Democracy in Mandate Palestine" (PhD diss., University of Toronto, 2017). Bonné's name was included in the list of *Brith Shalom* members. See "Roll of Members of the Brith Shalom [*sic*] society, 1931," CZA A 187/5. We would like to thank Adi Gordon for providing us with this reference.

46. Joan G. Roland, *The Jewish Communities of India: Identity in a Colonial Era*, 2nd ed. (New Brunswick, NJ: Transaction, 1998), chapter 4. After 1948, Pollack was appointed Israel's first trade commissioner to the Far East. Given that Pollack was a member of the *Blau-Weiss* youth movement, we have good reason to believe that his acquaintance with Bonné, Bergmann, and the other German-speaking members of the delegation predates 1947.

47. Shimoni also authored a number of studies of Palestinian society and Asian affairs, including *The Arabs of the Land of Israel* (Tel Aviv: Am Oved, 1947) [Hebrew]; *Contemporary Asia: A Political History* (Tel Aviv: Yizre'el, 1961) [Hebrew]. For discussion, see Eyal, *The Disenchantment of the Orient*, chapter 3.

48. Hacohen's autobiographical notes were published posthumously in David Hacohen, *Time to Tell: An Israeli Life, 1898–1984*, trans. Menachem Dagut (New York: Cornwall Books, 1985). His recollections of his visit to India were put in writing in Habas and Hacohen, *Twenty Days in India*.

49. Habas's name does not appear in some reports, as well as in Bergmann's articles on the conference that appeared in the daily *Ha'aretz*, which may suggest that she was not considered one of the official delegates but was invited as Hacohen's spouse. Interestingly enough, she left one of the most detailed descriptions of the events.

50. Born in Winnipeg, Canada, and trained at Columbia University, May Bere in 1929 married Yisrael Mereminsky, the Histadrut's representative in the United States. Though little is known about Anna Brachyhahu, it is worth mentioning that her spouse was the physician Moderchai Brachyhahu (Borochov, 1882–1959), who laid the foundations of hygiene education and preventative medicine and authored numerous studies promoting what he termed "spiritual hygiene." As Dafna Hirsch has argued, Brachyhahu played a key role in the scientification and medicalization of hygiene discourses and practices, which were inseparable from negative images of "Easternness." See Dafna Hirsch, *"We Are Here to Bring the West": Hygiene Education and Culture Building in the Jewish Society of Mandate Palestine* (Sde Boker: Makhon Ben-Gurion, 2014) [Hebrew].

51. His Indian experience was mentioned only briefly in his posthumous memoir, Ben-Zion Ilan, *An American Soldier/Pioneer in Israel* (New York: Labor Zionist Letters, 1979). We would like to thank Maya Ashkenazi, the director of the kibbutz Afikim archive, for confirming this information. Unfortunately, we failed to trace additional sources shedding light on Ilan's experiences in India.

52. Gyan Prakash, "Writing Post-Orientalist Histories of the Third World: Perspectives from Indian Historiography," *Comparative Studies in Society and History* 32 (1990): 383–408, here 389.

53. *Asian Relations*, 64.

54. Ibid., 64–65.

55. *Davar*, April 4, 1947.

56. Samuel Hugo Bergmann, "Hebrew Letters from the Pan-Asian Conference in New Delhi," *Ha'aretz*, March 25, 1947 [Hebrew]; "New Delhi Hears Palestine Woman," *The Palestine Post*, March 31, 1947.

57. "The case in New Delhi is not the first. Nor is it even the most respected and serious event of them all...The incident at Mount Sinai, which was eternally publicized. An incident of a Jew on an Asiatic stage. (Already then Egypt was involved)!" Nathan Alterman, "Incident at New Delhi," *Davar*, March 28, 1947 [Hebrew].

58. "Marginalia," *Davar*, April 27, 1947 [Hebrew].

59. "Day to Day: Palestine and the East," *Ha'aretz*, April 15, 1947 [Hebrew].

60. Bergmann and Shimoni, "Report on the Inter-Asian Conference," 7.

61. Michele L. Louro, *Comrades against Imperialism: Nehru, India, and Interwar Internationalism* (Cambridge, UK: Cambridge University Press, 2018).

62. Mahatma K. Gandhi, "The Jews," in *Collected Works of Mahatma Gandhi*, vol. 74 (Delhi: Government of India, 2000), 137–41 (originally published in *Harijan*, November 20, 1938). Gandhi's Open Letter triggered Martin Buber to write his own famous response: Martin Buber to Mohandas Gandhi, Jerusalem, February 24, 1939, in *The Letters of Martin Buber: A Life of Dialogue*, ed. Nahum N. Glatzer and Paul Mendes-Flohr, trans. Richard and Clara Winston and Harry Zohn (New York: Schocken, 1991), 476–82. Bergmann, no doubt, was familiar with this sharp exchange due to his proximity to Buber. For discussion, see Blair B. Kling, "Gandhi, Nonviolence, and the Holocaust," *Peace & Change* 16 (1991): 176–96; Aishwary Kumar, *Radical Equality: Ambedkar, Gandhi, and the Risk of Democracy* (Stanford, CA: Stanford University Press, 2015), chapter 4.

63. Shmuel Hugo Bergman[n], "The Inter-Asian Relations Conference," *The Jewish*

Frontier, June 1947, 13–15. We would like to thank Dr. Enrico Lucca for providing us with a copy of this article.

64. Habas and Hacohen, *Twenty Days in India*, 83.
65. Ibid., 64.
66. Ibid., 7–8.
67. Ibid., 52.
68. Ibid., 58.
69. Ibid., 55–56.
70. Ibid., 56.
71. "Letter from India," *Davar*, January 4, 1947.
72. Rami Ginat, "India and the Palestine Question: The Emergence of the Asio-Arab Bloc and India's Quest for Hegemony in the Post-Colonial Third World," *Middle Eastern Studies* 40, no. 6 (2004): 189–218.
73. Jamie Mackie, "The Bandung Conference and Afro-Asian Solidarity: Indonesian Aspects," in *Bandung 1955: Little Histories*, ed. Antonia Finnane and Derek McDougall (Caulfield East: Monash University Press, 2010), 9–26, here 11.
74. Moshe Yegar, *The Long Journey to Asia: A Chapter in the Diplomatic History of Israel* (Haifa: University of Haifa Press, 2004), 58 [Hebrew].
75. Schechtman to Eban et al., July 20, 1948, Israel State Archives Jerusalem (henceforth ISA), HZ-1/2414. Also see Eilat to Sharett, March 3, 1950, ISA, HZ-31/2391. According to Eilat, Das was "among the most ardent Zionists in the Indian delegation in America."
76. Agarwal (All India Spinners' Association) to Shimoni, June 25, 1947, CZA S25/9029; Sinha (Radical Democratic Party) to Shimoni, July 24, 1947, CZA, S25/9029; Greenberg to Bergmann, May 20, 1947, CZA, S25/9029.
77. *Davar* ran a piece praising the journal. See "India and Israel," *Davar*, April 21, 1949.
78. See, for instance, "India's Recognition of Israel," *Davar*, September 18, 1950; "Special Recognition Issue," *India and Israel*, October 15, 1950; "True Independence Is the Condition to Take Advantage of India's Recognition," *Herut*, September 19, 1950; "What Does the Indian Recognition of Israel Introduce," *Ma'ariv*, September 18, 1950.
79. Arazi to Sasson, December 26, 1950, ISA, HZ-30/2385.
80. Pandit to Eban, August 14, 1951, ISA, HZ-1/2414.
81. "Visit of Director to India," March 18, 1952, ISA, HZ-1/2414; Sharett to Nehru, May 21, 1954, CZA, A245/60; Sharett to Hacohen, May 18, 1954, CZA, A245/60; Levin to Doron, May 24, 1954, ISA, HZ-9/458.
82. Ben-Gurion Diary, April 17, 1949, Ben-Gurion Archive.
83. Eilat to Eytan, March 25, 1952, ISA, HZ-1/2414; Eilat to Comay, September 3, 1952, ISA, HZ/2382.
84. Keenleyside, "Nationalist Indian Attitudes Towards Asia," 224–25.
85. Eshed to Doron, September 13, 1953, ISA, HZ-9/458.
86. "Moshe Shertok's Speech at the Political Assembly of the UN," *Davar*, May 16, 1947.
87. "What Did Israeli Youngsters Learn from Their Meetings with Members of Asia?" *Davar*, April 14, 1952; "Conference of Jurists from Asian Countries," *Davar*, December 25, 1953. Shabtai Rosenne represented Israel at the New Delhi Conference; see Levin to Levavi, January 12, 1954, ISA, HZ-1/2414; Rosenne to Asia, January 22, 1954, ISA,

HZ-1/2414; "Israel Participated in a UN Seminar for Housing in India," *Davar*, April 13, 1954; *India and Israel*, April 20, 1953.

88. See "Beginning of Relations between Israel and the State of Asia," *Davar*, March 14, 1954.

89. "Trade with Asia Is Expanding," *Davar*, December 26, 1954.

90. See Uri Bialer, *Between East and West: Israel's Foreign Policy Orientation, 1948–1956* (Cambridge, UK: Cambridge University Press, 2008), 31. See also Eytan's memo "India and Israel," July 1952, ISA, HZ-1/2414.

91. David Kimche, *The Afro-Asian Movement: Ideology and Foreign Policy of the Third World* (Jerusalem: Israel Universities Press, 1973), 37. Between 1953 and 1980 Kimche served in the Mossad, Israel's intelligence agency, reaching the rank of a deputy director. Regarding Israeli voting in the UN, also see Roland Burke, *Decolonization and the Evolution of International Human Rights* (Philadelphia: University of Pennsylvania Press, 2010), 95; Mary Keynes, "The Arab-Asian Bloc," *International Relations* 1 (1957): 238–50, here 243. Keynes notes that beginning in 1951 Israel began to draw away from the bloc and often abstained on issues relating to French North Africa.

92. "Israel and the Asian States," *Davar*, September 19, 1952.

93. Christopher J. Lee, *Making a World after Empire: The Bandung Moment and Its Political Afterlives* (Athens: Ohio University Press, 2010); Naoko Shimazu, "Diplomacy as Theatre: Staging the Bandung Conference of 1955," *Modern Asian Studies* 48 (2014): 225–52. Lee goes so far as to argue that, thanks to Bandung, Nasser was able to ascend to a status equivalent to that of Nehru, a position to be confirmed by the 1956 Suez Crisis.

94. Carlos Romulo, *The Meaning of Bandung* (Chapel Hill: University of North Carolina Press, 1956), 33. Romulo, the Filipino diplomat, noted, "It was a revealing commentary on the changing times and shifting scenes of the Asian-African story that Mr. Nehru, at Bandung, cut an altogether different figure from the serene, imperturbable man who deeply impressed delegates to the New Delhi Conference in 1947."

95. Ibid., 3; Jansen captured this most poignantly: "Two conferences were held at Bandung in April 1955. One was the real conference, about which not very much is known, about which people care even less, and which has faded away like a bad dream. The other was a quite different conference, a crystallisation of what people wanted to believe had happened which, as a myth, took on reality in the Bandung Principles and, later, in the Bandung Spirit." Jansen, *Afro-Asia and Non-Alignment*, 182.

96. George McTurnan Kahin, *The Asian-African Conference, Bandung, Indonesia, April 1955* (Ithaca, NY: Cornell University Press, 1956), 11; Robert Vitalis, "The Midnight Ride of Kwame Nkrumah and Other Fables of Bandung (Ban-Doong)," *Humanity* 4 (2013): 261–88.

97. Kahin, *The Asian-African Conference*, 11–32.

98. Sinderpal Singh, "From Delhi to Bandung: Nehru, 'Indian-ness' and 'Pan-Asian-ness,'" *South Asia* 34 (2011): 51–64, here 59.

99. B. V. A. Röling, *International Law in an Expanded World* (Amsterdam: Djambatan, 1960), 69.

100. Zach Levey, *Israel and the Western Powers, 1952–1960* (Chapel Hill: University of North Carolina Press, 2011); Bialer, *Between East and West*.

101. The use of the term to describe Bandung is anachronistic and glosses over the many alternative terms invoked at the time to describe different configurations of the nascent states. See Vitalis, "The Midnight Ride of Kwame Nkrumah." The person credited with coining the term "Third World" in its contemporary geopolitical sense is the French demographer Alfred Sauvy, who in 1952 compared former colonies to the "third estate" of the French Revolution (the people). It is important to note that at the time this was not considered a pejorative term.

102. Cindy Ewing, "The Colombo Powers: Crafting Diplomacy in the Third World and Launching Afro-Asia at Bandung," *Cold War History* 19 (2019): 1–19, here 14.

103. Carlebach to Sharett, January 21, 1955, ISA, HZ-9/458. For more on Carlebach's trip to India, see Azriel Carlebach, *India: Journal of Visit* (Tel Aviv: Sifriyat Ma'ariv, 1986) [Hebrew].

104. Shimoni to Eytan, March 1, 1955, ISA, HZ-9/458.

105. David Hacohen to Asia Division, January 5, 1955, ISA HZ-9/458.

106. Eytan to All Consulates and Embassies, April 14, 1955, ISA, HZ-9/458.

107. Centre for the Study of Asian-African and Developing Countries (Indonesia), ed., *Collected Documents of the Asian-African Conference: April 18–24, 1955* (Jakarta: Agency for Research and Development, Department of Foreign Affairs, 1983), 64.

108. After discussing the colonial subjugation of North Africans and racial discrimination in South Africa, Zhou said, "The problem of Arab refugees of Palestine still remains to be solved," ibid., 40–41. The Chinese continued along this same line in closed sessions and equated America's support for Israel with its support for Taiwan. See on this matter Roeslan Abdulgani, *The Bandung Connection: The Asia-Africa Conference in Bandung in 1955*, trans. Molly Bodan (Singapore: Gunung Agung, 1981), 110. For the general shift in the People's Republic of China's policy toward the Israeli-Arab conflict and its manifestations at Bandung, see Yufeng Mao, "When Zhou Enlai Met Gamal Abdel Nasser: Sino-Egyptian Relations and the Bandung Conference," in Finnane and McDougall, *Bandung 1955*, 89–108.

109. *Collected Documents of the Asian-African Conference*, 141–42. This chapter also included a resolution supporting Indonesian claims in West Irian over those of the Netherlands and one supporting Yemeni claims over Aden and the Southern Protectorate.

110. Minister to Eytan, April 26, 1955, ISA, HZ-29/2413.

111. "Israel's Absence from the Bandung Conference," *Davar*, April 20, 1955; "The Decision of the Bandung Conference," *Davar*, April 22, 1955.

112. Minutes of Israeli Government Meeting no. 41, April 24, 1955, 10, ISA.

113. "Anti-Israel Decision at Bandung," *Hatzofeh*, April 24, 1955.

114. "Bandung," *Molad*, May 1955.

115. Bhabha, *The Location of Culture*, 86, 88 (italics in the original).

116. Daniel Boyarin, "The Colonial Drag: Zionism, Gender, and Mimicry," in *The Pre-Occupation of Postcolonial Studies*, ed. Fawzia Afzal-Khan and Kalpana Seshadri-Crooks (Durham, NC: Duke University Press, 2000), 234–65, here 258.

117. Étienne Balibar, "Paradoxes of Universality," in *Anatomy of Racism*, ed. David Theo Goldberg (Minneapolis: University of Minnesota Press, 1990), 283–94, here 285.

118. Mark H. Gelber, *Melancholy Pride: Nation, Race, and Gender in the German Literature of Cultural Zionism* (Tübingen: Niemeyer, 2000), 137.

119. Bergmann and Shimoni, "Report on the Inter-Asian Conference," 11.

120. David Walker, "Nervous Outsiders: Australia and the 1955 Asia-Africa Conference in Bandung," *Australian Historical Studies* 37 (2005): 40–59.

121. Ussama Samir Makdisi, *Age of Coexistence: The Ecumenical Frame and the Making of the Modern Arab World* (Oakland: University of California Press), 2019.

122. Zygmunt Bauman, "Allosemitism: Premodern, Modern, Postmodern," in *Modernity, Culture, and "the Jew,"* ed. Bryan Cheyette and Laura Marcus (Cambridge, UK: Polity Press, 1998), 143–56, here 148.

123. Shira Robinson, *Citizens Strangers: Palestinians and the Birth of Israel's Liberal Settler State* (Stanford, CA: Stanford University Press, 2013), 158.

124. [Uri Avnery and Natan Yelin-Mor], *The Hebrew Manifesto* (Tel Aviv: Central Committee, Semitic Action, 1958) [Hebrew].

Part IV
Conversations

12

An Interview with Dipesh Chakrabarty

Dipesh Chakrabarty is one of most distinguished and important postcolonial thinkers today. As a trained historian, he has been among the founding members of the Subaltern Studies Group, one of the original nuclei of postcolonial studies, and he is currently a professor of history at the University of Chicago. He is also a founding editor of *Postcolonial Studies* and a consulting editor of *Critical Inquiry*, two preeminent journals in this field. He is probably best known for his book *Provincializing Europe* (2000), which has been translated into numerous languages and continues to influence historians, philosophers, and cultural critiques around the world. The interview was conducted in the summer of 2020 via email by Stefan Vogt.

STEFAN VOGT. The subtitle of this book is "Postcolonial Studies and the Historiography of Zionism." "Postcolonial Studies" is of course a particularly vague and broad term. Could you describe some essential aspects of your understanding of "Postcolonial Studies" or of "The Postcolonial"? Is this a temporal concept for you, or, as Stuart Hall, for instance, has argued, rather a systematic approach to the histories, cultures, and societies shaped by colonialism? How strictly is it limited in your view to the societies and cultures of the former colonies?

DIPESH CHAKRABARTY. The postcolonial for me is both a temporal concept and not. The prefix "post" clearly refers to a before-after relationship. The question is what comes before what, and what comes after. Conceptually, the "post" refers to a set of critical relationship to questions of modernity that can come only *after* those relations have achieved some dominance or hegemony in the prevalent discourses. So, if one thinks of colonization as an ironical narrative of domination whereby the colonized comes to develop a desire to possess as their own precisely the institutions and knowledge systems that were deployed by the colonizer as instruments of domination—such as the modern nation-state, judiciary, military, industry and technology, and modern academic institutions and their disciplines—then the "post" in postcolonialism would signal the beginning of a critical relationship to such objects of desire. Such a critical relationship could come only *after* the colonized developed a desire for modernization and its trappings. Critical stances like these could develop even during colonial rule, as in the cases of Franz Fanon and Mahatma Gandhi. The expression "post-colonial," however, could also refer to things and events that either follow the establishment of colonial rule or come into existence after colonial rule is formally ended. For the sake of convenience, I will here use "postcolonial" to refer to the quality or property of a particular mode of thinking, and "post-colonial" as a specific period-marker in history (*after* the coming of colonial rule; and *after* the formal cessation of colonial rule).

You ask if the expression should be limited to cases where former colonies of European powers are under discussion. One runs into a familiar problem in wanting to legislate the use of such powerful words as "colonialism" or "postcolonialism." These words became powerful in the twentieth century. In the nineteenth century and before, "to colonize" carried an older, Roman meaning: It referred to the act of taking over a piece of land to create a settlement there. In that sense, only the settler-colonies of European powers were colonies. India was part of the British Empire but not, strictly speaking, a colony, as the British never meant to settle there (while early in their stay some Indian leaders did want them to settle in the same way that Europeans had done in Latin America). In the twentieth century, however—since Lenin's interest in the role that "national liberation" movements could play in the overthrow of global capitalism—we did learn to speak of India as a "colony" and of the British practicing "colonialism" in the subcontinent. Key political words coined at particular moments in history thus go on to change and expand their meanings.

"Colonialism" now works not only as reference to historical forms of rule but also as a metaphor of a particular kind of domination. One speaks of someone's mind or intellectual categories being "colonized" or being in need of decolonization. Such metaphorical extension of the meaning of the verb "to colonize" has to be welcomed for it powerfully expresses one's relationship to the ideas or categories one might be thinking through. Other powerful words—such as race, power, hegemony—undergo similar extensions of their semantic fields, enabling feelings of political solidarity across many historical differences. Take the case of Fanon. The political leaders of the indigenous peoples of Australia, for instance, were reading *The Wretched of the Earth* in the 1960s and 1970s in order to develop their own ideas of sovereignty in the context of what they saw as their own "colonized" condition. Was the "native" of Fanon's Algeria the same as the indigene of Australia in the twentieth century? No, and yet the rhetoric of Fanon's prose must have helped them to express some of their sentiments of resistance.

We have to accept and work with these multiple meanings that some of the key words in our critical vocabulary will inevitably acquire.

STEFAN VOGT. Let us move a little closer to the topic of the book. While it asks for the applicability of concepts of postcolonial studies, it is primarily a book about Jewish history. In his essay "The West and the Rest," Stuart Hall called the Jews the West's "own internal others." The notion that Jews were a colonized group within Europe, that they were subject to colonial ideologies and practices, has been taken up in recent years by a number of scholars of Jewish studies, such as Susannah Heschel, Bryan Cheyette, or John Efron. Would you agree to this interpretation? In which ways would you consider the history of the Jews in Europe as part of colonial history?

DIPESH CHAKRABARTY. I have to begin by reminding you that I am not a scholar of Jewish history. But even so, I know that while at one level the horrendous and murderous antisemitic developments of the mid-twentieth century kindled a spirit of solidarity among diverse groups that made up the Jewish population of the world, there still remain Jews of very different kinds. One thinks of the division not only between the Orthodox and secular Jews but also of divisions between the Jewry of Western and Eastern Europe of the mid-twentieth century as well as of the divisions, let us say, between Moroccan Jews and European Jews in present-day Israel. But, still, the history of oppression of European Jewry reminds you of many themes that mark histories of colonial rule: racism, systematic oppression of target groups, and even the creation of so-called "assimilated Jews" of late-nineteenth and early-twentieth-century Europe. Stuart Hall's description of the Jews as "the internal others" of the West seems right. In recent times, on the other hand, some scholars have pointed to the parallels between the practices of settler-colonial states and those of the Israeli state toward Arab Palestinians (treated as "internal others"). Overall, there are apparent similarities across many contexts but there are also crucial differences. One cannot think of the older Jewish communities of Morocco or India as colonized. So, I would not stretch the metaphor too far.

STEFAN VOGT. The postcolonial scholar Aamir Mufti was the first to develop this into a comprehensive theory that connects the colonial and postcolonial experience with the European Jewish experience. He argues that the European Jews' confrontation with the Enlightenment, with emancipation, and with the developing bourgeois societies has been an early and paradigmatic incarnation of what he calls the "crisis of minority," that is the incapability of European modernity to accommodate difference. In this sense, European Jewish history is seen as a model and even part of colonial history. Mufti claims that connecting Jewish history with colonial and postcolonial history in such a way will help us to understand the implications of European modernity for both the Jews and the colony. Do you agree? How is your reading of Mufti's theses and how does this relate to your own work on the contradictions of European modernity in your seminal book, *Provincializing Europe*?

DIPESH CHAKRABARTY. Mufti's work has pioneered the efforts to build bridges between Jewish history and the political cultural history of the subcontinent. Faisal Devji is another trail-blazing scholar in this area. Mufti read quite deeply into some aspects of the history of Jewish emancipation in Europe to develop his thesis about the "crisis of minority" within the global project of modernity. In other words, European Jewry, for him, is an early instance of modernity's failure to deal with difference, a failure that he then reads through the literature (Urdu) and history of the modern Muslim in colonial India to explain the partition of the country in 1947 and the consequent forced migration of millions of Muslims and Hindus. Devji does the same from a different angle: He shows how much the Jewish conception of "homeland" drove the nation-making imagination of the leaders of the Muslim community in colonial India. Pakistan, especially the western wing of the country (the eastern wing became Bangladesh in 1971), was conceived as a homeland for Muslims from any part of the subcontinent. This marked a significant difference from the "blood and soil" kind of nationalism that the Hindu mainstream—and I might add, the Bengali Muslims of East Pakistan—developed. The ideology of the ruling party in India today—the ideology of *Hindutva* (the attributes of being Hindu)—owes a lot to a text that was inspired by the idea of a homeland for Hindus.

That said, we have to think about another aspect of the Jewish question in Europe, an aspect Hannah Arendt tried to capture by the use of the Anglicized form of a Tamil word: pariah. "The status of the Jews in Europe," she wrote, "has been not only that of an oppressed people but also of what Max Weber has called a 'pariah people'...."[1] In Tamil, the word "pariah" refers to a low-caste person, someone who is despised and shunned. It entered the English language through Portuguese in the sixteenth century and came to mean a low-caste person who is also "low in habits, frequently eating carrion and other objectionable food, and addicted to drink."[2] It is true that the Jews were often otherized in Europe but it was also an other that was hated. As Arendt put it, discussing Herzl's Zionism: "Their [Europeans'] hatred of others became a fixation displaced upon a false object: the Jewish substance."[3] Arendt would move on to create the ethical figure of the "conscious pariah." I will have more to say about that later. Let me just say here that this makes the equation of the Jewish question with the minority question in late-colonial India doubly complicated. First, the Muslims in India had never been pariahs, nor despised through the centuries of Muslim rule and later. Thus, there is an aspect to the Jewish question that the minority question in India did not have in the case of Muslims (the Dalit case would be different). Secondly, the stigma and disgust that the Jews suffered were comparable—as the use of the word "pariah" suggests—to what the so-called low-caste and "untouchable" groups suffered at the hands of dominant castes. These points, I think, complicate the pioneering narratives of Mufti and Devji. There are moves afoot in contemporary India to stigmatize and despise the Muslim community and make them into social "pariahs," but that is a different and a much more recent development.

STEFAN VOGT. In *Provincializing Europe*, you do not discuss the role of Jews, or Jewish history, for the critique of the concept of European modernity and for the goal of "provincializing" this concept. However, it seems to me that the book provides a lot of points from which we could also think in productive ways about this role. For instance, the contradictions between the Enlightenment's claim to universalism and the practical denial of this universalism can also be witnessed in the debates about Jewish emancipation. I also think that your theses about the different temporalities that are at work in colonial contexts could apply, to some degree at least, to Jewish history. Would you think that this is a legitimate way to use your theses? How would you integrate, if at all, Jewish history into your understanding of European modernity and of the necessity to provincialize Europe?

Of course, Jewish history did not only take place in Europe, but also in the colonies. Several contributions to this book address the history of Jews in North Africa and the Middle East or in the Caribbean. At the same time, it is more than problematic to subsume the different experiences of Jews in the various parts of Europe, not to speak of North America, into a single category of "European Jewry." Would you think that looking at Jewish history could thus help to provincialize Europe? Moreover, would you think that looking at this history, and especially at the history of Zionism, which might be considered a project of colonization by a colonized group, could support postcolonial studies in their endeavor to complicate the concept of the colonial? Would you agree that this should be a goal of postcolonial studies?

DIPESH CHAKRABARTY. True, I do not discuss Jewish history in *Provincializing Europe*, but German-Jewish thought informs it in many ways.

You are, for instance, absolutely right to raise the question of time. My critique of the empty notion of time that underlies the secular chronology of academic historical narratives clearly owes a direct and major debt to Walter Benjamin's last important piece of writing, *Theses on the Philosophy of History*, and to his thoughts on messianic time that derive no doubt from Jewish traditions of mysticism. To recall some of his famous lines:

> A historical materialist approaches a historical subject only where he encounters it as a monad. In this structure he recognizes the sign of a Messianic cessation of happening, or, put differently, a revolutionary chance in the fight for oppressed past. He takes cognizance of it in order to blast a specific era out of the homogenous course of history—blasting a specific life out of the era or a specific work out of the lifework.[4]

Benjamin's biographers, Howard Eiland and Michael W. Jennings, point out how many of Benjamin's thoughts on the relationship between the empty and homogeneous chronological history and messianic time arose out of his "intensive discussions with Arendt and Blücher in winter 1939–40 of Scholem's *Major Trends in Jewish Mysticism*, which Scholem had sent Benjamin in manuscript."[5] All this, as Arendt points out in her introduction to *Illuminations*, was central to the "Jewish question" that, understandably, so engaged Benjamin and other German-Jewish intellectuals of his generation that it constituted, in Kafka's words, their "terrible inner condition."[6]

Speaking of Kafka, he is another Jewish thinker from the German-speaking world—apart from Marx, who refused to recognize his Jewishness—who had a quiet but crucial influence on *Provincializing Europe*. This goes back to the question of "minor/minority" that I discussed in the chapter entitled "Minority Histories, Subaltern Pasts." Kafka's importance for our times was, of course, emphasized by Deleuze in his work on "minor literature." The "minor" came to signify an ethical position, as aspiration to resist the majoritarian politics of the majority in such a way as to renounce the very desire ever to speak in the voice of the majority.

So, clearly, certain churnings in the traditions of German-Jewish thought were absolutely critical to my project of provincializing what I called "Europe," a hyperreal entity that I argued was a product of both Europe's work in India and the modernizing imagination of India's anticolonial nationalism. This is a debt I have to acknowledge. But you ask: Can Jewish history help provincialize Europe? The answer, as you acknowledge, is complicated by two facts: (a) the plural nature of global Jewish community and their differentiated histories, and (b) the role the so-called "emancipated" Jewish families played—before Nazism—in the creation of European empires. But Kafka's conception of the "minor" or Arendt's idea of the "conscious pariah" may provide some threads of thought here that I will try and pick up below while answering your other questions.

STEFAN VOGT. One important postcolonial scholar, who was also a Jew from the colonies, was Albert Memmi. So, beginning with him, I would like to speak with you about several attempts by postcolonial scholars to address the history of Zionism, as a specific aspect of Jewish history, within their own conceptual framework. Memmi spoke about parallels between the debates of Jews and Blacks about identity and belonging and noted the influence of the ideas of Négritude on his own thinking about "Judéité." Questions of identity have been at the heart of postcolonial studies from the very beginning. Another particularly interesting way to conceptualize this, in my view, is Stuart Hall's understanding of identity as positioning. In my own work, I try to use Hall's concept of positioning to analyze the location of Zionism within the field of European, and specifically German, nationalism. Paul Gilroy, finally, went further than any other postcolonial thinker in calling for an integration not only of Jewish history, but also of the history of Zionism into the framework of postcolonial studies. In his book *The Black Atlantic*, he noted that Zionism and Black nationalism "share many of its aspirations and some of its rhetoric." I know of course that African history or Black nationalism is not your field of research, but I was wondering what you think of Gilroy's contentions and if you think that they could be applied more generally to the histories of anticolonial movements and postcolonial political developments. More generally, how would you think about possible parallels, similarities, or connections between Jewish, or even Zionist, and anti- or postcolonial discourses and practices of identity?

Closer to your own field, the British postcolonial historian Faisal Devji has studied the creation of Pakistani nationalist ideology and the establishment of the state of Pakistan. In his *Muslim Zion*, he argues that not only were there strong parallels between Pakistani Muslim nationalism and Zionism, but also the processes that led to the independence of Pakistan and Israel respectively bore remarkable similarities This also sheds new light on Israel's own postcoloniality. What are your thoughts about Devji's theses, based on your own work on Indian history? Do you see similarities also between Indian anti- and postcolonial nationalism and the history of Zionism and of Israel?

DIPESH CHAKRABARTY. I cannot, unfortunately, comment on all the individual critics and the contributors you have mentioned here. I have already commented on the usefulness of the link Devji draws between the idea of a homeland for Jews and the Indian Muslim demand for a homeland for the Muslims of the subcontinent. That was indeed a generative move. And our general debts to the insights of scholars of the stature of Stuart Hall and Paul Gilroy are undeniable. But the larger point you make in all of your statement has to do with a question that appears to have structured this whole volume as such: the degree to which Jewish history may be amenable to postcolonial approaches. Given certain features of Jewish history, particularly in Europe from the Middle Ages on—the diasporic nature of the community, the long history of persecution, the limited and insecure nature of the "emancipation" of the nineteenth century, and then, of course, the Holocaust of the mid-twentieth century—there is no question that, as Zygmunt Bauman showed a long time ago with his book, *Modernity and the Holocaust* (1989), Jewish history is central to all critical understanding of modernity. And to the extent that postcolonial/decolonial approaches often entail critical encounters with the assumptions of modernity and modernization—think of the work of Ashis Nandy or Enrique Dussel or Walter Mignolo—there are clearly some important overlaps between Jewish histories and the histories of those who have suffered the negative consequences of colonial/nationalist modernization of their societies and institutions.

What complicates matters here, however, is the fact that the European Jewry, since their "emancipation" and their rise to positions of influence in the worlds of finance, media, and intellection in the nineteenth and twentieth centuries in both Western Europe and America, have fallen on both sides of the story of European empires and their drive for domination of the world. They have been with both the victors and the victims and themselves paid a terrible price for their "successful" participation in the rise of Germany. Jewish bankers funded the absolutist states of Europe. They helped the Habsburgs when the Thirty Years War broke out in 1618 and in turn benefited themselves.[7] Jewish entrepreneurs also played a significant role enabling Europe to "expand" and to set in motion the process of colonization, i.e., the "Europeanization" of the earth. As Paul Johnson's best-selling *A History of the Jews* has it:

> [T]he Jews were well prepared to take advantage of the growth in the world economy which marked the sixteenth century; in view of their exclusion from the Spanish peninsula ... To the West, Columbus' voyages were not the only ones which had a Jewish and *marrano* background in finance and technology. Expelled Jews went to the Americas as the earliest traders. They set up factories.... They controlled the trade in precious and semi-precious stones. Jews expelled from Brazil in 1654 helped to create the sugar industry in Barbados and Jamaica. The new British colonies in the West welcomed them.[8]

Moreover, one cannot forget that the establishment of the nation-state of Israel was facilitated by the existence of the British Empire.

Yet so much of nineteenth- and twentieth-century critical European thought is unthinkable without the contribution of intellectuals of the European Jewry—Marx, Freud, and Einstein just stand out as some of the greatest names here. We are all, everywhere in the world, in their debt. How and why Jewish intellectuals, in spite of all the obstacles that were thrown their way, rose to such commanding heights of almost every sector of human thought in the last two centuries is an extremely rich, complex, and inspiring story in its own right. But it is also true that, unlike in the case of their counterparts among the colonized people, some great Jewish entrepreneurs participated in and benefited from the European imperial machinery in many parts of the world, including in Europe. And the two stories are not unconnected.

Since you mention Memmi, you will remember how he discusses this being-caught-in-the-middle position of the Jewish elite in colonial Tunisia.

His words are worth repeating at some length as he wrote from his personal experience of his own people:

> The situation of the Jewish population—eternally hesitant candidates refusing assimilation—can be viewed in a similar light [as in his discussion of the Italians]. Their constant and very justifiable ambition is to escape from their colonized condition, an additional burden in an already oppressed status. To that end, they endeavor to resemble the colonizer in the frank hope that he may cease to consider them different from him. Hence their efforts to forget the past, to change collective habits, and their enthusiastic adoption of Western language, culture and customs. But if the colonizer does not always discourage these candidates to develop that resemblance, he never permits them to attain it either. They thus live in painful and constant ambiguity. Rejected by the colonizer, they share in part the physical conditions of the colonized and have a communion of interests with them; on the other hand, they reject the values of the colonized as belonging to a decayed world from which they eventually hope to escape.[9]

This has some strong parallels with the in-between situation of the Jewry in Europe. Hannah Arendt, I think, is one of the best theorists of this peculiar condition of the Jews of Western Europe, and we will return to her thoughts in answering the next couple of questions.

STEFAN VOGT. I now want to turn to your own work and its possible implications on the study of the history of Zionism. You have developed the concept of "subaltern pasts" as a concept that would not only bring hidden histories into the light, but also subvert the historicist understanding of history, modernity, and time itself. Could Jewish history—or specific Jewish pasts—be considered examples of those time-knots that you described in *Provincializing Europe* as something that enables us to see the limits of a "European" perspective on history? Can the history of Zionism, as part of this Jewish history, be included in this?

The central argument of *Provincializing Europe*, as I understand it, is that the concepts and categories developed in European thought in order to make sense of history are themselves implicated in the project of submitting the world to European dominance, and that these concepts, while being indispensable, are utterly insufficient to understand Indian, and, by extension, non-European history. The idea to "provincialize" Europe therefore would mean to be aware of these implications and insufficiencies, and to allow subaltern pasts to complicate and unsettle such a historicist view. To what extent would you think that this also applies to inner-European history and, more specifically, to European Jewish history? I am asking because if this were the case, *Provincializing Europe* would have tremendous implication also on how to understand this history, including the position of Zionism within it. It would, for instance, provide important stimulation for the ongoing debate on how to reconceptualize older and obviously problematic notions of a Jewish "contribution" to European culture. What are your thoughts on these questions?

DIPESH CHAKRABARTY. Constraints of space and time will not allow me to do justice to the richness of all the questions you pose here. Let me just say that I have already argued—in the 2007 preface to the second edition of *Provincializing Europe*—that there was no reason why one could not provincialize Europe from within. Several friends from Eastern Europe used to tell me, jokingly, that I should have named the book *Provincializing Western Europe*. But, more seriously, if my fundamental argument was right, then Europeans in different parts of Europe would have had to translate many of their own pre- or non-modern categories of thought into the fundamental categories of modernity in order to experience themselves as modern and therefore as "superior" to others, including many fellow Europeans. And, in my terms, this would have meant the hegemony of History 1 over several other European History 2s. Ashis Nandy's *Intimate Enemy* offers a fascinating illustration of this process in the course of discussing how, in the training that boys received in English public schools in the nineteenth and twentieth centuries, any "feminine" or soft side of the English personality had to yield place to a "hypermasculine" construction of the English persona in order to facilitate the acquisition of the traits of an imperial ruling race. That is just one example. But any game of domination of one people by another scars the history of those who want to dominate. And Jewish history, both internally and with regard to the history of imperial Europe, would not be an exception to this statement.

So, the simple answer to your question is: Yes, it should be possible to use elements of Jewish history to provincialize Europe. In addition, there is something very special about modern Jewish thought. It is integral to modern European thought and also provides a ground for critique. I have already discussed this point. Think, additionally, of the revival of Spinoza that we see today. He is now seen as central to many projects of critique, including Hardt and Negri's—Deleuze-influenced—analysis of the "multitude" in their book, *Empire* (2000).

STEFAN VOGT. The relationship between the academic fields of Zionist history and postcolonial studies has not been an easy one in the past, to say the least. For a long time there has been almost no conversation between scholars of these fields. Only recently have scholars of the history of Zionism begun to turn to concepts of postcolonial studies. Especially with regard to the history of European Zionism, this is still far from being a commonly accepted approach in this field. In the field of postcolonial studies, the history of Zionism is still almost a nonentity. If at all, Zionism figures as part of the colonial structures of domination. It is easy to identify the reason for this. It is of course an echo of the polarized positions that also in the academy dominate the discourse about the Israeli-Palestinian conflict. What do you think about this non-dialogue between postcolonial studies and the historiography of Zionism? Do you see ways to overcome it?

DIPESH CHAKRABARTY. The Israel-Palestine conflict divides scholars for understandable reasons. And just as I do not wish to minimize the centuries-old suffering and persecution of the Jewish people, I do not also minimize the sufferings of the Palestinian people today. But that should not stop any possible dialogue between postcolonial studies and the historiography of Zionism. There is in fact a moment in the history of twentieth-century Jewish thinking around the idea of a Jewish homeland that I find ethical and utopian at the same time. The thought was utopian in that it was not capable of resisting the onslaught of events in the domain of realpolitik. (Hitler's "final solution" in many ways forced the hands of many European and Jewish politicians and facilitated the formation of an Israeli state premised on the problematic idea of a permanent demographic majority of the Jews.) But I find the thought also ethical, for it represents a point in Jewish thought where addressing the suffering of the Jewish minority in Europe did not call on the Jewry of the world to practice their own version of "majoritarianism" over an Arab minority. This ethical moment resonates across the work of many postcolonial thinkers, not least that of Mufti and Devji, the two scholars in South Asian studies with whom we began this discussion. They are both interested in developing what I think of as traditions of "minority" thinking, and it is no surprise that the figure of Kafka should preside over this moment.

This moment is beautifully captured for me in certain writings of Hannah Arendt on the question of a homeland for the Jews in Palestine. As you know, she thought that the best form of Jewish homeland would be within a federal arrangement in which the Arabs would be equal partners:

> The advocates of the Jewish commonwealth or state, [she wrote in 1943], want a Jewish majority and are prepared to guarantee the Arabs their rights as a minority, whereas the existence of binational state within an Arab federation would mean instead it would be the Jews who have a minority status. Both proposals cling to the idea of a sovereign state or empire whose majority people identify with the state.... The truth is, to speak in sweeping generalities, that Palestine can be saved as the national homeland for Jews only if (like other small countries and nationalities) it is integrated into a federation.[10]

Along with this opposition to the nation-state form went the image of an ethical Jewish persona that she saw illustrated in the figure of what she called—following Bernard Lazare—a "conscious pariah"—someone who never sought the status of a "parvenu" and who never therefore disavowed his or her Jewishness in order to "assimilate" into a host culture. "Modern Jewish history, having started with court Jews and continuing with Jewish millionaires and philanthropists, is apt to forget about this other thread of Jewish tradition—the tradition of Heine, Rahel Varnhagen, Sholem Aleichem, of Bernard Lazare, Franz Kafka, or even Charlie Chaplin." Continuing, she added: "It is the tradition of a minority of Jews who have not wanted to become upstarts, who preferred the status of 'conscious pariah.' All vaunted Jewish qualities—the 'Jewish heart,' humanity, humor, disinterested intelligence—are pariah qualities."[11]

Postcolonial scholars can gather in solidarity around Arendt's figure of the "conscious pariah" who refuses to be a "parvenu" partner in projects of domination. Arendt thus shows how the history of Zionism and the quest for a Jewish homeland can be excavated to discover points where the historiography of Zionism and the ethical-political concerns of postcolonial studies can indeed converge and generate a productive and imaginative conversation pointing to possible and more just human futures.

NOTES

1. Hannah Arendt, "The Jew as Pariah: A Hidden Tradition," in *The Jewish Writings*, ed. Jerome Kohn and Ron H. Feldman (New York: Schocken Books, 2007), 275–97, here 276.
2. See the entry for "pariah," "parraiar," in Henry Yule and A. C. Burnell, *Hobson-Jobson: A Glossary of Colloquial Anglo-Indian Words and Phrases, and of Kindred Terms, Etymological, Historical, Geographical and Discursive* (Delhi: Munshi Manoharlal, 1994 [1903]), 678. The word originally meant a "drummer," a low-caste occupation.
3. Hannah Arendt, "Antisemitism," in *The Jewish Writings*, 46–121, here 54.
4. Walter Benjamin, *Illuminations*, ed. and with an introduction by Hannah Arendt, trans. Harry Zohn (New York: Schocken Books, 1968), 263 [first published in German in 1955].
5. Howard Eiland and Michael W. Jennings, *Walter Benjamin: A Critical Life* (Cambridge, MA: Harvard University Press, 2014), 659.
6. Arendt, "Introduction," in Benjamin, *Illuminations*, 1–51, here 30.
7. Paul Johnson, *A History of the Jews* (New York: Harper, 1988), 254–55.
8. Ibid., 249–50. I understand that Johnson's particular facts are not always reliable but the general point about Jews falling on both sides of the colonial divide would appear indisputable.
9. Albert Memmi, *The Colonizer and the Colonized*, expanded ed., trans. Howard Greenfeld (Boston: Beacon Press, 1991), 15–16 [first published in French in 1957].
10. Hannah Arendt, "Can the Jewish-Arab Question Be Solved?" (1943), in *The Jewish Writings*, 193–98, here 194–95.
11. Hannah Arendt, "We Refugees," ibid., 264–74, here 274. See also the 1944 essay, "The Jew as Pariah: A Hidden Tradition," ibid., 275–97, for an elaboration of Arendt's point.

Afterword
Intellectual Journeys

ATO QUAYSON

What *Unacknowledged Kinships* does with great adroitness and insight is to bring together a series of comparative case studies that sift through various concepts to be used for exploring the intersections between the history of Zionism and postcolonial studies. While Vogt, Penslar, and Saposnik's introduction shows the intersectional character of postcolonial concepts such as colonialism, subalternity, and resistance as they apply to Zionism, it is the call they make for us not to take anything for granted but to consistently be prepared to shift perspectives in response to the subject in question that makes this volume so valuable for instigating a productive conversation between the two fields. For the chapters in this book serve to show the resonance of postcolonial concepts for exploring the complexity of Zionism itself, but from viewpoints that are novel and refreshing. More importantly, I think, *Unacknowledged Kinships* also provides a template for comparative work in postcolonial studies that might start with Zionism or Israel but goes well beyond them. Taking Israel as an example of contesting yet mutually reinforcing nationalisms, what might it look like to do a thorough comparative analysis of the histories of Ireland and India, both of which were for centuries under the impress of colonial Britain and yet also diverge fundamentally in their postcolonial configurations? What do developments in the Irish diaspora since 1842 have to tell us about the Lebanese diaspora since the close of the nineteenth century, and how are these two to be understood in relation to the modern Jewish Diaspora since

World War I? Was the fallout of the collapse of the Ottoman Empire for Israel and the Middle East the same as what pertained to the decolonization processes in the French and English Empires? Is the State of Israel a colonial state or a developmental state with colonial features? Is it of the Global North or of the Global South? And if the way in which it has managed its contending Arab and Jewish populations echoes similar practices during the high point of empire, what might be the value of comparing Israeli policies, say, to today's China, which still insists on being called a developmental state in international forums but exercises clear colonial features with respect to its Uyghur population? Are the Uyghurs China's Palestinians, and if so, how are Palestinian (and Arab) provocations against Israel to be compared to the life-and-death protests of the Uyghurs in China? Do these comparisons illuminate various events in various parts of the world, or do they simply serve to obfuscate local contests?

I want to start off my reflections on the confluence between postcolonialism and studies of Zionist history with a personal narrative of how I came to develop an interest in Jewish studies more generally from a postcolonial perspective. I have always felt that as an African scholar it was somehow inauthentic of me to make any serious statements concerning Jewish studies. The reason for this is at once straightforward and yet quite complicated. A long-standing complaint about scholarship in African studies is that Euro-American scholars are able to build substantial careers in the field without learning any African languages.[1] This is something that would not be countenanced in studies of Russian, or French, or Chinese, for example. And so, coming from a combined African studies and postcolonial background, I have often wondered whether I can ever make any statements to be taken seriously about anything in Jewish studies without having even the most rudimentary knowledge of Hebrew, Yiddish, Ladino, and other Jewish languages that have been so fundamental to shaping the Jewish tradition of scholarship. Of course, this proposition might be countered with the fact that German, English, Russian, and French are now also Jewish languages of scholarship. This resonates with similar positions on opposite sides of the argument by Chinua Achebe and Ngũgĩ wa Thiong'o, the first arguing that to write only in African languages was like being ambidextrous yet refusing to use one of your hands, while the second argued passionately that the only way to truly develop the field of African literature was to write exclusively in African languages. Ngũgĩ has thus written several novels in his native Gikuyu but has also translated them into English. Until his death, Achebe wrote his literary works exclusively in English, but amply leavened with inspirations from his native Igbo wisdom traditions, as anyone who has read *Things Fall Apart* would readily attest to.

Despite this continuing anxiety about how I might make acceptable statements about Jewish life and scholarship without sharing in the Jewish tradition, a gradual shift has occurred in my thinking over roughly the past decade and a half. It started first with the principles I adopted with colleagues when establishing the Centre for Diaspora Studies (CDTS) at the University of Toronto in 2005, of which I was director for its first twelve years. We held the view from the beginning that while the application of the term "diaspora" to various cultural and ethnic groups is much welcome, that it was also of signal importance to pay serious attention to the Jewish Diaspora as providing if not the template, then historically the most extensive experience and philosophical discussion of the term.[2] To graduate from the undergraduate program in Diaspora and Transnational Studies, students were required to take both humanities and social science courses and also to study at least two diaspora groups. The first principle was to ensure that they adopted an interdisciplinary view of diasporas and the second was so that they would not immerse themselves entirely in their heritage diasporas (that is to say, a Caribbean student could not graduate only by studying the Caribbean, or an Armenian only by studying things pertaining to Armenian dispersal). Examples from the Jewish Diaspora were consistently presented in both the compulsory 200-level "Introduction to Diaspora Studies" course, as well as in individual gateway level-400 courses such as "Jewish Diaspora Storytelling" and "Cognates of Cosmopolitanism: Diaspora and Representation," among others.[3]

However, what I can now describe as my "pivot" into an earnest interest in Jewish studies was what I happily discovered to be the shared fascination that my colleague Anna Shternshis and I had in the subject of storytelling. This developed slowly and serendipitously over a number of years. Our offices were across from each other at the Centre and we both had the habit of leaving our office doors open while we were in them. We often drifted into each other's offices to ask for views on one thing or another, and with time also started talking about the things we were reading when the other one dropped in unannounced. Anna used to feed me random Jewish stories as well as books on the Jewish storytelling tradition she happened to be working on and I reciprocated in kind with African stories of my own. After a while I discovered that Jewish storytelling bore some uncanny resemblances to African storytelling and that they shared many features of orality between them. On Anna's promptings, and somewhat hesitantly, I began attending the annual Association of Jewish Studies conferences, where I sat in on panels on things that fell well outside my standard areas of expertise. It was a great learning experience about the differences between Jewish studies and African and postcolonial studies. For one thing, Jewish scholars all seemed to be functionally multilingual in various European and non-European languages. This also gave them the advantage of being able to compare texts or phenomena across language traditions as a matter of habit. There was also a great pride in parsing Jewish-language words. The only language group I am aware of in African studies with the same etymological approach to their language are the Yoruba. Like many Jewish scholars, the Yoruba regularly draw on traditional proverbs and wise sayings at will and use these to anchor their various arguments. This is not something you find as a standard practice in monolingual scholars of, say, English or French.

Sometime in the course of my scholarly exchanges with Anna, but completely unrelated, I took on the task of actively getting Marc Caplan's *How Strange the Change* accepted for publication at Stanford University Press.[4] I was one of the manuscript reviewers. The argument of the book was basically that there were structural similarities between the peripheral modernisms of the nineteenth- and early-twentieth-century Yiddish work of writers such as Reb Nachman of Bratslav and Sholem Yankev Abramovitsch (Mendele Mokher Seforim) and others on the one hand, and the early cohort of African writers in the mid-twentieth century such as Amos Tutuola, Chinua Achebe, Camara Laye, Cheikh Hamidou Kane, and others. Anna was equally excited about *How Strange the Change* when it came out, and yet it is clear that most of my colleagues in African and postcolonial literary studies did not share our enthusiasm for Caplan's argument. When I first saw the manuscript, I thought the comparison between Yiddish and African peripheral modernisms to be so blatantly obvious that I wondered how anyone could have failed to see it.

Caplan's example got me thinking about how the Jewish and African traditions might be compared from a historical postcolonial perspective, but my first serious scholarly dive into Jewish studies only took place when I co-edited a special issue on Jewish studies and postcolonialism with Willi Goetschel at the University of Toronto's Department of Philosophy, with whom even though not sharing offices at CDTS I have had countless conversations on Jewish philosophy. And for the special issue we co-edited I finally wrote an essay comparing Sholem Aleichem's *Tevye the Milkman* and Chinua Achebe's *Arrow of God* in terms of the modes of orality that were discernible in their writings.[5] This then brought to full circle the conversations on storytelling that I had long been having with Anna. Thus, Anna Shternshis, Willi Goetschel, and Marc Caplan have been instrumental in shaping the kinds of intersections I have been able to discover between Jewish and postcolonial studies.[6]

I tell this personal narrative of my introduction to Jewish studies to illustrate a number of themes, all of which are not untypical for most postcolonial studies scholars I can think of. The first is that while I have always had an interest in concepts elaborated by Jewish scholars and thinkers, somehow I did not think of them as Jewish but simply as thinkers whose work I found highly stimulating and productive. The names of Karl Marx, Sigmund Freud, Theodor Adorno, Walter Benjamin, Hannah Arendt, Erich Auerbach, and Jacques Derrida readily come to mind among the ones I regularly return to, and all of whose views are readily deployed in postcolonial studies without any acknowledgment of their Jewish heritage. Now, without wanting to appear in any way obtuse, I would like to say that the reason for this is that Jewish thinkers are more easily segregated from their cultural and ethnic background and adopted as universal than, say, Black thinkers, whose race is bound to color their reception. And so, while I can consider Freud and the other thinkers I have mentioned simply as thinkers, when I invoke the work of Du Bois, Stuart Hall, Paul Gilroy, and Achille Mbembe, they emerge as Black thinkers. In other words, for the second group their race is not so easily separable from their identity, while for Jewish thinkers this is readily to be found. But, why, we might ask, is this so? The reason, I think, is as obvious as it is complicated, and that is that to non-Jews such as myself Jewish thinkers are considered first and foremost as white. This is especially so in the cases of the thinkers that

I have just named, whose discourses, even if starting with Jewish examples, readily create thinking that transcends Jewish culture itself. In fact, the idea of the Jewish sources of universalism is one that would be fruitful to investigate seriously, bringing together scholars from different cultural traditions to revisit the entire question. There are of course serious problems with the point I have just made, not the least is that it represents a certain assimilation of Jewish identity into the larger category of whiteness. The point, however, is that because Jewish thinkers are considered white, they are received fundamentally as de-ethnicized thinkers. The ignorant assumption underlying this position is only assuaged when these Jewish thinkers are placed in their historical contexts. It is only then that we find that irrespective of their universalism they have routinely been subject to antisemitic persecution and that they have often found themselves peripheral to the national discourses they sought to contribute to. Exile has been the cost for many of them, especially in the twentieth century.

The second point I want to illustrate with my scholarly trajectory is how little my personal and scholarly background had prepared me to think about anything to do with Jewish studies before I met and interacted with my Jewish colleagues. It is these interactions that helped to gradually illuminate the complexity of the traditions that animated their backgrounds. The Bible might be said to have done part of this job for me already, but given the degree to which it has been appropriated for all kinds of agendas, including antisemitism, it is no longer reliable by itself as a measure of Jewish traditions. For this, familiarity with other sources of Jewish life and thought are required, including the traditions of the Kabbalah, the Talmud, and for understanding the shtetls, the *yizker bikher* that Marianne Hirsch writes about so eloquently in *The Generation of Postmemory* and elsewhere.[7] It is my interaction and friendship with Jewish scholars that led me to deepen my understanding of Jewish studies and the traditions from which it had arisen. It would be interesting to find out how many undergraduate programs worldwide systematically introduce their students to a model of critical race studies that encompasses both Jewish and Black histories in equal measure. As we glean from Michael Rothberg's *Multidirectional Memory*, the arguments regarding commemorations of the traumatic history of various groups seem to turn on the principle of "I suffered, therefore I am," placing the Cartesian *cogito ergo sum* firmly in the vicinity of feelings and affects and making that the justification of foundational speech acts that then come to shape zero-sum calculations about whose memory should be allowed to be acknowledged and memorialized in the public sphere.[8] These ethnic and cultural determinants then come to impact on the design of memory studies, and indeed in the design of undergraduate and graduate programs in general. It is entirely possible for students to go through their entire undergraduate degree and learn nothing about Black culture, never mind about Jewish life and history. This counts for undergraduate programs in many parts of the world, including in Africa, and not just in the Euro-American university. The term "equity-seeking groups" stands for all those who feel themselves politically and socially marginalized by the political systems in which they live and for which they seek forms of equitable representation (in all senses of the word). At a minimal level, a list of equity-seeking groups would include the following: people of color and racial minorities, persons with disabilities, persons with non-heteronormative sexual orientations, formerly colonized people, Native peoples (pertaining specifically to the settler communities of Australia, Canada, and the United States), women, Jews, and Muslims, among others. Each of these gains salience within particular historical configurations. But the point to note is that they are rarely studied systematically together. In my own case, it is only on interacting regularly with my Jewish studies colleagues that I came to realize the number of overlaps between my areas of expertise in African and postcolonial studies and theirs.

The final point relates closely to the previous one and has to do with specific approaches to interdisciplinary case studies. As I am primarily a literary scholar, the primary cases for my entry into Jewish studies were those of the storytelling traditions that Anna Shternshis and I shared over several years. It was out of these conversations that I came to see a whole vista of research possibilities not just to do with literature, but also with broader cultural products and expressions more generally. The question of interdisciplinary case studies is an important one, because it is through specific cases that we build the foundations for understanding the relationships among different domains, whether these are entire fields, such as Jewish and postcolonial studies, or simply those of the overlapping experiences between different cultural groups.

To switch the focus from Jewish studies to the State of Israel, we have to note how it always interposes itself between Jewish studies and postcolonial studies, not the least because even well-meaning critics of Israel are frequently accused of being antisemitic. This imposes a mode of censorship on any statements that might be said about Israel, but this has not stopped postcolonial scholars from adopting stringent anti-Israeli standpoints. Israel's unsteady standing among what should have been early Third World fellow travelers was registered as early as the Bandung Conference in 1955, when the twenty-nine Asian and African participants adopted an anti-Israel resolution in support of the Arab states that took part in the conference. By the 1960s, however, Israel was much lauded as providing technical support in the form of agricultural extension officers in places such as my homeland Ghana and in other parts of West Africa. The heyday of Israeli development involvement in Africa was roughly from the late 1950s to 1973. The 1973 war was a major turning point in Africa-Israel relations, with many African countries breaking off relations thereafter. Even though many of these relations were restored in the 1990s, the hiatus led to much animosity toward Israel's foreign relations position. In a way the relationship with sub-Saharan Africa was dictated by Israel's relationship with North African Arab states such as Egypt, Morocco, and Algeria, among others.

For me and my friends in Ghana, however, the Palestinian killing of eight Israeli competitors at the 1972 Munich Games was a stomach-churning set of events, and one that placed our sympathies firmly with the Israelis. On a personal note, and in contrast to the foreign policy positions being taken by African states, the successful raid on Entebbe to free the hostages taken from the Air France Airbus in Athens and the film that was made out of it in 1977 served to consolidate the Israelis as heroes in our young eyes even further. But by the same token, Israel's image got tarnished in the popular imagination following the Sabra and Shatila massacres of 1982, when the Maronite Phalange militia entered the refugee camps to randomly kill an estimated three thousand Palestinians, reportedly with the tacit permission of, and a short distance from, Israeli military positions. The complex geopolitical calculus that led to the massacres also involved Iran, which had Lebanese surrogates among Palestinians in the two camps for several years before the massacre.[9] It was partly with the objective of purging these Iran surrogates from the two camps that the massacres took place. The public relations disaster that followed the Israeli military's apparent complicity created a bitter taste toward Israel for many people in the postcolonial world, and I recall that at the time young people in my own country started wearing the kaffiyeh as a fashion accessory and as a way of identifying with the Palestinians.

As Israel gained an upper hand in the vicious cycle of revenge reprisals against Palestinian and Arab attacks on Israeli interests and on their own soil, and following the First and Second Intifadas in 1987 and 2000, respectively, there developed in the international community an "on-the-one-hand-on-the-other hand" discourse regarding Israel's treatment of the Palestinians in their midst and also in the occupied territories. Thus, on the one hand Israel has every right to protect itself, and on the other hand the Palestinians feel they are waging a war against a much stronger aggressor. On the one hand Hamas's rockets are intolerable to Israel's sense of security, and on the other hand the rockets are the symptom of a much larger question regarding Israel's right to exist, which has been called into question by Arab factions over the past seventy years. One element that refutes this even-handed kind of evaluation are the statistics of the number of deaths on both sides, because however the even-handed narrative is spun, the number of deaths is predominantly on the Palestinian side. And the images from news feeds keeps confirming the vastly asymmetrical nature of the military engagement. For example, in the eleven days of fighting that took place between Israel and its Palestinian neighbors in May of 2021, a reported 256 Palestinians were killed, including 66 children. The Gaza Ministry of Health reported 1,900 Palestinians injured. The contrast with Israel's casualties is quite stark; for them 13 people were reported killed, including 2 children, with over 200 injured as of May 12.[10] As Israel has won its military battles against the Palestinians over the decades, it also progressively lost the public relations war. This has been responsible for many postcolonial scholars' support of the BDS (Boycott, Divestment, and Sanctions) movement, something that I personally think precipitously abandons the possibility of dialogue and collaboration with progressive Israel-based scholars. To critique the Israeli government is one thing, but to completely abandon Israeli and even in certain cases the Palestinian scholars who are working assiduously in favor of a more equitable and just order is somewhat unfortunate. Analogies with the boycott of apartheid

South Africa have often been made, but the historical differences between the two scenarios are such as to have spawned disagreements even among proponents of BDS.[11]

* * *

I am reminded in closing of what Erich Auerbach wrote from Princeton in 1952:

> [N]ew outlooks on history and on reality have been revealed, and the view of the structure of inter-human processes has been enriched and renewed. We have participated—indeed, we are still participating—in a practical seminar on world history... In any event, our philological home is the earth: it can no longer be the nation.[12]

More recently, in an interview with Sarah Ladipo Manyika as part of the Conversations Across the Diaspora Series, Henry Louis Gates also opined that there are two rivers that flow under Western culture: one is antisemitic and the other is anti-Black.[13] If we take these two views as cross-fertilizing each other, they might help us conceive of a seminar of world history that fully accounts for the relationship between the conditions of differently oppressed peoples in world history. And *Unacknowledged Kinships* would be of primary significance in this regard. As Chinua Achebe puts it in his novel *Arrow of God*: "The world is like a mask dancing. If you want to see it well, you do not stand in one place."

NOTES

1. A strong variant of this sentiment was recently launched at scholars of early modern studies by the Princeton African studies scholar Wendy Belcher, herself a specialist on Ethiopian literature. See her "Are We Global Yet? Africa and the Future of Early Modern Studies," *Eighteenth-Century Fiction* 33 (2021): 413–46. Belcher's reflections did not go down well in the field of Shakespeare studies, where it generated something of a Twitter storm among scholars based in Europe and the US.

2. This position is not entirely without support in the field of modern diaspora studies. See, for example, Robin Cohen, *Global Diasporas: An Introduction*, 2nd ed. (London: Routledge, 2008); Stéphane Dufoix, *Diasporas*, trans. William Rodamor (Berkeley: University of California Press, 2008); Daniel Cullocciello Barber, *On Diaspora: Christianity, Religion, and Secularity* (Eugene, OR: Cascade Books, 2011); Khachig Tölölyan, "The

Contemporary Discourse of Diaspora Studies," *Comparative Studies of South Asia, Africa and the Middle East* 27 (2007): 647–55; Ato Quayson and Girish Daswani, "Diaspora and Transnationalism: Scapes, Scales and Scopes," in *A Companion to Diaspora and Transnationalism*, ed. Ato Quayson and Girish Daswani (New York: Blackwell, 2013), 1–26.

3. I want to thank my former colleagues at DTS Anna Shternshis, Kevin O'Neill, Hui Kwee Huang, Ken MacDonald, and Antonela Arhin for providing such a fertile environment in which to think about all things diaspora. For the current work of the Centre, see https://cdts.utoronto.ca.

4. See Marc Caplan, *How Strange the Change: Language, Temporality, and Narrative Forms in Peripheral Modernism* (Stanford, CA: Stanford University Press, 2011).

5. Willi Goetschel and Ato Quayson, "Jewish Studies and Postcolonialism," *The Cambridge Journal of Postcolonial Literary Inquiry* 3 (2016). My own contribution was entitled "Comparative Postcolonialisms: Storytelling and Community in Sholem Aleichem and Chinua Achebe," 55–77. The special issue also had essays by Willi Goetschel, Natalie Zemon Davis, Nils Roemer, Marc Caplan, and Sarah Philips Casteel, along with an introduction by the two co-editors laying out the stakes of bringing the two fields together.

6. I mention these three only because they are the ones that I have most regularly had face-to-face conversations with, but in fact the list of interlocutors on the intersections between the two fields is much more extensive and would at the very least have to include Bryan Cheyette, Gabrielle Safran, Naomi Seidman, and Aamir Mufti, among various others. I am very grateful to all these scholars for sharing with me their perspectives on Jewish studies.

7. Marianne Hirsch, *The Generation of Postmemory: Writing and Visual Culture After the Holocaust* (New York: Columbia University Press, 2012).

8. Michael Rothberg, *Multidirectional Memory: Remembering the Holocaust in the Age of Decolonization* (Stanford, CA: Stanford University Press, 2009). Rothberg's argument is much more subtle than my rendition here, but I have often wondered whether the debates on public memory don't echo Descartes to a certain degree.

9. Iran's quite complicated geopolitical calculus in the region since the 1979 Revolution is spelled out in great and fascinating detail in Arash Azizi, *The Shadow Commander: Soleimani, The U.S., and Iran's Global Ambitions* (New York: One World, 2020).

10. See Weiyi Cai, et al., "The Toll of Eight Days of Conflict in Gaza ad Israel," *New York Times*, May 17, 2021, https://www.nytimes.com/interactive/2021/05/17/world/middleeast/israel-palestine-gaza-conflict-death-toll.html. See also "2021 Israel-Palestine Crisis," https://en.wikipedia.org/wiki/2021_Israel%E2%80%93Palestine_crisis#:~:text=As%20a%20result%20of%20the,at%20least%20200%20injured%20Israelis.

11. Noam Chomsky has to me what seems to be the most sophisticated position on BDS. He argues variously for careful targeting in the occupied territories rather than blanket cultural boycotts of Israel. See, for example, his "On Israel-Palestine and BDS," *The Nation*, July 2, 2014, https://www.thenation.com/article/archive/israel-palestine-and-bds/, and his speech at the United Nations and subsequent interview with Amy Goodman in 2014, https://www.democracynow.org/2014/10/22/noam_chomsky_at_united_nations_it.

12. Erich Auerbach, "Philology and *Weltliteratur*," *The Centennial Review* 13 (1969): 1–17, here 11, 17.

13. Sarah Manyika's interview with Skip Gates was under the auspices of the Museum of the African American Diaspora (MOAD)'s Conversations Across the Diasporas Series and took place on April 9, 2021. See Conversations Across the Diaspora with guest Dr. Henry Louis Gates, Jr., https://www.youtube.com/watch?v=gGphmh7EfYw.

Bibliography

Aaronsohn, Ran. "Settlement in Eretz Israel—A Colonialist Enterprise? 'Critical' Scholarship and Historical Geography." *Israel Studies* 1 (1996): 214–29.

Aaronsohn, Ran. "Settlement in Palestine: A Colonial Endeavour?" In *Zionism: A Contemporary Controversy*. Edited by Pinhas Ginossar and Avi Bareli, 340–54. Sde Boker: Ben-Gurion Research Center, 1996 [Hebrew].

Abdulgani, Roeslan. *The Bandung Connection: The Asia-Africa Conference in Bandung in 1955*. Translated by Molly Bodan. Singapore: Gunung Agung, 1981.

Achcar, Gilbert. *The Arabs and the Holocaust: The Arab-Israeli War of Narratives*. New York: Metropolitan Books, 2010.

Adler, Kathleen. *Camille Pissarro: A Biography*. London: B. T. Batsford Ltd., 1978.

Adriaansen, Robbert-Jan. *The Rhythm of Eternity: The German Youth Movement and the Experience of the Past, 1900–1933*. New York: Berghahn Books, 2015.

Alcalay, Ammiel. *After Jews and Arabs: Remaking Levantine Culture*. Minneapolis: University of Minnesota Press, 1993.

Anidjar, Gil. "Jewish Mysticism Alterable and Unalterable: On Orienting Kabbalah Studies and the 'Zohar of Christian Spain.'" *Jewish Social Studies* 3 (1996): 89–157.

Anidjar, Gil. *Our Place in al-Andalus: Kabbalah, Philosophy, Literature in Arab Jewish Letters*. Stanford, CA: Stanford University Press, 2002.

Anzi, Menashe. "From Biblical Criticism to Criticism of the Kabbalah: Colonialism and Interreligious Interactions in the Indian Ocean and Yemen." *Journal of Levantine Studies* 10 (2020): 91–110.

Aran, Gideon. *Kookism. The Roots of Gush Emunim: Settler Culture, Zionist Theology and Contemporary Messianism*. Jerusalem: Carmel, 2013.

Arendt, Hannah. *The Jewish Writings*. Edited by Jerome Kohn and Ron H. Feldman. New York: Schocken Books, 2007.

Aschheim, Steven E. *Brothers and Strangers: The Eastern European Jew in German and German-Jewish Consciousness, 1800–1923*. Madison: University of Wisconsin Press, 1982.

Aschheim, Steven E. "German History and German Jewry: Boundaries, Junctions and Interdependence." *Leo Baeck Institute Year Book* 43 (1998): 315–22.

Aschheim, Steven E. "German Jews Beyond *Bildung* and Liberalism: The Radical Jewish Revival in the Weimar Republic." In *Culture and Catastrophe: German and Jewish Confrontations with National Socialism and Other Crises*, 31–44. New York: New York University Press, 1996.

Aschheim, Steven E., and Vivian Liska, eds. *The German-Jewish Experience Revisited*. Berlin: De Gruyter, 2015.

Ashcroft, Bill, Gareth Griffith, and Helen Tiffin, eds. *The Empire Writes Back: Theory and Practice in Post-Colonial Literatures*. London: Routledge, 1994.

Ashcroft, Bill, Gareth Griffith, and Helen Tiffin, eds. *The Post-Colonial Studies Reader*. London: Routledge, 1995.

Atia, Nadia, and Kate Houlden, eds. *Popular Postcolonialisms: Discourses of Empire and Popular Culture*. London: Routledge, 2019.

Auerbach, Erich. "Philology and *Weltliteratur*." *The Centennial Review* 13 (1969): 1–17.

Aydin, Cemil. *The Politics of Anti-Westernism in Asia: Visions of World Order in Pan-Islamic and Pan-Asian Thought*. New York: Columbia University Press, 2007.

Azizi, Arash. *The Shadow Commander: Soleimani, The U.S., and Iran's Global Ambitions*. New York: One World, 2020.

Baer, Marc David. *German, Jew, Muslim, Gay: The Life and Things of Hugo Marcus*. New York: Columbia University Press, 2020.

Baldwin, P. M. "Liberalism, Nationalism, and Degeneration: The Case of Max Nordau." *Central European History* 13 (1980): 99–120.

Balibar, Étienne. "Paradoxes of Universality." In *Anatomy of Racism*. Edited by David Theo Goldberg, 283–94. Minneapolis: University of Minnesota Press, 1990.

Bamberg, Michael. "Considering Counter-Narratives." In *Considering Counter-Narratives: Narrating, Resisting, Making Sense*. Edited by Michael Bamberg and Molly Andrews, 351–71. Amsterdam: John Benjamins Publishing Company, 2004.

Barak, Oren. *State Expansion and Conflict: In and Between Israel/Palestine and Lebanon*. Cambridge, UK: Cambridge University Press, 2017.

Barber, Daniel Cullocciello. *On Diaspora: Christianity, Religion, and Secularity*. Eugene, OR: Cascade Books, 2011.

Bareli, Avi. "Forgetting Europe: Perspectives on the Debate about Zionism and Colonialism." *The Journal of Israeli History* 20 (2001): 99–120.

Baron, Beth. *The Orphan Scandal: Christian Missionaries and the Rise of the Muslim Brotherhood*. Stanford, CA: Stanford University Press, 2014.

Bartal, Israel. *Cossack and Bedouin: Land and People in Jewish Nationalism*. Tel Aviv: Am Oved, 2007 [Hebrew].

Bartal, Israel. *The Jews of Eastern Europe, 1772–1881*. Philadelphia: University of Pennsylvania Press, 2005. Original Hebrew edition: Tel Aviv: Ministry of Defense Publishing House, 2002.

Bartal, Israel, and Anthony Polonsky. "Introduction. The Jews of Galicia under the Habsburg Empire." *Polin. Studies in Polish Jewry* 12 (1999): 4–23.

Bar-Yosef, Eitan. *A Villa in the Jungle: Africa in Israeli Culture*. Jerusalem: Van Leer Institute/Kubbutz HaMeuchad, 2014 [Hebrew].

Bar-Yosef, Eitan. "A Villa in the Jungle: Herzl, Zionist Culture, and the Great African Adventure." In *Theodor Herzl: From Europe to Zion*. Edited by Mark H. Gelber and Vivian Liska, 85–102. Tübingen: Niemeyer, 2007.

Bar-Yosef, Eitan, and Nadia Valman, eds. *"The Jew" in Late-Victorian and Edwardian Culture: Between the East End and East Africa*. Basingstoke: Palgrave Macmillan, 2009.

Bashkin, Orit. "The Arab Revival, Archaeology, and the Ancient Middle Eastern History." In *Pioneers to the Past: American Archaeologists in the Middle East, 1919–1920*. Edited by Geoff Emberling, 91–101. Chicago: The Oriental Institute Museum Publications, 2010.

Bashkin, Orit. "Introduction to a Roundtable: Jewish Identities in the Middle East, 1876–1956: The Middle Eastern Shift and Provincializing Zionism." *International Journal of Middle East Studies* 46 (2014): 577–80.

Bashkin, Orit. "My Sister Esther: Reflections on Judaism, Ottomanism, and the Empire of Egypt in the Works of Farah Antun." In *The Long 1890s in Egypt: Colonial Quiescence, Subterranean Resistance*. Edited by Marilyn Booth and Anthony Gorman, 315–41. Edinburgh: Edinburgh University Press, 2014.

Bashkin, Orit. *New Babylonians: A History of Jews in Modern Iraq*. Stanford, CA: Stanford University Press, 2012.

Bashkin, Orit. "On Noble and Inherited Virtues: Discussions of the Semitic Race in the Levant and Egypt, 1876–1918." *Humanities* 10 (2021). https://doi.org/10.3390/h10030088.

Bashkin, Orit. "Why Did Baghdadi Jews Stop Writing to Their Brethren in Mainz? Some Comments about the Reading Practices of Iraqi Jews in the 19th Century." *Journal of Semitic Studies* 15 (2004): 95–111.

Beatty, Aidan. "Zionism and Irish Nationalism: Ideology and Identity on the Borders of Europe." *The Journal of Imperial and Commonwealth History* 45 (2017): 315–38.

Becke, Johannes. "Beyond Allozionism: Exceptionalizing and De-Exceptionalizing the Zionist Project." *Israel Studies* 23, no. 2 (2018): 168–93.

Becke, Johannes. "Dismantling the Villa in the Jungle: Matzpen, Zochrot, and the Whitening of Israel." *Interventions* 21 (2019): 874–91.

Becke, Johannes. "Land and Redemption: The Zionist Project in Comparative Perspective." *Trumah* 23 (2016): 1–13.

Becke, Johannes. *The Land Beyond the Border: State Formation and Territorial Expansion in Syria, Morocco, and Israel*. Albany: State University of New York Press, 2021.

Becke, Johannes. "Towards a De-Occidentalist Perspective on Israel. The Case of the Occupation." *Journal of Israeli History* 33 (2014): 1–23.

Becke, Johannes. "Varieties of Expansionism: A Comparative-Historical Approach to the Study of State Expansion and State Contraction." *Political Geography* 72 (2019): 64–75.

Becker, Howard Saul. *Outsiders: Studies in the Sociology of Deviance*. New York: Free Press, 1963.

Behar, Almog, and Yuval Evri. "From Saadia to Yahuda: Reviving Arab Jewish Intellectual Models in a Time of Partitions." *Jewish Quarterly Review* 109 (2019): 458–63.

Behar, Moshe, and Zvi Ben-Dor Benite, eds. *Modern Middle Eastern Jewish Thought: Writing on Identity, Politics and Culture, 1893–1958*. Waltham, MA: Brandies University Press, 2013.

Beinin, Joel. *The Dispersion of Egyptian Jewry: Culture, Politics, and the Formation of a Modern Diaspora*. Berkeley: University of California Press, 1998.

Beinin, Joel. [Book review.] "*Nazi Propaganda for the Arab World* by Jeffrey Herf; *From Empathy to Denial: Arab Responses to the Holocaust* by Meir Litvak and Esther Webman." *International Journal of Middle East Studies* 42 (2010): 689–92.

Beinin, Joel, and Zachary Lockman. *Workers on the Nile: Nationalism, Communism, Islam, and the Egyptian Working Class, 1882–1954*. Princeton, NJ: Princeton University Press, 1987.

Belcher, Wendy. "Are We Global Yet? Africa and the Future of Early Modern Studies." *Eighteenth-Century Fiction* 33 (2021): 413–46.

Ben-Ari, Nitsa. *Romanze mit der Vergangenheit. Der deutsch-jüdische historische Roman des 19. Jahrhunderts und seine Bedeutung für die Entstehung einer neuen jüdischen Nationalliteratur*. Tübingen: Niemeyer, 2006.

Bendix, Regina. *In Search of Authenticity: The Formation of Folklore Studies*. Madison: University of Wisconsin Press, 1997.

Benjamin, Walter. *Illuminations*. Edited and with an introduction by Hannah Arendt. Translated by Harry Zohn. New York: Schocken Books, 1968.

Berkowitz, Michael. *The Jewish Self-Image in the West*. New York: New York University Press, 2000.

Berkowitz, Michael. "Transcending 'Tzimmes and Sweetness': Recovering the History of Zionist Women in Central and Western Europe, 1897–1933." In *Active Voices. Women in Jewish Culture*. Edited by Maurie Sacks, 41–62. Urbana: University of Illinois Press, 1995.

Berkowitz, Michael. *Zionist Culture and West European Jewry before the First World War*. Chapel Hill: University of North Carolina Press, 1993.

Bhabha, Homi K. *The Location of Culture*. London: Routledge, 1994.

Biale, David. *Gershom Scholem: Kabbalah and Counter-History*. Cambridge, MA: Harvard University Press, 1979.

Bialer, Uri. *Between East and West: Israel's Foreign Policy Orientation, 1948–1956*. Cambridge, UK: Cambridge University Press, 2008.

Biger, Gideon. "The Names and Boundaries of Eretz-Israel (Palestine) as Reflections of Stages in Its History." In *The Land That Became Israel: Studies in Historical Geography*. Edited by Ruth Kark, 1–22. New Haven, CT: Yale University Press, 1990.

Block, Nick. "On Nathan Birnbaum's Messianism and Translating the Jewish Other." *Leo Baeck Institute Year Book* 60 (2015): 61–78.

Bloom, Harold. *The Anxiety of Influence: A Theory of Poetry*. Oxford: Oxford University Press, 1997.

Bömelburg, Hans-Jürgen. *Friedrich II. zwischen Deutschland und Polen: Ereignis- und Erinnerungsgeschichte*. Stuttgart: Alfred Kröner Verlag, 2011.

Booth, Marilyn. *May Her Likes Be Multiplied: Biography and Gender Politics in Egypt*. Berkeley: University of California Press, 2001.

Bornstein, George. *The Colors of Zion: Blacks, Jews, and Irish from 1845 to 1945*. Cambridge, MA: Harvard University Press, 2011.

Boyarin, Daniel. "The Colonial Drag: Zionism, Gender, and Mimicry." In *The Pre-Occupation of Postcolonial Studies*. Edited by Fawzia Afzal-Khan and Kalpana Seshadri-Crooks, 234–65. Durham, NC: Duke University Press, 2000.

Boyarin, Daniel, and Jonathan Boyarin. "Diaspora: Generation and the Ground of Jewish Identity." *Critical Inquiry* 19 (1993): 693–725.

Brenner, David A. *Marketing Identities: The Invention of Jewish Ethnicity in "Ost und West."* Detroit: Wayne State University Press, 1998.

Brenner, Michael. *Jüdische Kultur in der Weimarer Republik*. Munich: Beck, 2000.

Brenner, Michael, Stefi Jersch-Wenzel, and Michael A. Meyer, eds. *Deutsch-jüdische Geschichte in der Neuzeit 1780–1871*. Vol. 2. Munich: Beck, 2000.

Bretell, Richard R. "Camille Pissarro and St. Thomas: The Story of an Exhibition." In *Camille Pissarro in the Caribbean, 1850–1855: Drawings from the Collection at Olana*. Edited by Richard R. Bretell and Karen Zukowski, 8–17. New York: New York State Office of Parks, 1996.

Bretell, Richard R., and Karen Zukowski. *Camille Pissarro in the Caribbean, 1850–1855: Drawings from the Collection at Olana*. New York: New York State Office of Parks, 1996.

Broder, Henryk M. "Nicht alle Wege führen nach Jerusalem: Nathan Birnbaum—von der Geschichte vergessen." In *Die jüdische Moderne: Frühe zionistische Schriften*. Edited by Nathan Birnbaum, 7–15. Augsburg: Ölbaum-Verlag, 1989.

Brunotte, Ulrike, Anna-Dorothea Ludewig, and Axel Stähler, eds. *Orientalism, Gender, and the Jews: Literary and Artistic Transformations of European National Discourses.* Berlin: De Gryter, 2015.

Brunotte, Ulrike, Jürgen Mohn, and Christina Späti, eds. *Internal Outsiders – Imagined Orientals? Antisemitism, Colonialism and Modern Constructions of Jewish Identity.* Würzburg: Ergon, 2017.

Burke, Roland. *Decolonization and the Evolution of International Human Rights.* Philadelphia: University of Pennsylvania Press, 2010.

Campos, Michelle U. *Ottoman Brothers: Muslims, Christians, and Jews in Early Twentieth-Century Palestine.* Stanford, CA: Stanford University Press, 2011.

Caplan, Marc. *How Strange the Change: Language, Temporality, and Narrative Forms in Peripheral Modernism.* Stanford, CA: Stanford University Press, 2011.

Césaire, Aimé. *Discourse on Colonialism.* Translated by Joan Pinkham. New York: Monthly Review Press, 1972.

Chakrabarty, Dipesh. *Provincializing Europe: Postcolonial Thought and Historical Difference.* Princeton, NJ: Princeton University Press, 2000.

Charmé, Stuart Z. "Varieties of Authenticity in Contemporary Jewish Identity." *Jewish Social Studies* 6 (2000): 133–55.

Chatterjee, Partha. *Nationalist Thought and the Colonial World. A Derivative Discourse?* London: Zed Books, 1986.

Chatterjee, Partha. *The Nation and Its Fragments: Colonial and Postcolonial Histories.* Princeton, NJ: Princeton University Press, 1993.

Cheyette, Bryan. *Diasporas of the Mind: Jewish and Postcolonial Writing and the Nightmare of History.* New Haven, CT: Yale University Press, 2013.

Cheyette, Bryan, and Laura Marcus, eds. *Modernity, Culture and "the Jew."* Cambridge, UK: Polity Press, 1998.

Chomsky, Noam. "On Israel-Palestine and BDS." *The Nation*, July 2, 2014. https://www.thenation.com/article/archive/israel-palestine-and-bds.

Cocks, Joan. "Jewish Nationalism and the Question of Palestine." *Interventions* 8 (2006): 29–30.

Cohen, Hillel. *Year Zero of the Arab-Israeli Conflict 1929.* Waltham, MA: Brandeis University Press, 2015.

Cohen, Judah M. *Through the Sands of Time: A History of the Jewish Community of St. Thomas, U.S. Virgin Islands.* Waltham, MA: Brandeis University Press, 2004.

Cohen, Julia Phillips. *Becoming Ottomans: Sephardi Jews and Imperial Citizenship in the Modern Era.* Oxford: Oxford University Press, 2014.

Cohen, Julia Phillips, and Sarah Abrevaya Stein. *Sephardi Lives: A Documentary History, 1700–1950.* Stanford, CA: Stanford University Press, 2014.

Cohen, Robin. *Global Diasporas: An Introduction.* 2nd ed. London: Routledge, 2008.

Collet, Dominic. "Hunger ist der beste Unterhändler des Friedens: Die Hungerkrise

1770–1772 und die erste Teilung Polens." In *Die Teilungen Polen-Litauens: Inklusions und Exclusionsmechanismen, Traditionsbildung, Vergleichsebenen*. Edited by Hans-Jürgen Bömelburg, Andreas Gestric, and Helga Schnabel-Schüle, 155–70. Oldenburg: Fibre Verlag, 2013.

Collins, Michael. *Empire, Nationalism and the Postcolonial World: Rabindranath Tagore's Writings on History, Politics and Society*. London: Routledge, 2012.

Conklin, Alice L. *A Mission to Civilize: The Republican Idea of Empire in France and West Africa 1895–1930*. Stanford, CA: Stanford University Press 1998.

Costantini, Dino. *Mission civilisatrice: Le rôle de l'histoire coloniale dans la construction de l'identité politique française*. Paris: La Découverte, 2008.

Crawford, Neta C. *Argument and Change in World Politics: Ethics, Decolonization, and Humanitarian Intervention*. Cambridge, UK: Cambridge University Press, 2002.

Dawidowicz, Lucy S. *The Golden Tradition: Jewish Life and Thought in Eastern Europe*. New York: Holt, Rinehart and Winston, 1967.

Dawn, Ernest C. "The Formation of Pan-Arab Ideology in the Inter-war Years." *International Journal of Middle East Studies* 20 (1988): 67–91.

Dekel, Mikhal. "'Who Taught This Foreign Woman About the Ways and Lives of the Jews?': George Eliot and the Hebrew Renaissance." *English Literary History* 74 (2007): 783–98.

Deshingkar, Giri. "The Construction of Asia in India." *Asian Studies Review* 23 (1999): 173–180.

Devji, Feisal. *Muslim Zion: Pakistan as a Political Idea*. Cambridge, MA: Harvard University Press, 2013.

Doğan, Mehmet Ali, and Heather J. Sharkey, eds. *American Missionaries and the Middle East: Foundational Encounters*. Salt Lake City: University of Utah Press, 2011.

Downs, Roger M., and David Stea. *Maps in Minds: Reflections on Cognitive Mapping*. New York: Harper & Row, 1977.

Dubnov, Arie M. "Notes on the Zionist Passage to India, or: The Analogical Imagination and its Boundaries." *Journal of Israeli History* 35 (2016): 177–214.

Dubnov, Arie M. "On Vertical Alliances, 'Perfidious Albion' and the Security Paradigm: Reflections on the Balfour Declaration Centennial and the Winding Road to Israeli Independence." *European Judaism* 52 (2019): 67–110.

Dubnov, Arie M. "'True Art Makes for the Integration of the Race': Israel Zangwill and the Varieties of the Jewish Normalization Discourse in Fin-De-Siècle Britain." In *New Directions in Anglo-Jewish History*. Edited by Geoffrey Alderman, 101–34. Brighton, MA: Academic Studies Press, 2010.

Dubnov, Arie M., and Laura Robson, eds. *Partitions: A Transnational History of Twentieth-Century Territorial Separatism*. Stanford, CA: Stanford University Press, 2019.

Dufoix, Stéphane. *Diasporas*. Translated by William Rodamor. Berkeley: University of California Press, 2008.

Echeruo, Michael J. C. "Edward W. Blyden, 'The Jewish Question,' and the Diaspora: Theory and Practice." *Journal of Black Studies* 40 (2010): 544–65.

Efron, John M. *Defenders of the Race: Jewish Doctors and Race Science in Fin-de-Siècle Europe*. New Haven, CT: Yale University Press, 1994.

Efron, John M. *German Jewry and the Allure of the Sephardic*. Princeton, NJ: Princeton University Press, 2016.

Eiland, Howard, and Michael W. Jenning. *Walter Benjamin: A Critical Life*. Cambridge, MA: Harvard University Press, 2014.

El-Ariss, Tarek. *Trials of Arab Modernity*. New York: Fordham University Press, 2013.

El-Husseini, Rola. *Pax Syriana: Elite Politics in Postwar Lebanon*. Syracuse, NY: Syracuse University Press, 2012.

Endelman, Todd M. "Benjamin Disraeli and the Myth of Sephardi Superiority." *Jewish History* 10 (1996): 21–35.

Engel, Amir. *Gershom Scholem: An Intellectual Biography*. Chicago: University of Chicago Press, 2017.

Ewing, Cindy. "The Colombo Powers: Crafting Diplomacy in the Third World and Launching Afro-Asia at Bandung." *Cold War History* 19 (2019): 1–19.

Eyal, Gil. *The Disenchantment of the Orient: Expertise in Arab Affairs and the Israeli State*. Stanford, CA: Stanford University Press, 2006.

Fahmy, Ziad. *Ordinary Egyptians: Creating the Modern Nation through Popular Culture*. Stanford, CA: Stanford University Press, 2011.

Fanon, Frantz. *Black Skin, White Masks*. Translated by Richard Philcox. New York: Grove Press, 2007.

Fanon, Frantz. "Racism and Culture." *Toward the African Revolution*. Translated by Haakon Chevalier. New York: Grove Press, 1988, 29–44.

Fanon, Frantz. *The Wretched of the Earth*. Translated by Richard Philcox. New York: Grove Press, 2004.

Feichtinger, Johannes, Ursula Prutsch, and Moritz Csáky, eds. *Habsburg postcolonial: Machtstrukturen und kollektives Gedächnis*. Innsbruck: StudienVerlag, 2003.

Feldman, David. "The British Empire and the Jews, c. 1900." *History Workshop Journal* 63 (2007): 70–89.

Finnane, Antonia, and Derek McDougall, eds. *Bandung 1955: Little Histories*. Caulfield East: Monash University Press, 2010.

Fishman, Joshua. *Ideology, Society & Language: The Strange Odyssey of Nathan Birnbaum*. Ann Arbor, MI: Karoma Publishers, 1987.

Florence, Ronald. *Blood Libel: The Damascus Affair of 1840*. Madison: University of Wisconsin Press, 2004.

Forman, Seth. *Blacks in the Jewish Mind: A Crisis of Liberalism.* New York: New York University Press, 1998.

Fox, Robin. *The Search for Society: Quest for a Biosocial Science and Morality.* New Brunswick, NJ: Rutgers University Press, 1989.

Fraenkel, Josef. *Dubnow, Herzl, and Ahad Ha-Am: Political and Cultural Zionism.* London: Ararat Publishing Society, 1963.

Frankel, Jonathan. *The Damascus Affair: "Ritual Murder," Politics, and the Jews in 1840.* Cambridge, UK: Cambridge University Press, 1997.

Freitag, Ulrike, and Israel Gershoni. "The Politics of Memory: The Necessity for Historical Investigation into Arab Responses to Fascism and Nazism." *Geschichte und Gesellschaft* 37 (2011): 311–31.

Freud, Sigmund. "The Uncanny." In *The Standard Edition of the Complete Psychological Works of Sigmund Freud,* 219–56. Vol. 17. Translated by James Strachey. London: Hogarth Press, 1981.

Friedman, Maurice. "Martin Buber and Asia." *Philosophy East and West* 26 (1976): 411–26.

Friedman, Michal Rose. "Orientalism between Empires: Abraham Shalom Yahuda at the Intersection of Sepharad, Zionism, and Imperialism." *Jewish Quarterly Review* 109 (2019): 435–45.

Furas, Yoni. "We the Semites: Reading Ancient History in Mandate Palestine." *Contemporary Levant* 5 (2020): 33–43.

Gans, Haim. *A Political Theory for the Jewish People.* Oxford: Oxford University Press, 2016.

Gates, Henry Louis. "Critical Fanonism." *Critical Inquiry* 17 (1991): 457–70.

Gelber, Mark H. *Melancholy Pride: Nation, Race, and Gender in the German Literature of Cultural Zionism.* Tübingen: Niemeyer, 2000.

Gelber, Yoav. "The History of Zionist Historiography: From Apologetics to Denial." In *Making Israel.* Edited by Benny Morris, 47–80. Ann Arbor: University of Michigan Press, 2007.

Gelber, Yoav. "Zionism and Colonialism." *Nekuda* 245 (2001): 44–47 [Hebrew].

Geldenhuys, Deon. *Contested States in World Politics.* Houndmills: Palgrave Macmillan, 2009.

Gershoni, Israel, ed. *Arab Responses to Fascism and Nazism.* Austin: Texas University Press, 2014.

Gershoni, Israel, and James Jankowski. *Confronting Fascism in Egypt: Dictatorship versus Democracy in the 1930s.* Stanford, CA: Stanford University Press, 2009.

Ghanem, As'ad. *Ethnic Politics in Israel: The Margins and the Ashkenazi Center.* London: Routledge, 2010.

Gietzelt, Dale. "The Indonesianization of West Papua." *Oceania* 59 (1989): 201–21.

Gilman, Sander L. *Jüdischer Selbsthaß: Antisemitismus und verborgene Sprache der Juden*. Frankfurt am Main: Jüdischer Verlag, 1993.

Gilman, Sander L. *Multiculturalism and the Jews*. London: Routledge, 2006.

Gilroy, Paul. *Between Camps: Nations, Cultures and the Allure of Race*. London: Routledge, 2000.

Gilroy, Paul. *The Black Atlantic: Modernity and Double Consciousness*. Cambridge, MA: Harvard University Press, 1993.

Gilroy, Paul. *There Ain't No Blck in the Union Jack: The Cultural Politics of Race and Nation*. London: Hutchinson, 1987.

Ginat, Rami. *A History of Egyptian Communism: Jews and Their Compatriots in Quest of Revolution*. Boulder, CO: Lynne Rienner, 2011.

Ginat, Rami. "India and the Palestine Question: The Emergence of the Asio-Arab Bloc and India's Quest for Hegemony in the Post-Colonial Third World." *Middle Eastern Studies* 40, no. 6 (2004): 189–218.

Golomb, Jacob. *In Search of Authenticity: From Kierkegaard to Camus*. London: Routledge, 1995.

Gonzalez, Allyson. "Abraham S. Yahuda (1877–1951) and the Politics of Modern Jewish Scholarship." *Jewish Quarterly Review* 109 (2019): 406–33.

Gordon, Adi, ed. *Brith Shalom and Bi-National Zionism: The "Arab Question" as a Jewish Question*. Jerusalem: Carmel, 2008 [Hebrew].

Gordon, Daniel. "Telling the Whole Truth: Albert Memmi." *Jewish Review of Books* 9 (Spring 2018): 27–30.

Gorenberg, Gershom. *The Accidental Empire: Israel and the Birth of the Settlements, 1967–1977*. New York: Times Books, 2006.

Govrin, Nurith. *Forgotten Traveler: Schlomith F. Flaum: Her Life and Work*. Jerusalem: Karmel, 2005 [Hebrew].

Green, Abigail. "The British Empire and the Jews: An Imperialism of Human Rights?" *Past and Present* 199, no. 1 (2008): 175–205.

Green, Abigail. *Moses Montefiore: Jewish Liberator, Imperial Hero*. Cambridge, MA: Belknap Press of Harvard University Press, 2010.

Greene, Annie. "Burying a Rabbi in Baghdad: The Limits of Ottomanism for Ottoman-Iraqi Jews in the Late Nineteenth Century." *Journal of Jewish Identities* 12 (2019): 97–123.

Greene, Annie Leah. "Provincial, Not Peripheral: Ottoman-Iraqi Intellectuals and Cultural Networks, 1863–1914." PhD diss., University of Chicago, 2018.

Gribetz, Jonathan Marc. "An Arabic-Zionist Talmud: Shimon Moyal's At-Talmud." *Jewish Social Studies* 17 (2010): 1–30.

Gribetz, Jonathan Marc. *Defining Neighbors: Religion, Race, and the Early Zionist-Arab Encounter*. Princeton, NJ: Princeton University Press, 2014.

Gribetz, Jonathan Marc. "'Their Blood Is Eastern': Shahin Makaryus and Fin-de-Siècle Arab Pride in the Jewish 'Race.'" *Middle Eastern Studies* 49 (2013): 143–61.

Guha, Ranajit, and Gayatri Chakravorty Spivak, eds. *Selected Subaltern Studies*. New York: Oxford University Press, 1988.

Guignon, Charles B. *On Being Authentic*. London: Routledge, 2004.

Gupta, Sisir. *India and Regional Integration in Asia*. Bombay: Asia Publishing House, 1964.

Haddour, Azzedine. "Sartre and Fanon: On Négritude and Political Participation." *Sartre Studies International* 11 (2005): 286–301.

Hagen, William W. *Anti-Jewish Violence in Poland, 1914–1920*. Cambridge, UK: Cambridge University Press, 2018.

Haim, Sylvia G. "Arabic Antisemitic Literature: Some Preliminary Notes." *Jewish Social Studies* 17 (1955): 307–12.

Haklai, Oded, and Neophytos Loizides, eds. *Settlers in Contested Lands: Territorial Disputes and Ethnic Conflicts*. Stanford, CA: Stanford University Press, 2015.

Hall, Stuart. "Cultural Identity and Diaspora." In *Identity: Community, Culture, Difference*. Edited by Jonathan Rutherford, 222–37. London: Lawrence & Wishart, 1990.

Hall, Stuart. "Introduction: Who Needs 'Identity'?" In *Questions of Cultural Identity*. Edited by Stuart Hall and Paul Du Gay, 1–17. London: Sage, 1996.

Hall, Stuart. "New Ethnicities." In *Black Film, British Cinema*. Edited by Kobena Mercer, 27–31. London: Institute of Contemporary Arts, 1988.

Hall, Stuart. "Notes on Deconstructing 'the Popular.'" In *People's History and Socialist Theory*. Edited by Raphael Samuel, 227–40. London: Routledge, 1982.

Hall, Stuart. "Politics of Identity." In *Culture, Identity, and Politics: Ethnic Minorities in Britain*. Edited by Terence Ranger, Yunas Samad, and Ossie Stuart, 129–35. Aldershot: Avebury, 1996.

Hall, Stuart. *Representation: Cultural Representation and Signifying Practices*. London: Sage, 1997.

Hall, Stuart. "The West and the Rest: Discourse and Power." In *Formations of Modernity*. Edited by Stuart Hall and Bram Gieben, 276–320. Cambridge, MA: Polity Press, 1992.

Hall, Stuart. "When Was 'the Post-Colonial'? Thinking at the Limit." In *The Postcolonial Question: Common Skies, Divided Horizons*. Edited by Iain Chambers and Lidia Curti, 242–60. London: Routledge, 1996.

Halperin, Liora R. *Babel in Zion: Jews, Nationalism, and Language Diversity in Palestine, 1920–1948*. New Haven, CT: Yale University Press, 2015.

Hannan, Jim. "Crossing Couplets: Making Form the Matter of Walcott's *Tiepolo's Hound*." *New Literary History* 33 (2002): 559–79.

Hansen, Mette Halskov. "The Call of Mao or Money? Han Chinese Settlers on China's South-Western Borders." *The China Quarterly* 158 (1999): 394–413.

Hanssen, Jens, and Max Weiss, eds. *Arabic Thought beyond the Liberal Age: Towards an Intellectual History of the Nahda*. Cambridge, UK: Cambridge University Press, 2016.

Harel, Yaron. "The First Jews from Aleppo in Manchester: New Documentary Evidence." *AJS Review* 23 (1998): 191–202.

Harel, Yaron. *Syrian Jewry in Transition, 1840–1880*. Oxford: Littman Library of Jewish Civilization, 2010.

Harif, Hanan. *For We Be Brethren: The Turn to the East in Zionist Thought*. Jerusalem: The Zalman Shazar Center, 2019 [Hebrew].

Harkabi, Yehoshafat. *Palestinians and Israel*. Jerusalem: Keter, 1974.

Harley, J. B., and Paul Laxton. *The New Nature of Maps: Essays in the History of Cartography*. Baltimore, MD: Johns Hopkins University Press, 2001.

Harrison, Olivia C. *Transcolonial Maghreb: Imagining Palestine in the Era of Decolonization*. Stanford, CA: Stanford University Press, 2015.

Heid, Ludger. *Maloche—nicht Mildtätigkeit: Ostjüdische Arbeiter in Deutschland 1914–1923*. Hildesheim: Olms, 1995.

Herrmann, Manja. "Emotions in Jewish Nationalist Garb. Wilhelm Herzberg's Novel Jewish Family Papers: Letters of a Missionary (1868)." In *Wegweiser und Grenzgänger: Studien zur deutsch-jüdischen Kultur- und Literaturgeschichte*. Edited by Stefan Vogt, Hans Otto Horch, Vivian Liska, and Małgorzata A. Maksymiak, 261–271. Vienna: Böhlau, 2018.

Herrmann, Manja. "The Power of Authenticity: Individualism, Gender, and Politics in Early German Zionism." *Modern Judaism* 39 (2019): 93–113.

Herrmann, Manja. "Proto-Zionism Reconsidered: Wilhelm Herzberg's Early German-Jewish Nationalist Novel 'Jewish Family Papers' and the Discourse of Authenticity." *Leo Baeck Institute Year Book* 62 (2017): 179–95.

Herrmann, Manja. *Zionismus und Authentizität: Gegennarrative des Authentischen im frühen zionistischen Diskurs*. Berlin: De Gruyter, 2018.

Heschel, Susannah. *Abraham Geiger and the Jewish Jesus*. Chicago: University of Chicago Press, 1998.

Heschel, Susannah. "Jewish Studies as Counterhistory." In *Insider/Outsider: American Jews and Multiculturalism*. Edited by David Biale, Michael Galchinsky, and Susannah Heschel, 101–15. Berkeley: University of California Press, 1998.

Hess, Jonathan M. *Germans, Jews and the Claims of Modernity*. New Haven, CT: Yale University Press, 2002.

Hess, Jonathan M. "'Sugar Island Jews'? Jewish Colonialism and the Rhetoric of 'Civic Improvement' in Eighteenth-Century Germany." *Eighteenth-Century Studies* 32 (1998): 92–100.

Hever, Hannan. "Yitzhak Shami: Ethnicity as an Unresolved Conflict." *Shofar* 24, no. 2 (2006): 124–39.

Hever, Hannan, Yehouda Shenhav, and Pnina Motzafi-Haller, eds. *Mizrachim in Israel: A Critical Observation into Israel's Ethnicity*. Jerusalem: Van Leer/Tel Aviv: Ha-Kibbutz ha-me'uhad, 2002 [Hebrew].

Hicks, David. *Rhetoric and the Decolonization and Recolonization of East Timor*. London: Routledge, 2015.

Hill, Peter. *Utopia and Civilisation in the Arab Nahda*. Cambridge, UK: Cambridge University Press, 2020.

Hirsch, Dafna: *"We Are Here to Bring the West": Hygiene Education and Culture Building in the Jewish Society of Mandate Palestine*. Sde Boker: Mahon Ben-Gurion, 2014 [Hebrew].

Hirsch, Marianne. *The Generation of Postmemory: Writing and Visual Culture After the Holocaust*. New York: Columbia University Press, 2012.

Hirschhorn, Sara Yael. *City on a Hilltop: American Jews and the Israeli Settler Movement*. Cambridge, MA: Harvard University Press, 2017.

Hochberg, Gil. *In Spite of Partition: Jews, Arabs, and the Limits of Separatist Imagination*. Princeton, NJ: Princeton University Press, 2007.

Hodges, Tony. *Western Sahara: The Roots of a Desert War*. Chicago: Lawrence Hill Books, 1983.

Hourani, Albert. *Arabic Thought in the Liberal Age*. London: Oxford University Press, 1962.

Hundert, Gershon D. *Jews in Poland-Lithuania in the Eighteenth Century: A Genealogy of Modernity*. Berkeley: University of California Press, 2004.

Hurvitz, Nimrod. "Muhibb al-Din al-Khatib's Semitic Wave Theory and Pan Arabism." *Middle Eastern Studies* 29 (1993): 118–34.

Huss, Boaz. "Ask No Questions: Gershom Scholem and the Study of Contemporary Jewish Mysticism." *Modern Judaism* 25 (2005): 141–58.

Hussein, Mostafa. "The Integration of Arabo-Islamic Culture into the Emergent Hebrew Culture in Late Ottoman Palestine." *Jewish Quarterly Review* 109 (2019): 464–69.

Hussein, Mostafa. "Intertwined Landscape: The Integration of Arabo-Islamic Culture in Pre-State Palestine." *Israel Studies Review* 33 (2018): 51–65.

Hyman, Paula E. *Gender and Assimilation in Modern Jewish History: The Roles and Representation of Women*. Seattle: University of Washington Press, 1995.

Ilan, Ben-Zion. *An American Soldier/Pioneer in Israel*. New York: Labor Zionist Letters, 1979.

Ilany, Ofri. "'Is Judah Indeed the Teutonic Fatherland?' The Debate over the Hebrew Legacy at the Turn of the 18th Century." *Naharaim* 8 (2014): 31–47.

Isenberg, Noah. *Between Redemption and Doom: The Strains of German-Jewish Modernism*. Lincoln: University of Nebraska Press, 1999.

Israeli, Raphael. "The New Muslim Anti-Semitism: Exploring Novel Avenues of Hatred." *Jewish Political Studies Review* 17 (2005). https://jcpa.org/article/the-new-muslim-anti-semitism-exploring-novel-avenues-of-hatred.

Iyob, Ruth. *The Eritrean Struggle for Independence: Domination, Resistance, Nationalism, 1941–1993*. Cambridge, UK: Cambridge University Press, 1995.

Jacobson, Abigail. *From Empire to Empire: Jerusalem between Ottoman and British Rule*. Syracuse, NY: Syracuse University Press, 2011.

Jankowski, James, and Israel Gershoni. *Rethinking Nationalism in the Arab Middle East*. New York: Columbia University Press, 1997.

Jansen, G. H. *Afro-Asia and Non-Alignment*. London: Faber and Faber, 1966.

Johnson, Paul. *A History of the Jews*. New York: Harper, 1988.

Judson, Pieter. *The Habsburg Empire: A New History*. Cambridge, MA: Belknap Press/Harvard University Press, 2016.

Kahin, George McTurnan. *The Asian-African Conference, Bandung, Indonesia, April 1955*. Ithaca, NY: Cornell University Press, 1956.

Kalmar, Ivan Davidson, and Derek J. Penslar, eds. *Orientalism and the Jews*. Waltham, MA: Brandeis University Press, 2005.

Kamczycki, Artur. "Orientalism: Herzl and his Beard." *Journal of Modern Jewish Studies* 12 (2013): 90–116.

Kaplan, Marion. *The Making of the Jewish Middle Class: Women, Family, and Identity in Imperial Germany*. Oxford: Oxford University Press, 1991.

Katz, Ethan B. *The Burdens of Brotherhood: Jews and Muslims from North Africa to France*. Cambridge, MA: Harvard University Press, 2015.

Katz, Ethan B., Lisa Moses Leff, and Maud S. Mandel, eds. *Colonialism and the Jews*. Bloomington: Indiana University Press, 2017.

Katz, Jacob. *Zwischen Messianismus und Zionismus: Zur jüdischen Sozialgeschichte*. Frankfurt am Main: Jüdischer Verlag, 1993.

Kaufman, Asher. *Reviving Phoenicia: The Search for Identity in Lebanon*. London: I. B. Tauris, 2004.

Kayali, Hasan. *Arabs and Young Turks: Ottomanism, Arabism, and Islamism in the Ottoman Empire, 1908–1918*. Berkeley: University of California Press, 1997.

Kedourie, Elie. "The Jews of Baghdad in 1910." *Middle Eastern Studies* 7 (1971): 355–61.

Kedourie, Elie. *Nationalism*. 4th expanded ed. Cambridge, MA: Blackwell, 1996.

Keenleyside, T. A. "Nationalist Indian Attitudes Towards Asia: A Troublesome Legacy for Post-Independence Indian Foreign Policy." *Pacific Affairs* 55 (1982): 210–30.

Kemp, Adriana. "Talking Borders: The Construction of a Poilitical Territory in Israel, 1949–1957." PhD diss., Tel Aviv University, 1997 [Hebrew].

Keynes, Mary. "The Arab-Asian Bloc." *International Relations* 1 (1957): 238–50.

Khalidi, Rashid. "Arab Nationalism: Historical Problems in the Literature." *The American Historical Review* 96 (1991): 1363–73.

Khazzoom, Aziza. "The Great Chain of Orientalism: Jewish Identity, Stigma Management, and Ethnic Exclusion in Israel." *American Sociological Review* 68 (2003): 481–510.

Khazzoom, Aziza. *Shifting Ethnic Boundaries and Inequality in Israel: Or, How the Polish Peddler Became a German Intellectual*. Stanford, CA: Stanford University Press, 2008.

Khuri-Makdisi, Ilham. *The Eastern Mediterranean and the Making of Global Radicalism, 1860–1914*. Berkeley: University of California Press, 2010.

Kimche, David. *The Afro-Asian Movement: Ideology and Foreign Policy of the Third World*. Jerusalem: Israel Universities Press, 1973.

Kirasirova, Masha. "An Egyptian Communist Family Romance: Revolution and Gender in the Transnational Life of Charlotte Rosenthal." In *The Wider Arc of Revolution, Part 1*. Edited by Choi Chatterjee, Steven G. Marks, Mary Neuburger, and Steven Sabol, 309–36. Bloomington, IN: Slavica Publishers, 2019.

Kirchhoff, Markus. "Erweiterter Orientalismus: Zu euro-christlichen Identifikationen und jüdischer Gegengeschichte im 19. Jahrhundert." In *Jüdische Geschichte als allgemeine Geschichte*. Edited by Raphael Gross and Yfaat Weiss, 99–119. Göttingen: Wallstein, 2006.

Klein, Menachem. "Arab Jew in Palestine." *Israel Studies* 19 (2014): 134–53.

Kling, Blair B. "Gandhi, Nonviolence, and the Holocaust." *Peace & Change* 16 (1991): 176–96.

Krobb, Florian. *Kollektivautobiographien, Wunschautobiographien: Marranenschicksal im deutsch-jüdischen historischen Roman*. Würzburg: Königshausen & Neumann, 2002.

Krutikov, Mikhail. *From Kabbalah to Class Struggle: Expressionism, Marxism, and Yiddish Literature in the Life and Work of Meir Wiener*. Stanford, CA: Stanford University Press, 2011.

Kumar, Aishwary. *Radical Equality: Ambedkar, Gandhi, and the Risk of Democracy*. Stanford, CA: Stanford University Press, 2015.

Kupfert Heller, Daniel. "Israeli Aid and the 'African Woman': The Gendered Politics of International Development, 1958–73." *Jewish Social Studies* 25 (2020): 49–78.

Lavsky, Hagit. *Before Catastrophe: The Distinctive Path of German Zionism*. 2nd ed. Jerusalem: Magnes, 1998.

Lawrence, Mark A. "Pacific Dreams: The Institute of Pacific Relations and the Struggle for the Mind of Asia." PhD diss., University of Texas at Austin, 2009.

Lee, Christopher J. *Making a World after Empire: The Bandung Moment and Its Political Afterlives*. Athens: Ohio University Press, 2010.

Lemberg, Hans. "Zur Entstehung des Osteuropabegriffs im 19. Jahrhundert: Vom 'Norden' zum 'Osten' Europas." *Jahrbücher für Geschichte Osteuropas* 33 (1985): 48–91.

Lev, Shimon. "'Clear Are the Paths of India': The Representation of Tagore in Jewish Literature." *The Journal of Indo-Judaic Studies* 15 (2015): 31–48.

Lev, Shimon. *From Lithuania to Santiniketan: Schlomith Flaum & Rabindranath Tagore*. New Delhi: Lithuanian Embassy in New Delhi, 2018.

Levey, Zach. *Israel and the Western Powers, 1952–1960*. Chapel Hill: University of North Carolina Press, 2011.

Levy, Lital. "Historicizing the Concept of Arab Jews in the Mashriq." *Jewish Quarterly Review* 98 (2008): 452–69.

Levy, Lital. "Jewish Writers in the Arab East: Literature, History, and the Politics of Enlightenment, 1863–1914." PhD diss., University of California, Berkeley, 2007.

Lewis, Bernard. *The Jews of Islam*. Princeton, NJ: Princeton University Press, 1984.

Liberles, Robert. "From Toleration to Verbesserung: German and English Debates on the Jews in the Eighteenth Century." *Central European History* 22 (1989): 3–32.

Lieberman, Lisa. "Albert Memmi's About-Face." *Michigan Quarterly Review* 46 (2007). http://hdl.handle.net/2027/spo.act2080.0046.326.

Lin, Nimrod. "People Who Count: Zionism, Demography and Democracy in Mandate Palestine." PhD diss., University of Toronto, 2017.

Linfield, Susie. *The Lions' Den: Zionism and the Left from Hannah Arendt to Noam Chomsky*. New Haven, CT: Yale University Press, 2019.

Litvak, Meir, and Esther Webman, eds. *From Empathy to Denial: Arab Responses to the Holocaust*. New York: Columbia University Press, 2009.

Livingstone, Thomas. *Education and Race: A Biography of Edward Wilmot Blyden*. San Francisco: The Glendessary Press, 1975.

Lockman, Zachary. *Comrades and Enemies: Arab and Jewish Workers in Palestine, 1906–1948*. Berkeley: University of California Press, 1996.

Louro, Michele L. *Comrades against Imperialism: Nehru, India, and Interwar Internationalism*. Cambridge, UK: Cambridge University Press, 2018.

Lubin, Alex. *Geographies of Liberation: The Making of an Afro-Arab Political Imaginary*. Chapel Hill: University of North Carolina Press, 2014.

Lustick, Ian S. *Unsettled States, Disputed Lands: Britain and Ireland, France and Algeria, Israel and the West Bank-Gaza*. Ithaca, NY: Cornell University Press, 1993.

Lynch, Hollis R. *Edward Wilmot Blyden: Pan-Negro Patriot 1832–1912*. London: Oxford University Press, 1967.

Macey, David. *Frantz Fanon: A Biography*. London: Verso, 2012.

Mack, Michael. *German Idealism and the Jew: The Inner Anti-Semitism of Philosophy and German Jewish Responses*. Chicago: University of Chicago Press, 2013.

MacLeod, Jason. *Merdeka and the Morning Star: Civil Resistance in West Papua*. St. Lucia: University of Queensland Press, 2015.

Mahla, Daniel. *Orthodox Judaism and the Politics of Religion: From Prewar Europe to the State of Israel*. Cambridge, UK: Cambridge University Press 2020.

Makdisi, Ussama. *The Culture of Sectarianism: Community, History, and Violence in Nineteenth-Century Ottoman Lebanon*. Berkeley: University of California Press, 2000.

Makdisi, Ussama. "Ottoman Orientalism." *The American Historical Review* 107 (2002): 768–96.

Makdisi, Ussama Samir. *Age of Coexistence: The Ecumenical Frame and the Making of the Modern Arab World*. Oakland: University of California Press, 2019.

Maksymiak, Małgorzata A. "Beggars, Nymphomaniac Women, Miracle Rabbis and Other East European Jews: The East as a Category of Social Difference." *Journal of Modern Jewish Studies* 19 (2020): 434–49.

Maksymiak, Małgorzata A. *Mental Maps im Zionismus: Ost und West in Konzepten einer jüdischen Nation vor 1914*. Bremen: Edition Lumière, 2015.

Malinovich, Nadia. "Orientalism and the Construction of Jewish Identity in France, 1900–1932." *Jewish Culture and History* 2 (1999): 1–25.

Mandel, Maud S. *Muslims and Jews in France: History of a Conflict*. Princeton, NJ: Princeton University Press, 2014.

Manor, Dalia. *Art in Zion: The Genesis of Modern National Art in Jewish Palestine*. London: Routledge, 2005.

Manthorne, Katherine. "Caribbean Beginnings: Camille Pissarro." *Latin American Art* 2, no. 3 (1990): 30–35.

Maor, Zohar. "Hans Kohn and the Dialectics of Colonialism: Insights on Nationalism and Colonialism from Within." *Leo Baeck Institute Year Book* 55 (2010): 255–71.

Masalha, Nur. *The Palestine Nakba: Decolonising History, Narrating the Subaltern, Reclaiming Memory*. London: Zed Books, 2012.

Massad, Joseph A. *The Persistence of the Palestinian Question: Essays on Zionism and the Palestinians*. London: Routledge, 2006.

Masters, Bruce. *Christians and Jews in the Ottoman Arab World: The Roots of Sectarianism*. Cambridge, UK: Cambridge University Press, 2001.

Maurer, Trude. *Ostjuden in Deutschland, 1918–1933*. Hamburg: Christians, 1986.

Mbembe, Achille. "Necropolitics." *Political Culture* 15 (2003): 11–14.

Me'ir-Glitsenshtain, Esther. *Zionism in an Arab Country: Jews in Iraq in the 1940s*. London: Routledge, 2004.

Memmi, Albert. *The Colonizer and the Colonized*. Translated by Howard Greenfeld. London: Earthscan, 2003. Originally published as *Portrait du colonisé, précédé du portrait du colonisateur*. Paris: Buchet/Chastel, 1957.

Memmi, Albert. "The Impossible Life of Frantz Fanon." *The Massachusetts Review* 14 (1973): 9–39. Originally published as "La vie impossible de Frantz Fanon." *Esprit* 406 (1971): 248–73.

Memmi, Albert. *Jews and Arabs*. Translated by Eleanor Levieux. Chicago: J. Philip O'Hara, 1975.

Memmi, Albert. *The Liberation of the Jew*. Translated by Judy Hyun. New York: Viking Press, 1973.

Memmi, Albert. "Négritude et Judéité." *African Arts* 1, no. 4 (1968): 26–123.

Memmi, Albert. *The Pillar of Salt*. Translated by Edouard Roditi. Boston: Beacon Press, 1992.

Memmi, Albert. *Portrait of a Jew*. Translated by Elisabeth Abbott. New York: Orion Press, 1962.

Mendel, Yonathan, and Ronald Ranta. *From the Arab Other to the Israeli Self: Palestinian Culture in the Making of Israeli National Identity*. Farnham: Ashgate, 2016.

Mendelsohn, Ezra, Stefani Hoffman, and Richard I. Cohen, eds. *Against the Grain: Jewish Intellectuals in Hard Times*. New York: Berghahn Books, 2014.

Mendes-Flohr, Paul R. *Divided Passions: Jewish Intellectuals and the Experience of Modernity*. Detroit: Wayne State University Press, 1991.

Mendes-Flohr, Paul. "Fin-de-Siècle Orientalism, the Ostjuden and the Aesthetics of Jewish Self-Affirmation." *Studies in Contemporary Jewry* 1 (1984): 96–139.

Mendes-Flohr, Paul. *From Mysticism to Dialogue: Martin Buber's Transformation of German Social Thought*. Detroit: Wayne State University Press, 1989.

Meyer, Michael A., ed. *German-Jewish History in Modern Times*. Vol. 3, *Integration in Dispute, 1871–1918*. New York: Columbia University Press, 1997.

Michael, Reuven. "Dr. Wilhelm Herzberg (1827–1897). Eine lückenhafte Biographie." *Bulletin des Leo Baeck Instituts* 65 (1983): 53–85.

Mirzoeff, Nicholas, ed. *Diaspora and Visual Culture: Representing Africans and Jews*. London: Routledge, 2000.

Mishra, Pankaj. *From the Ruins of Empire: The Revolt against the West and the Remaking of Asia*. London: Penguin, 2013.

Mooreville, Anat. "Eyeing Africa: The Politics of Israeli Ocular Expertise and International Aid, 1959–1973." *Jewish Social Studies* 21 (2016): 31–71.

Mosès, Stéphane. "Scholem and Rosenzweig: The Dialectics of History." Translated by Ora Wiskind. *History and Memory* 2, no. 2 (1990): 100–16.

Motta, Giuseppe. *The Great War against Eastern European Jewry, 1914–1920*. Newcastle upon Tyne: Cambridge Scholars Publisher, 2018.

Moyn, Samuel. "German Jewry and the Question of Identity: Historiography and Theory." *Leo Baeck Institute Year Book* 41 (1996): 291–308.

Mudimbe, V. Y. *The Invention of Africa: Gnosis, Philosophy, and the Order of Knowledge.* Bloomington: Indian University Press, 1988.

Mueller, Monika. *George Eliot U.S.: Transatlantic Literary and Cultural Perspectives.* Madison, NJ: Fairleigh Dickinson University Press, 2005.

Mufti, Aamir. *Enlightenment in the Colony: The Jewish Question and the Crisis of Postcolonial Critique.* Princeton, NJ: Princeton University Press, 2007.

Mundy, Jacob. "Moroccan Settlers in Western Sahara: Colonists or Fifth Column?" *The Arab World Geographer* 15 (2012): 95–126.

Myers, David N. *Between Jew and Arab: The Lost Voice of Simon Rawidowicz.* Hanover, NH: Brandeis University Press, 2008.

Myers, David N. *Re-Inventing the Jewish Past: European Jewish Intellectuals and the Zionist Return to History.* New York: Oxford University Press, 1995.

Naor, Moshe. *Oriental Neighbors: Middle Eastern Jews and Arabs in Mandatory Palestine.* Waltham, MA: Brandeis University Press, 2017.

Nemtsov, Jascha. *Der Zionismus in der Musik: Jüdische Musik und nationale Idee.* Wiesbaden: Hassarowitz, 2009.

Neuberger, Benyamin. "Early African Nationalism, Judaism and Zionism: Edward Wilmot Blyden." *Jewish Social Studies* 47 (1985): 151–66.

Nicosia, Francis R. *Zionism and Anti-Semitism in Nazi Germany.* Cambridge, UK: Cambridge University Press, 2008.

Nicosia, Francis R., and Boğaç A. Ergene, eds. *Nazis, the Holocaust, and the Middle East: Arab and Turkish Responses.* New York: Berghahn, 2018.

Nord, Philip. "The New Painting and the Dreyfus Affair." *Historical Reflections/Reflexions Historiques* 24 (1998): 115–36.

Nordbruch, Götz. "‚Cultural Fusion' of Thought and Ambitions? Memory, Politics and the History of Arab–Nazi German Encounters." *Middle Eastern Studies* 47 (2011): 183–94.

Nordbruch, Götz. *Nazism in Syria and Lebanon: The Ambivalence of the German Option, 1933–1945.* London: Routledge, 2009.

O'Leary, Brendan. "The Elements of Right-Sizing and Right-Peopling the State." In *Right-Sizing the State: The Politics of Moving Borders.* Edited by Brendan O'Leary, Ian S. Lustick, and Thomas Callaghy, 15–73. Oxford: Oxford University Press, 2001.

Olson, Jess. *Nathan Birnbaum and Jewish Modernity: Architect of Zionism, Yiddishism, and Orthodoxy.* Stanford, CA: Stanford University Press, 2013.

Or, Tamara. *Vorkämpferinnen und Mütter des Zionismus: Die deutsch-zionistischen Frauenorganisation 1897–1938.* Frankfurt am Main: Lang, 2009.

Orlowski, Hubert. *"Polnische Wirtschaft": Zum Polendiskurs der Neuzeit*. Wiesbaden: Harrassowitz Verlag, 1996.

Owen, Roger. *State, Power and Politics in the Making of the Modern Middle East*. 2nd ed. London: Routledge, 2000.

Pappé, Ilan. *A History of Modern Palestine: One Land, Two Peoples*. Cambridge, UK: Cambridge University Press, 2004.

Pappé, Ilan, ed. *Israel and South Africa: TheMany Faces of Apartheid*. London: Zed Books, 2015.

Parfitt, Tudor. *Black Jews in Africa and the Americas*. Cambridge, MA: Harvard University Press, 2013.

Peleg, Yaron. *Orientalism and the Hebrew Imagination*. Ithaca, NY: Cornell University Press, 2005.

Pellegrini, Ann. *Performance Anxieties: Staging Psychoanalysis, Staging Race*. London: Routledge, 1997.

Penslar, Derek J. "Declarations of (In)Dependence: Tensions within Zionist Statecraft, 1896–1948." *Journal of Levantine Studies* 8 (2018): 13–34.

Penslar, Derek J. *Israel in History: The Jewish State in Comparative Perspective*. London: Routledge, 2007.

Penslar, Derek J. *Theodor Herzl: The Charismatic Leader*. New Haven, CT: Yale University Press, 2020.

Penslar, Derek J. *Zionism and Technocracy: The Engineering of Jewish Settlement in Palestine, 1870–1918*. Bloomington: Indiana University Press, 1991.

Penslar, Derek J. "Zionism, Colonialism and Postcolonialism." *Journal of Israeli History* 20 (2001): 84–98.

Penslar, Derek J. "Zionism, Colonialism, and Technocracy: Otto Warburg and the Commission for the Exploration of Palestine, 1903–1907." *Journal of Contemporary History* 25 (1990): 142–60.

Phillips Casteel, Sarah. *Calypso Jews: Jewishness in the Caribbean Literary Imagination*. New York: Columbia University Press, 2016.

Pianko, Noam. *Zionism and the Roads Not Taken: Rawidowicz, Kaplan, Kohn*. Bloomington: Indiana University Press, 2010.

Pollock, Sheldon. "Deep Orientalism? Notes on Sanskrit and Power Beyond the Raj." In *Orientalism and the Postcolonial Predicament: Perspectives on South Asia*. Edited by Carol A. Breckenridge and Peter van der Veer, 76–133. Philadelphia: University of Pennsylvania Press, 1993.

Pomeranz, Kenneth. "Empire & 'Civilizing' Missions, Past & Present." *Daedalus* 134, no. 2 (2005): 34–45.

Portugali, Yuval. "Inter-Representations Networks and Cognitive Maps." In *The Construction of Cognitive Maps. Edited by Yuval Portugali, 11–43. Dordrecht: Springer, 1996.

Pötzl, Viktoria. "From Pan-Asianism to Safari-Zionism: Gendered Orientalism in Jewish-Austrian Literature." *Journal of Modern Jewish Studies* 19 (2020): 205–23.

Prakash, Gyan. "Writing Post-Orientalist Histories of the Third World: Perspectives from Indian Historiography." *Comparative Studies in Society and History* 32 (1990): 383–408.

Prashad, Vijay. *The Darker Nations: A People's History of the Third World*. New York: New Press, 2007.

Provence, Michael. *The Last Ottoman Generation and the Making of the Modern Middle East*. Cambridge, UK: Cambridge University Press, 2017.

Quayson, Ato. "Comparative Postcolonialisms: Storytelling and Community in Sholem Aleichem and Chinua Achebe." *The Cambridge Journal of Postcolonial Literary Inquiry* 3 (2016): 55–77.

Quayson, Ato, and Girish Daswani. "Diaspora and Transnationalism: Scapes, Scales and Scopes." In *A Companion to Diaspora and Transnationalism*. Edited by Aro Quayson and Girish Daswani, 1–26. New York: Blackwell, 2013.

Rabinovici, Doron, Ulrich Speck, and Natan Sznaijder, eds. *Neuer Antisemitismus? Eine globale Debatte*. Frankfurt am Main: Suhrkamp, 2004.

Rachum, Stephanie. "Camille Pissarro's Jewish Identity." *ASSAPH Studies in Art History* 5 (2000): 3–29.

Raz-Krakotzkin, Amnon. "Between 'Brith Shalom' and the Temple: Redemption and Messianism in the Zionist Discourse—A Reading of the Writings of Gershom Scholem." *Theory and Criticism* 20 (2002): 87–112 [Hebrew].

Regev, Motti, and Edwin Seroussi. *Popular Music and National Culture in Israel*. Berkeley: California University Press, 2004.

Reichmann, Shalom, and Shlomo Hasson. "A Cross-Cultural Diffusion of Colonization: From Posen to Palestine." *Annals of the Association of American Geographers* 74 (1984): 57–70.

Reinharz, Jehuda. "Ideology and Structure in German Zionism, 1882–1933." *Jewish Social Studies* 42 (1980): 119–46.

Reinharz, Jehuda, and Yaacov Shavit. *Glorious, Accursed Europe: An Essay on Jewish Ambivalence*. Waltham, MA: Brandeis University Press, 2010.

Reiss, Tom. *The Orientalist: Solving the Mystery of a Strange and a Dangerous Life*. New York: Random House, 2005.

Rhoy, Abik. "Martin Buber and Rabindranath Tagore: A Meeting of Two Great Minds." *Comparative Literature East & West* 25 (2016): 30–42.

Rivlin, Benjamin, and Jacques Fomerand. "Changing Third World Perspectives and

Policies Towards Israel." In *Israel in the Third World*. Edited by Michael Curtis and Susan Aurelia Gitelson, 318–60. New Brunswick, NJ: Transaction Books, 1976.

Robinson, Shira. *Citizen Strangers: Palestinians and the Birth of Israel's Liberal Settler State*. Stanford, CA: Stanford University Press, 2013.

Rodinson, Maxime. *Israel: A Colonial Settler-State?* New York: Monad Press, 1973.

Rodrigue, Aron. *French Jews, Turkish Jews: The Alliance Israélite Universelle and the Politics of Jewish Schooling in Turkey, 1860–1925*. Bloomington: Indiana University Press, 1990.

Rodrigue, Aron. *Jews and Muslims: Images of Sephardi and Eastern Jewries in Modern Times*. Seattle: University of Washington Press, 2003.

Rodrigue, Aron, ed. *Ottoman and Turkish Jewry: Community and Leadership*. Bloomington: Indiana University Press, 1992.

Rodrigue, Aron, and Esther Benbassa. *Sephardi Jewry: A History of the Judeo-Spanish Community, 14th–20th Centuries*. Berkeley: University of California Press, 2000.

Rodrigue, Aron, and Esther Benbassa, eds. *A Sephardi Life in Southeastern Europe: The Autobiography and Journal of Gabriel Arié*. Seattle: University of Washington Press, 1998.

Rodrigue, Aron, and Sarah Abrevaya Stein, eds. *A Jewish Voice from Ottoman Salonica: The Ladino Memoir of Sa'adi Besalel a-Levi*. Stanford, CA: Stanford University Press, 2012.

Rohde, Achim. "Der Innere Orient. Orientalismus, Antisemitismus und Geschlecht im Deutschland des 18. bis 20. Jahrhunderts." *Die Welt Des Islams* 5 (2005): 370–411.

Roland, Joan G. *The Jewish Communities of India: Identity in a Colonial Era*. 2nd ed. New Brunswick, NJ: Transaction, 1998.

Röling, B. V. A. *International Law in an Expanded World*. Amsterdam: Djambatan, 1960.

Romulo, Carlos. *The Meaning of Bandung*. Chapel Hill: University of North Carolina Press, 1956.

Rotbard, Sharon. "Wall and Tower (Homa Umigdal): The Mold of Israeli Architecture." In *A Civilian Occupation: The Politics of Israeli Architecture*. Edited by Rafi Segal and Eyal Weizman, 39–56. London: Verso, 2003.

Rothberg, Michael. *Multidirectional Memory: Remembering the Holocaust in the Age of Decolonization*. Stanford, CA: Stanford University Press, 2009.

Said, Edward W. *Culture and Imperialism*. New York: Alfred A. Knopf, 1993.

Said, Edward W. *The End of the Peace Process: Oslo and After*. New York: Vintage Books, 2001.

Said, Edward W. *Orientalism*. New York: Vintage Books, 1979.

Said, Edward W. *Out of Place: A Memoir*. London: Granta Books, 2000.

Salmon, Yosef. "Zionism and Anti-Zionism in Eastern Europe." In *Zionism and Reli-*

gion. Edited by Shmuel Almog, Jehuda Reinharz, and Anita Shapira, 25–43. Hanover, NH: Brandeis University Press.

Salomon, Francisca. *Blicke auf das galizische Judentum: Haskala, Assimilation und Zionismus bei Nathan Samuely, Karl Emil Franzos und Saul Raphael Landau*. Vienna: Literatur-Verlag, 2012.

Salzman, Philip Carl, and Donna Robinson Divine, eds. *Postcolonial Theory and the Arab-Israeli Conflict*. London: Routledge, 2008.

Saposnik, Arieh Bruce. *Becoming Hebrew: The Creation of a Jewish National Culture in Ottoman Palestine*. New York: Oxford University Press, 2008.

Saposnik, Arieh Bruce. "Europe and Its Orients in Zionist Culture Before the First World War." *The Historical Journal* 49 (2006): 1105–23.

Satia, Priya. "Byron, Gandhi and the Thompsons: The Making of British Social History and Unmaking of Indian History." *History Workshop Journal* 81 (2016): 135–70.

Sautman, Barry. "Colonialism, Genocide, and Tibet." *Asian Ethnicity* 7 (2006): 243–65.

Schechter, Ronald. *Obstinate Hebrews: Representations of Jews in France, 1715–1815*. Berkeley: University of California Press, 2003.

Schlaepfer, Aline. "Between Cultural and National Nahda: Jewish Intellectuals in Baghdad and the Nation-Building Process in Iraq (1921–1932)." *Journal of Levantine Studies* 1 (2011): 59–74.

Schlaepfer, Aline. *Les intellectuels juifs de Bagdad. Discours et allégeances (1908–1951)*. Leiden: Brill 2016.

Schorsch, Jonathan. *Jews and Blacks in the Early Modern World*. Cambridge, UK: Cambridge University Press, 2004.

Schulte, Christoph. *Psychopathologie des Fin de siècle: Der Kulturkritiker, Arzt und Zionist Max Nordau*. Frankfurt am Main: Fischer, 1997.

Schulte, Marion. *Preußische Offiziere über Judentum und Emanzipation, 1762–1815*. Berlin: De Gruyter Oldenbourg, 2018.

Sciarcon, Jonathan. "Unfulfilled Promises: Ottomanism, the 1908 Revolution and Baghdadi Jews." *International Journal of Contemporary Iraqi Studies* 3 (2009): 155–68.

Scott, James C. *Seeing Like a State. How Certain Schemes to Improve the Human Condition Have Failed*. New Haven, CT: Yale University Press, 1988.

Segal, Miryam. *A New Sound in Hebrew Poetry: Poetics, Politics, Accent*. Bloomington: Indiana University Press, 2010.

Sehayyek, Sha'ul. "The Figure of the Jew in the Arab Press in the Years 1858–1908." PhD diss., Hebrew University Jerusalem, 1991 [Hebrew].

Seroussi, Edwin, and Meir Stern. "Songs That Young Gershom Scholem May Have Heard: Jacob Beimel's *Jüdische Melodieen*, Jung Juda, and Jewish Musical Predicaments in Early Twentieth-Century Berlin." *Jewish Quarterly Review* 110 (2020): 64–101.

Sevitch, Benjamin. "W. E. B. Du Bois as America's Foremost Black Zionist." In *The Souls of W. E. B. Du Bois: New Essays and Reflections*. Edited by Edward Blum and Jason Young, 244–45. Fairfax, VA: George Mason University Press, 2009.

Shafir, Gershon. *Land, Labour and the Origins of the Israeli-Palestinian Conflict 1882–1914*. Cambridge, UK: Cambridge University Press, 1989.

Shahar, Galili. "'A Third Reading': The German, the Hebrew and (the Arab)." *Prooftexts* 33 (2013): 133–39.

Shalom Chetrit, Sami. *Intra-Jewish Conflict in Israel: White Jews, Black Jews*. London: Routledge, 2010.

Shamir, Ronen. *The Colonies of Law: Colonialism, Zionism and Law in Early Mandate Palestine*. Cambridge, UK: Cambridge University Press, 2000.

Shanes, Joshua. *Diaspora Nationalism and Jewish Identity in Habsburg Galicia*. Cambridge, UK: Cambridge University Press, 2012.

Sharkey, Heather J. *American Evangelicals in Egypt: Missionary Encounters in an Age of Empire*. Princeton, NJ: Princeton University Press, 2008.

Shenhav, Ghilad H. "Between Abgrund and Urwirbel: The Story of One Word in the Buber-Rosenzweig Bible Translation." *Naharaim* 14 (2020): 83–102.

Shenhav, Yehouda. *The Arab Jews: A Postcolonial Reading of Nationalism, Religion, and Ethnicity*. Stanford, CA: Stanford University Press, 2006.

Shenhav, Yehouda. "The Jews of Iraq, Zionist Ideology, and the Property of the Palestinian Refugees of 1948: An Anomaly of National Accounting." *International Journal of Middle East Studies* 31 (1999): 605–30.

Shiblak, Abbas. *The Lure of Zion: The Case of Iraqi Jews*. London: al-Saqi Books, 1986.

Shikes, Ralph, and Paula Harper. *Pissarro: His Life and Work*. New York: Horizon Press, 1980.

Shimazu, Naoko. "Diplomacy as Theatre: Staging the Bandung Conference of 1955." *Modern Asian Studies* 48 (2014): 225–52.

Shohat, Ella. "The Invention of the Mizrahim." *Journal of Palestine Studies* 29 (1999): 5–20.

Shohat, Ella. *Israeli Cinema: East/West and the Politics of Representation*. Austin: University of Texas Press, 1989.

Shohat, Ella Habiba. *On the Arab Jew, Palestine, and Other Displacement: Selected Writings*. London: Pluto Press, 2017.

Shohat, Ella. "Sephardim in Israel: Zionism from the Standpoint of Its Jewish Victims." *Social Text* 19 (1988): 1–35.

Shohat, Ella. *Taboo Memories, Diasporic Voices*. Durham, NC: Duke University Press, 2006.

Shulvass, Moses A. *From East to West: The Westward Migration of Jews from Eastern*

Europe During the Seventeenth and Eighteenth Centuries. Detroit: Wayne State University Press, 1971.

Shumsky, Dmitry. *Beyond the Nation-State: The Zionist Political Imagination from Pinsker to Ben-Gurion*. New Haven, CT: Yale University Press, 2018.

Sicher, Efraim. *Under Postcolonial Eyes. Figuring the "Jew" in Contemporary British Writing*. Lincoln: University of Nebraska Press, 2012.

Simon, Reeva. *Iraq between Two World Wars: The Creation and Implementation of a Nationalist Ideology*. New York: Columbia University Press, 1986.

Singh, Sinderpal. "From Delhi to Bandung: Nehru, 'Indian-ness' and 'Pan-Asian-ness.'" *South Asia* 34 (2011): 51–64.

Slabodsky, Santiago. *Decolonial Judaism: Triumphal Failures of Barbaric Thinking*. New York: Palgrave Macmillan, 2014.

Snir, Reuven. *Arab-Jewish Literature: The Birth and Demise of the Arabic Short Story*. Leiden: Brill, 2019.

Somekh, Sasson, and Deborah Starr, eds. *Mongrels or Marvels: The Levantine Writings of Jacqueline Shohet Kahanoff*. Stanford, CA: Stanford University Press, 2011.

Spector, Scott. "Another Zionism: Hugo Bergmann's Circumscription of Spiritual Territory." *Journal of Contemporary History* 34 (1999): 85–106.

Spector, Scott. *Modernism without Jews? German-Jewish Subjects and Histories*. Bloomington: Indiana University Press, 2001.

Spector, Scott. *Prague Territories: National Conflict and Cultural Innovation in Franz Kafka's Fin de Siècle*. Berkeley: University of California Press, 2000.

Spector, Scott. "The Return of the Prodigal Galician Sons: An Austro-Jewish Dialectic." *Austrian Studies* 28 (2020): 47–63.

Spivak, Gayatri Chakravorty. "Can the Subaltern Speak?" In *Marxism and the Interpretation of Culture*. Edited by Cary Nelson and Lawrence Grossberg, 271–313. Basingstoke: Macmillan, 1988.

Stähler, Axel. *Zionism, the German Empire, and Africa: Jewish Metamorphoses and the Colors of Difference*. Berlin: De Gryter, 2019.

Steffen, Katrin. "Zur Europäizität der Geschichte der Juden im östlichen Europa." *H-Soz-Kult* June 6, 2006. https://www.hsozkult.de/article/id/artikel-742.

Stein, Gerd, ed. *Kulturfiguren und Sozialcharaktere des 19. und 20. Jahrhunderts*. Vol. 4, *Philister – Kleinbürger – Spießer. Normalität und Selbstbehauptung*. Frankfurt am Main: Fischer, 1985.

Stein, Sarah Abrevaya. *Saharan Jews and the Fate of French Algeria*. Chicago: University of Chicago Press, 2014.

Stillman, Norman A. *The Language and Culture of the Jews of Sefrou*. Manchester: University of Manchester Press, 1987.

Stoler, Ann Laura, and Frederick Copper. "Between Metropole and Colony: Rethinking a Research Agenda." In *Tensions of Empire: Colonial Cultures in a Bourgeois World*. Edited by Frederick Copper and Ann Laura Stoler, 1–56. Berkeley: University of California Press, 1997.

Swarts, Lynne M. *Gender, Orientalism and the Jewish Nation: Women in the Work of Ephraim Moses Lilien at the German Fin-de-Siècle*. New York: Bloomsbury Visual Arts, 2020.

Szarota, Tomas. "Pole, Polen und Polnisch in den deutschen Mundartenlexika und Sprichwörterbüchern." *Acta Poloniae Historica* 50 (1984): 81–114.

Tamari, Salim. *Mountain against the Sea: Essays on Palestinian Society and Culture*. Berkeley: University of California Press, 2009.

Taverson, Andrew, and Sara Upstone, eds. *Postcolonial Spaces: The Politics of Place in Contemporary Culture*. Basingstoke: Palgrave Macmillan, 2011.

Taylor, Charles. "The Politics of Recognition." In *Multiculturalism: Examining the Politics of Recognition*. Edited by Amy Gutmann, 25–73. Princeton, NJ: Princeton University Press, 1994.

Thakur, Vineet. "An Asian Drama: The Asian Relations Conference, 1947." *The International History Review* 41 (2019): 673–95.

Thobhani, Akbarali. *Western Sahara Since 1975 under Moroccan Administration: Social, Economic, and Political Transformation*. Lewiston, NY: Edwin Mellen Press, 2002.

Thompson, Virginia, and Richard Adloff. *The Western Saharans*. London: Croom Helm, 1980.

Tibebu, Teshale. *Edward Wilmot Blyden and the Racial Nationalist Imagination*. Rochester, NY: University of Rochester Press, 2012.

Tölölyan, Khachig. "The Contemporary Discourse of Diaspora Studies." *Comparative Studies of South Asia, Africa and the Middle East* 27 (2007): 647–55.

Trilling, Lionel. *Sincerity and Authenticity*. Cambridge, MA: Harvard University Press, 1972.

Troen, S. Ilan. *Imagining Zion: Dreams, Designs, and Realities in a Century of Jewish Settlement*. New Haven, CT: Yale University Press, 2003.

Trollope, Anthony. *The West Indies and the Spanish Main*. London: Chapman & Hall, 1860.

Troutt Powell, Eve M. *A Different Shade of Colonialism: Egypt, Great Britain, and the Mastery of the Sudan*. Berkeley: University of California Press, 2003.

van Rahden, Till. "Jews and the Ambivalences of Civil Society in Germany, 1800 to 1933: Assessment and Reassessment." *Journal of Modern History* 77 (2005): 1024–47.

Varga, Somogy. *Authenticity as an Ethical Ideal*. London: Routledge, 2012.

Veeser, H. Aram. *Edward Said: The Charisma of Criticism*. London: Routledge, 2010.

Veidlinger, Jeffrey. *In the Midst of Civilized Europe: The Pogroms of 1918–1921 and the Onset of the Holocaust*. New York: Metropolitan Books, 2021.

Vergès, Françoise. "Creole Skin, Black Mask: Fanon and Disavowal." *Critical Inquiry* 23 (1997): 578–95.

Vitalis, Robert. "The Midnight Ride of Kwame Nkrumah and Other Fables of Bandung (Ban-Doong)." *Humanity* 4 (2013): 261–88.

Vogt, Stefan, ed. *Colonialism and the Jews in German History: From the Middle Ages to the 20th Century*. London: Bloomsbury Academic, 2022.

Vogt, Stefan. "The Postcolonial Buber: Orientalism, Subalternity, and Identity Politics in Martin Buber's Political Thought." *Jewish Social Studies* 22 (2016): 161–86.

Vogt, Stefan. "Robert Weltsch and the Paradoxes of Anti-Nationalist Nationalism." *Jewish Social Studies* 16 (2010): 85–115.

Vogt, Stefan. *Subalterne Positionierungen: Der deutsche Zionismus im Feld des Nationalismus in Deutschland, 1890–1933*. Göttingen: Wallstein, 2016.

Vogt, Stefan. "Zionismusgeschichte und postcolonial studies: Überlegungen zu einem uneingestandenen Verwandtschaftsverhältnis." *Werkstatt Geschichte* 76 (2017): 43–58.

Volkov, Shulamit. "Antisemitism as a Cultural Code: Reflections on the History and Historiography of Antisemitism in Imperial Germany." *Leo Baeck Institute Year Book* 23 (1978): 25–46.

Walker, David. "Nervous Outsiders: Australia and the 1955 Asia-Africa Conference in Bandung." *Australian Historical Studies* 37 (2005): 40–59.

Wallas, Armin A. "Der Pförtner des Ostens: Eugen Hoeflich. Panasiat und Expressionist." In *Von Franzos zu Canetti. Jüdische Autoren aus Österreich. Neue Studien*. Edited by Mark H. Gelber, Hans Otto Horch, and Sigurd Paul Scheichl, 305–44. Tübingen: Niemeyer, 1996.

Weiner, Hanna. "Gershom Scholem and the Jung Juda Youth Group in Berlin, 1913–1918." *Studies in Zionism* 5 (1984): 29–42.

Weiss, Yfaat. "Central European Ethnonationalism and Zionist Binationalism." *Jewish Social Studies* 11 (2004): 93–117.

Weizman, Eyal. *Hollow Land: Israel's Architecture of Occupation*. London: Verso, 2007.

Weldemichael, Awet Tewelde. *Third World Colonialism and Strategies of Liberation. Eritrea and East Timor Compared*. Cambridge, UK: Cambridge University Press, 2013.

Welter, Volker M. "The 1925 Master Plan for Tel-Aviv by Patrick Geddes." In *Tel-Aviv, the First Century: Visions, Designs, Actualities*. Edited by Maoz Azaryahu and S. Ilan Troen, 299–326. Bloomington: Indiana University Press, 2012.

Werses, Shmuel. "Daniel Deronda in the Hebrew Press and Literature." *Molad* 8 (1980): 39–40 [Hebrew].

Wertheimer, Jack. *Unwelcome Strangers: East European Jews in Imperial Germany.* New York: Oxford University Press, 1987.

Wien, Peter. "Arabs and Fascism: Empirical and Theoretical Perspectives." *Die Welt Des Islams* 52 (2012): 331–50.

Wien, Peter. "Coming to Terms with the Past: German Academia and Historical Relations between the Arab Lands and Nazi Germany." *International Journal of Middle East Studies* 42 (2010): 311–21.

Wien, Peter. *Iraqi Arab Nationalism: Authoritarian, Totalitarian and Profascist Inclinations, 1932–1941.* London: Routledge, 2006.

Wiese, Christian. *Challenging Colonial Discourse: Jewish Studies and Protestant Theology in Wilhelmine Germany.* Leiden: Brill, 2005.

Wiese, Christian. "'Doppelgesichtigkeit des Nationalismus': Die Ambivalenz zionistischer Identität bei Robert Weltsch und Hans Kohn." In *Janusfiguren: 'Jüdische Heimstätte', Exil und Nation im deutschen Zionismus*. Edited by Andrea Schatz and Christian Wiese, 213–52. Berlin: Metropol, 2006.

Wiese, Christian. "The Janus Face of Nationalism: The Ambivalence of Zionist Identity in Robert Weltsch and Hans Kohn." *Leo Baeck Institute Year Book* 51 (2006): 103–30.

Wild, Stefan. "National Socialism in the Arab Near East between 1933 and 1939." *Die Welt des Islams* 1 (1985): 126–73.

Wilder, Gary. *The French Imperial Nation-State: Négritude and Colonial Humanism Between the Two World Wars.* Chicago: University of Chicago Press, 2005.

Wilder, Gary, and Albert Memmi. "Irreconcilable Differences." *Transition* 71 (1996): 158–77.

Williams, Louise Blakeney. *Modernism and the Ideology of History: Literature, Politics, and the Past.* Cambridge, UK: Cambridge University Press, 2009.

Wistrich, Robert S. *Anti-Zionism and Antisemitism in the Contemporary World.* New York: New York University Press, 1990.

Wistrich, Robert S. *The Jews of Vienna in the Age of Franz Joseph.* Oxford: The Littman Library of Jewish Civilization, 1989.

Wolff, Larry. *The Idea of Galicia: History and Fantasy in Habsburg Political Culture.* Stanford, CA: Stanford University Press, 2010.

Yamamura, Midori, and Yu-Chieh Li, eds. *Visual Representations of the Postcolonial Struggles: Art in East and Southeast Asia.* London: Routledge, 2021.

Yegar, Moshe. *The Long Journey to Asia: A Chapter in the Diplomatic History of Israel.* Haifa: University of Haifa Press, 2004 [Hebrew].

Ye'or, Bat. *Juifs et chrétiens sous l'Islam: Les dhimmis face au défi intégriste.* Paris: Berg International, 1994.

Yiftachel, Oren, and Avinoam Meir. *Ethnic Frontiers and Peripheries: Landscapes of Development and Inequality in Israel.* Boulder, CO: Westview Press, 1998.

Young, Robert J. C. *Postcolonialism: A Very Short Introduction*. Oxford: Oxford University Press, 2003.

Young, Robert J. C. *Postcolonialism: An Historical Introduction*. Oxford: Blackwell, 2001.

Zertal, Idith, and Akiva Eldar. *Lords of the Land: The War for Israel's Settlements in the Occupied Territories, 1967–2007*. New York: Nation Books, 2007.

Zipperstein, Steven J. *Elusive Prophet: Ahad Ha'am and the Origins of Zionism*. Berkeley: University of California Press, 1993.

Zohar, Zvi. *Rabbinic Creativity in the Modern Middle East*. New York: Bloomsbury Publishing, 2013.

Zudrell, Petra. *Der Kulturkritiker und Schriftsteller Max Nordau. Zwischen Zionismus, Deutschtum und Judentum*. Würzburg: Königshausen & Neumann, 2003.

Contributors

ORIT BASHKIN is a historian who works on the intellectual, social, and cultural history of the modern Middle East. She got her PhD from Princeton University (2004) and has since been working as a professor of modern Middle Eastern history in the Department of Near Eastern Languages and Civilizations at the University of Chicago. Her publications deal with Iraqi history, the history of Iraqi Jews, the Arab cultural revival movement (the nahda) in the late nineteenth century, and the connections between modern Arab history and Arabic literature. Among her recent publications are *Impossible Exodus: Iraqi Jews in Israel* (Stanford University Press, 2017) and *New Babylonians: A History of the Jews in Iraq* (Stanford University Press, 2012). Her current research project explores the lives of Iraqi Jews in Israel.

JOHANNES BECKE is professor of Israel and Middle East studies at the Heidelberg Center for Jewish Studies (Hochschule für Jüdische Studien Heidelberg) in Germany. His research interests focus on comparative perspectives on Zionism and Israeli statehood. He is currently heading a research group at Heidelberg University comparing Jewish, Kurdish, and Berber nation-building. Recent publications include *Israel Studien: Geschichte, Methoden, Paradigmen* (Wallstein, 2020, in German, co-edited with Michael Brenner and Daniel Mahla) and *The Land Beyond the Border: State Formation and Territorial Expansion in Syria, Morocco, and Israel* (SUNY Press, 2021).

DIPESH CHAKRABARTY is the Lawrence A. Kimpton Distinguished Service Professor of History and South Asian Studies at the University of Chicago. He has been a founding member of the editorial collective of *Subaltern Studies* and a founding editor of *Postcolonial Studies*. He is the author of seven monographs, including *Provincializing Europe: Postcolonial Thought and Historical Difference* (Princeton University Press, 2000; 2008), *The Crisis of Civilization: Exploring Global and Planetary Histories* (Oxford University Press, 2018), and *The Climate of History in a Planetary Age* (Chicago University Press, 2021). His new book, *One Planet, Many Worlds*, is forthcoming with Brandeis University Press.

334 | CONTRIBUTORS

ARIE M. DUBNOV is an associate professor of history and the Max Ticktin Chair of Israel Studies at George Washington University. Among his publications are the intellectual biography *Isaiah Berlin: The Journey of a Jewish Liberal* (Palgrave Macmillan, 2012); two edited volumes, *Zionism—A View from the Outside* (The Bialik Institute, 2010, in Hebrew), seeking to put Zionist history in a larger comparative trajectory; and *Partitions: A Transnational History of Twentieth-Century Territorial Separatism* (Stanford University Press, 2019, co-edited with Laura Robson), tracing the genealogy of the idea of partition in the British interwar imperial context and reconstructing the links connecting partition plans in Ireland, Palestine/Israel, and India/Pakistan. In addition, he has published numerous essays in leading venues, including *Nations & Nationalism, Modern Intellectual History, Theoria u'vikoret* (*Theory & Criticism*), *Rethinking History, Jewish Social Studies, The Journal of Israeli History*, and more. His current research project, tentatively entitled *Dreamers of the Third Empire/Temple*, examines ties between Zionist and British imperial thinkers in interwar years and seeks to uncover alternative, neglected federalist political schemes for the future of the region that were circulating at the time.

MANJA HERRMANN is a research associate at the Selma Stern Center for Jewish Studies Berlin-Brandenburg and the Technical University Berlin (Center for Research on Antisemitism). She is the leader of the "The 'Righteous Among the Nations' in Comparative Perspective" research group. Herrmann received her PhD from Ben-Gurion University in Beer Sheva (Israel) in 2015 with a dissertation on the concept of authenticity in early German Zionism, which was published as *Zionismus und Authentizität: Gegennarrative des Authentischen im frühen zionistischen Diskurs* (De Gruyter, 2018). From April 2020 to March 2021, Herrmann was the Lilli and Michael Sommerfreund guest professor at the Hochschule für Jüdische Studien Heidelberg. The results of her research have been published in the *Leo Baeck Institute Year Book, Modern Judaism*, and *German History*, among others. Most recently, she has published the collected volume *Wilhelm Herzberg's Jewish Family Papers (1868): Interdisciplinary Readings of a Forgotten Bestseller* (De Gruyter, 2021).

MAŁGORZATA A. MAKSYMIAK received her PhD in 2009 from Ben Gurion University in Beer Sheva (Israel). Her dissertation has been published in German as *Mental Maps in Zionimus: Ost und West in Konzepten einer jüdischen Nation vor 1914* (Edition Lumière, 2015). She is currently working on a monograph on the German fear of the East and the emergence of the image of the "Ostjude" in the period between 1772 and 1897. She is a lecturer in the Department for Early Modern History at the University of Rostock.

CONTRIBUTORS | 335

DEREK J. PENSLAR is the William Lee Frost Professor of Jewish History at Harvard University. Penslar's books include *Israel in History: The Jewish State in Comparative Perspective* (Routledge, 2006), *The Origins of Israel: A Documentary History* (with Eran Kaplan, University of Wisconsin Press, 2011), *Jews and the Military: A History* (Princeton University Press, 2013), *Theodor Herzl: The Charismatic Leader* (Yale University Press, 2020), and the forthcoming *Zionism: An Emotional State* (Rutgers University Press, 2023).

SARAH PHILLIPS CASTEEL is professor of English at Carleton University, where she is cross-appointed to the Institute of African Studies and the Institute for Comparative Studies in Literature, Art and Culture. She is the author of *Second Arrivals: Landscape and Belonging in Contemporary Writing of the Americas* (University of Virginia Press, 2007) and *Calypso Jews: Jewishness in the Caribbean Literary Imagination* (Columbia University Press, 2016), which won a Canadian Jewish literary award. She has also co-edited *Canada and Its Americas: Transnational Navigations* (McGill-Queen's University Press, 2010) and *Caribbean-Jewish Crossings: Literary History and Creative Practice* (University of Virginia Press, 2019). She has been a visiting fellow at the Zentrum Jüdische Studien Berlin-Brandenburg and the United States Holocaust Memorial Museum and has taught at the Universities of Mainz, Vienna, and Potsdam, where she held the Potsdam Postcolonial Chair in Global Modernities in 2021. She is currently working on a book entitled *Making History Visible: Black Lives under Nazism in Literature and Art*.

ATO QUAYSON is the Jean G. and Morris M. Doyle Professor in Interdisciplinary Studies and professor of English at Stanford University. He studied for his undergraduate degree at the University of Ghana and took his PhD from the University of Cambridge, after which he became reader in Commonwealth and postcolonial literature in the faculty of English at Cambridge from 1995 to 2005. He was also director of the Centre for African Studies while at Cambridge. Prior to Stanford he was professor of African and postcolonial Literature at New York University (2017–2019) and professor of English and inaugural director of the Centre for Diaspora and Transnational Studies at the University of Toronto (2005–2017). His most recent book is *Tragedy and Postcolonial Literature* (Cambridge University Press, 2021). Earlier monographs include *Postcolonialism: Theory, Practice, or Process?* (Polity Press, 2000) and *Oxford Street, Accra: City Life and the Itineraries of Transnationalism* (Duke University Press, 2014). Edited volumes include *Relocating Postcolonialism* (with David Goldberg, Blackwell Publishers, 2001) and the two-volume *Cambridge History of Postcolonial Literature* (Cambridge University Press, 2012). Ato Quayson is also the editor of the *Cambridge*

Journal of Postcolonial Literary Inquiry, for which in 2015 he compiled, together with Willi Goetschel, a special issue on *Jewish Studies and Postcolonialism*.

ABRAHAM RUBIN is assistant professor of modern Jewish religious thought and history at the University of Dayton. Before coming to Dayton, he held postdoctoral positions in the Martin Buber Society of Fellows at the Hebrew University of Jerusalem; Lawrence University in Wisconsin; and Goethe University, Frankfurt am Main. He received his PhD in comparative literature from the City University of New York. He is currently completing a monograph entitled *Conversion in the Shadow of Catastrophe: The Consolations of Christianity in German-Jewish Émigré Autobiography*. His scholarly work has appeared in such journals as *Literature & Theology*, *The AJS Review*, *The Jewish Quarterly Review*, and *Jewish Social Studies*.

ARIEH SAPOSNIK is associate professor at the Ben-Gurion Institute for the Study of Israel and Zionism at Ben-Gurion University in the Negev. Prior to joining the faculty at Ben-Gurion University, he was the founding director of the Nazarian Center for Israel Studies at UCLA. A historian of Zionism and Jewish nationalism, Saposnik is interested in the construction of national cultures and identities in the modern world. He is the author of *Becoming Hebrew: The Creation of a Jewish National Culture in Ottoman Palestine* (Oxford University Press, 2008) and *Zionism's Redemptions: Images of the Past and Visions of the Future in Jewish Nationalism* (Cambridge University Press, 2021). He is currently working on a book that explores modern efforts to reshape the Jewish relationship to space and place and on an intellectual biography of Joseph Klausner.

GHILAD H. SHENHAV is a postdoctoral fellow in the department for religious studies at the University of Potsdam. He is currently at work on his first book about language, tradition, and gender in the writings of Gershom Scholem. Shenhav has written several articles in the fields of modern Jewish thought and literature, among them "Jacques Derrida and the Desertification of the Messianic" (*Jewish Studies Quarterly*, 2022) and "The Sound(s) of Silence: Gershom Scholem's 'Laments Project' and the Question of Gender" (*Journal of Jewish Studies*, forthcoming).

SCOTT SPECTOR is the Rudolf Mrázek Collegiate Professor of History and German Studies at the University of Michigan. He is a cultural and intellectual historian of modern Central and East Central Europe, specializing in Habsburg and Jewish culture, sexual science and sensational culture, and fin-de-siècle studies. He is the author of *Prague Territories: National Conflict and Cultural Innovation in Franz Kafka's Fin de Siècle* (University of California Press, 2000), *Violent Sensations: Sexuality, Crime, and Utopia in Vienna and Berlin, 1860–1914* (University of Chicago Press, 2016), and

Modernism without Jews? German-Jewish Subjects and Histories (University of Indiana, 2017), and has co-edited *After the History of Sexuality: German Genealogies with and beyond Foucault* (Berghahn, 2012). He has held fellowships in recent years at the Center for Urban History of East-Central Europe, Lviv (Ukraine); the Ukraine in European Dialogue program at the Institut für die Wissenschaften vom Menschen/ Institute for Human Sciences (IWM), Vienna; the Institut für jüdische Studien und Religionswissenschaft, University of Potsdam; and the International Research Center in Cultural Studies (IFK), Vienna. He is currently working on a manuscript on the layers of national, imperial, and global belonging in cities of the former Habsburg empire and its successor states.

REPHAEL G. STERN is a PhD candidate in history at Harvard University. He is also the 2022–2023 Samuel I. Golieb Fellow in Legal History at NYU Law School. He earned a JD from Harvard Law School, an MA from Princeton University, and a BA from Brandeis University. His dissertation explores the formation of administrative and constitutional legal regimes in the twentieth-century Middle East and, especially, Israel/Palestine.

STEFAN VOGT is professor for Jewish History and research coordinator at the Buber-Rosenzweig Institute for Modern and Contemporary Jewish Intellectual and Cultural History at Goethe University in Frankfurt am Main. He received his PhD in history from the Free University Berlin in 2004 and has previously worked at the University of Amsterdam, at New York University, and at Ben Gurion University of the Negev. His main research areas are German-Jewish history and the intersections of Jewish history with the history of colonialism. He is the author of two monographs, *Subalterne Positionierungen: Der deutsche Zionismus im Feld des Nationalismus in Deutschland, 1890–1933* (Wallstein, 2016) and *Nationaler Sozialismus und Soziale Demokratie: Die sozialdemokratische Junge Rechte 1918–1945* (Dietz, 2006), and of a number of articles on the history of Zionism, German-Jewish history, and the history of nationalism and antisemitism. He is also the editor of the volume *Colonialism and the Jews in German History: From the Middle Ages to the Twentieth Century* (Bloomsbury Academic, 2022).

Index

Page numbers in *italics* indicate illustrations. Titles of authored works are found under the name of the author.

'Abduh, Muḥammad, 200
Abraham Accords (2020), 227
Abramovitsch, Sholem Yankev (Mendele Mokher Seforim), 294
A[c]had Ha'am (Asher Zvi Hirsch Ginsberg), 95, 130–31, 145, 167
Achcar, Gilbert, 206
Achebe, Chinua, 292, 294, 295, 300; *Arrow of God*, 295, 300; *Things Fall Apart*, 293
Acher, Matthias. *See* Birnbaum, Nathan
Adler, Felix, 102, 117n48
Adler, Herman, 101
Adorno, Theodor, 295
al-Afghānī, Jamāl al-Dīn, 200
Africa/African states: comparative study of Yiddish and African peripheral modernisms, 294–95; Entebbe raid, 298; Israel's technical assistance to (in 1960s/1970s), 14, 298; languages of, and African studies scholars, 292–93, 294; Memmi on Négritude and, 80; political relationships between Israel and, 298–99; Uganda debate (1903), 137n42. *See also specific states*
Agnon, S. Y., 171
Agudas Yisroel party, 147
Ahavath Zion, 142
Alcalay, Ammiel, 190; *After Jews and Arabs*, 190
Alemayu, Haddis, 221
Algeria: Fanon's involvement in, 76–78, 81, 85–86; Memmi on, 151, 152; Moroccan claims on portions of, 220; Zionism compared to French colonial regime in, 219
Aliyah, 148–49, 154
Allgemeine Zeitung des Judentums (AZJ), 124
Alliance Israélite Universelle, 192, 196, 199
Almoni, Pawel, 137n42
Alterman, Nathan, 246–47, 267n57
Anderson, Benedict, 201
Anidjar, Gil, 162–63, 180n5

anti-nationalist nationalism, Zionism viewed as, 70n45
antisemitism: affinities of Zionism with some aspects of antisemitic ideology, 64; diaspora, viewed as inevitable consequence of, 59; mentally ill Jew, concept of, 124; Middle East, experience of Jews in, 187–88, 200, 206, 209n2; Orientalist, 57; Palestinian resistance/criticism of Israel depicted as, 207, 298; subaltern, 7, 23n31; Zionism and rise of, in Middle East, 188–89; Zionist identity politics and, 52, 59–61
Anṭūn, Faraḥ, 199
Anzi, Menashe, 212n46
Arabic language, viewed as threat to Hebrew by Scholem, 173–74
Arab-Israeli conflict. *See* Palestinian-Israeli conflict
Arab League, 246, 262n1
Arabs and Jews: Galician Zionist perception of Arabs, 137n40; Hoeflich's pan-Semitism, 150; in interwar period, 201–2; Memmi's rejection of Arab-Jewish identity, 78–80; Muslim/Arab nationalism and nation-states, 187–91, 201–9; in Ottoman Empire and British Mandate Palestine, 195–96; pre-modern forms of Arab-Jewish coexistence, collapse of, 187; Scholem on Hebrew language and, 164–66
Arendt, Hannah, 279, 282, 285, 288–89, 295; *Illuminations*, 281
Armenia, territorial enclaves established by, 225
Arndt-Kurnberg, Friedrich (Omar al-Rashid Bey), 239
Aschheim, Steven, 119
Asia, Zionist perceptions of, 18, 233–62; after 1950s, 260–62; Bandung Conference (1955), Israel's non-invitation to, 18, 215,

339

Asia, Israel's non-invitation to (*continued*), 236, 252–57, 259–60, 298; in context of Jewish, European, and colonial history, 236–42; cultural ambivalence about Jewish otherness and, 234–35, 258–59; in first year of Israeli statehood, 236, 250–52; India and UNEF, 259–60, *261*; nation-statism and, 258–59; "Orient," "East," and "Asia," lack of clear distinction between, 236, 258; pan-Asianism, 241–43; pan-Semitism/pan-Asiatic Zionism of Hoeflich, 150, 151–52, 154, 241; parameters of, 235–36; sartorial choices, politics of, 233–34, *235*; UN votes on partition and Israel's membership in UN, 250. *See also specific Asian countries*
Asian Relations Conference (1947), 18, 233–34, *235*, 236, 242–50, *249*, 258–59
Asian Relations Conference (1949), 250
Assad, Talal, 189
assimilation: authenticity as counternarrative to, 31, 34–36; Birnbaum's rejection of, 143; "conscious pariah," concept of, 288; Galician criticism of, 131, 132; Herzl and Nordau rejecting, 140; Jewish women as assimilationists, 40–44, 49n67; liberalism, associated with, 34–35, 45; Pissarro's assimilationist trajectory, 108, 110–13; Zionism as rejection of, 154
Association of Jewish Studies, 294
Auerbach, Erich, 295, 300
Austrian Jewish National Party, 144
Austro-Hungarian Dual Monarchy. *See* Habsburg colonial imaginary and Central European Zionism
authenticity as counternarrative, 15, 29–45; to assimilation, 31, 34–36; Birnbaum's use of, 144; to Christianity and Christian culture, 30–31, 32–34; concept of authenticity, 31–32; concept of counternarrative, 30–31; for Galician Zionists, 129–31; gender and, 31, 40–44, 49n67; in German-Jewish Zionist thought, 29–31, 44–45; within Judaism, 46n2; master narratives or dominant discourses, 30, 46n3; to "new Marranos," 31, 36–39, *37*, 48n49; Orientalism and, 45–46n1; to "Philistines," 31, 39–41
Avnery, Uri, 261

Bader, Gershom (Gustav), 130–31
Baghdad Pact, 253
Bahrain, 227
Balfour Declaration, 150–51, 241
Balibar, Étienne, 258
Bandung Conference (1955), 18, 215, 236, 252–57, 259–60, 298

Barak, Ehud, 14
Bareli, Avi, 3
Baron, Beth, 199
Bashkin, Orit, 17, 187, 203, 333
Bauman, Zygmunt, 260; *Modernity and the Holocaust*, 283
Becke, Johannes, 17–18, 215, 333
Behar, Almog, 205
Behar, Moshe, 199, 207–8
Beinin, Joel, 188, 193–94, 202, 203
Belcher, Wendy, 300n1
Ben Aboud, Mehdi, 220
Ben-Avi, Itamar, 239
Benbassa, Esther, 188
Bendix, Regina, 30, 31
Ben Dor, Zvi, 199, 207–8
Ben-Gavriêl, Moshe Ya'akov. *See* Hoeflich, Eugen
Ben-Gurion, David, 218, 251
Benjamin, Walter, 177–78, 295; *Illuminations*, 281; *Theses on the Philosophy of History*, 281
Ben-Yehuda, Eliezer, 166, 167, 172–73, 239
Bergman[n], Shmuel Hugo: at Asian Relations Conference (1947), 234, *235*, 242–48, 258–59, 265–66n42; Buber in Prague and, 148; traveling to Eastern Habsburg Empire, 153
Bernfeld, Simon, 237
Bhabha, Homi K., 3, 10, 189, 237, 257
Biale, David, 46n4
Bialer, Uri, 254
Bialik, Haim Nachman, 167
Birnbaum, Nathan (Matthias Acher): *Fun an apikoyres gevorn a maymin* (From Apostate to Believer), 142; Habsburg colonial imaginary and, 142–47, 153, 154; Hoeflich and, 149; the *Ostjude* and, 35, 125–26, 133, 134, 136n34, 137n38, 146; religious orthodoxy, turn to, 147; Yiddishism, turn to, 125, 137n38, 145–46, 147, 157n34; Zionism of, 144–46, 157n26
Black and Jewish experience, 8, 51, 95–97, 115n1, 282, 295–96, 300. *See also* Fanon, Frantz; Memmi, Albert; slaves and slavery; St. Thomas, diaspora experience of Blacks and Jews of
the black Sabbath (Operation Agatha), 245
Blau-Weiß youth movement, 167–69, 170, 266n46
blood libel, 188, 200
Bloom, Harold, 88n5
Blumenfeld, Kurt, 29, 59
Blyden, Edward Wilmot: *Christianity, Islam and the Negro Race*, 97; Gilroy's study of, 96–97, 102–4, 108, 117n55; *The Jewish*

Question, 97–99, 100–102; in Liberia, 98, 108, 112; pan-Africanism and embrace of Zionism, 97–102, 114; parallel lives of Blyden and Pissarro on St. Thomas, 96, 104, 106–8, 116n41; Venezuela, Blyden and Pissarro in, 105, 107, 110; *From West Africa to Palestine*, 97, 100. *See also* St. Thomas, diaspora experience of Blacks and Jews of
Boehm, Max Hildebert, 68n33
Bogor Conference (1954), 254
Bonné, Alfred, 244–45, 266n45
Boucetta, M'hammed, 220
Boyarin, Daniel, 3, 257
Boyarin, Jonathan, 3
Boycott, Divestment, and Sanctions (BDS) movement, 19n2, 299–300, 301n11
Brachyahu, Anna (Hannah Borochov), 245, 246, 267n50
Brenner, David A., 46n1
Brenner, Michael, 46n1
Bretell, Richard R., 104–5
Britain: comparative studies of collapse of empires, 292; George Eliot and *Daniel Deronda*, 97, 237–38, 263nn11–12; Irish rebellion against, 247–48; Suez War (1956), 234, 254; Zionist Asianism and, 237–39, 263nn11–12
Brith Shalom movement, 149, 154, 158n39, 158n45, 160n60, 164, 240, 244
British Mandate Palestine: Arab-Jewish relations in, 195–96; Asianism, Zionist, and, 238; Balfour Declaration, 150–51, 241; communism in, 203; India and, 241–42; Jewish emigration to, 148–49, 150, 154; Jewish population of (*see* Yishuv); Palestine national revolt (1929), 205–6; Peel Commission (1937), 242; restriction of Jewish emigration by British, 151, 247; Scholem in, 163
Brod, Max, 149
Buber, Martin: authenticity as counternarrative and, 42–43; on Gandhi, 267n62; *Der Geist des Orients und das Judentum*, 56, 68n18; Habsburg colonial imaginary and, 147–49, 153, 158n45; Orientalism of, 6, 55–58, 61, 63, 68n17, 239–41, 258; Tagore and, 24n42
Bukovinian Jews, 133, 140, 146, 153
Burma, 234, 243, 250, 252, 254, 255, 262n1

Calvary, Moses, 40
Camp David peace talks (2000), 1
Campos, Michelle, 205; *Ottoman Brothers*, 195
Caplan, Marc, 301n5; *How Strange the Change*, 294–95

Caribbean: Memmi on Fanon's Black West Indian identity, 76–80; Négritude movement, 80–82, 89–90n29, 97, 282; St. Croix slave revolt, 96, 108. *See also* St. Thomas, diaspora experience of Blacks and Jews of
Celler, Emanuel, 243
Centre for Diaspora Studies (CTDS), University of Toronto, 293, 295
Césaire, Aimé, 76, 80, 97, 102
Cézanne, Paul, 111
Chakrabarty, Dipesh, 2, 11–12, 18–19, 275–89, 333; *Provincializing Europe*, 11, 275, 278, 280, 285–87
Chaplin, Charlie, 288
Charmé, Stuart Z., 46n2
Chatterjee, Partha, 19n2, 71n57
Chetrit, Sami Shalom, 188
Cheyette, Bryan, 4, 73, 114, 277, 301n6
China: at Asian Relations Conference (1947), 243, 262n1; Bandung Conference and, 253, 270n108; compared to Israel, 292; on Palestinian-Israeli conflict, 270n108; pan-Asianism, Hoeflich on, 241; recognition of Israel by, 250; Third World colonialism of, 18, 216–19, 222, 223, 227; UN votes on partition and Israel's membership in UN, 250; Uyghurs, 292
Chomsky, Noam, 301n11
Christianity and Christian culture: antisemitism introduced into Arab states by Christian missionaries, 187–88; authenticity as counternarrative to, 30–31, 32–34; missionary education in Middle East, 199; in Ottoman Empire and Mandate Palestine, 193, 196–97
civil rights movement, conflation of Black and Jewish experience in, 115n1
Clarke, Thomas, 237
Cock, Joan, 74
Cohen, Hillel, 205–6
Cohen, Judah, 100
Cold War, 7, 251, 253, 254
Colombo Powers, 254
communism: Bandung Conference on neocolonialism of, 253; in British Mandate Palestine and Israel, 203–4; Middle East, Jews in, 203–5, 208
"conscious pariah," concept of, 279, 288–89
Conversations Across the Diaspora series, 300
Cooper, Frederick, 5
counternarratives. *See* authenticity as counternarrative
Crawford, Neta, 231n44
Crimean War, 124

Critical Inquiry (journal), 275
cultural Zionism, 146, 147–49, 150, 154, 157n26, 158n45
Czernowitz Conference (1908), 146

Das, Taraknath, 250
Davar (newspaper), 246, *249*, 255–56
Davis, Natalie Zemon, 301n5
Dawn, C. Ernest, 198
Dayyan, Rabbi Yitzhak, 200
decolonization: defined, 231n44; Fanon and, 76; Memmi on, 75, 78; processes and consequences of, 9, 14, 215, 217, 222, 223. *See also* Third World colonialism and Israel's settlement project
Degas, Edgar, 111
Deleuze, Gilles, 281, 287
Derrida, Jacques, 295
Descartes, René, 296, 301
Devji, Faisal, 278–79, 280, 282–83, 288; *Muslim Zion*, 283
diaspora: antisemitism viewed as inevitable consequence of, 59; comparative studies in, 291–92; interdisciplinary approach to diaspora studies, 293–94; Memmi on Jewish life in, 79, 81–83; Négritude movement, development of, 81; postcolonial approaches to, 4, 8. *See also* St. Thomas, diaspora experience of Blacks and Jews of
Disraeli, Benjamin (Lord Beaconsfield), 239; *Tancred* (Disraeli), 263n12
Domhardt, Johann Friedrich von, 121
"Dosh" (Katriel Gordosh), 259–60, *261*
double consciousness, 143
Downs, Roger M., 121–22
Dreyfus Affair, 96, 108, 111–12, 117n52
Du Bois, W. E. B., 97, 99, 108, 115n14, 117n52, 295
Dubnov, Arie M., 18, 20n7, 233, 334
Dussel, Enrique, 283

East/West dichotomy, 16–17. *See also* Habsburg colonial imaginary and Central European Zionism; Orientalism; *Ostjude*; Scholem, Gershom; St. Thomas, diaspora experience of Blacks and Jews of
Ebenbürtigkeit, 60, 69n39
Efron, John, 181n14, 277
Egypt: at Asian Relations Conference (1947), 234; New Delhi Incident, Asian Relations Conference, 246; Suez War (1956), 234, 254
Egyptian Jews: in interwar period, 202; in Ottoman Empire and under British colonial rule, 193–94, 196–200
Eiland, Howard, 281
Eilat, Eliahu, 251
Einstein, Albert, 284
Elad (City of David Foundation), 226
Eliot, George, 97; *Daniel Deronda*, 237–38, 263nn11–12
England. *See* Britain; British Mandate Palestine
Entebbe raid, 298
equity-seeking groups, 297
Eritrea, 221, 222
Ervi, Yuval, 205
Ethical Culture movement, 102
Ethiopia: Italian occupation of, 206; Third World colonialism of, 217, 221, 222
Etzel (Irgun), 261
Europe, Zionism, and [post]colonialism, 4–7, 11–14; authenticity as counternarrative and, 34; Blyden on, 101–2; Chakrabarty on, 277–78, 280–82; imperialism of Europe, Jewish role in/victimization by, 283–84; Jews as Europe's "internal others," 8, 51, 277–78; positioning, identity politics as, 51; Syrian and Lebanese Jews migrating to Europe, 194; in Walcott's verse biography of Pissarro, 110. *See also specific European countries*
Evron, Boaz, 260
Expressionism, 149, 158n41
Eytan, Walter, 251

Fahmy, Ziad, 199
Fanon, Frantz, 15–16, 73–87; affinities between Memmi and Fanon, 73–74, 79–80, 86–87; Algerian nationalism, Fanon's involvement in, 76–78, 81, 85–86; *Black Skin, White Masks*, 74, 81; Black West Indian identity, failure to come to terms with, 76–80; Chakrabarty on postcolonialism and, 276, 277; conceptual connection between Jewish marginality and condition of colonial domination, 75–76; France, disavowal of, 76, 77, 78; Israel of Memmi as parallel for Fanon's Algeria, 83–86; nativism and, 80, 81, 82, 84; on Négritude, 80–82, 89–90n29; pan-Africanism of, 76, 77; universalism and, 74, 78–80, 82–84, 90n40, 90n46; *The Wretched of the Earth*, 74, 77, 78, 81, 86, 277
Fascism and Nazism in Middle East, 206–7, 208
al-Fassi, 'Allal, 228
Fiewel, Berthold, 41–42
Fink, Dr., 136n35
First Intifada, 15, 299
First Pan-African Congresses (1900), 95
Flaum, Schlomith F., 242, 265n31
Forman, Seth, 115n1
France: comparative studies of collapse of empires, 292; difference attributed to

colonialism of, 141; Dreyfus Affair, 96, 108, 111–12, 117n52; Fanon's disavowal of, 76, 77, 78; Memmi settling in, 84; mentally ill Jew, concept of, 124; Négritude movement, development of, 80–81; Pissarro's assimilationist trajectory in, 108, 110–13; *Radio Levant France Libre*, 245; Suez War (1956), 234, 254. *See also* Algeria
Franzos, Karl Emil, 127, 146, 155n11; *Halb-Asien*, 124
Frederick II of Prussia, 121, 122, 135n9, 135n20
Freitag, Ulrike, 207
Freud, Sigmund, 175, 219, 284, 295
Frischmann, David, 238–39, 264n17

Galicia: Arabs, Galician Zionist perception of, 137n40; emigration of Jews from, 123–24, 146; Habsburg colonial imaginary and Central European Zionism in, 140, 141–44, 146, 148, 150–51, 153; heterogeneous culture of, 126–27; invention of, 120–21; novels and stories about, 124–25; *Ostjude* concept and Galician Zionists, 125–32; territorial composition, 127; Uganda debate (1903), Galician Zionists on, 137n42
Gandhi, Mohandas/Mahatma, 239, 240, 244, 247–48, 267n62, 276
Gans, Chaim, 228
Garvey, Marcus, 97
Gates, Henry Louis, Jr., 300
Gauguin, Paul, 113
Gazety Pisane (newspaper), 124
Geddes, Patrick, 242
Gellner, Ernest, 201
gender: Asian Relations Conference, women representatives of Yishuv at, 245, 266n49; authenticity as counternarrative and, 31, 40–44, 49n67; Pan-Asiatic Women's Conference (1947), 246; Zionist movement and, 205
German colonial movement, 63
German Hebraist movement, Scholem on, 169, 180n4
German-Jewish thought: on authenticity as counternarrative, 29–31, 44–45 (*see also* authenticity as counternarrative); Chakrabarty influenced by, 280–82; East, perceptions of, 120, 123–25; self-Orientalization in, 239–41
Germany, demographics of Jews in, 122, 135–36n21
German Zionist Association (*Zionistische Vereinigung für Deutschland*), 60–61
German-Zionist youth movements, 167–69, 171, 181n22

Gershoni, Israel, 201, 206, 207
Gilman, Sander L., 136n32
Gilroy, Paul, 3, 8, 295; *The Black Atlantic*, 31, 102–4, 282; comparison of Walcott and, 108–9, 112; *Modernity, Culture and "the Jew,"* 95; on Pissarro, 102–4, 108–9, 112, 117n55
Ginat, Rami, 203
Goetschel, Willi, 295, 301n5
Goldsmid, Albert W., 263n12
Golem, Scholem on modern spoken Hebrew as, 172–73
Gordon, Adi, 158n39, 160n60
Gordosh, Katriel ("Dosh"), 259–60, *261*
Greene, Annie Leah, 197, 200, 210n15
Gribetz, Jonathan, 198, 205
Gronemann, Samy, 138n61
Grünbaum, J., 131
Guedalla, Haim, 263n11
Gulf War (1990), 222
Gush Emunim, 219, 222

Ha'aretz (newspaper), 247
Habas, Bracha, 234, 245, 248–50, 266n49
Habsburg colonial imaginary and Central European Zionism, 16–17, 139–55; Birnbaum and, 142–47, 153, 154; Buber and, 147–49, 153, 158n45; Cisleithanian focus of, 140; cultural Zionism, importance of, 146, 147–49, 150, 154, 157n26, 158n45; Galicia in, 140, 141–44, 146, 148, 150–51, 153; Hoeflich (Ben-Gavriêl) and, 149–52, 153; Memmi's *Colonizer and the Colonized*, 140–41, 151, 154, 155n3; mythology of, 141; Orientalism of, 142, 150, 152, 153, 154; origins of Zionism in Habsburg Empire, 141–45; the *Ostjude* in, 146–47; Ottoman Empire, Austro-Hungarian alliance with, 152; Palestinian-Israeli conflict and, 152
Hacohen, David, 234, *235*, 245, 247, 248, 250, 266n49
Hacohen, Mordechai Ben-Hillel, 237
Haganah, 245
Haim, Sylvia, 209n2
Hall, Stuart: as Black thinker, 295; on Caribbean model of diaspora, 103; Chakrabarty on, 275, 278, 282, 283; *Cultural Identity and Diaspora*, 52; positioning, identity politics as, 15, 51–55, 58, 61, 62, 64, 66; postcolonial approaches to historiography of Zionism and, 8–11, 19n2
Hamann, Johann Georg, 169
Hamas, 299
ha-Mizrah he-Hadash (journal), 251
Hardt, Michael, and Antonio Negri, *Empire*, 287
Harel, Yaron, 194, 199

Harif, Hanan, 241
Harper, Paula, 105, 117n46
Harrison, Olivia, 84–85
Harrison, Olivia C., 218
Hasidim, 124, 129, 142
Haskalah (Jewish Enlightenment), 142, 189, 200
Hatzofeh, 256
Hebraist movement, 169, 180n4
Hebrew language: A[c]had Ha'am and, 130; Birnbaum's initial embrace of, 144; Blyden's study of, 97; Buber on Jewish woman and, 43; emergence of Jewish literature in, 125; Galician Zionists and, 125, 130, 132; Middle Eastern Jews and, 192–93; secular spoken language, modern transition to, 161–62; "Sephardic" accent, transition to, 161, 165–66, 167, 181n12, 181n14; Sokolov writing in, 37; Zionist youth movements and, 167–69, 171, 181n22. *See also* Scholem, Gershom
Hebrew Language Council, 165–66, 181n12
Hebrew Manifesto, 261
Hebrew University of Jerusalem, 18, 165, 234, 242, 243, 244, 246, 250
Hegel, Georg Wilhelm Friedrich, 240
Heid, Ludger, 119
Heine, Heinrich, 124, 288
Heinrich (Prussian prince), 122
Herder, Johann Gottfried, 31, 169
Herrmann, Manja, 15, 29, 334
Herzberg, Wilhelm, 32–34, 45, 47n19; *Jüdische Familienpapiere* (Jewish Family Papers), 32–34, 45, 47n19
Herzberg-Fränkel, Leo, 146
Herzl, Theodor: *Altneuland*, 131; Arendt on, 279; Asia, Zionist perceptions of, 236, 237–38, 240–41, 262n6, 263n12; authenticity as counternarrative and, 35; Habsburg colonial imaginary and, 139–40, 145, 148; the *Ostjude* and, 129, 131; St. Thomas, diaspora experience of Blacks and Jews of, 95, 101
Heschel, Susannah, 3, 4, 30, 277; *Abraham Geiger and the Jewish Jesus* (Heschel), 30
Hess, Jonathan, 5
Hess, Moses, *Rome and Jerusalem*, 32
Hirsch, Dafna, 267n50
Hirsch, Marianne, *The Generation of Postmemory*, 296
Hitler, Adolf, 247
Hobsbawm, Eric, 201
Hochberg, Gil, 89n22
Hoeflich, Eugen (Moshe Ya'akov Ben-Gavriêl), 149–52, 153, 154, 241; *The Way into the Land*, 151
Holocaust, 134, 248
Holocaust analogies, 96, 115n3

Hovevei Zion/Hibbat Zion, 142
Hroch, Miroslav, 201
Hurvitz, Nimrod, 198
al-Ḥusaynī, Amīn, 206
Huss, Boaz, 163
Hussein, Mostafa, 205
Hyman, Paula F., 49n67

identity politics, concept of, 10–11. *See also* positioning, identity politics as
Ilan, Benjamin (Ben-Zion), 245, 267n51
Imber, Naphtali Herz, *Barkai the Third*, 238, 263n13
India: Asian Relations Conference (1947) and, 233–34, 235, 242–43, 246–50; Bandung Conference and, 253; British occupation of Palestine and, 241–42; diplomatic relations with Israel by, 250; Flaum's Asianism and, 242; Gandhi, Jews, and Zionism, 239, 240, 244, 247–48; in Hebrew Manifesto, 261; Kashmir conflict, 224, 251, 259, 261; Palestinians, support for, 240, 244; partition and Muslim minority in, 279–80; recognition of/diplomatic relations with Israel, 250–51; UNEF (United Nations Emergency Force) and, 259–60, 261; UN partition proposal, voting against, 250;
Indian National Congress, 244
Indonesia: at Asian Relations Conference (1947), 262n1; Third World colonialism of, 216–18, 220–22, 223, 227–28
Iraq: Fascism in, 206; interwar years in, 202–3; Ottomanism in, 196–97; Third World colonialism of, 221, 222
Ireland: Britain, rebellion against, 247–48; India compared, 291; Lebanese diaspora and, 291
Irgun, 261
irredentist ideologies, 216, 220, 222, 223, 228, 242
Islam. *See specific entries at* Muslim
Israel, state of: Asian relations in first year of Israeli statehood, 236, 250–52; Bandung Conference (1955), non-invitation to, 18, 215, 236, 252–57; China compared to, 292; communism in, 203–4; decolonization, Memmi associating establishment with, 75; geographic and political terminology for, 231n38; South Africa compared to, 14, 215, 239, 270n108, 300; UN votes on partition and Israel's membership in UN, 250. *See also* Palestinian-Israeli conflict; Third World colonialism and Israel's settlement project; *specific wars*
Israeli, Raphael, 188

INDEX | 345

Jabotinsky, Ze'ev (Vladimir), 228, 236, 262n6
Jacobson, Abigail, 195, 205
Jankowski, James, 206
Jansen, G. H., 269n95
Japan, 150, 154, 158n45, 238, 241–43, 252, 255, 263n13
Japonisme, 241
Jennings, Michael W., 281
Jewish Agency, 205, 244
Johnson, Paul, 289n8; *A History of the Jews*, 284
Der Jude (journal), 167–68, 239
Die Jüdische Volkszeitung (periodical), 144

Kabbalah, 162, 163, 179, 296
Kadimah, 143–44, 156–57n20
Kafka, Franz, 148, 234, 281, 282, 288
Kahanoff, Jacqueline, 208
Kakuzō, Okakura, *The Ideals of the East*, 241
Kallenbach, Hermann, 239
Kane, Cheikh Hamidou, 294
Kanowitz, Siegfried, 60
Kant, Immanuel, 240
Katowice Conference (1884), 156n12
Katz, Jacob, 123
Kedourie, Elie, 32, 196
Keenleyside, T. A., 251
Keynes, Mary, 269n91
Khalidi, Rashid, 197
Khazoom, Aziza, 235
Khuri-Makdisi, Ilham, 194
Kimche, David, 269n91
Kishinev pogrom, 263n13
Kohn, Hans, 154, 158n45, 160n60
Korah, biblical story of, 177–78, 182n39
Korean War, 251, 253
Krobb, Florian, 48n32
Krushchev, Nikita, 220
Krutikov, Mikhail, 158n41
Kuwait, 221, 222

Labor Zionist movement, 245, 260
Landau, Noa, 227
Laqueur, Zeev (Walter), 256
Laye, Camara, 294
Lazare, Bernard, 288
League Against Imperialism, 242
Lebanon: Europe, Lebanese Jews migrating to, 194; Fascism in, 206; IDF withdrawal from (2000), 1; Irish diaspora and, 291; in Ottoman period, 192; Sabra and Shatila massacres (1982), 298–99; Syrian occupation of, 217, 221, 222
Lee, Christopher, 253, 269n93
Lehi (Stern gang), 261
Lenin (V. I.), 276

Levey, Zach, 254
Levy, Lital, 190, 198, 199, 200
Lewis, Bernard, 190; *The Jews of Islam*, 187
liberalism: affinities of Zionism with some aspects of antisemitic ideology, critique of, 69n33; assimilation associated with, 34–35, 45; authenticity as counternarrative to, 45; emancipation project in Europe, 155
Livingstone, Thomas, 116n41
Lockman, Zachary, 194, 203
Lubecki, J. A., 129, 131, 138n55
Luce-Celler Act (USA, 1946), 243
Lynch, Hollis, 97

Maimon, Moshe, *The Marranos*, 37, 37–38, 39
Makdisi, Ussama, 191–92, 197, 260
Maksymiak, Małgorzata A., 16, 119, 334
Mandatory Palestine. *See* British Mandate Palestine
Manthorne, Katherine, 117n48
Manyika, Sarah Ladipo, 300
Mapai party, 245
Marranos, as cipher for emancipated/baptized Jew, 31, 36–39, 37, 48n49
Marx, Karl, 281, 284, 295
Marxism, 141, 196, 215
Mashriqi Jews, 192–93, 196–98, 200, 204, 208
Masters, Bruce, 193
Maurer, Trude, 119
Mauritania, 217, 220, 221, 222
Mbembe, Achille, 295
Meir, Golda, 221
Meissner, Otto, 47n19
Melbye, Fritz, 107, 110, 111
Memmi, Albert, 15–16, 73–87: abstract anticolonial politics, critiquing/mirroring, 82–83; affinities between Memmi and Fanon, 73–74, 79–80, 86–87; on Algeria, 151, 152; Chakrabarty on, 282, 284–85; *The Colonizer and the Colonized*, 16, 74, 89n26, 140, 154, 155n3; conceptual connection between Jewish marginality and condition of colonial domination, 75–76; diaspora Jewish life, critique of, 79, 81–83; Habsburg colonial imaginary and, 140–41, 151, 154, 155n8; Israel of Memmi as parallel for Fanon's Algeria, 83–86; *The Liberation of the Jew*, 78, 81, 83–85; nativism and, 80, 81, 82, 84; on Négritude, 80–82, 89–90n29; *The Pillar of Salt*, 74, 78, 84, 85; *Portrait of a Jew*, 78, 84; on postcolonial studies, 74–75; statist view on Zionism, 89–90n29; Tunisian experience, rejection of Arab-Jewish identity, and turn to Zionism, 78–80, 84–86, 89n22, 151, 284–85; universalism and, 74, 78–80, 82–84, 90n40, 90n46

Menczel, Philipp, 129
Mendelssohn, Ezra, 119
mental mapping, 120, 121–22, 126, 133–34
Merminsky (Merom), May Bere, 245, 246, 267n50
Michael, Reuven, 47n19
Michaelis, Johann David, 135n12
Middle East, historiography of Jews in, 17–18, 187–209; antisemitism, 187–88, 200, 206, 209n2; communism/leftist ideologies, 203–5, 208; interwar period, 201–9; Muslim/Arab nationalism and, 187–91, 201–9; Nazism and Fascism, 206–7, 208; Ottoman Empire, 191–201; patriotism, local, 201, 202–3, 204–5, 208; Zionism, 188–89, 190, 201, 203, 204–6, 208. *See also* Arabs and Jews; Asia, Zionist perceptions of; British Mandate Palestine; Palestinian-Israeli conflict; Third World colonialism and Israel's settlement project; *specific countries*
Mignolo, Walter, 283
Mirzoeff, Nicholas, 105–6, 108, 117n55
modernity: authenticity as counternarrative to, 33–34, 46n2; comparative study of Yiddish and African peripheral modernisms, 294–95; Middle East, Jews in, 187, 190, 191, 201; monumentalist state projects and Third World colonialism, 216, 217, 223
Montagu, Edwin, 241–42
Montefiore, Sir Moses, 263n11
monumentalism. *See* Third World colonialism and Israel's settlement project
Moreh, Shmuel, 206
Morel, Benedict Augustin, 36
Moriah (magazine), 128, 129–30
Moria Literary Society for Jewish Girls, 43
Morocco: normalization of relations with Israel, 227; Third World colonialism of, 18, 216–23, 227–28
Mosès, Stéphane, 182n36
Mossad, 269n91
Al Moudjihad (newspaper), 78
Mountbatten, Lord, 266n42
Moyal, Esther, 198
Moyal, Shim'on, 198
Moyn, Samuel, 3
Mufti, Amir, 278–80, 288, 301n6; *Enlightenment in the Colony*, 8
Munich Games (1972), 80
Munich Pact, 247
Muslim League, 243
Muslim minority in India, 279–80
Muslim nationalism and nation-states, 187–91, 201–9

Nachman of Breslav, Reb, 294
nahḍa, 197–98, 200
Nandy, Ashis, 283
Na'or, Moshe, 205
Naqqash, Samir, 190
Nasser, Gamal Abdel, 253, 269n93
national "schools" of Zionism, 139
nativism, 80, 81, 82, 84, 196, 219, 222, 228
Navon, Arie, 249
Nazism and Fascism in Middle East, 206–7, 208
Negri, Antonio, and Michael Hardt, *Empire*, 287
Négritude, 80–82, 89–90n29, 97, 282
Nehru, Jawaharlal: at Asian Relations Conference (1947), 233, 234, 235, 242–44, 246, 247, 250; at Bandung Conference, 251, 253, 254, 269n94; Hebrew Manifesto on, 261; Nasser and, 253, 269n93
Nehru, Vijaya Lakshmi, 243
neo-colonialism: communism viewed as, 253; of postcolonial countries (*see* Third World colonialism and Israel's settlement project)
Neo-Orthodoxy, 46n2
Netanyahu, Benyamin, 227
Neuberger, Benyamin, 101
New Delhi Incident, Asian Relations Conference, 246–47, 249
"new Marranos," authenticity as counternarrative to, 31, 36–39, 37, 48n49
Ngũgĩ wa Thiong'o, 292–93
Non-Aligned Movement, 215–16, 261
Nordau, Max, 35–37, 39, 40–41, 42, 129, 131, 138n55, 139–40; *Degeneration*, 36; *Muskeljude*, 136n32; *Paradoxes*, 40
Nordbruch, Götz, 206
Nussimbaum, Lev (Essed Bey), 239

Occidentalization, 216, 218–19
Olson, Jess, 156n15
Olsvanger, Immanuel, 244, 266n44
Omar, Hajji Farah Ali, 221
Operation Agatha (the black Sabbath), 245
Operation Suzanna, 205
Oppenheim, Hans, 168, 169
Orientalism: Arabs, Galician Zionist perception of, 137n40; of Buber, 6, 55–58, 61, 63, 68n17, 239–41, 258; concept of, 3, 6, 56; European Orientalist discourse, 57, 200; in Germany and Austria, 134n7; Habsburg colonial imaginary and Central European Zionism, 142, 150, 152, 153, 154; Hebrew language, Gershom Scholem on, 162–63, 164, 166, 172, 174, 179; internal Jewish Orientalist discourse, 205; Jewish

INDEX | 347

authenticity and, 45–46n1; Ottoman, 197; Poles and Polish Jews, as colonized and Orientalized others, 121–25, 134; self-Orientalization, Jewish, 57, 239–41, 258; Zionist appropriation of, 13, 52, 55–58

Oslo Peace Accords, 19

the *Ostjude*, 16, 119–34; Asianism, Zionist, and, 236–37; Birnbaum and, 35, 125–26, 133, 134, 136n34, 137n38, 146; coded terms for, 125; development of concept of, 125–26, 132–34; emigration of Polish and Galician Jews, 121, 123–24, 146; German-Jewish perceptions of, 120, 123–25; in Habsburg colonial imaginary and Central European Zionism, 146–47; mental mapping of, 120, 121–22, 126, 133–34; Poles and Polish Jews, as colonized and Orientalized others, 121–25, 134; Prussia's expansion to the east, 119, 120–23; social distinction between designations of East and West, 128–29; West European Jews/Zionists viewed as inauthentic, 128–31; Zionists on, 125–32. *See also* Galicia; Poland

Ost und West (journal), 125, 239

Ottoman Empire: Austro-Hungarian alliance with, 152; comparative studies of collapse of, 292; new historiography of Jews in, 191–201; Orientalism in, 197; revolution of 1908, 193, 194, 196–97; *Tanẓīmāt* (1839–1876), 192–94, 196

Ottomanism, 194–95, 196, 198

Pachachi, Adnan, 221

Pale of Settlement, 142, 157n34, 237

Palestine, British Mandate for. *See* British Mandate Palestine

Palestine national revolt (1929), 205–6

Palestinian-Israeli conflict: antisemitism, Palestinian resistance depicted as, 207; at Asian Relations Conference, 246–48, *249*; at Bandung Conference, 255, 270n108; Bandung Conference and, 253; Entebbe raid, 80; First and Second Intifadas, 15, 299; Habsburg colonial imaginary and, 152; Indian support for, 240, 244; Munich Games (1972), 80; postcolonialist support for Palestinians, 15, 19n2, 24n49, 287, 297–300; Sabra and Shatila massacres (1982), 298–99; Uyghurs compared, 292. *See also* Third World colonialism and Israel's settlement project

Palestinians: India's support for, 240, 244; Muslim/Arab nationalism and, 187–91, 201–9; Palestinian resistance/criticism of Israel depicted as antisemitism, 207, 298; patriotism, local, 201, 202–3, 204–5, 208; Sabra and Shatila massacres (1982), 298–99. *See also* Arabs and Jews

pan-Africanism, 76, 77, 95, 96, 97, 99, 103, 108

pan-Arab nationalism (*qawmiyya*), 201

pan-Asianism, 241–43

Pan-Asiatic Women's Conference (1947), 246

pan-Islamism, 199

pan-Semitism/pan-Asiatic Zionism, 150, 151–52, 154, 241

Peel Commission (1937), 242

Penslar, Derek J., 1, 216, 228, 263n12, 291, 335

Philippson, Phöbus, *Die Marannen*, 36, 48n49

"Philistines," authenticity as counternarrative to, 31, 39–41

Phillips Casteel, Sarah, 16, 95, 301n5, 335

Pinsker, Leon, 144, 156n12; *Autoemancipation*, 144

Pissarro, Camille: assimilationist path in France, 108, 110–13; engagement with Caribbean Blackness, 104–8, *106*, *107*; Mirzoeff's reading of, 105–6, 108, 117n55; opposition to slavery, 105–6, 117n48; parallel lives of Blyden and Pissarro on St. Thomas, 96, 104, 106–8, 116n41; *Portrait of a Boy*, 105; *Two Women Chatting by the Sea*, 105–6, *107*; Venezuela, Blyden and Pissarro in, 105, 107, 110; *Woman Carrying a Pitcher on Her Head*, 105, *106*. *See also* St. Thomas, diaspora experience of Blacks and Jews of

Pissarro, Frédéric (father of Camille), 104

Pissarro, Pierre Rodrigues Alvares (grandfather of Camille), 104

Pissarro, Rachel Pomié Petit (mother of Camille), 104, 105

pogroms, 125, 142, 263n13

Poland: demographics of Jews in, 122, 135–36n21; disorder, coded as, 122; emigration of Polish Jews from, 121, 123–24, 146; first partition of (1772), 119, 120, 121, 124, 132; German-Jewish perception of Polish Jews, 123–25; Poles and Polish Jews, as colonized and Orientalized others, 121–25, 134

political Zionism, 145, 150–51

Pollack, Fritz W., 245, 266n46

Pommerantz, Kenneth, 155n9

Portugali, Yuval, 122

positioning, identity politics as, 15, 51–67; antisemitism, Zionist strategy against, 52, 59–61; Buber's Orientalism and, 55–58, 61, 63, 68n17; character of Zionist nationalism and, 64–65; concept of identities, 52–54; concept of identity politics, 10–11; concept of positioning, 54; context of Zionism in European cultures and, 65–66;

positioning, cultural identities, defined (*continued*), 52; Hall's approach to, 15, 51–55, 58, 61, 62, 64, 66; Orientalism, Zionist appropriation of, 52, 55–58; political strategy, understanding identity as, 55; relationship of Zionism to anticolonial/postcolonial identity politics, 59, 66–67; as self-representation versus hegemonial culture's representation of minority, 58, 68n29; Zionism as positioning, 61–64

postcolonial approaches to historiography of Zionism, 1–25; defining postcolonialism, 9, 275–77; defining Zionism, 29; Europe, relationship to, 4–7, 11–14 (*see also* Europe, Zionism, and [post]colonialism); Jewish/Israeli history and culture, use of postcolonial concepts in study of, 3–8, 51, 277–89; political factors involved in, 14–15, 19n2, 24n49, 297–300 (*see also* Palestinian-Israeli conflict); unacknowledged kinship between Zionist and postcolonialist studies, 1–3, 9–14. *See also* authenticity as counternarrative; Black and Jewish experience; Habsburg colonial imaginary and Central European Zionism; Middle East, historiography of Jews in; Orientalism; *Ostjude*; positioning, identity politics as; Scholem, Gershom; St. Thomas, diaspora experience of Blacks and Jews of

Postcolonial Studies (journal), 275
Powell, Eve Toutt, 198
practical Zionism, 145, 146, 148
Protocols of the Elders of Zion, 188
Prussia, eastward expansion of, 119, 120–23
Przyszłość, 126, 129

qawmiyya (pan-Arab nationalism), 201
Quayson, Ato, 2, 18–19, 291–300, 335–36

Rachmones-Zionists, 131, 138n61
Rachum, Stephanie, 117n53
racial issues, 216, 218–19, 234, 237, 258, 259–60, 295–96
Radio Levant France Libre, 245
Rand, Frieda, 43–44
Raz-Krakotzkin, Amnon, 90n40, 180n9
Reform Judaism, 46n2
Renoir, Auguste, 111
Revisionist Zionists, 245
revolutionary Zionism, 150
Ringelblum, Emanuel, 124
Rodrigue, Aron, 188
Roemer, Nils, 301n5
Romulo, Carlos, 269n94
Rosenblüth, Felix (Pinchas Rosen), 64

Rosenzweig, Franz, 164–65, 174–77, 180n10, 182n36
Roth, Joseph, 153
Rothberg, Michael, 4, 301n8; *Multidirectional Memory*, 296
Rothschild, Lord, 239
Rozenthal, Joseph, 194
Rubin, Abraham, 15–16, 73, 336

Sa'adā, Antūn, 206
Sabra and Shatila massacres (1982), 298–99
Sacher-Masoch, Leopold von, 124–25, 127
Safran, Gabrielle, 301n6
Sahrawi Arab Democratic Republic. *See* Western Sahara
Said, Edward, 3, 6, 8, 13, 19n2, 24n49, 56, 57, 134, 134n7, 153, 228, 258; *Orientalism*, 1, 120
al-Sa'id, Karima, 246
Salmon, Yosef, 142
Şannū', Ya'qūb, 198–99
Saposnik, Arieh, 1, 291, 336
Sartre, Jean-Paul, 140–41, 155n3
Sauvy, Alfred, 270n101
Schach, Fabius, 125
Schlaepfer, Aline, 202–3
Scholem, Gershom, 17, 161–80; apocalyptic tone of, 176–79; Arabic language, viewed as threat to Hebrew, 173–74; Arab-Jewish relations and, 164–66; Golem, modern spoken Hebrew regarded as, 172–73; Hebraist movement and, 169, 180n4; ideological deafness to spoken manifestations of modern Hebrew, 171–74, 175, 179; Kabbalah, study of, 162, 163, 179; Korah, biblical story of, 177–78; *Major Trends in Jewish Mysticism*, 162, 281; Orientalism and, 162–63, 164, 166, 172, 174, 179; religious and spiritual versus secular use, prioritization of, 162, 164–65, 166–71, 172; Rosenzweig, Scholem's letter (in German) to, 164–65, 174–77, 180n10, 182n36; silence, philosophical/theological account of, 168–70; theological stance regarding secularization of, 174–79; written over spoken Hebrew, prioritization of, 164, 168, 171, 172
Sciarcon, Jonathan, 196
Scott, James, 216, 223
Second Intifada, 15, 299
Segal, Miryam, 166
Sehayek, Shaul, 197–98
Seidman, Naomi, 301n6
Sejm Wielki (newspaper), 124
Selbst-Emancipation (periodical), 35, 126–27, 144

Selig, Gottfried, 122
Senghor, Léopold Sédar, 80, 97
Sephardim: Hebrew language, transition to "Sephardic" accent in, 161, 165–66, 167, 181n12, 181n14; Pissarro, Blyden, and Sephardic Caribbean (*see* St. Thomas, diaspora experience of Blacks and Jews of)
settlements, Israeli. *See* Third World colonialism and Israel's settlement project
settler colonialism, 215, 219
Shahar, Galili, 181n11
Shakwat, Sāmī, 206
Shāmī, Isḥāq, 196
Sharett, Moshe, 251, 256
Sharkey, Heather, 199
Shenhav, Gilad H., 17, 161, 336
Shenhav, Yehuda, 188–90
Shertok, Moshe, 252
Shikes, Ralph, 105, 117n46
Shimazu, Naoko, 253
Shimoni, Ya'akov, 245, 247, 254, 266n47
Shohat, Ella, 90n40, 188–90, 235
Sholem Aleichem, 288, 295; *Tevye the Milkman*, 295
Shternshis, Anna, 293–95, 297
Simon, Oswald John, 98, 102
Six Day War (1967), 14, 215, 221
slaves and slavery: emancipation of slaves on St. Thomas, 105, 110; Jewish involvement in slave system on St. Thomas, 101, 105; Pissarro's opposition to, 105–6, 117n48; St. Croix slave revolt, 96, 108
Smith, Anthony, 201
Smolenskin, Peretz, 142, 143
Snir, Reuven, 202
Sokolov [Sokolow], Nahum, 37–39, 238
al-Solh, Taqieddin, 246
Solomon, Louis, 98, 115n10
Somalia, 221, 222
Sombart, Werner, 240
Somekh, Rabbi 'Abdallah, 200
Somekh, Sasson, 208
South Africa compared to Israel, 14, 215, 239, 270n108, 300
Southeast Asia Treaty Organization (SEATO), 253
Spector, Scott, 16–17, 139, 336–37
Spinoza, Baruch, 287
Spitzer, Solomon, 142
Spivak, Gayatri Chakravorty, 3
"Srulik," 259–60, *261*
Stähler, Ahad, 95, 115n2
Stand, Adolf, 127–28, 137n40
Stapel, Wilhelm, 68n33
Starr, Deborah, 208

St. Croix slave revolt, 96
Stea, David, 121–22
Steiner, Franz Baermann, *Taboo*, 240
Stern, Raphael G., 18, 233, 337
Stern gang, 261
Stillman, Norman, 188
Stoler, Ann, 5, 19n2
St. Thomas, diaspora experience of Blacks and Jews of, 16, 95–114; Black nationalism and Zionism, cross-cultural exchange between, 95–97; Dreyfus Affair, 96, 108, 111–12, 117n52; emancipation of slaves on St. Thomas, 105, 110; Jewish involvement in slave system, 101, 105; multilingual and cosmopolitan nature of island culture, 99–100; parallel lives of Blyden and Pissarro on St. Thomas, 96, 104, 106–8, 116n41; St. Croix slave revolt, 96, 108. *See also* Blyden, Edward Wilmot; Gilroy, Paul; Pissarro, Camille; Walcott, Derek
subaltern antisemitisms, 7, 23n31
Subaltern Studies Group, 275
Suez War (1956), 234, 254, 259, 260
Sukarno (president of Indonesia), 220–21
Syrian occupation of Lebanon, 217, 221, 222

Tagore, Rabindranath, 24n42, 238, 242
Tamari, Salim, 196
Tanzīmāt (1839–1876), 192–94, 196
Taubes, S., 128
Taylor, Charles, 31–32
Theory and Criticism (journal), 3
Third World, concept of, 254, 270n101
Third World colonialism and Israel's settlement project, 17–18, 215–28; analytical benefits of studying, 227–28; definition of Third World colonialism, 216, 217–18; irredentist ideologies, 216, 220, 222, 223, 228, 242; Israeli fusion of political monumentalism and architectural miniaturization/museumization, 216, 223–27; monumentalist state projects and, 216, 222–24; postcolonial states, separation of Israel from study of, 215, 217–20; settler colonialism, Israeli settlements defined as, 215, 219; shared features of expansionist projects of postcolonial states, 216, 220–22
Thirty Years War, 284
Thon, Osias (Jehoshua, Ozjasz), 130
Tibet: at Asian Relations Conference (1947), 262n1; China's colonization of, 13, 216–19, 222, 223
Tilling, Lionel, 31
Treitschke, Heinrich von, *Unsere Aussichten*, 57
Trollope, Anthony, 99–100

Tunisia, Memmi in, 78–80, 84–86, 151, 284–85
Turkey, territorial enclaves established by, 225
Tutuola, Amos, 294

Uganda debate (1903), 137n42
United Arab Emirates (UAE), 227
United Kingdom. *See* Britain; British Mandate Palestine
United Nations: Declaration on the Granting of Independence to Colonial Countries and Peoples (1960), 220; Economic Commission for Asia and the Far East, 252; Israel's votes in, 252, 269n91; membership of Israel, vote on (1949), 250; partition, calls for implementation of, 255; partition, vote on (1947), 250
United Nations Emergency Force (UNEF), 259
United States Holocaust Memorial Museum, 96, 115n3
universalism: of European Enlightenment, 8, 280; of Jewish condition, 83, 90n40; Memmi/Fanon and, 74, 78–80, 82–84, 90n40, 90n46
Uyghurs, 292

Va'ad Leumi (Zionist National Council), 243–44
Varnhagen, Rahel, 288
Vogt, Stefan, 1, 15, 51, 240, 275–87, 291, 337

Wagner, Richard, 240
Walcott, Derek: comparison of Gilroy and, 108–9, 112; *Dream on Monkey Mountain*, 118n82; on Europe, Zionism, and [post]colonialism, 110; *O Babylon!*, 118n82; *Tiepolo's Hound*, 95, 108–14, 118n82; verse biography of Pissarro, 95, 96–97, 104, 108–14, 117n55, 118n82
Wandervogel movement, 167
Warburg, Otto, 63
Weber, Max, 279
Weizmann, Chaim, 266n42
Weldemichael, Awet Tewelde, 216, 217–18
Die Welt (newspaper), 37, 125–26
Weltsch, Felix, 149
Weltsch, Robert, 68n33, 70n45
Wertheimer, Jack, 119
Western Sahara, 13, 216–23
Wien, Peter, 206
Wiese, Christian, 4
Winz, Leo, 125
Wissenschaft des Judentums, 30, 46n2, 163, 180n5
Wolf, Larry, 120
women. *See* gender
World War I: Asia, Zionist perceptions of, 234, 241; Habsburg colonial imaginary and Central European Zionism, 143, 145–46, 149–50, 156n18, 159n53; Jewish diaspora after, 292; Middle East, Jews in, 187, 191, 195; the *Ostjude*, conceptualization of, 16, 146
World War II: Asia, Zionist perceptions of, 244, 248, 262; Holocaust, 134, 248; Memmi on Fanon and, 78, 87; Nazism and Fascism in Middle East, 206–7, 208; the *Ostjude*, conceptualization of, 119, 134; Zionism, development of, 13
World Zionist Organization, 37
Wschód (journal), 128, 130–31

Yelin-Mor, Natan, 260–61
Yellin, David, 181n12
Yiddish: Birnbaum's turn to, 125, 137n38, 145–46, 147, 157n34; comparative study of Yiddish and African peripheral modernisms, 294–95; the *Ostjude* associated with, 123, 125, 127, 133; Scholem's approach to Hebrew language and, 167
Yishuv: at Asian Relations Conference (1947), 18, 233–34, *235*, 236, 242–50, *249*; colonial paradigm applied to, 20n10; postcolonial approaches to, 4
Yom Kippur War (1973), 298
Young, Robert, 217
youth movements, German-Zionist, 167–69, 171, 181n22

Zaydān, Jurjī, 198
Zhou Enlai, 253, 270n108
Zionism. *See* postcolonial approaches to historiography of Zionism
Zionist Congresses: First Congress (1897), 35, 36, 98, 145; Fourth Congress (1900), 95; Second Congress (1898), 98; Uganda debate (1903), 137n42
Zipper, Gerschon, 132, 137n40
Zohar, Zvi, 199–200
Zola, Emile, 111